Dimitris Tziovas is Professor of Modern Greek Studies at the University of Birmingham. He has served as Director of the Centre for Byzantine, Ottoman and Modern Greek Studies at the University of Birmingham and as Secretary of the European Association of Modern Greek Studies. He is the author of *The Other Self: Selfhood and Society in Modern Greek Fiction* (2003) and editor of *Re-imagining the Past: Antiquity and Modern Greek Culture* (2014).

'At last a book in English on the Greek crisis that goes beyond the narrowly economic. These chapters conjure up recent Greek experience reflected in the country's music, street art, fiction, museums, rural life and many other aspects.'

Professor Robert Holland, Centre for Hellenic Studies, King's College London

GREECE IN CRISIS

The Cultural Politics of Austerity

Edited by
DIMITRIS TZIOVAS

I.B.TAURIS
LONDON • NEW YORK • OXFORD • NEW DELHI • SYDNEY

I.B. TAURIS
Bloomsbury Publishing Plc
50 Bedford Square, London, WC1B 3DP, UK
1385 Broadway, New York, NY 10018, USA

BLOOMSBURY, I.B. TAURIS and the I.B. Tauris logo
are trademarks of Bloomsbury Publishing Plc

First published in Great Britain 2017
This paperback edition published 2020

A catalogue record for this book is available from the British Library.

A catalog record for this book is available from the Library of Congress.

ISBN: HB: 978-1-7845-3845-3
PB: 978-0-7556-0109-7
ePDF: 978-1-7867-3252-1
eBook: 978-1-7867-2252-2

Series: International Library of Historical Studies

Typeset by OKS Prepress Services, Chennai, India

To find out more about our authors and books visit www.bloomsbury.com and sign up for our newsletters.

Arts & Humanities Research Council

The chapters in this volume were commissioned or delivered at a workshop held in May 2015 at the University of Birmingham as part of a research network project sponsored by the Arts and Humanities Research Council (AHRC) on 'The cultural politics of the Greek crisis' [grant number AH/L01498X/1].

CONTENTS

LIST OF ILLUSTRATIONS

Figures

Charts

Tables

NOTES ON CONTRIBUTORS

Yiorgos Anagnostou is Professor in the Modern Greek Programme at The Ohio State University. His research interests include Greek transnational studies and American ethnic studies, with an emphasis on Greek America. He has published in a range of scholarly journals and is the author of *Contours of White Ethnicity: Popular Ethnography and the Making of Usable Pasts in Greek America* (2009, forthcoming in Greek). He has published two poetry collections, *Διασπορικές Διαδρομές* (2012) and «*Λόγοι Χ Επαφής, Επιστολές εξ Αμερικής*» (2016).

Patricia Felisa Barbeito is Professor of American Literatures at the Rhode Island School of Design and a translator of Greek fiction and poetry. Her research focuses primarily on race and ethnicity in American literature and culture and she is currently working on a book about the African-American author Chester Himes.

Maria Boletsi is Assistant Professor at the Film and Comparative Literature Department of Leiden University. She has published on several topics, such as the concept of barbarism, post-9/11 literature and political rhetoric, Modern Greek literature, street art and subjectivity in the context of the Greek crisis. Her most recent book publications include *Barbarism and Its Discontents* (2013) and the co-edited volume *Barbarism Revisited: New Perspectives on an Old Concept* (2015). She is also main partner in an international project on the modern conceptual history of barbarism, funded by the Netherlands Organization for Scientific Research (NWO) and the Swiss National Science Foundation (SNSF).

Andromache Gazi is Assistant Professor of Museum Studies at the Department of Communication, Media and Culture at Panteion University, Athens. Prior to entering academia, she worked as a museum consultant. She has lectured and published extensively on museum issues, and is the co-author of three books. Her recent research focuses on memory and oral history in museums, and museum text. She holds a BA in Archaeology from the University of Thessaloniki, an MPhil in Archaeology from the University of Cambridge, and a PhD in Museum Studies from the University of Leicester.

Dionysis Goutsos is Professor of Text Linguistics at the National and Kapodistrian University of Athens. He has also taught at the University of Birmingham and the University of Cyprus. He has published several articles on linguistics, as well as a series of books, among others: *Modeling Discourse Topic* (1997), *Discourse Analysis: An Introduction* (1997/2004), *The Discourse of Translation* (2001, in Greek) and *Language: Text, Variety, System* (2012, in Greek). He has been research coordinator for the research projects leading to the compilation of the *Corpus of Greek Texts* and the *Diachronic Corpus of Greek of the 20th Century*.

Ourania Hatzidaki is Assistant Professor of English Language and Linguistics at the Hellenic Air Force Academy. She has also taught at the Universities of Birmingham and Athens, and the Ionian University. She specializes in and has published articles on English and Greek corpus linguistics, especially corpus-based phraseology. In recent works she has systematically pursued the integration of corpus linguistics with (critical) discourse analysis, especially in the areas of gender, politics (esp. party and anti-establishment discourse), the media, and the military. She is partner of the LINDSEI project (*Louvain International Database of Spoken English Interlanguage*), for which she has compiled the Greek component (spoken corpus of Greek learners of English, 2010).

Lois Labrianidis is Secretary General for Strategic and Private Investments of the Greek Ministry of Economy, Development and Tourism, and Professor in the Department of Economics, University of Macedonia, Greece. He is an economic geographer, has a BA from the Aristotle University of Thessaloniki, an MA from the University of Sussex and a PhD from the London School of Economics. He has done research and published on topics such as industrial location, the spatial aspects of subcontracting, development of rural areas, rural entrepreneurship, delocalization of economic activities and international migration.

Katerina Levidou is Visiting Research Fellow at the Centre for Hellenic Studies, King's College London and Tutor on the master's programme at the Faculty of Music Studies, University of Athens. Previously she held postdoctoral research fellowships at the Universities of Oxford, Lausanne and Athens. Her publications focus on Greek and Russian music of the twentieth and twenty-first centuries as well as the reception of Greek antiquity in music.

Lydia Papadimitriou is Reader in Film Studies at Liverpool John Moores University. She is the author of numerous academic articles published in journals and edited collections, as well as a monograph on *The Greek Film Musical* (2006). She is the editor of *Greek Cinema: Texts, Histories, Identities* (2011) and the principal editor of the *Journal of Greek Media and Culture*. Her research focuses on different aspects of Greek and Balkan cinema, as well as documentary, film festivals and distribution.

Dimitris Plantzos is Associate Professor of Classical Archaeology at the National and Kapodistrian University of Athens. His research focuses primarily on Greek art, archaeological theory, and modern receptions of classical antiquity. He is the author of *Greek Art and Archaeology, 1200–30 BC* (2016) and co-editor (with TJ Smith) of *A Companion to Greek Art* (2012).

Manolis Pratsinakis is a Marie Curie IF postdoctoral fellow at the University of Macedonia, Greece, studying the new crisis-driven Greek emigration, and a research fellow at the University of Amsterdam where he previously worked as a lecturer in Sociology. He holds a BA in Human Geography, an MA in Sociology and a PhD in Anthropology and has researched and published on migration, ethnicity and everyday nationhood.

Julia Tulke conducts research on street art and graffiti as mediums of expression and dissent in cities undergoing social and political crises.

In this context she has been conducting ethnographic fieldwork in Athens since 2013 (more at aestheticsofcrisis.org). Julia holds a BA in Social and Cultural Anthropology and Political Sciences from the Free University Berlin and an MA in European Ethnology from Humboldt University of Berlin. Since 2015 she has been pursuing a PhD in Visual and Cultural Studies at the University of Rochester, New York.

Trine Stauning Willert earned her PhD in Modern Greek Studies from the University of Copenhagen with a comparative study of Greek and Danish schoolchildren's perceptions of Europe and European identity. Her publications include the monograph *New Voices in Greek Orthodox Thought: Untying the Bond between Nation and Religion* (2014) and the co-edited volumes *Innovation in the Orthodox Christian Tradition? The Question of Change in Greek Orthodox Thought and Practice* (2012) and *Rethinking the Space for Religion: New Actors in Central and Southeast Europe on Religion, Authenticity and Belonging* (2012). In 2015 she was a Stanley F. Seeger visiting fellow at the Centre for Hellenic Studies at Princeton University where she worked on her forthcoming monograph with the working title *The New Ottoman Greece: From the Turkish Yoke to Pluralistic Coexistence in History and Fiction*.

INTRODUCTION

Dimitris Tziovas

Greece may have defaulted on its debts on several occasions in the past (1827, 1843, 1893, 1932), but since 2010 it has been experiencing the longest period of austerity and economic downturn in its recent history, further compounded by the influx of refugees and migrants. It has suffered more severely from the economic crisis than any other European country with harsh austerity measures, high unemployment and capital controls. What has happened in Greece since 2010 has occurred nowhere else in the developed world. In five years the country's GDP shrank by 25 per cent, over one million people became unemployed and more than 250,000 young professionals left the country. All indicators of economic activity in Greece point to a more significant decline than in the rest of the Eurozone and social inequalities have been exacerbated due to the crisis.[1] Some fear that the syndrome of a failed society may become widespread, recovery will be hard to achieve and a persecution mentality may become entrenched. Resignation and despair could become everyday conditions. Given the food and fuel poverty and the general economic meltdown, there is widespread concern about returning to a past perceived as pre-modern.

Greece's predicament has acquired global significance, judging from the unprecedented international media attention it has received and the fact that the former finance minister Yanis Varoufakis became for a time, according to the *Daily Telegraph*, 'the emerging rock star of Europe's anti-austerity uprising' or according to other European newspapers 'the bad boy of European politics'.[2] As Mark Mazower has pointed out, we usually think of Greece in terms of the home of Plato and Pericles but 'for the past 200 years, Greece has been at the forefront of Europe's evolution' and the present crisis continues exactly this pattern.[3] The consequences of the 'audit culture' and the perception of Greece as a 'debt colony' has also increased the willingness of some radical critics 'to examine the possibility that Greece is in a colonial relationship with the West'.[4] According to them the continent is implementing for the first time the neo-colonial strategies invented for and imposed on Africa and Latin America.[5] Such a view reinforces Zygmunt Bauman's argument that what differentiates the present wider crisis from its historical precedents is the 'divorce between power and politics'.[6]

The Greek crisis has emerged as the main perspective through which recent Greek artistic activity is discussed and analysed both at home and abroad. It is occasionally treated as a kind of colonial spectacle by foreign commentators and artists. Yet the dominance of the label 'Greek crisis' in the international media discourse risks producing facile and blanket readings of Greek cultural developments, which do not acknowledge different narratives or diverse cultural discourses. With this caveat in mind, this volume explores both local and transnational transmutations of the economic crisis by focusing on artistic and literary production, cultural institutions and changes in national self-perceptions, while examining the Greek crisis in a European and diasporic context. Despite the fact that there are a number of studies on the economics of the Greek crisis, no study has been made of its cultural impact. It is to be hoped that the analysis of the interaction between culture, identity and economics undertaken in this book will attract a readership beyond academia. By bringing together scholars from a range of disciplines, we are aiming to appeal to researchers whose work relates to other countries that are going through or have experienced austerity, helping them explore the cultural politics of economic challenges.

There have been a number of accounts of the economic crisis in Greece by financial and political analysts (e.g. M. Mitsopoulos & T. Pelagidis, *Understanding the Crisis in Greece: from Boom to Bust*, 2012, G. Tzogopoulos, *The Greek Crisis in the Media*, 2013 Anna Triandafyllidou, Ruby Gropas & Hara Kouki (eds), *The Greek Crisis and European Modernity*, 2013, G. Karyotis & R. Gerodimos, *The Politics of Extreme Austerity: Greece in the Eurozone Crisis*, 2015, and various contributions by the economist Yanis Varoufakis) or philosophers (Costas Douzinas, *Philosophy and Resistance in the Crisis*, 2013), as well as more personal or journalistic accounts (e.g. Yannis Palaiologos, *The 13th Labour of Hercules: Inside the Greek Crisis*, 2014, Vrasidas Karalis, *The Demons of Athens: Reports from the Great Devastation*, 2014). I am listing here only some books in English; there are many more in Greek. Articles have also been published on the impact of austerity on the Greek health and welfare systems, on crime, on Greek farming and other areas.[7] On the whole, the crisis tends to invite two scholarly approaches: one which can be described as ethnographic autopsy, focusing on empathetic experience and visuality and the other which seeks to analyse the logistics or interpret the causes and the consequences of the crisis. However, the impact of the crisis on culture and identity has not hitherto been properly considered. Obviously one could argue that it is too early to assess this kind of impact. Nevertheless these essays will try to prepare the ground for more in-depth assessments in the future and offer some sort of orientation for further research.

This volume is the outcome of a two-year research project 'The cultural politics of the Greek Crisis' funded by the Arts and Humanities Research Council (AHRC). The overall aim of the project was to stimulate debate among academics, research students, journalists, artists and writers on the implications of the economic crisis for Greek culture and identity and foster an interdisciplinary dialogue among historians, literature and performing arts scholars, cultural theorists, political scientists and anthropologists on the ways in which economic crises impact on cultural practices and the construction of identities. The project's website is http://culpolgreekcrisis.com/, where details of its programmes and videos of three workshops can be found.

Crises are moments of disruption and periodization watersheds, inviting analysts to explore their impact in different areas and compare it with that of other momentous events. To what extent can a crisis be captured and represented by art and literature? Is the cultural impact of the economic crisis, for example, similar to that of a war? How far can we talk about post-crisis literature or art in the same way that Greek critics and scholars have talked about postwar literature or art? Some parallels might also be drawn with the climate crisis, which can be framed as a matter of intergenerational debt the consequences of which may be spread over too extended a timescale to grab the public's attention. Economic changes may be happening very fast and be more visible, but the cultural effects of the crisis may take longer to emerge.

Culture, like sport, is a shared experience. It encourages community and solidarity, something vital in testing times, challenging arguments about funding for cultural activities being a luxury in an age of austerity. The unleashing of creativity in a period of crisis is not simply a coping strategy in the face of the withdrawal of public funding, it also has to do with the understanding of austerity 'not as a temporary measure for dealing with government debt, but as an enduring commitment to reshape social relations'.[8] Austerity differs from endemic underdevelopment and poverty; it involves the dynamics of reversal after losing earlier standards of living and associated social status.[9] In austerity culture the idea of community as nostalgia or as something lost which needs to be restored gives way to new forms of sociality and community. Yet some activists have argued that austerity promotes a particular form of creativity which is about resourcefulness and restoring what is seen to be lost, rather than challenging the state or becoming mobilized to hold it to account.[10]

Despite funding difficulties, an explosion of creativity has been witnessed in Greece during the crisis, particularly in the areas of theatre, film and performance. Readings, recitals, music, dance and other artistic activities have brought together spectators and performers in a number of public performances, confirming Jacques Rancière's conclusion that the emancipation of the spectator involves 'the blurring of the boundary between those who act and those who look'.[11] These performances promote intermedial hybridity and audience involvement, moving beyond the page or the closed space. With very little money and sometimes with voluntary contributions from the audience, young artists have staged exciting performances and responded to the crisis in imaginative and provocative ways. Athens became the focus of artistic activity with the Documenta 14 exhibition being the highlight. This international event with the title 'Learning from Athens', prepared for years under the artistic direction of Adam Szymczyk, opened in Athens in April 2017 and Kassel (its host city since its inception in 1955) in June 2017. Both cities hosted the exhibition on an equal footing with Kassel relinquishing its hitherto undisputed position as the central exhibition venue in favour of Athens.

Recent Greek films, in particular, have received international attention, going some way to counterbalance the negative media coverage of the crisis and offering a trope for understanding its social and artistic repercussions (see Papadimitriou, Chapter 5).[12] A debatable, if catchy, label – 'Greek Weird Wave' – has even been coined for these films by Steve Rose who also raised the question: 'Is it just coincidence that the world's most messed-up country is making the world's most messed-up cinema?'[13] Films like Yorgos Lanthimos's *Dogtooth* (2009) or Athina Rachel Tsangari's *Attenberg* (2010), Alexandros Avranas' *Miss Violence* (2013) and others use narratives about dysfunctional families and an austere visual language to convey a sense of social crisis revolving around claustrophobic domesticity, violence, young people and the legacy they have been handed.[14] On an institutional and commercial level the crisis has brought about a long-awaited restructuring of the funding of Greek cinema and encouraged filmmakers to seek new opportunities for international exposure. Despite the general austerity, it has been claimed that 'Greek film has benefited from both the changes in state funding and the more "creative" financing routes that have opened up'.[15]

In the hope that in times of austerity literature might record the lived experience of Greeks today in an inventive way and show their resourcefulness in living with less, fiction writers have even been commissioned to write stories about the crisis.[16] Interestingly, crime fiction has gained momentum thanks to its main practitioner and writer on the crisis Petros Markaris (see Barbeito, Chapter 10),[17] short-story writing is thriving once again (probably because it is a more 'economical' form) and creative writing classes have offered people opportunities to transcend the crisis woes.[18] In her introduction to the poetry anthology *Austerity Measures* (2016), Karen van Dyck sums up how Greek poetry production is defying economic recession:

> Poets writing graffiti on walls, poets reading in public squares, theatres and empty lots, poets performing in slams, chanting slogans, and singing songs at rallies, poets blogging and posting on the internet, poets teaming up with artists and musicians, poets teaching workshops to schoolchildren and migrants. In all of the misery and mess, new poetry is everywhere, too large and too various a body of writing to fit neatly on either side of any ideological rift.[19]

This abundance of poetry in a period of austerity makes little reference to classical statues, ancient myths, light or the sea, such as is found in the poetry of the Nobel laureates George Seferis and Odysseas Elytis. Instead poets seek to represent hard lives and uncertain futures in times of social and economic precarity.

Culture does not simply encapsulate the impact of hard times, it sometimes adumbrates it. Adopting the view that 'literature often tells us what will happen before history has time to unfold',[20] some have argued that in contrast to the political and economic euphoria of the period since the fall of the military junta in 1974, literature gradually anticipated the upcoming crisis and gave early warnings by portraying a society becoming more cynical, materialistic and consumerist while charting the decline of collective visions and grand narratives.[21] It is easy enough with the benefit of hindsight to express such views, but in a period of austerity and in an atmosphere of blame and recrimination, culture aspires to offer a new vision or an often comforting outlet for creativity.

Notwithstanding the cultural efflorescence mentioned above and the opening of small and independent publishers or bookshops during the crisis, the book market has suffered considerably and its turnover has almost halved.[22] Since 2011, 700 school libraries throughout Greece and the Athens-based European Centre for Literary Translation have closed. In 2013–2014, the Greek government decided to suspend the operation of the National Book Centre of Greece (EKEBI) and this has adversely impacted the availability of statistics on Greek publishing and the organization and funding of the International Thessaloniki Book Fair. Also the fixed book price law, which came into force in Greece in 1997, was modified in 2014 allowing unregulated discounts. The earlier policy obliged publishers to set a retail price and in the first two years after publication booksellers were only permitted to vary this price by a discount of up to 10 per cent or a maximum surcharge of 5 per cent. Though this policy still applies to literary and children's books, its discontinuation in all other areas of the trade and the subsequent deregulation of the book market has hit small, independent bookshops hard, favouring supermarkets and no more than a couple of 'heavy discount' booksellers. The increase of VAT in all the intermediate stages of book production from 6.5 per cent to 23 per cent and the capital controls imposed in the summer of 2015 have made the situation even worse for the book market.

Cultural production thrives in difficult or critical periods, and the current age of austerity is no exception. Poets, artists and filmmakers try to capture the zeitgeist of the crisis at the same time as challenging it creatively. Culture also became more accessible with the State Orchestra of Athens performing in public places and some theatre performances are free or alternatively offered in return for voluntary contributions of food for those in need. In this time of crisis it has not been the written word that has expressed the anger and frustration of ordinary people so much as the image. Photography became the international voice of the dispossessed as well as of human solidarity; it captured the agony and plight of many suffering people, including migrants and refugees, and conveyed it all over the world. Images of demonstrations, street art, homeless people or those queuing for food were more powerful than newspaper articles or social media commentaries.[23] The lack of public funding for culture allowed private, not-for-profit organizations such as the Niarchos and Onassis Foundations or Daskalopoulos' NEON to step in and play the role of patrons of the arts by sponsoring exhibitions, staging performances, purchasing archives, funding translations (e.g. the complete works of Aristotle) or the construction of new buildings for the National Opera and Library of Greece.[24]

The issue here is not simply how culture copes with and responds to austerity but how the impact of the crisis in other areas can reverberate in cultural developments or the image of the country. For example, during the crisis the public switched to using social media, abandoning newspapers and traditional outlets of information. This was partly due to economic reasons and partly to a mistrust of the established media. Blog posts, twitter feeds, independent web-based outlets supplanted conventional media while the internet became an ever growing open-access archive of the crisis. The digital mediascape became not only a source of alternative information but also the vehicle for cultural expression, humour and critique. Despite its gloom and doom, the crisis has produced a good deal of laughter and humorous reflection in the social media and on the streets (graffiti) (see Tulke, Chapter 8). The discontent with austerity does not simply challenge hegemonic constellations of political power, it becomes a state of mind involving indignation, defensive nationalism, xenophobia and resistance. During the crisis the numerous protests and the anti-austerity mobilization, the Greek version of Spain's Los Indignados (known in Greek as the *aganaktismenoi*), re-energized an agonistic and antisystemic culture.[25] European politicians, such as David Cameron and Nicolas Sarkozy, used social unrest in Greece as a bogeyman to warn their own citizens of how things might be if they did not consent to austerity policies.

Thus Greece became, on the one hand, the international symbol of resistance to neoliberal policies and, on the other, a European outcast, an example to be avoided. This, in turn, led Greeks to feel increasingly disillusioned with Europe and raised questions about the cultural orientation of the country and its identity. The crisis has indeed woken up the 'sleeping giant' of popular Euroscepticism, a latent force in Greece, which had previously failed to reach its full potential.[26] Greek popular Euroscepticism, for decades below the EU average, now significantly exceeded it, due to the involvement of the European Commission and the European Central Bank in the harsh austerity programme imposed by the 'Troika' of international lenders. Though the crisis accelerated an already upward trend, there was an impressive rise in support for Eurosceptic parties 'not seen in Greece for more than a quarter century'.[27] From being one of the most pro-European societies in the EU, Greece has been transformed into one of the most Eurosceptic – or rather 'Euro-critical', given the support for Eurozone membership among the Greeks. This rise in Euroscepticism could potentially have a challenging impact on a hitherto increasingly Europhile culture and encourage a re-emergence of the old questions as to whether Greece is closer to the West or the East. The economic crisis appears as a defining period, a national trauma, analogous to other traumatic periods such as that of 1967–1974. All these fostered a self-reflective and self-questioning trend, revisiting the past and searching for new national narratives and explanations as to what had gone wrong (see Tziovas, Chapter 1). The Memoranda (Mnimonia), as the master documents of austerity, are seen as a retrogression on many fronts; a reversal of the natural order of things, cancelling the prospect of an ever-increasing prosperity.

Another indirect cultural impact is the emigration of young scientists, artists and professionals looking for work outside Greece. The fact that the number of emigrants to OECD countries (i.e. those which are members of the Organisation for Economic Cooperation and Development) shot up from 19,912 in 2010 to 52,078 in 2012, decreasing slightly in 2013 (46,377), is indicative of the brain drain due to the crisis.[28] Despite the awkward relations between the two countries, most of the Greeks who emigrated settled in Germany (12,256 in 2010 and more than 32,088 in 2013). According to a study carried out by the OECD 'International Survey on Careers of Doctorate Holders-CDH', Greece has a high proportion of doctorate holders per 1,000 residents but most of them have left the country because of the economic crisis. According to a recent study conducted by the University of Macedonia, of the 185,388 Greek university graduates who left Greece between 1990 and 2015, 139,041 have left since 2010 (see Labrianidis and Pratsinakis, Chapter 3).[29] This is the biggest brain drain in an advanced Western economy in modern times and has been called Generation G: young, gifted and Greek.[30]

Yet this brain drain transforms traditional notions of the Greek diaspora and leads to the formation of new diaspora communities consisting of young professionals and academics, who develop different kinds of relationships with their home country from earlier patterns. These could involve virtual or digital storytelling communities, where Greek 'neomigrants' can submit their own 'open letters', photos and videos from all over the world. The New Diaspora (http://www.newdiaspora.com) project is an online platform that aims to host mini-documentaries and all kinds of user-generated content revolving around the multiple aspects of the diaspora experience. In this way the Greek diaspora is developing into a global network sharing stories and ideas. It has even been argued that in the current economic climate 'Greece may be best served by encouraging diaspora involvement in Greek economic development from overseas rather than encouraging return at present'.[31] What is more, some have tried to shift the focus from the Helladic state to the elusive notion of Hellenism, implicitly contrasting the failures of Greece as a country with the creative drive of Greeks worldwide (see Anagnostou, Chapter 4).[32] Despite the international interest in the Greek crisis and the recent influx of refugees and migrants to the country, the decrease in the number of registered foreigners – from about 610,800 in 2009 to 450,000 in June 2014[33] – suggests that Greece is gradually losing its recently acquired multiculturalism and becoming a more inward looking society due to the crisis. The crisis also makes the social and cultural integration of the newly arrived migrants and refugees, who might otherwise decide to seek asylum in the country, more difficult.

This insularity could be exacerbated by another consequence of the crisis: Greece is becoming an ageing society. According to a study conducted by the New York-based NGO 'HelpAge International', Greece is a 'demographic ticking time bomb'.[34] In 2030 one in every three Greeks will be a pensioner, while by 2050 the proportion of over-60s is expected to have increased to 40.8 per cent of the population.[35] Greece is ranked among the top 6 countries for fastest ageing of the population along with Italy, Portugal, Spain, Japan and South Korea. Due to the worsening economic conditions it has been experiencing over the past five years, Greece is ranked overall 79th out of the 96 countries included in the study, and is the lowest ranked country in western Europe.[36]

Greece has long suffered with an ageing population, but seven years of austerity have significantly exacerbated these disturbing trends. Fertility rates are dropping as young couples, affected by unemployment and falling incomes, are postponing having children.[37] Greek society is not only ageing but is also becoming unhealthy and obese.[38] The financial distress has forced people to eat cheap food and has led to high rates of obesity, particularly among children. An OECD report in 2014 ranked Greece first among member countries for high levels of childhood obesity, with a staggering 44 per cent of Greek children classed as overweight or obese.[39] These demographic and social changes inevitably have a cultural impact because an ageing and unhealthy society cannot dynamically promote inventiveness or openness to new trends and ideas, and young artists are seeking creative opportunities outside the country.

In an ageing and melancholic Greek society, can culture become the driving force and offer the hope, the innovation and the excitement required to reverse the downturn? Can culture play an uplifting role similar to the spirit of the war years or the dictatorship? In challenging periods is the role of art to comfort, to inspire or just to question? Or, in the words of a poem by Stamatis Polenakis (2012), does poetry not suffice?

> Gentlemen, don't let anything,
> anyone, deceive you:
> we were not bankrupted today,
> we have been bankrupt for a long time now.
> Today it's easy enough
> for anyone to walk on water:

the empty bottles bob on the surface
without carrying any secret messages.
The sirens don't sing, nor are they silent,
they merely stay motionless,
dumbstruck by the privatization
of the waves and no
poetry doesn't suffice since the sea filled up
with trash and condoms.
Let him write as many sonnets as he wants about Faliro
that Lorentzos Mavilis.[40]

This edited volume will analyse previously virtually uncharted cultural aspects of the Greek economic crisis by exploring the connections between austerity and culture and how the crisis has led Greeks to rethink or question cultural discourses and conceptions of identity. The link between cultural and identity politics will be highlighted through an examination of Greek diaspora attitudes towards the crisis and of how various perceptions of the ancient past have been deployed during the crisis. By discussing literary, artistic and visual representations of the crisis, it will look at how contemporary Greek culture is responding to or coping with austerity. It will also address the impact of the crisis on Greek attitudes to Europe and the national imaginary and how Greek cultural agents and institutions are being affected by the economic downturn.

This volume includes a range of chapters focusing on different aspects of the cultural politics of the crisis, such as the uses of the past (Chapter 1), archaeology (Chapter 2), the brain drain and the Greek diaspora (Chapter 3 and Chapter 4), Greek cinema (Chapter 5), museums (Chapter 6), music festivals (Chapter 7), street art (Chapter 8), the nostalgia for a return to the countryside (Chapter 9), literature (Chapter 10 and Chapter 11), the discourses and counter-discourses of the Greek crisis (Chapter 12). Obviously the volume does not promise comprehensive coverage of the cultural politics of austerity but it aims to prepare the ground for further research into the cultural impact of the Greek crisis and its long-term effects. The aim here is to generate a dialogue with the work of other scholars who have worked on the crisis and chart new opportunities for interdisciplinary or comparative approaches to the crisis in Greece and beyond.

Notes

1. See the report by T. Giannitsis and S. Zografakis, 'Greece: solidarity and adjustment in times of crisis', Hans-Böckler-Stiftung, IMK Studies, Nr. 38, Düsseldorf: March 2015. This report is an attempt to examine the impact of the crisis and crisis policies on incomes, inequality and poverty in Greece.
2. Mick Brown, 'Yanis Varoufakis: "Europe is too important to be left to its clueless rulers"', *Telegraph*, 1 March 2016. Available at http://www.telegraph.co.uk/men/thinking-man/yanis-varoufakis-europe-is-too-important-to-be-left-to-its-cluel/ (accessed 17 July 2016).
3. Mark Mazower, 'Democracy's Cradle, Rocking the World', *New York Times*, 29 June 2011. Available at http://www.nytimes.com/2011/06/30/opinion/30mazower.html?_r=0 (accessed 15 July 2016).
4. Michael Herzfeld, 'Crisis Attack: Impromptu Ethnography in the Greek Maelstrom', *Anthropology Today* 27/5 (2011), p. 25 and 'The European Crisis and Cultural Intimacy', *Studies in Ethnicity and Nationalism* 13/3 (2013), p. 492.
5. Costas Douzinas, *Philosophy and Resistance in the Crisis* (Cambridge, 2013), p. 101.
6. Zygmunt Bauman and Carlo Bordoni, *State of Crisis* (Cambridge, 2014), p. 12.
7. Alexander Kentikelenis & Irene Papanikolas, 'Economic crisis, austerity and the Greek public health', *European Journal of Public Health* 22/1 (2011), pp. 4–5, S. Xenakis & L. K. Cheliotis 'Crime and Economic Downturn: The Complexity of Crime and Crime Politics in Greece since 2009', *British Journal of Criminology* 53/5 (2013), pp. 719–745, Sofia Vasilopoulou, Daphne Halikiopoulou & Theofanis Exadaktylos, 'Greece in Crisis: Austerity, Populism and the Politics of Blame', *Journal of Common Market Studies* 52/2 (2014), pp. 388–402, David Wills, 'Reinventing Paradise: the Greek crisis and contemporary British travel narratives', *Byzantine and Modern Greek Studies* 39/2 (2015), pp. 286–301, Athanasios Ragkos, Stavariani Koutsou and Theodoros Manousidis, 'In Search of Strategies to Face the Economic Crisis: Evidence from Greek Farms', *South European Society and Politics* 21/3 (2016), pp. 319–337.
8. Rebecca Bramall, 'Introduction: The Future of Austerity', *New Formations* 87 (2016), p. 2.
9. Daniel M. Knight & Charles Stewart, 'Ethnographies of Austerity: Temporality, Crisis and Affect in Southern Europe', *History and Anthropology* 27/1 (2016), pp. 1–18.
10. Kirsten Forkert, 'Austere Creativity and Volunteer-run Public Services: the Case of Lewisham's Libraries', *New Formations* 87 (2016), pp. 11–28.
11. Jacques Rancière, *The Emancipated Spectator*, trans. Gregory Elliott (London 2011), p. 19.
12. Lydia Papadimitriou, 'Locating Contemporary Greek Film Cultures: Past, Present, Future and the Crisis', *Filmicon: Journal of Greek Film Studies* 2 (September 2014), pp. 1–19.

13. Steve Rose, 'Attenberg, Dogtooth and the weird wave of Greek cinema', *Guardian*, 27 August 2011. Available at http://www.theguardian.com/film/2011/aug/27/attenberg-dogtooth-greece-cinema (accessed 1 July 2016).
14. See Alex Lykidis, 'Crisis of sovereignty in recent Greek cinema', *Journal of Greek Media & Culture* 1/1 (2015), pp. 9–27.
15. Olga Kourelou, Mariana Liz and Belén Vidal, 'Crisis and creativity: The new cinemas of Portugal, Greece and Spain', *New Cinemas: Journal of Contemporary Film* 12/1 & 2 (2014), p. 140.
16. Eleni Boura & Mikela Hartoulari, *Το αποτύπωμα της κρίσης* [The trace of crisis] (Athens, 2012).
17. Filippos Filippou, 'Crime fiction during the crisis' and Marlena Politopoulou, 'When the Crisis Wears Noir' in Natasha Lemos & Eleni Yannakakis (eds), *Critical Times, Critical Thoughts: Contemporary Greek Writers Discuss Facts and Fiction* (Newcastle upon Tyne, 2015), pp. 144–173.
18. Lambrini Kouzeli, 'Εργαστήρια δημιουργικής γραφής' [Workshops of creative writing], *To Vima*, 4 October 2015. Available at http://www.tovima.gr/books-ideas/article/?aid=742810 (accessed 25 July 2016).
19. Karen van Dyck (ed.), *Austerity Measures* (London 2016), pp. xvii–xviii.
20. Ibid., p. xix. Theodoros Chiotis thinks that Manolis Anagnostakis' poem 'Thessaloniki, Days of 1969 AD (1970)' 'reads like an omen of a future foretold' (*Futures: Poetry of the Greek crisis*, edited and translated by Theodoros Chiotis, London, 2015, p. ii).
21. Titika Dimitroulia 'Η προαναγγελία της παρακμής' [Advance notice of the decline], *I Kathimerini*, 10 June 2012, available at http://www.dimitroulia.gr/proanaggelia_tis_parakmis-article-307.html?category_id=66 (accessed 15 July 2016) and Dimosthenis Kourtovic, 'Υπήρξα ελεύθερος σκοπευτής' [I was a sniper], *Ta Nea*, 25 April 2015, available at http://www.tanea.gr/news/nsin/books/article/5231966/yphrksa-eleytheros-skopeyths/ (accessed 15 July 2016).
22. Manolis Pimplis, 'Κρίση και εκδοτικοί οίκοι' [Crisis and publishers], *Ta Nea*, 30 July 2016, available at http://www.tanea.gr/opinions/all-opinions/article/5378493/krish-kai-ekdotikoi-oikoi/ (accessed 5 August 2016) and Nikolas Zois, 'Βιβλία: τίτλοι τέλους τον καιρό της κρίσης' [It's curtains for books during the crisis], *Ta Nea*, 28–29 May 2016. Available at http://www.tanea.gr/news/nsin/article/5362046/titloi-teloys-ton-kairo-ths-krishs/ (accessed 12 July 2016).
23. See the special issue on Uncertain Visions: Crisis, Ambiguity and Visual Culture in Greece, *Visual Anthropology Review* 32/1 (Spring 2016).
24. Mikela Hartoulari, 'Είναι δικαίωμα ο πολιτισμός ή όχι;' [Do we have a right to culture?], *Chronos*, 23, March 2015. Available at http://www.chronosmag.eu/index.php/l-e-pls.html (accessed 10 July 2016).
25. For an anthropological analysis of the local voices of discontent see Dimitrios Theodossopoulos, 'Infuriated with the Infuriated? Blaming Tactics and Discontent about the Greek Financial Crisis', *Current Anthropology* 54/2 (2013), 200–221 and Dimitrios Theodossopoulos, 'The Ambivalence of Anti-Austerity

Indignation in Greece: Resistance, Hegemony and Complicity', *History and Anthropology* 25/4 (2014), pp. 488–506.

26. Susannah Verney, 'Waking the "sleeping giant" or expressing domestic dissent? Mainstreaming Euroscepticism in crisis-stricken Greece', *International Political Science Review* 36/3 (2015), pp. 279–295.
27. Ibid., p. 285.
28. Organization for Economic Cooperation and Development (OECD), *Connecting with Emigrants: A Global Profile of Diasporas 2015*, http://www.oecd.org/publications/connecting-with-emigrants-9789264239845-en.htm (accessed 15 July 2016).
29. Apostolos Lakasas, 'Educated Greeks can't catch a break at home', *Kathimerini* (English Edition), 24 June 2016, available at http://www.ekathimerini.com/209841/article/ekathimerini/community/educated-greeks-cant-catch-a-break-at-home (accessed 15 July 2016) and Lois Labrianidis and Manolis Pratsinakis, *Greece's New Emigration at Times of Crisis*, May 2016 http://www.lse.ac.uk/europeanInstitute/research/hellenicObservatory/CMS%20pdf/Publications/GreeSE/GreeSE-No.99.pdf.
30. Helena Smith, 'Young, gifted and Greek: Generation G – the world's biggest brain drain', *Guardian*, 19 January 2015. Available at http://www.theguardian.com/world/2015/jan/19/young-talented-greek-generation-g-worlds-biggest-brain-drain (accessed 23 July 2016).
31. Jennifer Cavounidis, *The Changing Face of Emigration: Harnessing the Potential of the New Greek Diaspora*, Transatlantic Council on Migration & Migration Policy Institute, December 2015, p. 11, http://www.migrationpolicy.org/research/changing-face-emigration-harnessing-potential-new-greek-diaspora (accessed 15 July 2016).
32. Victor Roudometof, 'Η επιστροφή του Ελληνισμού' [The return of Hellenism], *Ta Nea*, 16 March 2016. Available at http://www.tanea.gr/triti-apopsi/article/5343234/h-epistrofh-toy-ellhnismoy/ (accessed 12 July 2016).
33. Organization for Economic Cooperation and Development (OECD), *International Migration Outlook 2015* (Paris: OECD Publishing, 2015), www.oecd.org/migration/international-migration-outlook-1999124x.htm (accessed 15 July 2016). The figures are not always reliable and the number of registered migrants seems to have risen in May 2015 (527,264) and again in April 2016 (557,476). See Panagiota Bistika, 'Ο «χάρτης» των 557.476 νόμιμων μεταναστών [The 'map' of 557.476 legal migrants]', *To Vima*, 27 April 2016. Available at http://www.tovima.gr/society/article/?aid=795716 (accessed 25 July 2016).
34. Global Age Watch Index 2015 http://www.helpage.org/global-agewatch/population-ageing-data/country-ageing-data/?country=Greece See also Nikos Konstandaras, 'Greece's Dismal Demographics', *New York Times*, 9 December 2013. Available at http://www.nytimes.com/2013/12/10/opinion/greeces-dismal-demographics.html?_r=1 (accessed 15 July 2016).

35. Roula Salourou, 'Greece's demographic time bomb is about to go off', *Kathimerini*, English edition, 3 October 2015. Available at http://www.ekathimerini.com/202171/article/ekathimerini/business/greeces-demographic-time-bomb-is-about-to-go-off (accessed 20 July 2016).
36. Global AgeWatch Index 2015, http://www.helpage.org/global-agewatch/reports/global-agewatch-index-2015-insight-report-summary-and-methodology/ (accessed 16 July 2016).
37. According to demographers a population requires a fertility rate of 2.1 to replenish the previous generation. Based on data from 2011 the rate in Greece has dropped to 1.4 and many experts believe that the situation is even worse today. 2011 became the first year in which deaths exceeded births (by 4,671). According to the statistical service of the European Union this figure jumped to 16,300 in 2012 with net migration causing Greece's population to drop by another 44,200.
38. For the health effects of austerity see Alexander Kentikelenis, Marina Karanikolos, Aaron Reeves, Martin McKee, David Stuckler, 'Greece's health crisis: from austerity to denialism', *Lancet* 383 (22 February 2014), pp. 748–753.
39. OECD, Obesity Update, June 2014, http://www.oecd.org/health/Obesity-Update-2014.pdf and Felicity Capon, 'Financial distress in Greece said to be fuelling childhood obesity', *Newsweek* 21 July 2015. Available at http://europe.newsweek.com/financial-distress-greece-said-be-fueling-childhood-obesity-330613 (accessed 15 July 2016).
40. Karen van Dyck (ed.), *Austerity Measures*, p. 231.

PART I

CRISIS NARRATIVES AND CULTURAL POLITICS

CHAPTER 1

NARRATIVES OF THE GREEK CRISIS AND THE POLITICS OF THE PAST

Dimitris Tziovas

For the past seven years the European and American media have been inundated with stories about the Greek economic or debt crisis. The word 'economic' or 'debt' (the choice of word depending on the point of view of the speaker or writer) was soon dropped, and most talked simply about the 'Greek crisis', suggesting its wider ramifications and international implications.[1] Western analysts often referred to a 'Greek tragedy' and encapsulated the crisis in exaggerated media headlines such as 'Greek drama is far from over', 'Greece pulls back from the brink of euro exit' or 'Greece is facing a Herculean task', while one left-wing commentator described the political situation in Greece as 'exciting' compared to the 'inertia' of the English and something that offered hope to a Europe facing austerity.[2] The crisis attracted immense international attention and was played out in the Western media in a range of reports, opinion pieces, images and comments. The media have been instrumental in constructing the narratives of the Greek crisis, and hence this paper places particular emphasis on newspaper articles and other media reports and images.

During the crisis many people's concern has been what will happen in the future and how soon austerity will be over. Opinion polls suggest that Greeks are pessimistic about or even fearful of the future. And that this uncertainty about the future might spawn some sort of national introversion and defensive retrogression or a nostalgic escape to the past. We witness returns to and of the past for different reasons: as an attempt to trace the roots of the crisis or its early signs, as a source of national pride or an opportunity for reflection, contrast or reclamation. Yet the crisis has made many talk about a new 'narrative' for Greece, a departure from the failed practices of the past, a kind of national catharsis and replenishment. It has also induced Greek society to rethink its values, to revisit its founding myths and to re-examine its earlier certainties. This involves to some extent a narrativization of the traumas of history, an interrogation of past practices and a critical searching for what went wrong, using the past as a guide. The past is destabilized and at the same time acts as a source of strength. This twofold role of the past is analysed in this chapter by examining case studies from different areas (politics, international relations, history, media, archaeology, literature and performance).

Throughout the crisis there has been an attempt by scholars and the media to answer the question of whether history plays a role in the Greek crisis. Recently Stathis Kalyvas has described the historical trajectory of modern Greece as a succession of seven major boom, bust and bailout cycles and the crisis of 2009 as just the latest of these. He claimed that ambitious Greek projects and subsequent travails had received considerable global attention disproportionate to the size of the country, while outsiders had always stepped in to correct Greek mistakes. Because they always expect help from outside, he suggests, Greeks have been encouraged to take risks rather than investing in sound institutions. In turn, this has probably reinforced the ambitions of various Greek elites and has fed these successive boom-bust-bailout cycles. He concludes by pointing out that 'the past points to a pattern that allows us to both better understand Greece's present predicament as well as to reach a more informed assessment about its future trajectory'.[3] Thus Kalyvas treats the crisis as part of a recurring pattern and the latest episode in a historical cycle. On the other hand, the crisis could also be conceptualized in terms of what Alain Badiou calls an 'event', a kind of rupture, which disrupts the current situation and opens up a space to rethink the dominant social order.[4] Each event sets a new beginning in time, a break in history's continuum or a moment of disengagement from past experiences, which is both traumatic and exhilaratingly transformative for the participants.

In one way or another the crisis leads to a re-envisioning of the past and in turn the past informs the experience of the crisis. The past is invoked, remembered and re-interpreted, stimulating temporal thinking and historicization. People tend to look at present difficulties and potential futures through the prism of the past and try to develop coping strategies. Here the notion of 'preposterous history', introduced by Mieke Bal, could be useful to reflect on the dialogics of past and present and the interdependence of 'before' and 'after' during the Greek crisis.[5] What came before the crisis and what has come after play off against one another, altering each other so that neither is what it would be without the other. The 'pre' and the 'post' mark one another and change their corresponding statuses, as 'history' fluctuates in the in-between. The re-envisioning of the past entails its reciprocal interaction and hybrid confluence with the present.[6] Through such dialogue between past and present, Bal argues for a notion of 'preposterous history', where events or works that are earlier in time operate as after effects caused by the images of subsequent events or artefacts. For Bal, 'preposterous history' brings together the 'pre' and the 'post' of history in a hybrid recycling that re-visions the past (in her case, the Baroque era).

The crisis not only disturbs temporalities; it makes people think 'preposterously'.[7] Condensing multiple moments of the past, the crisis seems to have fractured time and re-enacted repressed memories or narratives of traumatic past events. Like trauma, the crisis involves a kind of double telling, the oscillation 'between the story of the unbearable nature of an event and the story of the unbearable nature of its survival'.[8] As a reflective process, trauma links past to present through representations and imagination.[9] This reliving of the past and the intergenerational transmission of traumatic experiences produces a kind of 'cultural trauma' involving the remembrance of the traumatic effect rather than the experience. The crisis has generated a retrospective discourse of cultural trauma, which is a process of reawakening earlier traumatic events ingrained in the collective memory. Past and present also coalesced into a body of knowledge during the dictatorship (1967–1974). Iakovos Kambanellis' play *Το Μεγάλο Τσίρκο* [*Our Grand Circus*] paralleled aspects of Modern Greek history with the Colonels' regime and US neocolonialism and alluded to the past suffering of the Greek people at the hands of both foreign and domestic rulers.

Following Michel Serres, Daniel Knight deploys the term 'cultural proximity' to define how certain past events resonate with the experiences of the current crisis.[10] He argues that 'cultural proximity is the ability for the individual or collectivity to recognize, and eventually embody, representations of the past within the context of the present'.[11] The crisis acts as a filter, making some past events feel culturally proximate. The embodiment of the past in the present suggests that the experience of the crisis includes multiple past moments and is a 'polytemporal' event. This chapter aims to explore how and to what extent the crisis has had an impact on the ways Greeks and others read, revisit or revise the past of the country in the light of the crisis. The different approaches to the role of the past can first be traced in the competing narratives as to the causes of the crisis.

Competing narratives and European visions

The narratives about the Greek crisis parallel the division of the Greek people into supporters and opponents of the bailout agreement. What is interesting is that both narratives have a time dimension in the sense that they see the crisis as a relatively synchronic event or as a culmination of a long process of incompetence and state failure.

The first narrative, which tends to find supporters in the ranks of the left, treats the Greek crisis as part of a wider European one. Back in 2010 Costas Lapavitsas, in trying to answer the question of what caused the crisis, identified as the primary reason 'the structural bias of the Eurozone stemming from the way the Eurozone has been set up', with what happened to Greece having 'nothing to do with state profligacy'.[12] Along the same lines, Yanis Varoufakis argued that 'there is a European and global crisis, of which Greece is an interesting part' and contended that the current crisis had nothing whatsoever to do with the malignancy of the country's state and private sectors. This was 'simply a convenient excuse for European leaders in denial'.[13] Greek society's ills were legion, he maintained, but '*do not* explain the current free fall'.[14] As he put it, 'the reason for our insolvency was simple: the Eurozone was incapable of absorbing the shockwaves of the 2008 global earthquake'.[15]

According to this narrative Greece is not the only country that has a huge debt; the whole of Europe is heavily in debt, and therefore the only solution is its mutualization. The crisis, in turn, is seen more as a recent phenomenon and a result of the malfunction of the Eurozone and its architecture. Even the term 'Greek crisis' that territorializes a global phenomenon is avoided as an appellation.[16] This narrative aspires to remind Europeans that they have 'become Greeks once again', not by going back in history in Shelley's sense of succumbing to the charms of classical literature or Churchill's idea of emulating Greek heroism, but by bringing to the fore Europe's denial of its current systemic failures, responsible for the Greek derailment. It is implied here that an orientalist and colonialist perspective is being ushered in, dividing European countries into modern and not-yet-modern countries.

The treatment of the Greek crisis as a symptom of a wider malaise finds supporters among non-Greeks too. Slavoj Žižek, for example, argues that the Greeks 'are at war with the European economic establishment, and what they need is solidarity in their struggle, because it is our struggle too'.[17] According to him, Greece has become the main testing ground for a depoliticized technocracy in which bankers and other experts are allowed to demolish democracy. What is at stake for him is the European legacy – democracy, trust in people, egalitarian solidarity – and he claims that by saving 'Greece from its so-called saviours, we also save Europe itself'. Greece may foreshadow the future of Europe, as the latter is following Greece both in its catastrophic downward spiral and in the rise of popular protest.[18] The country is becoming the testing ground for the transition from democracy to 'demo-crisis' or post-democracy.

The rival narrative adopts a more historical perspective by suggesting that Greece aspires to the Western lifestyle but still maintains oriental attitudes and institutions.[19] The crisis is seen as an opportunity to make Greece a 'normal' country and terminate Greek exceptionalism. In trying to answer the question 'How did Greece get into this position?', political scientists point the finger at the 'nature of the Greek state', which is 'on its way to being a failed state' and 'barely fit for purpose'.[20] It is claimed that the long-standing clientelistic relationship of the state with wider society and the economy is fundamental to the nature of the crisis. This, in turn, leads to the conclusion that the crisis was 'ultimately invented in Athens' and that there is a cultural setting that has led to the profligacy of the state.[21] More recently Edmund Phelps, the 2006 Nobel laureate in economics, has argued that neither austerity nor government cutbacks can be blamed for the economic ills of the country, because they are 'rooted in the values and beliefs of Greek society'.[22]

Continuing in the same vein, P.M. Kitromilides historicizes even further the origins of the Greek crisis. He points out that, instead of 'blaming as usual everybody else except the Greeks themselves for the country's problems', one has to look back 'at the origins of Greek political culture and the ideological traditions that shaped the Greek political community in the nineteenth century' to understand the present crisis. The answer to the origins of contemporary problems, according to him, goes back to what he calls the 'failure of liberalism' in Greece, which in turn bred intolerance and resulted in 'the replacement of the discredited culture of national values by a new authoritarianism, deriving from leftist ideology'.[23] This narrative often becomes self-disparaging and points to the assumption, still plaguing Greeks and obstructing any attempt towards self-understanding, 'that the Europeans are not creditors – both literally and culturally – but debtors'.[24] What is interesting here is that in both narratives the role of Europe is crucial, either by reminding Europeans that they 'have become Greeks once again' or by emphasizing their role as agents of modernization. Athens for some has become the laboratory of the past and future of Europe, while the cradle of civilization could end up as the graveyard of past assumptions about Europe.[25]

Between these narrative polarities (broadly defined as globalist and culturalist respectively), there is a third narrative that attempts to apportion blame between Greek politicians and voters and Greece's European partners and the EU institutions.[26] Along with the inadequacies of the Greek administration, it acknowledges that the crisis has brought to the surface the imperfections of the EU and that 'the crisis was, to varying degrees and in different ways, mismanaged both *within Greece and at the European level*'.[27] However, such a balanced and dispassionate narrative cannot deter a number of commentators from pointing out that there is an 'enduring history of a sense of victimhood' that has been in evidence from the origins of the modern Greek state to the present day.[28]

Though this notion of victimhood can be traced back to well before 2009, the widespread reporting of the crisis has had the effect of expanding it into new areas. It stems from the centrality of Greece in the Western historical narrative and imagining the modern country as having fallen from the tree of Western tradition. Current depictions of Greece in the media are eerily similar to those painted by the European philhellenes in the early modern period, who thought of Greece in terms of binary oppositions: Western–Eastern, Hellenic–Romaic and Modern–Ancient. The media image of modern Greece, for example as an unwelcome 'cancer' in the body of the Eurozone, resonates with a metaphor used by John Galt in 1813 portraying Greeks as vermin in the 'skeleton of a deceased hero'.[29] These defamatory views question the country's credentials, its claim to a place in the West and its validity as a nation state: 'the idea of Greeks as childlike people experimenting with statehood [. . .] has not been easily erased from the collective attitudes of Northern Europeans'.[30] Just as modern Greece is perceived to threaten the sanctity of Western culture, so the Greek economy presents a threat to the stability of Europe and its economic union. And this adds a historical dimension to the narrative, which tends to see the crisis as the outcome of recent European failures.

It has been argued that Greeks continue to see modern Europe in terms of the nineteenth century, when Delacroix depicted the 'Massacre of Chios' and Byron, Shelley, François-René de Chateaubriand and Victor Hugo expressed their philhellenic feelings.[31] Philhellenism has become an integral part of the modern Greek identity, and the crisis has encouraged a sentimental and romanticized approach to international relations. European leaders are judged by their philhellenism, and the statement, purportedly made by the former French president Valéry Giscard d'Estaing, that 'the descendants of Plato cannot play in the second league' has received considerable publicity in the Greek media.

Since the beginning of the crisis foreign media have been asking 'Are the Greeks really Europeans?'.[32] When SYRIZA came to power in January 2015, and more especially following Alexis Tsipras's visit to Moscow in April 2015, Western commentators once again raised the question of whether Greeks were 'Westerners' and argued that Greece and Russia were breathing new life into their ancient 'eastern' alliance. Going back to the Ottoman Empire, these commentators argue that 'Greece has, in fact, a more Asiatic flavour', while former subjects of the Austro-Hungarian Empire which are predominantly Roman Catholic, such as Slovenia and Croatia, have more historical continuity with Europe.[33] This has allowed them to adapt to the norms of the EU more easily than Greece, a much older member state. It has also been pointed out that Russia has spent considerable sums projecting its soft power into Greece since the crisis, and the TV channel Russia Today has gained the hearts and minds of quite a few Greeks since 2011.[34] In May 2014 members of Golden Dawn, the neo-Nazi party, even met with Alexander Dugin, an intellectual with close ties to the Kremlin and a driving force behind neo-Eurasianism and the restoration of the Russian Empire.

Here, perhaps, we need to consider a reading of the crisis along the East–West religious divide and in terms of two contrasting moral worldviews that point to different attitudes towards economics in general and capitalism in particular.[35] For eastern Christian theologians, all the important action happens at the Resurrection, not the Crucifixion. The West, and above all Catholicism, fetishizes suffering and criticizes Orthodox theology for having a 'free lunch' view of salvation. For Western theology the message of salvation is that Christ paid the price for man's sins, whereas the Eastern Church is not so obsessed with sin. This explains why Orthodox Christian art, unlike Western Christian art, is not obsessed with the bleeding crucified Jesus. Salvation is not merely payback; it is about life triumphing over death, and this cosmic accountancy determines attitudes to making reparation for debt/sin. Greeks want to escape death-dealing debt; Westerners believe it must be paid back, no matter how much blood and pain is involved.

The crisis has sparked off a debate about Europe and a rethinking of its identity, cultural values and orientation. Harking back to an elusive ideal of European humanism, which has been gradually eroded due to neoliberal austerity and the shrinking of the welfare state, it is claimed that the crisis precipitated the clash of two visions of Europe: an older and rather idealized Europe of human solidarity and democratic values, and a Europe envisioned by technocrats and managers, that ends in social exclusion and restricted access to education. This clash suggests that many Greeks see Europe as moving away from past ideals, and its future unity and identity is increasingly in doubt. The early twenty-first-century euphoria about Europe seems to be giving way to a return to older Greek suspicions about foreign conspiracies and interventions.[36] In short, earlier humanist aspirations for an integrated Europe now seem to be contrasted with an uncertain future undermined by nationalism and the North–South divide.

Since the crisis, the opposition between ethnocentrism and Europeanism has been exacerbated in Greece and elsewhere and these polarized attitudes tend to cut across the Right–Left divide. An aggressive, emotional and polarizing nationalism marks a defensive regression to the past and an attempt to find in the past a means of boosting national pride. In one way or another the crisis involves a (re-) reading of the past. Even those who claim that it is a wider European phenomenon and that its causes lie in the way the Eurozone has been set up trace it back to Germany's debt relief in 1953 or link Germany's war reparations with the Greek bailout.

The tyranny of Greece or the ghosts of history

After the fall of the junta in Greece in 1974 anti-Americanism was at its peak, since the Americans were considered to have masterminded the military coup. American bases in Greece were treated as representing a form of neo-colonial control, while the popularity of American culture was often equated with cultural imperialism.[37] Later, President Clinton was even publicly put on trial in Syntagma Square in central Athens by the actor Kostas Kazakos for his role in the war in the former Yugoslavia. During the crisis this attitude has been turned around. The Germans have assumed the role of the 'enemy', while the Americans are seen as the ones trying to keep Greece in the Eurozone and pleading with Chancellor Merkel to this end.

In his *New York Times* blog, Paul Krugman reminded us of the title of a classic book by E.M. Butler, *The Tyranny of Greece over Germany*, published in 1934 and banned by the Nazis, in which Butler argued that German culture was warped by an obsession with ancient Greece and had succumbed to 'the tyranny of an ideal'.[38] During the crisis the Germans' view of Greece has been informed by an economic, rather than an aesthetic, ideal and by the popular view of themselves as prudent and hard working. A different tyranny, in the form of austerity, is now conditioning relations between the two countries, who have developed a certain bitterness towards one another. The Germans have revived their stereotypes about the lazy, feckless Greeks, while the latter have developed an antipathy towards the former and particularly the Federal Finance Minister Wolfgang Schäuble.

The anti-German predisposition of the Greek people has been given added impetus during the crisis by the revival of Greek claims for compensation for wartime damage done by the Germans and for a loan that the National Bank of Greece was forced to extend to Nazi Germany for the maintenance costs of the German army and further military activity in the Mediterranean during the period 1942–1944. In early

1945 high-ranking German economists calculated this 'German debt (*Reichsschuld*) to the Greek state' at 476m Reichsmarks, which would be roughly €10 billion today.[39] The issue of the war reparations triggered a debate and encouraged research into the archives, which brought to light documents outlining how ever since the 1950s German diplomacy has tried to avoid the responsibility of applying international law regarding war reparations, which were estimated by the Greek finance ministry at €279 billion in April 2015.[40]

The decision of the newly elected Greek government in March 2015 to air once again Greece's demand for war reparations from Germany has, predictably, soured Greco–German relations even further. Calls for reparations are often emotionally charged and seen as an attempt by 'bankrupt' Greeks to settle their debts, but the wartime loan is relatively free of moralistic baggage. The importance of revisiting these claims and remembering the past was made clear in Alexis Tsipras' emotional speech to the Greek parliament in March 2015:

> Some people ask us: 'Why do you tackle the past? Look at the future'. But what country, what people can have a future if it does not honour its history and its struggles? What people can move forward, erasing the collective memory and leaving historically unjustified its struggles and sacrifices? Indeed, not much time has passed since then, ladies and gentlemen. The generation of the Occupation and of the National Resistance is still living. And the pictures and sounds from the tortures and executions at Distomo and Kaisariani, at Kalavrita and at Vianno, are still fresh in the collective memory of our people.[41]

Such statements led commentators to ask whether 'World War II belongs to the recent or distant past – or whether the war ever really ended'.[42] Some commentators argue that mixing up the debt issue with German war guilt and hoping that the former could be written off as 'reparations' is not an intelligent negotiating strategy. It might prove a serious miscalculation on the part of the Greeks and could contribute to a disorderly exit from the euro.[43] Others add that the issue of the war reparations has already been settled in 1960 and then again in 1990 at the time of German unification. And these reparations cover the forced loan. And that, if it was not a forced loan, then it is a zero interest loan.[44]

War reparations fuel anti-German feelings among ordinary people and these feelings were reinforced by the showing for some days in April and May 2015 of a video, prepared by the Greek Ministry of Defence and endorsed by other Greek authorities, on screens throughout the Athens Metro. The video footage depicted atrocities and war crimes committed by the German armed forces during the Axis occupation of Greece (1941–1944). The short video begins 'We keep the memory – we do not forget' and ends with the words 'The case remains open'. It alleges that Germany owes 'war reparations', 'a repayment of the occupation loan', 'compensation to the victims' and 'the return of archaeological treasure'. The foreign media have widely criticized this as an attempt by the Greek government to entangle the issue of German World War II reparations with Greece's ongoing sovereign debt obligations, purportedly inciting anti-German hatred. Another Ministry of Defence video, first introduced at an event in Athens on 27 April 2015 marking the 74th anniversary of Hitler's invasion of the Greek capital, included footage from the invasion of Athens by German troops in 1941 and contained an audio clip of the last free broadcast aired from the Greek radio station, just hours before the arrival of the Wehrmacht troops in Athens. Some have argued that this was done for propagandistic reasons in order to draw parallels between past and present; and that associating the German occupation of the early 1940s with the current perception of Greece as a debt colony resisting German demands was aimed at playing up anti-German attitudes among ordinary Greeks.[45]

And it is not just the Greeks who are referring back to the Nazi occupation of their country. On the cover of the leading German news magazine *Der Spiegel* of 21 March 2015 a photo of Chancellor Angela Merkel on the Acropolis was juxtaposed with one of Nazi officers in front of the Parthenon during the period of occupation. Under the headline 'How Europeans look at the Germans – German Superiority', the magazine's lead article explained the troubled relations between the two countries due to the issue of war reparations.

These competing narratives have a moral dimension, as the Germans present themselves as having achieved economic success through self-sacrifice and hard work after World War II.[46] By following a sensible course of self-reliance and austerity their virtue has been rewarded, and this view of themselves is contrasted with the profligate, debt dependent and irresponsible course chosen by the Greeks. This has led to a war of symbols conducted through images, book and magazine covers or cartoons invoking antiquity or the Nazi past.[47] In February 2010 the German weekly magazine *Focus* presented the Venus de Milo making a rude gesture next to a headline reading 'Betrüger in der Euro-Familie' (Cheats in the Euro-family). The next day the Greek newspaper *Niki* showed a Nazi flag flying on the Brandenburg Gate in Berlin. In October 2012, in anti-German demonstrations during Angela Merkel's visit to Athens, the German Chancellor was presented as Hitler, while in February 2015 the Greek prime minister, Alexis Tsipras, apologized for a cartoon in the left-wing paper *Avgi* showing Wolfgang Schäuble dressed as a Nazi officer saying to the Greeks: 'I'll turn you into a soap.'[48] And in June 2015 a doctored photograph posted on his Facebook page by an MP for the Independent Greeks party, Dimitris Kammenos, angered the Central Board of Jewish Communities in Greece. The words on the sign over the Auschwitz gate, 'Arbeit Macht Frei', had been replaced with 'We stay in Europe' (Μένουμε Ευρώπη), the slogan of those campaigning for Greece to remain in the Eurozone. The board called this post 'shameful' and criticized it for trivializing the historical memory of the Holocaust.[49] In September 2015 this post, together with others he had posted on social media, cost Kammenos his short-lived ministerial career.

The increased sense of victimhood felt by Greeks during the crisis might also explain attitudes to the Holocaust. Victimhood encourages inward-looking reflection and forges an identity that 'generates biased responses against other groups whose status of victim is more widely accepted'.[50] The findings of a research project on attitudes to the Holocaust and anti-Semitism in Greece were presented at the British Embassy in Athens in March 2015 and demonstrate that the past matters for groups with a strong sense of collective victimhood.[51] These findings show that half of the interviewees said they associated the word 'holocaust' with Auschwitz and the other half with Distomo, Zalongo and Arkadi from Greek history. In responses to another question regarding which history topics should be part of the school curriculum the Holocaust was rated after the Asia Minor catastrophe, the Greek civil war and the Pontic genocide. On the basis of these findings the researchers argued that anti-Semitism and the low priority assigned by Greeks to the teaching of the Holocaust have to do with the logic of victimization adopted by Greek society.[52] This often leads to an inward-looking attitude and an ethnocentric perception of international events, and to antagonistic sentiments towards other people, such as the Jews, who were also victims of atrocities. The crisis has forced Greeks to reflect on racism and look back on anti-immigrant narratives. It has also led to the rediscovery of a lost solidarity and the promotion of counter-cultures of intimacy and empathy.

Re-energizing old traumas and the affective politics of memory

It is common for people to try to draw parallels between past and present momentous events and compare the present crisis with other debt crises or traumatic experiences.[53] History plays a significant role in the way Greeks negotiate the crisis, or in Cathy Caruth's words 'we could say that the traumatic nature of history means that events are only historical to the extent that they implicate others'.[54] Here we might think of Dominick LaCapra's distinction, based on psychoanalysis, between 'acting out' (melancholia) and 'working through' (mourning) as two processes through which individuals and societies deal with traumatic events.[55] In acting out, a repetitive process, one relives the past, whereas in working through one tries to gain critical distance and transcend the past. A crisis seems to reactivate earlier traumas and perpetuate an unsettling bond with the past. The embodiment of the past in the present suggests that the experience of the crisis is a 'polytemporal' event, involving past moments of suffering and the reactivation of the inherent latency of earlier traumatic experiences. Through the affective references to those moments, the crisis is historicized and temporalities collapse. As Walter Benjamin put it, 'every image of the past that is not recognized by the present as one of its own concerns threatens to disappear irretrievably'.[56]

In a way the crisis evokes Marianne Hirsch's term of 'postmemory',[57] which describes the relationship that the 'generation after' has with the personal, collective, and cultural trauma of those who came before, thus reflecting an uneasy oscillation between continuity and rupture and constituting a structure of transgenerational transmission of traumatic knowledge and experience. Postmemory's connection to the past is actually mediated not through recall but through imaginative investment, projection, and creation. It strives to reactivate and re-embody more distant memorial structures and provide an affective link to the past.

Some (including some classicists) argue that antiquity can offer insights into the crisis and suggest reading up on the tenets of ancient Stoicism to cope with the current difficulties or using the Solonic concept of *seisachtheia* to call for debt cancellation. Others argue that 'ancient Greek authors might have written insightfully about historical moments of crises and debt, but it would be absurd to argue that classicists are *a priori* in a better position to understand the current situation because they're familiar with the Melian Dialogue or Solon's reforms'.[58] Indeed the crisis has revived arguments about the proprietorship of the Greek classical past, going back to the fraught process of modern Greek nation building and has rehearsed claims that 'Greeks don't deserve Greece'. As we will see below classical antiquity has often been used to frame discussions on the crisis.

In the standoff between Greece and the EU some saw parallels with the encounter in 416 BC between the commanders of an Athenian fleet and the leaders of the small island of Melos.[59] In his history of the Peloponnesian War, Thucydides presents the Athenians demanding that the Melians join the Delian League – a kind of Athenian imperialism, since the democracy Athens practised at home did not extend to the governance of its League. Though the parallel falls short in many ways, what is highlighted here is the opposition between national sovereignty and supranational organizations; the Troika bureaucrats are seen as little different from the Athenian delegation. The resistance Greece puts up today in the name of freedom and dignity recapitulates the earlier response of the Melians, though force now comes in the form of economic diktats and monetary threats and not with phalanxes and triremes.

Classicists have explored other ancient Greek solutions to financial crises[60] and started comparing the present Greek crisis with the ways ancient Greek democracy resolved budgetary crises. Debt, as a financial, moral and cultural concept, has often been invoked in the context of the Greek crisis, bringing together the indebtedness to classical Greece of Greeks and Westerners as well as the moralizing discourse of repaying what is owed to creditors. Thus a dialectic of debt and credit is developing which further entangles antiquity in the discussions on the crisis. It has been pointed out that today's politicians could draw important lessons from ancient Athens, while public debate and frank discussion involving the voters could actually build consensus for tough reforms.[61] Ancient Greek politicians were thought to be brave enough to speak candidly about public finances, and voters regularly voted to put the collective good ahead of their personal interest.[62] Modern democracies, it has been suggested, could do the same, and modern politicians should abandon the view that voters could not tolerate the financial truth. In order to illustrate the ways in which debt has historically been used as a tool of control, plunder and predation, other historians argue that debt goes back millennia and focus on earlier Greek experiences of debt. The connection between ancient and modern Greece can also be seen in the documentary on the Greek crisis, *Agora: From Democracy to the Market* (2015), by the internationally acclaimed filmmaker Yorgos Avgeropoulos.

Though appeals to Thucydides or Plato can confer authority in real-world decision-making, Daniel Mendelsohn contends that scholars 'would be better off studying the centuries of subjugation and humiliation endured by the Greek people than reading the Melian Dialogue'.[63] For him it is Cavafy, and not Thucydides, that some Greeks have turned to to find the 'right' poem for the current Greek crisis, which has revived memories of past suffering and traumas. Yet older people did not turn to ancient history or poetry but started drawing comparisons between the experience of the crisis and the massacres of the Greek War of Independence (Chios), the 1922 Smyrna Catastrophe and the forced exchange of populations between Greece and Turkey that ensued, or the famine during the German occupation, and tried to fit the current situation into a trauma discourse.[64] The suffering of the past was revived and contrasted with the austerity of the present. Even the former Greek finance minister, Yanis Varoufakis, speaking to an Australian newspaper on the anniversary of the Greek junta of 1967, said that the Greek government had to face a new type of coup d'état, 'not with tanks, as in 1967, but through the banks'.[65]

For some people associations with the more recent famine of the early 1940s were vividly brought to mind. Soup kitchens and hungry school children brought back images of the food crisis of the German occupation (1941–1944). The famine killed at least five per cent of the population and was not a subject that Greeks were comfortable talking about in the 'good times'. But during the crisis it seems to have been coming up more and more in everyday conversation and in the news.[66] In times of austerity food becomes a metaphor of cultural belonging, solidarity and collective suffering. It provides a link to history and homeland.[67] Gastro-politics and anti-austerity slogans are often based on a shared understanding of history and politics. They are pinned to affective historical events, stitching together past events and present difficulties and bringing collectively recognized moments of the past back to life.[68] According to Rebecca Bramall, the austerity discourse creates new articulations and consolidates existing connections. It is also 'historical' in the sense that it activates and reasserts certain familiar histories or stories about the past by promoting an affective relationship with it.[69]

It is not only the famine of the early 1940s that invites comparisons with the crisis but also the events of the civil war (1946–1949). In her novel *The Scapegoat* (2015, Greek title: *Χορεύουν οι Ελέφαντες*, 2012), Sophia Nikolaidou connects the Greek civil war (with the murder of the American journalist George Polk in Thessaloniki in 1948 signalling the start of the Cold War) with the current Greek crisis, implicitly arguing that in both periods political decisions affecting Greece were taken outside the country. Both then and now people have indeed been powerless, their lives determined elsewhere and higher up. Ants cannot stand up to elephants, as the Greek title of the novel suggests. Written in alternating sections, in which the past resonates in the present, the book's mirroring of the two periods suggests that in Greece the scapegoating never stops and the injustices of the past go on resurfacing.

Two events from the Greek struggle for independence from the Ottomans (1821–1827) serve as metaphors to illustrate Greece's relationship with its Eurozone partners during the crisis. The first is the naval battle of Navarino, fought in October 1827, in which the allied British, French and Russian naval forces destroyed the combined Turkish and Egyptian armada. Without the decisive allied intervention, which marked the end of the Greek War of Independence, its outcome looked very uncertain. Parallels have been drawn between this first humanitarian Western intervention, which led to the emergence of the Greek nation state, and the bailout rescue agreements. The second event involves a stronghold in north-western Greece called Kougi. There in 1803 a group of Souliotes, led by a monk, blew themselves up rather than surrender to the Ottoman Turks. This heroic event has been used by Panos Kammenos, the nationalist coalition partner in the SYRIZA-led government in 2015, to suggest that the Greeks, like the Souliotes, might press the self-destruct button for themselves and the rest of the Eurozone.

In 2015 the annual celebration on 25 March to mark the beginning of the Greek War of Independence provided another opportunity to explore how the crisis is often seen in relation to or through the perspective of the past. The celebrations in 2015 were in stark contrast to the previous year's events, which had taken place under heavy security. In the morning Athenians watched a parade of tanks and fighter jets, followed by folk music and dancing, all aiming at evoking a sense of national pride and promoting social solidarity, thus reviving the spirit of 1821. At the same time inspectors were assessing the case for continued financial support for Europe's most-indebted nation. This attracted the following ironic comment: 'Greeks celebrate their independence Wednesday with a military parade and a folk-music festival sponsored by the Ministry of Defence, as European officials more than 1,000 miles away review the financial aid that will shape their future'.[70]

In the evening of the same day the Greek prime minister Alexis Tsipras, in a speech at the University of Athens, emphasized the usefulness of the past in understanding the present: 'Critical study of the past helps us to understand the present in order to open up to the horizons of the future and above all to do the right thing'.[71] In a sense he was attempting to project the present situation of Greece onto the past, suggesting that, just as in the early nineteenth century Greece had attracted the sympathy of European people, who in turn put pressure on their governments to assist the Greek cause, so today Europe should respond to the call of Greece by overcoming any neoliberal sentiments. In both cases Greece was fighting and continues to fight for the ideals of freedom, social justice and solidarity. By quoting a statement made by the historian Antonis Liakos claiming that today is 'the Greek hour of Europe and the European hour of Greece',[72] he rationalized the current international interest in Greece and stressed that Greek problems are also European ones. In his view this explained the European 'wave of solidarity' with Greece and its people. However, he was criticized for overlooking the striking differences between 1821 and 2015. The philhellenic movement of the early nineteenth century cannot be compared to any current allies or parties (e.g. Podemos, Die Linke) in Europe.[73] Though in his speech Tsipras was cautious about drawing historical parallels or creating transhistorical patterns, he tended to invite them, urging his audience to see the current crisis through the prism of the early nineteenth century.

The past here is closer to the concept of the 'practical past' which we carry around with us in our daily lives and draw upon. Following the British philosopher Michael Oakeshott and echoing Nietzsche's distinction between critical and monumental historiography, Hayden White drew a line between the cognitive (historical) and moral (practical) relationship to the past. While historians may typically be interested in knowing *about* the past, others are more concerned with how to deal *with* the past. The distinction between 'the historical past' and 'the practical past' 'is useful for distinguishing between modern professional historians' approaches to the study of the past and the ways in which lay persons and practitioners of other disciplines call upon, recall, or seek to use "the past" as a "space of experience"'.[74] The practical past is the kind of past ordinary people, politicians and others carry around with them as an 'imagined reality'. A storehouse of memory, ideals, examples and events worthy of remembrance and repetition, the practical past is not about establishing the facts but is intended to provide a basis on which to launch a plan of action in the present, whereas the historical past has little or no value when it comes to understanding or explaining the present.

Pride and prejudice: Archaeo-politics and the iconology of crisis

In his book *The Spectre of Comparisons: Nationalism, Southeast Asia, and the World*, Benedict Anderson refers to the novel *Noli Me Tangere* (1887) by José Rizal, who is considered one of the national heroes of the Philippines during the colonization of the country by Spain. In this novel a young mestizo hero returns to the Manila of the 1880s after a long sojourn in Europe and, looking at the municipal botanical gardens, he realizes that these gardens are overshadowed automatically and inescapably by images of their sister gardens in Europe. The novelist names the agent of this double vision 'el demonio de las comparaciones', or 'the spectre of comparisons', a kind of 'double-consciousness' that precludes one from experiencing one thing without immediately recalling the other. It is just such a 'spectre of comparisons' involving

Greek antiquity that shapes and underpins Western imaginings of Greece. Just as in Rizal's novel Crisóstomo Ibarra finds it 'impossible ever after to experience Berlin without at once thinking of Manila', so too 'the West' is unable to experience Greece without thinking of and invoking ancient Greece.[75] This 'spectre' of antiquity serves as the benchmark by which Western audiences and media judge the modern country. Like a spectre, the narrative of a European utopia, or de-historicized myth-space in which the West seeks to discover itself, haunts Western depictions of the modern nation and becomes the main portal to present-day Greece.

During the crisis many foreign commentators and journalists have used ancient Greek mythology or imagery in order to illustrate the dire economic situation of the country and the predicament of its people. It has been claimed that ancient myths lend context to the welter of acrimony and austerity, bailouts and brinkmanship, and have a good deal to say about hubris and ruin, order and chaos, boom and bust.[76] Here are two characteristic examples:

> Greece loves its epic tales and the greatest of them is the story of Odysseus, the hero who took 10 years to find his way back to Ithaca at the end of the Trojan war. A modern version of the Odyssey began in Greece five years ago this weekend when the government in Athens admitted that it had cooked the books to make its budget deficit look much smaller than it actually was. Few thought then that the scandal would have serious ramifications or that the journey through the stormy seas of crisis was to take so long.[77]

> And so Greece's conflict with its creditors drags on, threatening to make the decade-long Trojan war seem like a brief skirmish. Except this time, the Greeks are besieged and facing defeat.[78]

The association of economics with ancient imagery is characteristic of a number of articles in *The Economist*. One of them utilizes two cartoons that imitate the kind of ancient art found on classical red-figure pottery.[79] The first (Figure 1.1) shows a charioteer, resplendent in the EU flag, attempting to flee with piles of cash, while a man in a suit, cast as a hoplite, carries a shield emblazoned with a '€' sign. The second (Figure 1.2) shows two suited men holding up a marble slab bearing a

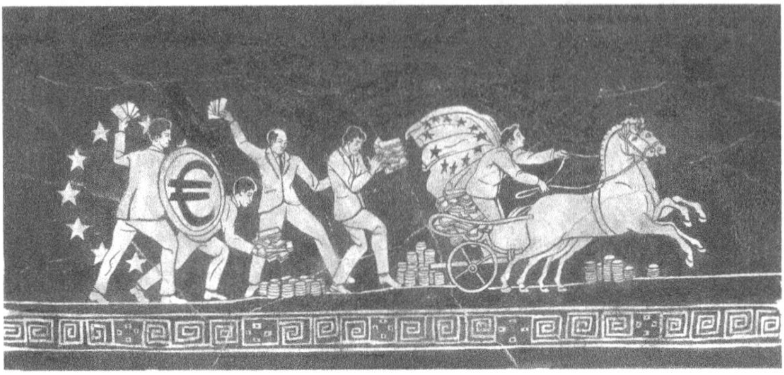

Figure 1.1 Illustration by Robert Venables (*The Economist*, 4 February 2010)

graph showing the decline of the Greek economy. On the right, a group of poorly clad Greek citizens 'wait at the door', looking like victims of exclusion and representing the suffering working and middle classes of Greece. In the background the lofty Acropolis – which both haunts and guards them – is being struck by lightning.[80] The Acropolis can serve both as an authority that sits in judgement and as an image that instantly conjures up ancient Greece and articulates the ever-present threat to the ancient Greek heritage. Depicting the Acropolis gives cartoonists and commentators 'a chance to contrast the lofty, venerated past with the local, downgraded surroundings that represent the present, the modern'.[81] The lightning, symbol of Olympian Zeus, implies that

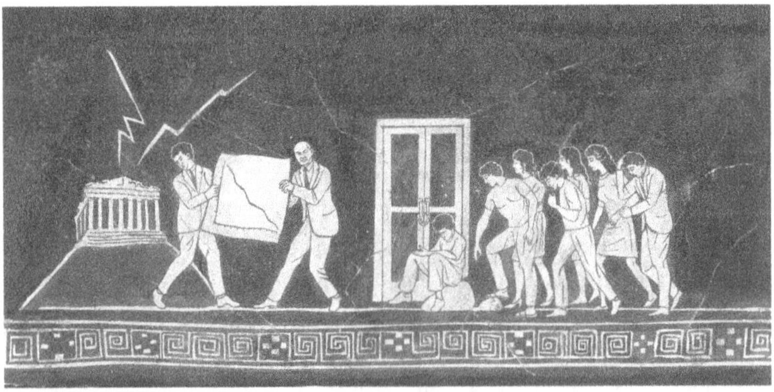

Figure 1.2 Illustration by Robert Venables (*The Economist*, 4 February 2010)

the ancient gods are angry because modern-day Greeks have somehow demeaned ancient Greece's heritage and cultural legacy. And the very language used in the article draws upon ancient themes. Subheadings such as 'Marathon not a sprint' and the punning 'Coming Acropolis', and the headings on the charts 'Spartan times ahead' and 'Olympic record', rely on popular references to antiquity. These, combined with the connotations of the images, encourage the audience to view Greece through this antiquarian prism.

It is clear from the above that Greek antiquity functions as a crucial symbolic resource in the critiquing of modern Greece. It is a trope through which the Western media, and by extension the West, approach and portray Greece in crisis. Symbols, monuments and heritage function as catalysts for understanding and recasting the modern in terms of the ancient. Audiences are invited to appreciate modernity through well-worn, accepted imaginings of the ancient Mediterranean world as the origin of civilization and home of the European spirit. Contemporary issues are, on the one hand, contextualized by universally recognized ancient Greek imagery and, on the other, de-contextualized through distance from the contemporary and the catch-all nature of the depictions. Such imagery is not confined to the realms of opinion pieces and travel writing, but permeates all genres. The portrait of an ancient Greek utopia, comprising a prestigious golden age of cultural excellence, is a commonplace. This 'glorious' ancient Greece is juxtaposed and contrasted with modernity. The modern and ancient are never in unison, nor in harmony; rather the ancient past is set against the 'failures' of modernity with a sense of irony. Antiquity is used to exclude modern Greeks from the discourse of Hellenic achievements, to make them the inefficient 'other' and to disengage the country's mythic status from its precarious present. The Greek crisis is translated against a Hellenic ideal, or even against an antique stereotype.

These frequent references to the ancient Greek world in relation to the crisis are rather surprising, considering that in other areas the ties between classical and modern Greece are presented as tenuous. Though the notion of cultural continuity has been promoted by the Greeks, it has been consistently resisted by many Westerners. It resurfaces only in periods of crisis and for the purposes of unfavourable reporting or commentary. Ancient myths might offer journalists and commentators the opportunity to illustrate their stories and perhaps make them more appealing to their audiences, but this deceptive connection aims at implicit criticism by contrasting ancient glory with contemporary failures. There are, of course, rare exceptions, like an editorial in the *Guardian* which, following Tsipras's comparison of SYRIZA's election victory to the inexorable forward march of an ancient drama, asked: 'Why do we keep returning to these ancient texts?', answering its own question by concluding that the ancient Greek way of thinking 'offers a dynamic means of trying to understand the other – a duty that, in today's world, has never seemed more pressing'.[82]

Though there are allusions to Greek antiquity in many articles in the Western media, there are even more in cartoons and covers of magazines deploying ancient Greek imagery to illustrate contemporary woes. With images ranging from Cerberus to Aphrodite and the Minotaur to Sisyphus, the iconology of crisis is very rich in the Western media. Greece is often presented as a country of ruins by the iconographic juxtaposition of ancient dilapidation with modern financial ruination. The visual impact of these images is more potent than any textual references and reinforces the narrative that it is the Greeks who are responsible for their financial problems.

These images typify the West's approach to the idea and the territory of Greece, a form of 'derealization', defined as 'the displacement of the real from one's own relation with the object on to the object itself'; in other words 'an analysis of the West's relation to Greece and never about Greece itself'.[83] In her study on the economic crisis and political cartoons, Lauren Talalay remarks that the 'cartoons may be suggesting something else as well: the West has long been conflicted about Greece's status as a fully "modern" and "European" nation; these cartoons, thinly disguised with humour, seem to reinforce the idea that Greece is still deemed situated at the margins of Europe.'[84] The impact of this imagery, particularly when deployed in a humorous, ironic or comparative fashion, marginalizes modern Greece, banishing it to the actual and metaphorical edge of Europe by casting the Greeks as failed, 'wayward descendants' of the European and Greek cultural legacy. It is often argued that the ancient past provides the yardstick against which the present is judged, and the prestige awarded to antiquity means that the modern is bound to be found lacking.[85] Talalay notes that few cartoons have 'sounded a note of concern for the rank and file' of Greece, and it is noticeable in the imagery used by the Western media that concern for and depiction of Greek heritage displaces concern for and depiction of the Greek people. In effect, Greece's antiquities and heritage displace Greeks as the inhabitants of Greece.[86]

By contrast, the Greeks themselves have used antiquity to boost their national self-confidence in the midst of economic woes and political uncertainty. Particularly during the second half of 2014, two events demonstrated the politicization of the past and the way it has been used to counter-balance the crisis blues: the archaeological finds at the Amphipolis tomb and the visit to Athens of Amal Clooney, which reignited the debate over the Parthenon sculptures and their return to Greece. The archaeological finds at Amphipolis caused a great deal of excitement and speculation as to who might be buried there. Greek bloggers and some media fantasized that Alexander the Great lay there, though many knew this was unlikely (see Plantzos, Chapter 2). As Professor James Romm put it, 'with their economy cratering and their government shaky, the Greeks are praying that Alexander the Great – or rather, his mother or son, or one of his generals – will come to their rescue'.[87] On the other hand, the suggestion by Professor Olga Palagia that the Amphipolis tomb might not be Macedonian but Roman, memorializing a Roman military victory in the area, was 'deeply disappointing to the Greek nationalist feelings that the excavation has aroused'.[88]

Turned into a media event and used as another piece of evidence for the Greekness of Macedonia, the excavation at Amphipolis was also deployed as a nationalist weapon in Greece's long-standing dispute with their northern neighbours. Thus archaeology emerged as a 'trustee of Hellenism', a champion of the exceptionalist discourse and a morale booster in the crisis. Some have suggested that it briefly became the equivalent of the nationalist 'Great Idea' of the nineteenth and early twentieth centuries. After years of economic austerity, political tumult and a humiliating international bailout, the then government was eager for some good news and the Greeks desperate for heroes. The then prime minister Antonis Samaras proudly displayed on his tablet the findings at the tomb to the German chancellor, Angela Merkel, while a promotional video marking the centenary of the Greek Tourist Organization, called *Gods, Myths, Heroes*, focuses almost exclusively on antiquity; only towards the end does it present a smooth, if debatable, transition to Christianity with 'the old gods taking on new names'. In a period of crisis the video celebrates the light and the landscape of Greece, creating the illusion that the country is inhabited by gods, not real people.

In October 2014 a young Anglo-Lebanese barrister, Amal Alamuddin-Clooney, recently married to a Hollywood star, reanimated the debate about the repatriation of the Parthenon sculptures. She visited Athens to offer her legal services and advise the Greek government on how to secure their return. In the dark days of the crisis, the support of celebrities such as the Clooneys for the campaign for the reunification of the sculptures was a badly needed boost to national pride. In response to this visit, the *Spectator* offered the following advice: 'Given the rioting, economic meltdown and general chaos of recent years, it would be easy to think that Greece had more immediate worries than the whereabouts of a set of decorative stones rescued in the early 19th century'. It went on to propose a compromise: 'We will return the Elgin Marbles once Greece has repaid the €240 billion of emergency loans made by EU states during the crisis, and honoured all its government bonds'.[89]

The Parthenon sculptures and the Amphipolis excavations are not the only story in town. References to Sparta have increased in number during the years of crisis due to its promotion by Golden Dawn, whose members organized regular ritual ceremonies in Thermopylae in front of the statue of Leonidas celebrating the spirit of Sparta. In one of them, in July 2008, Ilias Kasidiaris said this about the role of Golden Dawn:

> We are Sparta's shield, patiently guarding the body of Greece. We continue our lonely course, suffering persecution, slander, and continuous onslaughts from our enemies, who inflict deep cuts on our shield. We await the moment of the big counter attack, following in the steps of the ancient 'Krypteia', who soundlessly killed the city's internal enemies in complete darkness and silence.[90]

Some people did indeed see parallels between the racist attacks of Golden Dawn and the Spartan institution called the 'Krypteia', an elite troupe of initiates. There are two different versions of the latter's activities, one given by Plato and the other by Plutarch.[91] According to Plutarch, young Spartans enrolled in the Krypteia had the task of hiding by day and patrolling the Laconian countryside by night, murdering supposedly dangerous helots. Though the association of the Krypteia with helot-hunting has raised many questions, a number of historians have been seduced by Plutarch's version and have seen it as a kind of secret police whose function was to eliminate any helots marked out as likely troublemakers.[92] Among those obsessed with Sparta is the right-wing Eurosceptic Panagiotis Baltakos, who before the crisis had written two historical novels involving Sparta and the Krypteia: *Το τέλος του Εφιάλτη* (2004), translated as *300: The Hunt for Ephialtes* (2009), and *Ερμοκοπίδες* (*Hermokopidai*) (2006). Baltakos became cabinet secretary of the Samaras government and repeatedly expressed his Eurosceptic views along with his support for Spartan values, Byzantine culture, the Orthodox Church and the armed forces.[93] He was forced to resign his post in April 2014 after his secret talks with Golden Dawn members were revealed in a video.

Though the palingenetic and nationalist discourse of Golden Dawn glorifies other historical periods and heroic figures of Hellenism,[94] Thermopylae and Sparta are their staple symbols of purity and resistance to the decline of the capitalist West. In ancient Sparta, they argue, Lykourgos abolished gold and silver coins in order to promote virtue and stamp out corruption, and the Thermopylae 300 did not worship money and would not have supported the argument for 'the euro at all costs' or signed bailout agreements.[95] During the crisis the resistance at Thermopylae has been turned into a perennial symbol of resistance to creditors and their demands. For Golden Dawn the ideal of the nation transcends capitalism and the barbarism of consumerism and the moral superiority of the Greeks should be guided by the examples of the Spartans.[96]

As we can see, antiquity has been used in different ways by Westerners and Greeks during the crisis. The former refer back to it to illustrate modern failures; the latter deploy the ancient past as a source of pride and an opportunity for reflection. Cherry-picking from Greece's history, Greeks and non-Greeks have searched for explanations for and antidotes to the crisis, confirming the instrumental role of the past in engaging with the crisis.

The politics of monumentality: Graffiti and cultural heritage

During the crisis a proliferation of graffiti has swept over Greek cityscapes, particularly in Athens, while the slogan *vasanizomai* (literally 'I am in torment/being tortured')[97] has captured the attention of many visitors to Athens and has been turned into a symbol of the plight of a nation and a culture of empathy.[98] This powerful message of suffering articulates human despair and has been appropriated into crisis discourses by artists, bloggers, journalists and academics. Street art's *raison d'être* in the cityscape is in many ways about fostering a relationship between the artist, the viewer and the city.[99] The widespread use of politicized urban art in the urban landscape could be seen as one of the most emblematic manifestations of Agamben's 'state of exception' and as a barometer that registers levels of creativity and the spectrum of thought in hard times.[100] For some the graffitied slogans can represent a creative and challenging collapse of private and public space, a kind of 'social diary on public display'; for others the disrespect of the public space in Greece goes back a long way, since public and private have not co-existed harmoniously for many years. The former has invariably been subordinated to the latter due to the fact that Greeks have behaved primarily as individual property owners and not as citizens. However, both sides seem to agree that during the crisis graffiti and street art have emerged as a way of revising the past and Greece's cultural heritage, and thus have acquired symbolic significance. It is not so much aesthetics that matters here as historical significance.

In particular, the painting of the walls of the historic building of the National Technical University/Athens Polytechnic (a symbol of resistance against the military junta) by unknown artists stirred up a debate (Figure 1.3).[101] The monumental black and white graffiti art on the corner of Stournari Street and Patission Street was created in just one night in March 2015. Reactions were mixed. Those who did not see the graffiti as an artistic contribution but as a form of anti-social behaviour, an assault on the public space and a desecration of an historic building wondered whether the Acropolis could be next. They argued that in the past provocative artistic gestures or assaults on convention and good taste had not vandalized other artefacts or historic buildings (e.g. Marcel Duchamp, *Fountain*, 1917). For them writing on or painting the walls of public buildings was a form of private appropriation of the public space, similar to building without permission in a protected zone or in a conservation area, and not the artistic expression of a collectivity.

Others argued that the enigmatic mural does not invite aesthetic appreciation but aims to provoke and subvert bourgeois order and

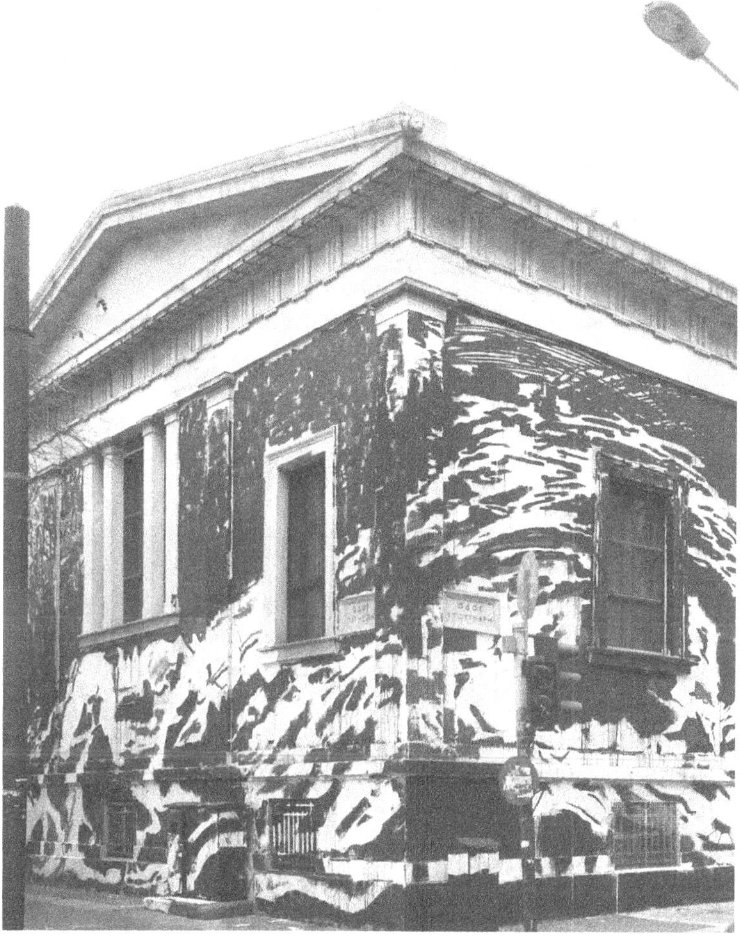

Figure 1.3 The National Technical University (Athens Polytechnic). Photo courtesy of Penelope Petsini

cleanliness. It de-territorialized the Polytechnic as 'a political topos of Hellenism'.[102] The black-and-white mural has been seen as making a statement about the failure of the Greek education system and representing the mood of a city in crisis. On social media it has even been suggested that the mural recalled Picasso's *Guernica* or a painting by Jackson Pollock, while others have interpreted the work as a 'heterotopia' to use Foucault's term. For some graffiti is a form of art and not of vandalism, and the independently managed Theatre of Embros called on its Facebook page for the removal of the graffiti, which they defined as an artistic 'monument', to be halted. Historic buildings are living monuments, places of creative interaction, and not fossilized spaces. Leaving aside the question of whether graffiti is vandalism or art, what is crucial here is that there was an attempt to engage with cultural heritage in a challenging way. The painting of a sculpture or a listed building is not necessarily a form of vandalism but could be seen as a revision of the past and its aesthetics.[103] The issue of community representation and engagement is crucial in public art discourse, shifting debates from aesthetics and design to social accountability.

The economic crisis complicated things even further in the case of the Polytechnic, the emblematic *lieu de mémoire* and the symbol of the fight against authoritarianism, by encouraging 'the complete dismissal of both the entire period of the transition to democracy and of the Polytechnic generation in particular'.[104] For attempting to exploit their credentials as resistance fighters against the junta the so-called 'Polytechnic generation' have become the target of a series of character assassinations in the noir novel *Ψωμί, Παιδεία, Ελευθερία* [*Bread, Education, Freedom*] (2012) by Petros Markaris (part of his Crisis Trilogy). In various ways, one of the foundational myths of the post-1974 Greek Republic has come under fire as a result of the scepticism and disillusionment caused by the crisis. Even in the 'December Events' of 2008 the majority of the activists tried to avoid being identified with past events, and the signs of imaginary links with a revolutionary heritage were rather ambiguous. Interestingly, the Polytechnic uprising of 1973, a point of reference for almost every youth movement since 1974, was not evoked consistently in the demonstrations that followed the killing of a 15-year-old student in Athens in December 2008.[105]

Lack of respect for historic buildings and statues has been exacerbated during the crisis, perhaps due to a desire to re-examine and reshape the past. Next to the Polytechnic building in Athens there is a statue of a young girl with her hands tied behind her back and her head raised. This sculpture, a symbol of the irredentist claims to Northern Epirus (Southern Albania), has been painted and provocatively transformed. Graffiti also appeared on the walls of the eleventh-century Church of Panagia Kapnikarea in Athens and on the neoclassical building and statues of Athens University, while the statue of the poet Kostis Palamas in central Athens and other statues and monuments have also been painted or damaged.[106] In another provocative act activists also dressed in orange the statue of the leading Cretan statesman Eleftherios Venizelos in the centre of Iraklio in Crete.

The vandalizing of churches such as the Holy Anargyroi and the Kapnikarea in Athens drew some comparisons with the desecration of Jewish cemeteries, places of worship of different religions, and even the destruction of Assyrian statues in the Museum of Mosul by the forces of the so-called Islamic State. It has been pointed out that, though there are vociferous protests about the other acts of desecration, no corresponding objections have been raised to the vandalizing of Christian churches, raising issues of religious freedom and the vexed issue of the relationship between narcissistic activism and cultural heritage. Though in the past similar acts have occurred, it seems that the crisis has generated a trend for revising cultural heritage by transforming works of art and architecture. It has fostered the desire to recreate the past by modernizing it, so that it could reflect a culture in crisis. Street art has become emblematic of a society revisiting its past and trying to express a precarious future.

Revisiting the past: Regression and revision

Urbanization, the dominant trend in Greek society during the twentieth century, led to a disproportionately overblown metropolitan population and the desertion of the countryside. For the first time in years the crisis has started reversing this process, with many young unemployed people returning to their villages, sometimes to cultivate the land of their ancestors. The countryside has become a kind of safe haven from the crisis-ridden urban space, and a return to the land and agriculture is considered an antidote to the unemployment caused by the economic situation.

In fiction this regression to the countryside is manifested in various ways. Sometimes it takes the form of a catharsis from the crisis-ridden cityscape or a search for some sort of authenticity, expiation or survival, as can be seen in the fiction of Yannis Makridakis (born 1971), associated with his native island of Chios, its ethos and local idiom. Considered one of the most significant writers of the crisis, his stories promote ecological activism and pit the self-sufficiency of nature and organic farming against a money-driven urban culture (see also Willert, Chapter 9). In particular, his novella *Το ζουμί του πετεινού* [*Cockerel Soup*] (2012) contrasts the crisis with the natural world. The main character lives, obliviously happy, on his remote farm with his wife, enjoying an 'authentic' life close to the land and away from city life. One day by chance he becomes aware of the consequences of the crisis and the possibility of the authorities selling off ancestral land to pay national debts. For three days his mental state is disturbed, leading to his smashing a television set in anger. However, he soon recovers and returns to his previous existence, cultivating his land and enjoying a life close to nature. Return to a pre-social, naive but authentic Arcadia is offered here as an alternative to the malaise of the crisis. Makridakis' narratives have a somewhat didactic tone and recall earlier rural stories, suggesting a utopian local ecology as an antidote to the crisis and globalization.

However, return to the local, not as a back-to-nature retreat but as a violent, lonely and dystopian setting, can be found in other fictional narratives of the crisis. For example, Christos Oikonomou (b. 1970), in his collection of stories *Το καλό θα 'ρθει από τη θάλασσα* [*All Good Things Will Come from the Sea*] (2014), explores the tension between locals and the Athenian incomers, who have arrived in an unnamed island due to the crisis. Here the island is transformed from an attractive tourist destination into a dark and evil place. Though there are no explicit references to the crisis in Michalis Markopoulos' noir novella *Το δέντρο του Ιούδα* [*The Judas tree*] (2014), his central character also returns to his village (Delvinaki) in Epirus after losing his job and his life in Athens breaks down. In this case we are dealing with a ritual of return, neither nostalgic nor escapist, but an encounter with the violent and harsh reality of a borderland.

One of the secondary characters of Rhea Galanaki's novel *Η Άκρα Ταπείνωση* [*Utmost Humiliation*] (2015) also returns to her village (tellingly called Apano Riza i.e. Upper Root) in Crete after her son has perpetrated a racist attack and she too has been stabbed by him. Her son defies the past and becomes a neo-Nazi, tarnishing her village and desecrating the history of her parents, who had suffered at the hands of the Germans during the war, and making her abandon 'crime-ridden' Athens for her native island. Though the setting of the novel is the Athens of the crisis, references to a mythical and historical past are clear to see. First, the book's title alludes to the Orthodox iconography of the Man of Sorrows; secondly, the way the novel is organized has been compared to the structure of an ancient tragedy;[107] and thirdly, the main female characters have modified their names to resemble ancient Greek ones (Thiresia/Teiresia and Theonymphe/Nymphe), while Theonymphe's son is called Orestes. There is also an inversion of the myths involving Zeus, the abduction of Europa and the Minotaur. Galanaki's novel may be about what has been going on in Athens during the crisis, but it goes back to the history of Greece, and particularly to the protests of 1965, to the events of the Athens Polytechnic in 1973 and the dramatic night of 12 February 2012. As the birthplace of ancient tragedy, Athens is presented in the novel as the setting of a contemporary drama without a director and actors: 'Athens ... cannot get rid of its past, it will remain across the centuries an open-air theatrical scene'.[108] The protected space of the care home where the two elderly female characters live is contrasted to the burning of a listed building in Athens during the episodes of February 2012. The two women escape from the home, dressed in a carnivalesque manner, feeling liberated and elated as they join the demonstrations in central Athens. The real and mythical Athens co-exist in the novel and the contrasting historical and modern images of the city add to the historical dimension of the novel.[109] Revolts against the past take different forms in the novel, opposing sons to mothers and modern revolutionaries to old heroes, and questioning the role of the older generation and the value of emblematic historic buildings. Galanaki's novel represents an eloquent case of the historical framing of a literary narrative.[110]

The crisis triggered off a self-reflective mode and its chroniclers have produced self-questioning fictional narratives. Using a quotation from Lawrence Durell on self-knowledge and Greece as the epigraph to his novel *Αλλάζει πουκάμισο το φίδι* [*The snake sheds its skin*] (2013), Kostas Akrivos searches the past in order to find out what makes him Greek and proud of his heritage in the midst of the crisis. His narrator travels all over Greece and revisits local history, music and literary texts as a kind of elementary lesson in the 'geography' of Greece (*patridognosia*) and a comforting counterweight to the crisis blues. A regression to the past and to a holistic lifestyle triggered by the crisis is intertwined here with an attempt to rediscover a hidden Greece and its cultural heritage.

Michalis Modinos' novel *Τελευταία Έξοδος Στυμφαλία* [*Last Exit to Stymphalia*] (2014) involves a narrator who is looking back at his personal life and the period before the crisis (referred to in the novel as a 'catastrophe'). This road novel-cum-chronicle consists of the narrator's monologue, as he contemplates suicide while travelling late at night on the Attica motorway, reflecting on what had gone wrong for him and his country. Adopting an ironic approach, Modinos questions national myths and reflects on what led to the crisis. This is a novel about the disintegration of a life and the possibility of a dystopian future, given that the action seems to take place when the catastrophe has reached its peak and the country has been devastated. Unlike Makridakis' viewpoint, the ecological perspective of Modinos is less optimistic and clear-cut. Ultimately he finds an uncertain escape from the devastation of the crisis in the mythological lake of Stymphalia, where it is suggested that the protagonist/narrator may find reconciliation with his son.

The crisis seems to promote on the one hand retrospection, including the revising of musical hits of previous decades, now perceived as a period of lost happiness,[111] while on the other it has encouraged a number of artists to revisit and destabilize the past in different ways by making political interventions. A revisionist attitude towards the past can be found in a radical adaptation of Giuseppe Verdi's opera *Aida*. Back in 2010 Bernhard Glocksin, the artistic director of Neuköllner Oper, an alternative but well-established musical theatre in Berlin, commissioned a Greek–German opera for the crisis, a co-production with The Beggars' Operas and the Thessaloniki Concert Hall. This led to a musically and dramaturgically revised version of Verdi's opera, a project brought to fruition by Glocksin in collaboration with Alexandros Efklidis, Charalambos Goyos and Dimitris Dimopoulos. The setting of this adaptation of *Aida*, a story of colonizers and colonized, was the headquarters of the European Central Bank in Frankfurt, and the work was premiered in January 2012 in Berlin under the title *Yasou Aida!*. The conflict between the Egyptians and the Ethiopians of the original opera is transferred to the setting of the European Union. Aida is renamed Elpida (Hope), who as a trainee Greek economist is pursuing a better future at the European Central Bank. Though the central issue of the new opera is the migration of young professionals due to the crisis, the opera avoids easy moralizing, offering an interesting Greco–German dialogue. The changes to the classic opera bring about a transnational critique and deconstruct in a postmodern fashion neo-colonial stereotypes (the 'hardworking' North and the 'lazy' South, the 'disciplined' Germans and the 'unruly' Greeks) in crisis-struck Europe, blurring the boundaries between composition and performance, tragedy and farce, classical and contemporary musical theatre. The Parthenon, *evzones* and images from the 2004 Athens Olympics also contribute to the ironic playfulness of *Yasou Aida!*.[112]

Another ironic reference to the past can be found in a series of paste-ups created by Dimitris Taxis on the walls of Athens with such titles as 'I wish you could learn something useful from the past'. The latter illustrates the Greek predicament by showing a hunched boy stuck between past and present, sitting on a stack of books with the names of Socrates, Plato and Democracy on their spines, while others entitled 'Athens means Luxury', 'Economics', 'No Future' and 'Survival Guide' weigh down on him from above. The boy, like Atlas, shows signs of resignation, but – caught between past and present – is unable to escape (Figure 1.4).

The crisis also transformed the Hellenic Festival, associated since its establishment in 1955 with performances in Athens (focused on contemporary theatre) and at the ancient theatre of Epidaurus. The cuts in its budget offered opportunities to younger artists and experimental theatre groups working on low-cost projects to challenge traditional views on performance and the sanctity of ancient texts. Though allusions to current events were not entirely lacking in earlier performances of ancient Greek drama, these have become more frequent during the crisis (e.g. Creon in *Antigone* has been compared to Wolfgang Schäuble), and particularly in performances of Aristophanes' plays. This opening up to alternative performances destabilized institutional frameworks and questioned the primacy of the ancient text in the drama performances at Epidaurus and by extension reverence for the ancient past. The political controversy and uncertainty surrounding the management of the Hellenic Festival in 2013 led to calls for the reinvention of the Epidaurus Festival and its separation from the Athens Festival in an attempt to protect the ancient drama (and, in turn, the ancient past) from being performed in derelict urban spaces or its violation by the sort of avant-garde productions that the cash-strapped Hellenic Festival had been obliged to encourage for reasons of economy.

Figure 1.4 'I wish you could learn something useful from the past'. Paste-up by Dimitris Taxis in Kerameikos, Athens. Photo: Julia Tulke/ aestheticsofcrisis.org

The reinvention of the Epidaurus Festival as an international festival of ancient drama in the midst of the crisis was aimed at celebrating continuity with antiquity and reinventing a cultural lineage.[113] What emerges from all the above is that the crisis has encouraged a re-examination and a creative re-thinking of the past, inviting Greeks and non-Greeks to reflect on the role of cultural heritage.

Conclusion

Though Greece represents around three per cent of the European economy, its cultural gravitas in the European project is much greater than its economic weight. Another country of similar size might have been forced to leave the Eurozone, but Greece still occupies a special place in the European imaginary. An article in the *Guardian* claimed that the Acropolis, as the symbol of the country's glorious past and of modern democracy, gives the Greek negotiating position huge moral strength: 'The eurozone's image and its cohesion would be irreparably damaged should the Acropolis come to represent the failure of EU institutions and not their success'.[114] In the same newspaper Jonathan Jones contended that 'A Europe without Greece would not feel like Europe at all. So Greece and Europe are stuck with each other, and the reasons are visible every time the Acropolis appears on the skyline in a news report. For Greece is not just a country. It is a living symbol of Europe'.[115]

As we have seen above, the crisis has encouraged Greeks to revisit and engage with the past in different, often critical or ironic, ways. Thus, they have ended up torn between evoking and overcoming it, remembering and forgetting, caught between a fear of regression to earlier, harsher times and optimism about renegotiating the way the past affects the present. In 1951 E.M. Forster reported the following reminiscences from his conversations with C.P. Cavafy:

> Half humorously, half seriously, he once compared the Greeks and the English. The two peoples are almost exactly alike, he argued; quick-witted, resourceful, adventurous. 'But there is one unfortunate difference between us, one little difference. We Greeks have lost our capital – and the results are what you see. Pray, my dear Forster, oh pray, that you never lose your capital'.[116]

Though Cavafy was likely to be referring to the capital of the Byzantine Empire, i.e. Constantinople, it is tempting to reinterpret this statement in the light of the present financial crisis. The Greeks may have ended up heavily in debt, having experienced their worst economic crisis to date, yet their past, as cultural capital, has emerged as an even more contested area. One might rightly expect economic crises to be about current difficulties and future solutions, but as I have shown here, with examples drawn from various areas – international relations, history-antiquity and contemporary culture – the past is part and parcel of the debates and the politics of the crisis. The past is employed as a tool for explaining the crisis, for engaging affectively or comparatively with history and for rethinking the uses of and challenges to cultural heritage. Generating a kind of 'preposterous history', the crisis has provided a perspective for revisiting the past and searching for causes, highlighting affective parallels, reviving memories and triggering hybrid approaches to cultural heritage. This dialogics of past and present involves the resignification of the past and the recontextualization of the present. In conclusion, the crisis has made the past more public, more controversial and more relevant.

Notes

1. Greece's debt saga has created its own crisis lexicon and led to a war over semantics. From the introduction of 'Grexit', coined in February 2012 and added to the Oxford dictionary in 2015, we have moved on to new shorthand terms such as 'Grimbo', 'Gredge' and 'Greekment' a few years later. In February 2015 'austerity' was replaced by 'current arrangements', 'troika' by 'institutions', 'bailout programme' by 'loan extension' and 'bridge loan' (Simon Kennedy, 'Grexit is so 2012. Citigroup introduces grimbo to crisis lexicon', *Bloomberg*, 23 April 2015, available at http://www.bloomberg.com/news/articles/2015-04-23/grexit-is-so-2012-citigroup-introduces-grimbo-to-crisis-lexicon and 'On the Gredge', The *Economist*, 25 April 2015, available at http://www.economist.com/node/21649466/print (accessed 17 July 2016).
2. Stuart Jeffries (interview with Tariq Ali), 'You can't just wait for something to happen. You have to do something', *Guardian*, 21 February 2015, p. 26. Available at http://www.theguardian.com/politics/2015/feb/20/tariq-ali-interview-renationalise-the-railways (accessed 15 July 2016).
3. Stathis N. Kalyvas, *Modern Greece: What Everyone Needs to Know* (Oxford, 2015), p. 204.
4. Alain Badiou, *Being and Event*, translated by Oliver Feltham (London, 2005).
5. Mieke Bal, *Quoting Caravaggio: Contemporary Art, Preposterous History* (Chicago, 1999).

6. Importantly, Mieke Bal cites T.S. Eliot at the outset: 'Whoever has approved this idea of order ... will not find it preposterous that the past should be altered by the present as much as the present is directed by the past'.
7. Even the December revolt of 2008 is described as 'the precise moment when an entire generation awoke to the realization that the muted stories of the past had always been part of the present', Dimitris Dalakoglou & Antonis Vradis, 'Introduction' in Antonis Vradis and Dimitris Dalakoglou, *Revolt and Crisis in Greece: Between a present yet to pass and a future still to come* (Oakland & Edinburgh, 2011), p. 14.
8. Cathy Caruth, *Unclaimed Experience: Trauma, Narrative, and History* (Baltimore 1996), p. 7.
9. Ron Eyerman, *Cultural Trauma: Slavery and the Formation of African American Identity* (Cambridge, 2001), p. 3.
10. Michel Serres, *Conversations on Science, Culture, and Time* (Ann Arbor, 1995).
11. Daniel Martyn Knight, 'Cultural proximity: crisis, time and social memory in central Greece', *History and Anthropology* 23/3 (2012), p. 350.
12. Costas Lapavitsas, 'The Greek crisis – politics, economics, ethics: a debate held at the Birkbeck Institute for the Humanities, Birkbeck College, University of London, 5 May 2010', *Journal of Modern Greek Studies* 28/2 (2010), pp. 293–294.
13. Yanis Varoufakis, 'We are all Greeks now! The crisis in Greece in its European and global context', in Anna Triandafyllidou, Ruby Gropas and Hara Kouki (eds), *The Greek Crisis and European Modernity* (New York, 2013), pp. 44, 52.
14. Ibid., p. 45.
15. Yanis Varoufakis, 'Being Greek and an economist while Greece is burning! An intimate account of a peculiar tragedy', *Journal of Modern Greek Studies* 32/1 (2014), p. 13.
16. Yannis Hamilakis, 'Some debts can never be repaid: the archaeo-politics of the crisis', *Journal of Modern Greek Studies* 34/2 (2016), p. 255.
17. Slavoj Žižek, 'Save us from the saviours', *London Review of Books*, 34:11, 7 June 2012. Available at http://www.lrb.co.uk/v34/n11/slavoj-zizek/save-us-from-the-saviours (accessed 10 August 2016).
18. Costas Douzinas, *Philosophy and Resistance in the Crisis* (Cambridge, 2013), p. 7.
19. The former president of France, Valéry Giscard d'Estaing, generally thought of as a friend of Greece, remarked in September 2012: 'Greece is basically an Oriental country' (Kalyvas, op.cit. 5).
20. Kevin Featherstone, 'The Greek crisis – politics, economics, ethics: a debate held at the Birkbeck Institute for the Humanities, Birkbeck College, University of London, 5 May 2010', op. cit., pp. 298–299. Elsewhere he argues: 'The 2010 crisis was the result, in significant part, of inherited state failure in Greece', Kevin Featherstone, 'The Greek sovereign debt crisis and EMU: a failing state in a skewed regime', *Journal of Common Market Studies* 49/2 (2011), p. 211. See also Elena Panaritis, 'The historical roots of Greece's

debt crisis: can the roots of today's debt crisis in Greece be traced as far back as the 1830s?', *The Globalist*, 13 May 2011, available at http://www.theglobalist.com/the-historical-roots-of-greeces-debt-crisis/ (accessed 15 July 2016) and Spyridon N. Litsas, 'The Greek failing state and its "smart power" prospects: a theoretical approach', *Mediterranean Quarterly* 26/3 (2014), pp. 52–73.

21. Featherstone, 'The Greek crisis – politics, economics, ethics', op. cit., pp. 299–301. Surveys (carried out between December 2010–June 2012) about the causes of the crisis indicate that almost all respondents (88 per cent) see corruption as by far the biggest contributing factor. See Georgios Karyotis and Wolfgang Rüdig, 'Protest Participation, Electoral Choices and Public Attitudes towards Austerity in Greece' in Georgios Karyotis & Roman Gerodimos (eds), *The Politics of Extreme Austerity: Greece in the Eurozone Crisis* (Basingstoke 2015), pp. 130–131.
22. Edmund S. Phelps, 'The foundations of Greece's failed economy', *Project Syndicate*, 4 September 2015. Available at https://www.project-syndicate.org/commentary/foundation-of-greeces-failed-economy-by-edmund-s–phelps-2015-09 (accessed 20 July 2016).
23. Paschalis M. Kitromilides, *Enlightenment and Revolution: The Making of Modern Greece* (Cambridge, Mass 2013), p. xii. Takis S. Pappas makes a similar argument by pointing out that the Greek crisis 'is fundamentally political, and that it has been long in the making. Greece's failure is the outcome of a long process during which populism prevailed over liberalism and became hegemonic in society' ('Why Greece failed', *Journal of Democracy* 24/2 (2013), p. 33). Roderick Beaton in an unpublished lecture on Lord Byron and the cultural and economic politics of Greece during the Greek War of Independence argues that the roots of the present economic and social crisis in Greece go deep into the historical and cultural foundations of the Greek nation-state in the early nineteenth century (http://www.megaron.gr/default.asp?pid=5&la=1&evID=3170).
24. Tolis Malakos, 'Greece facing herself: the past and present as fate', *Journal of Balkan and Near Eastern Studies*, 15/1 (2013), p. 3.
25. Neoliberalism and populism/clientelism are indictments made by one camp about the other.
26. Loukas Tsoukalis, 'International bubbles, European currency union, and national failures: the case of Greece and the euro crisis', in Anna Triandafyllidou, Ruby Gropas and Hara Kouki (eds), *The Greek Crisis and European Modernity*, op. cit., p. 29.
27. Roman Gerodimos and Georgios Karyotis, 'Austerity Politics and Crisis Governance: Lessons from Greece' in Georgios Karyotis & Roman Gerodimos (eds), *The Politics of Extreme Austerity: Greece in the Eurozone Crisis*, op.cit., p. 262.
28. Stephen Fidler, 'Greece vs. Germany: two competing national narratives', *Wall Street Journal*, 5 March 2015. Available at http://www.wsj.com/articles/greece-vs-germany-two-competing-national-narratives-1425591266 (accessed 14 July 2016).

29. John Galt, *Letters From the Levant: containing views of the state of society, manner, opinions and commerce in Greece and several of the principal islands of the archipelago* (London 1813), p. 78, cf. Paul Sheehan, 'Throw out cheating Greece before the rot cripples the rest of the world', *Sydney Morning Herald*, 15 September 2011. Available at http://www.smh.com.au/federal-politics/political-opinion/throw-out-cheating-greece-before-the-rot-cripples-rest-of-the-world-20110914-1k9lp.html (accessed 15 July 2016).
30. John Agnew, 'No borders, no nations: making Greece in Macedonia', *Annals of the Association of American Geographers*, 97/2 (2007), p. 410.
31. Takis Theodoropoulos, 'Η ελληνική ταυτότητα' (The Greek identity), *I Kathimerini*, 22 February 2015. Available at http://www.kathimerini.gr/804738/opinion/epikairothta/politikh/h-ellhnikh-taytothta (accessed 15 July 2016).
32. Palash Ghosh, 'Are Greeks really European?', *International Business Times*, 9 November 2011. Available at http://www.ibtimes.com/are-greeks-really-european-212891 (accessed 16 July 2016).
33. David Patrikarakos, 'The Greeks are not "Western"', *Politico*, 22 April 2015. Available at http://www.politico.eu/article/the-greeks-are-not-western/ (accessed 15 July 2016). See also Andreas Pappas, 'Η διαχρονική γοητεία του αντιδυτικισμού (The transhistorical charm of anti-Westernism), *To Vima*, 22 March 2015, available at http://www.tovima.gr/opinions/article/?aid=687923 (accessed 15 July 2016) and Takis Theodoropoulos, 'Κι αν δεν ανήκομεν εις την Δύσιν;' (And if we don't belong to the West?), *I Kathimerini*, 26 April 2015, available at http://www.kathimerini.gr/812898/opinion/epikairothta/politikh/ki-an-den-anhkomen-eis-thn-dysin (accessed 15 July 2016).
34. David Patrikarakos, 'The Greeks are not "Western"'.
35. Giles Fraser, 'Arguments over Greek debt echo ancient disputes about Easter', *Guardian*, 10 April 2015. Available at http://www.theguardian.com/commentisfree/belief/2015/apr/10/argument-about-greek-debt-echo-ancient-disputes-about-easter (accessed 11 July 2016).
36. Susannah Verney, 'Waking the "sleeping giant" or expressing domestic dissent? Mainstreaming Euroscepticism in crisis-stricken Greece', *International Political Science Review*, 36/3, 2015, pp. 279–295.
37. Ioannis D. Stefanidis, *Stirring the Greek Nation: Political Culture, Irredentism and Anti-Americanism in Post-war Greece, 1945–1967* (Aldershot 2007), and E. Kirtsoglou and D. Theodossopoulos, 'The poetics of anti-Americanism in Greece: rhetoric, agency, and local meaning', *Social Analysis* 54/1 (2010), pp. 106–124.
38. Paul Krugman, 'The tyranny of Greece over Germany', *New York Times*, 27 January 2015. Available at http://krugman.blogs.nytimes.com/2015/01/27/the-tyranny-of-greece-over-germany/ (accessed 15 July 2016).
39. Hagen Fleischer, 'Germany owes Greece money for the war – but morality needn't come into it', *Guardian*, 10 February 2015. Available at http://www.

theguardian.com/commentisfree/2015/feb/10/germany-greece-second-world-war-reparations. Germany is even being asked to repay the fares which 48,000 Greek Jews from Thessaloniki were forced to pay for their transportation to Auschwitz (http://www.tovima.gr/society/article/?aid=693960&wordsinarticle=εβραίοι%3bΘεσσαλονίκης) (accessed 14 July 2016).

40. Despina-Georgia Konstantinakou, *Πολεμικές οφειλές και εγκληματίες πολέμου στην Ελλάδα* [War reparations and war criminals in Greece] (Athens 2015), Nicos Christodoulakis, *Germany's War Debt to Greece: A Burden Unsettled* (Basingstoke 2014), Hagen Fleischer and Despina Konstantinakou, 'Ad calendas graecas? Griechenland und die deutsche Wiedergutmachung', in Hans Günter Hockerts, Claudia Moisel, and Tobias Winstel (eds) *Grenzen der Wiedergutmachung* (Göttingen, 2006), pp. 375–457, Karl Heinz Roth, *Griechenland am Abgrund. Die deutsche Reparationsschuld* (Hamburg, 2015).
41. For the full text of the Greek Prime Minster's speech in Greek see http://www.primeminister.gov.gr/2015/03/10/13387 (accessed 16 July 2016). Immediately after his civil swearing in, in a gesture of remembrance and of solidarity with the wartime left, Alexis Tsipras went to Kaisariani, where 200 left-wing resistance fighters were executed by the Nazis in 1944.
42. Leonid Bershidsky, 'Dear Greece: World War II ended 70 years ago', *Bloomberg View*, 12 March 2015. Available at http://www.bloombergview.com/articles/2015-03-12/dear-greece-world-war-ii-ended-70-years-ago (accessed 15 July 2016).
43. Gideon Rachman, 'Greece's reparations demand could bring the euro crisis to a head', *Financial Times*, 9 April 2015. Available at http://blogs.ft.com/the-world/2015/04/greeces-reparations-demand-could-bring-the-euro-crisis-to-a-head/ (accessed 15 July 2016).
44. Tim Worstall, 'Greece claims €279 Billion in German war reparations; they're not going to get it', *Forbes*, 7 April 2015, available at http://www.forbes.com/sites/timworstall/2015/04/07/greece-claims-e279-billion-in-german-war-reparations-theyre-not-going-to-get-it/ and Jérôme Gautheret, 'Réparations de guerre: quand Athènes joue avec le feu', *Le Monde*, 7 April 2015, available at http://www.lemonde.fr/europe/article/2015/03/25/reparations-de-guerre-quand-athenes-joue-avec-le-feu_4600550_3214.html (accessed 17 July 2016).
45. For the sexual connotations of anti-Germanism in Greece and the equation of Greekness with potent sexuality see Konstantinos Kalantzis, '"Fak Germani": materialities of nationhood and transgression in the Greek crisis', *Comparative Studies in Society and History* 57/4 (2015), pp. 1037–1069.
46. For a review of Greco-German relations see Philippe Douroux, 'Johann Chapoutot: "Pour les Allemands, les Grecs d'aujourd'hui ne sont pas à la hauteur des Grecs anciens"', *Liberation*, 15 July 2015. Available at http://www.liberation.fr/monde/2015/07/15/johann-chapoutot-pour-les-allemands-les-

grecs-d-aujourd-hui-ne-sont-pas-a-la-hauteur-des-grecs-ancie_1348468 (accessed 16 July 2016).

47. The German historian Heinz Richter, author of *Operation Mercury: The Invasion of Crete*, had been charged by a prosecutor on the island of Crete with denying the Nazi crimes committed against the Cretan people and debunking some myths about the resistance on the island during World War II. It all started in 2014 when the University of Crete decided to honour him with an honorary doctorate. Though he was cleared of all charges in 2016, his trial exacerbated widespread anti-German feelings in Greece during the crisis.
48. Louise Couvelaire, 'Allemands et Grecs s'affrontent à coup de caricatures', *Le Monde*, 5 March 2015. Available at http://www.lemonde.fr/m-actu/article/2015/03/05/allemands-et-grecs-se-chamaillent-a-coup-de-caricatures_4582862_4497186.html?xtmc=grece&xtcr=10 (accessed 20 July 2016).
49. More details are available at http://www.kis.gr/en/index.php?option=com_content&view=article&id=584:reactions-for-dimitris-kammenos-fb-posts-trivializing-holocaust-&catid=49:2009-05-11-09-28-23 (accessed 20 July 2016).
50. Giorgos Antoniou, Elias Dinas, Spyros Kosmidis and Leon Saltiel, 'Collective Victimhood and anti-Semitism', working paper, https://www.researchgate.net/profile/Elias_Dinas/publication/285236109_Collective_Victimhood_and_Social_Prejudice_A_Post-Holocaust_Theory_of_anti-Semitism/links/565cd59f08aefe619b254404.pdf/download?version=va p. 28 (accessed 15 July 2016).
51. Ibid. and 'Ανησυχητική αύξηση του αντισημιτισμού δείχνει έρευνα στην Ελλάδα' [A disturbing increase in anti-Semitism in Greece is shown in an opinion poll], *To Vima*, 19 March 2015, available at http://www.tovima.gr/society/article/?aid=687316 (accessed 20 July 2016) and Harry van Versendaal, 'Victimhood culture spawns Greek anti-Semitism, study finds', *ekathimerini.com*, 19 March 2015. Available at http://www.ekathimerini.com/168389/article/ekathimerini/community/victimhood-culture-spawns-greek-anti-semitism-study-finds (accessed 16 July 2016).
52. Giorgos Antoniou, Elias Dinas, Spyros Kosmidis and Leon Saltiel, 'Collective victimhood and anti-Semitism', op. cit.
53. The former Mayor of London, Boris Johnson, encouraged Greeks to rediscover the spirit of Marathon in order to break free from the shackles of Brussels ('Greece must rediscover the spirit of Marathon to burst its euro shackles', *Telegraph*, 12 July 2015. Available at http://www.telegraph.co.uk/finance/economics/11734869/Greece-must-rediscover-the-spirit-of-Marathon-to-burst-its-euro-shackles.html (accessed 15 July 2016).
54. Cathy Caruth, op. cit. p. 18.
55. Dominick LaCapra, *Writing History, Writing Trauma* (Baltimore & London 2001), pp. 65–67, 141–146.

56. Walter Benjamin, 'Theses on the philosophy of history', in *Illuminations*, trans. Harry Zohn (London 1979), p. 257.
57. Marianne Hirsch, 'The Generation of Postmemory', *Poetics Today* 29/1 (Spring 2008), pp. 103–128 and *Family frames: photography, narrative, and postmemory* (Cambridge, Mass. & London, 1997).
58. Johanna Hanink, 'Ode on a Grecian Crisis', *Eidolon*, 20 July 2015. Available at https://eidolon.pub/ode-on-a-grecian-crisis-de3c92595a97#.tt7k15no7 (accessed 7 May 2016).
59. Robert Zaretsky, 'What would Thucydides say about the crisis in Greece?', *New York Times*, 1 July 2015. Available at http://www.nytimes.com/2015/07/01/opinion/what-would-thucydides-say-about-the-crisis-in-greece.html?_r=1 (accessed 18 July 2016).
60. Armand D' Angour, 'Ancient Greek solution for debt crisis', BBC, 6 June 2012. Available at http://www.bbc.co.uk/news/business-18255039 (accessed 18 July 2016).
61. David M. Pritchard, 'If ancient Greeks could balance a budget, why can't we?' *Sydney Morning Herald*, 6 March 2015. Available at http://www.smh.com.au/comment/if-ancient-greeks-could-balance-a-budget-why-cant-we-20150306-13wzcb.html (accessed 21 March 2016).
62. Josiah Ober pointed out that 'because the ancient Greeks solved the question of integrating democracy, prosperity, and security, Greek culture survived long enough to be passed on to us' (Josiah Ober, 'Ancient Greece's Answer to the Financial Crisis', *The Daily Beast*, 13 July 2015. Available at http://www.thedailybeast.com/articles/2015/07/13/ancient-greece-s-answer-to-the-financial-crisis.html (accessed 12 September 2016).
63. Daniel Mendelsohn, 'Block that metaphor! The right poem', *New Yorker*, 27 July 2015, 19.
64. The description of Greece as a 'debt colony' has invited historical comparisons with the experience of foreign financial control in Egypt during the late 19th c. or Austria in the early 1920s. See Jamie Martin, 'The Colonial Origins of the Greek Bailout'. Available at http://imperialglobalexeter.com/2015/07/27/the-colonial-origins-of-the-greek-bailout/#_ftnref7 (accessed 18 July 2016).
65. Ioanna Zikakou, 'Greek FinMin Varoufakis sends message to Melbourne', *Greek Reporter*, 22 April 2015. Available at http://au.greekreporter.com/2015/04/22/greek-finmin-varoufakis-sends-message-to-melbourne/ (accessed 19 July 2016).
66. Daniel M. Knight, *History, Time, and Economic Crisis in Central Greece* (New York, 2015), and Violetta Hionidou, 'Greece: history repeating itself?', *History Workshop Online*, 2 January 2012, available at: http://webcache.googleusercontent.com/search?q=cache:xKLffD5MXaMJ:www.historyworkshop.org.uk/greece-history-repeating-itself/+&cd=1&hl=en&ct=clnk&gl=uk (accessed 20 July 2016) and Adam Lebor, 'The Greek crisis reveals a nation crushed by ancient history', *Newsweek*, 7 July 2015. Available at http://europe.newsweek.com/greek-crisis-reveals-nation-crushed-by-ancient-history-329918 (accessed 12 August 2016).

67. Daniel M. Knight, 'Turn of the screw: narratives of history and economy in the Greek crisis', *Journal of Mediterranean Studies* 21/1 (2012), pp. 53–76, and David Sutton, *Remembrance of Repasts: An Anthropology of Food and Memory* (Oxford, 2001).
68. Daniel M. Knight, 'Wit and Greece's economic crisis: ironic slogans, food, and antiausterity sentiments', *American Ethnologist* 42/2 (2015), pp. 230–246.
69. Rebecca Bramall, *The Cultural Politics of Austerity: Past and present in austere times* (Basingstoke, 2013), p. 53.
70. Nikos Chrysoloras and Antonis Galanopoulos, 'Greeks celebrate independence as EU creditors discuss their fate', *Bloomberg Business*, 25 March 2015. Available at http://www.bloomberg.com/news/articles/2015-03-25/greeks-celebrate-independence-as-eu-creditors-discuss-their-fate (accessed 19 July 2016). See also the satirical poem of Evripidis Garantoudis, '25η Μαρτίου 2015', *Athens Review of Books*, no. 61, April 2015, p. 8.
71. Alexis Tsipras, 'Η Ελληνική Επανάσταση ως ευρωπαϊκό γεγονός' [The Greek Revolution as a European event](speech delivered at the University of Athens, 25 March 2015). Available at http://www.primeminister.gov.gr/2015/03/26/13430 (accessed 20 July 2016).
72. Antonis Liakos, Interview with Stratis Bouranzos, *Avgi* (Enthemata), 11 January 2015, available at https://enthemata.wordpress.com/2015/01/11/liakos-11/ reprinted in the online journal *Chronos*, 21 January 2015. Available at http://www.chronosmag.eu/index.php/ls-ll-p-p-lle.html (accessed 20 July 2016).
73. N.K. Alivizatos, 'Η Ευρώπη του κ. Αλέξη Τσίπρα' [Alexis Tsipras' Europe], *I Kathimerini*, 29 March 2015. Available at http://www.kathimerini.gr/809321/opinion/epikairothta/politikh/h-eyrwph-toy-k-ale3h-tsipra (accessed 20 July 2016).
74. Hayden White, *The Practical Past* (Evanston, 2014), p. 15.
75. Benedict Anderson, *The Spectre of Comparisons: Nationalism, Southeast Asia, and the World* (London & New York, 1998), p. 229.
76. Christopher Torchia, 'Greek crisis: an odyssey seen through ancient myth', *Huffington Post*, 24 August 2012. Available at http://www.huffingtonpost.com/2012/06/24/greek-crisis-mythology_n_1622328.html (accessed 20 July 2016).
77. Larry Elliott, 'Eurozone crisis, five years on: no happy ending in sight for Greek odyssey', *Guardian*, 18 October 2014. Available at http://www.theguardian.com/business/2014/oct/17/eurozone-crisis-five-years-on-greek-odyssey (accessed 20 July 2016).
78. Alen Mattich, 'This Greek epic will run and run', *Wall Street Journal – Money Beat*, 5 June 2015. Available at http://blogs.wsj.com/moneybeat/2015/06/05/this-greek-epic-will-run-and-run/ (accessed 21 July 2016).
79. 'Greece's sovereign debt-crunch: a very European crisis', *The Economist*, 4 February 2010. Available at http://www.economist.com/node/15452594 (accessed 21 July 2016).

80. Eleana Yalouri, *The Acropolis: Global Fame, Local Claim* (Oxford 2001), p. 188.
81. Dimitris Tziovas, 'Beyond the Acropolis: rethinking neohellenism', *Journal of Modern Greek Studies* 19/2 (2001), p. 196.
82. Editorial, 'From Athens to London, ancient dramas open up questions too thorny to tackle head-on', *Guardian*, 31 January 2015. Available at http://www.theguardian.com/commentisfree/2015/jan/30/guardian-view-greek-tragedy-someting-old-new (accessed 21 July 2016).
83. Maria Koundoura, *The Greek Idea: The Formation of National and Transnational Identities* (London, 2007), p. 4.
84. Lauren Talalay, 'Drawing conclusions: Greek antiquity, the economic crisis, and political cartoons', *Journal of Modern Greek Studies* 31/2 (2013), p. 272.
85. Koundoura, op. cit., 107.
86. Talalay, op. cit, p. 270.
87. James Romm, 'Greek or Roman? Amphipolis tomb yields amazing finds but mysteries linger', *The Daily Beast*, 10 October 2014. Available at http://www.thedailybeast.com/articles/2014/10/17/amphipolis-tomb-yields-amazing-finds-but-mysteries-linger.html (accessed 21 July 2016). See also Leonidas Vournelis, 'Alexander's Great Treasure: Wonder and Mistrust in Neoliberal Greece', *History and Anthropology* 27/1 (2016), pp. 121–133.
88. Ibid. See also Hamilakis, 'Some debts can never be repaid: the archaeo-politics of the crisis', op.cit.
89. 'Let's make a deal, Mrs Clooney', *Spectator*, 18 October 2014. For the use of Greek antiquity as an instrument of protest against the government and the 'troika' see Dimitris Plantzos, 'The kouros of Keratea: Constructing subaltern pasts in contemporary Greece', *Journal of Social Anthropology* 12/ 2, 2012, pp. 220–244.
90. https://www.youtube.com/watch?v=hL2loK4HMxo.
91. There is very little information about the 'Krypteia', despite its importance in Ancient Sparta. The best starting point is the entry in *Brill's New Pauly* written by Paul Cartledge: http://referenceworks.brillonline.com/entries/brill-s-new-pauly/krypteia-e623750?s.num=0&s.f.s2_parent = s.f.book.brill-s-new-pauly&s.q=krypteia (accessed 21 July 2016).
92. For a detailed account of the 'Krypteia' as a complex phenomenon and the contradictory information available from the ancient sources see Jean Ducat, *Spartan Education: Youth and Society in the Classical Period* (Swansea, 2006), pp. 281–331.
93. Panagiotis Baltakos, 'Οίκαδε' [Homeward bound], *Η Καθημερινή*, 26 July 2015. Available at http://www.kathimerini.gr/825098/article/epikairothta/politikh/apoyh-oikade (accessed 5 August 2016).
94. Sofia Vasilopoulou and Daphne Halikiopoulou, *The Golden Dawn's 'Nationalist Solution': Explaining the Rise of the Far Right in Greece* (New York, 2015).

95. N.G. Mihaloliakos, 'Ευρώ πάση θυσία: 75%!' [Euro at all costs: 75%!], 9 May 2015. Available at http://www.xryshaygh.com/enimerosi/view/eurw-pash-thusia75-arthro-tou-n.-g.-michaloliakou (accessed 21 July 2016).
96. The Metaxas dictatorship (1936–41) also made references to Sparta. For details see Yannis Hamilakis, 'Spartan visions: antiquity and the Metaxas dictatorship', in his book *The Nation and its Ruins: Antiquity, Archaeology, and National Imagination in Greece* (Oxford, 2007), pp. 169–204.
97. It is difficult to translate it accurately because it can mean either that someone else is tormenting me or that I'm agonizing over something.
98. Maria Boletsi, 'From the subject of the crisis to the subject in crisis: Middle voice on Greek walls', *Journal of Greek Media and Culture* 2/1 (Spring 2016), pp. 3–28.
99. Anna Waclawek, *Graffiti and Street Art* (London, 2011), p. 84.
100. Giorgio Agamben, *State of Exception*, trans. Kevin Attell (Chicago and London, 2003).
101. Since 2008 many buildings in Athens have been damaged during protests, including the burning down of a historic building, which housed the Attikon cinema, in February 2012.
102. Artemis Leontis, 'Not Another Polytechnic Occupation! Reading the Graffiti on the Athens Polytechneio', March 2015', *Cultural Anthropology*, Greece is Burning, 21 April 2016. Available at http://culanth.org/fieldsights/862-not-another-polytechnic-occupation-reading-the-graffiti-on-the-athens-polytechneio-march-2015 (accessed 22 July 2016).
103. A mural close to Omonia Square, commissioned by the municipality of Athens and made by students of the Athens School of Fine Arts, shows the famous praying hands by Albrecht Dürer pointing down towards the city. The title of this artwork, 'Praying for Us', is a comment on the Greek crisis and a sarcastic statement about God being the solution.
104. Kostis Kornetis, *Children of the Dictatorship: Student Resistance, Cultural Politics, and the 'Long 1960s' in Greece* (New York, 2013), p. 327.
105. Kostis Kornetis, 'No more heroes? Rejection and reverberation of the past in the 2008 events in Greece', *Journal of Modern Greek Studies*, 28/2 (2010), pp. 173–197.
106. The Kostis Palamas Foundation protested about the vandalizing of the poet's statue and reminded people that his funeral, which took place during the German occupation, had mobilized thousands of Athenians in defiance of the German authorities (http://www.tovima.gr/politics/article/?aid=689680 accessed 22 July 2016).
107. Yannis Atzakas, 'Το έπος της μνημειακής πλατείας συντάγματος' [The epic of epoch-making Syntagma Square], *Chronos*, 25 May 2015. Available at http://chronosmag.eu/index.php/g-s-p-pl-sg.html (accessed 22 July 2016).
108. Rhea Galanaki, *Η Άκρα Ταπείνωση* [Ultimate Humiliation] (Athens, 2015), pp. 211–212.

109. See Rhea Galanaki, 'The Reality of Today in Today's Historical Novel' in Natasha Lemos & Eleni Yannakakis (eds), *Critical Times, Critical Thoughts: Contemporary Greek Writers Discuss Facts and Fiction* (Newcastle upon Tyne, 2015), pp. 109–110.
110. There are references to archaeological sites, arrows and conium (the potent infusion of the hemlock plant that killed Socrates) in Petros Markaris' noir novel *Περαίωση* [Termination] (2011) in which the killer of tax-evaders explains his preference for ancient weapons thus: 'It's to remind contemporary Greeks that their ancient ancestors knew how to punish' (p. 409).
111. Yorgos Skintzas, 'Η κρίση λατρεύει το ρετρό' [The crisis loves retro] *To Vima*, 17 February 2016. Available at http://www.tovima.gr/culture/article/?aid=774302 (accessed 22 July 2016).
112. Alexander Efklidis, '"Yasou Aida!" – An opera about the difficulties of dealing with easy truths'. Available at https://heimatkunde.boell.de/2013/11/18/"yasou-aida"-opera-about-difficulties-dealing-easy-truths (accessed 15 July 2016).
113. The cinema that has come to be associated with the crisis is generally known as 'The Greek New Wave' and is mainly concerned with the present, as opposed to the focus on history in the films of the previous generation of filmmakers and in particular those of Theo Angelopoulos. Adopting a critical stance towards contemporary Greece, the films of this new type of cinema focus on challenging issues revolving around domesticity, dysfunctional families and youth. In a sense some of these films, such as Lanthimos' *Dogtooth*, could be read as an indictment of the older generation. See Olga Kourelou, Mariana Liz and Belén Vidal, 'Crisis and creativity: the new cinemas of Portugal, Greece and Spain', *New Cinemas: Journal of Contemporary Film* 12/1&2 (2014), p. 139.
114. Philip Inman, Ian Traynor and Helena Smith, 'Greece bailout talks – the main actors in a modern-day epic', *Guardian*, 9 June 2015. Available at http://www.theguardian.com/business/2015/jun/09/greece-bailout-talks-the-main-actors-in-a-modern-day-epic (accessed 22 July 2016).
115. Jonathan Jones, 'Without Europe's generosity, Greece's museums are ancient history', *Guardian*, 13 July 2015. Available at http://www.theguardian.com/artanddesign/jonathanjonesblog/2015/jul/13/europes-generosity-greeces-museums-ancient-history (accessed 22 July 2016).
116. E.M. Forster, 'The Complete Poems of C.P. Cavafy', in *Two Cheers for Democracy* (London, 1951), p. 248.

CHAPTER 2

AMPHIPOLITICS: ARCHAEOLOGICAL PERFORMANCE AND GOVERNMENTALITY IN GREECE UNDER THE CRISIS

Dimitris Plantzos

On 12 August 2014, Konstantinos Tasoulas, the Greek Minister for Culture and Sports at the time, made a rather baffling statement: 'We (that is "the Greek nation at large") have been waiting for this tomb for 2,300 years', and he added: 'the big question is who is buried inside'.[1] The tomb the Minister was referring to was a yet unexcavated archaeological site expected to yield important finds; part of a massive tumulus, almost 500m in perimeter and covering a surface of 2 hectares, the anticipated tomb gave Amphipolis, the town in the vicinity of which it was discovered, sudden prominence and a badly wanted fame (Figure 2.1).[2] Amphipolis is a rather peripheral modern town in the northern Greek district of Macedonia, borrowing its name from a substantially more important predecessor of the classical era. Situated on the borderline between what in those days were the regions of Macedon and Thrace, and in a strategic position to control both the hinterland with its rich mines and access to the sea, Amphipolis became the main power base for the Athenians in the area (who had to compete for its control with their formidable adversaries, the Spartans) before becoming part of Philip's Macedonian realm. During Alexander's campaign against

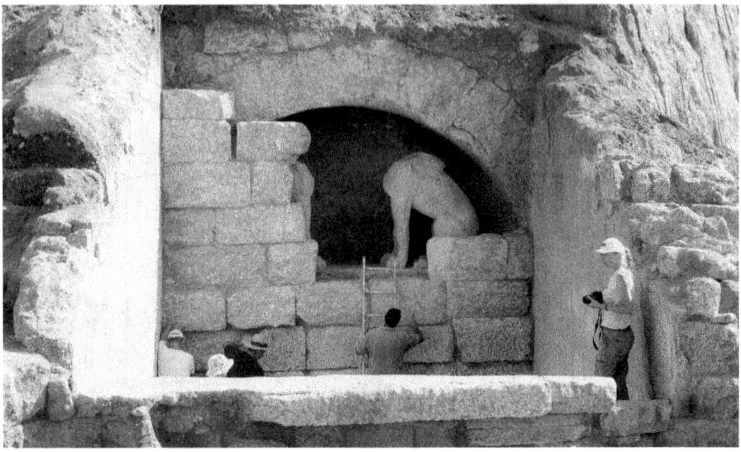

Figure 2.1 Early days of the Amphipolis dig in August 2014

the Kingdom of Persia, Amphipolis became an important naval base and the birthplace, we are told, of three of the most celebrated Macedonian admirals, including Nearchus, who famously sailed from the Indus River to the Persian Gulf following Alexander's Indian campaign in 326–324 BC. Its excavator, archaeologist Katerina Peristeri, had suggested already, in 2013, that the as yet unidentified tomb might be related to the family of Alexander the Great, reminding her audience that both Alexander's widow, Persian princess Roxanna, and his adolescent son, Alexander IV, had died in the later fourth century BC, precisely the period she thought the Amphipolis tomb ought to be dated.[3] She referred to this connection again in early 2014. Hence, when a monumental facade adorned with two confronted sphinxes, the entrance to what was presumed to be a tomb of the 'Macedonian' type, was discovered in early August of that year, the Greek media and the public at large sensed that there was about to be a fascinating discovery. Most daily papers spoke of an 'archaeological thriller',[4] a 'breath-taking tomb',[5] an important find related to Alexander the Great and his family. Greek cyberspace followed suit, exploring the political significance of the discovery;[6] very soon, most Greek bloggers and their keen commentators fantasized that the tomb belonged to Alexander the Great himself,[7] even though this was, both historically and archaeologically, highly improbable.[8]

The excavation that followed failed to fulfil those expectations. The much anticipated tomb was found to have been looted, and the meagre evidence from the scant skeletal remains proved inconclusive. The way this most spectacular and archaeologically significant find was excavated was soon exposed as cursory, disorganized and highly unprofessional, owing to the hastiness of the excavation and the erratic way its finds were disclosed to the public; by October 2015, an independent report by experts estimated that the date of the monument was later than once thought by its excavator, a view shared by many archaeologists at home and abroad but also challenged by many – and still is.[9] In this chapter, however, I am more concerned with the biopolitical uses of classical antiquity in the case of Amphipolis, and the way these help create a new sort of post-crisis governmentality in Greece. I turn therefore to this discussion in the sections that follow.

Truth regimes: Vergina revisited

Antonis Samaras, Prime Minister of Greece at the time, was among the first politicians to visit Amphipolis.[10] He was, in fact, the first person ever to address the public, through a television interview in front of the tumulus, where he described the find in true archaeological form – detailing its dimensions, typology, and date – and promising that the dig would be completed in a couple of days.[11] One should remember, furthermore, that all this is taking place on 12 August, that is only three days before the major religious holiday of the Dormition of the Virgin; as the Greeks were preparing to celebrate their beloved *Panaghia*, their Prime Minister appeared on TV performing as an archaeologist, promising a 'breath-taking' discovery of a 'unique burial monument'. This kind of improvised archaeological performance seemed on the one hand to introduce the elected delegate of the people as his people's own archaeologist and, on the other, to represent the Greek nation as the (sole) inheritor of classical culture as well as classical culture's most efficient manager.

In modern Greece, historical discourse has long ago acquired a patently archaeological structure: artefacts and monuments are systematically taken as the necessary triggers for the nation's imaginings and aspirations, from the country's accession to the European Community in the early 1980s and its capital's campaign for the hosting of the Olympic

Games in the 1990s to the current economic crisis and its predicament. Even if this may not be found to be unique to Greece, it may nevertheless be argued that as the modern nation state was designed as a neoclassical project in state-building, based on the glory that was Hellas as documented by the material remains of that glorious past, it soon became imperative for Greeks not only to own to their appointed heritage but also prove worthy of the privilege. Archaeology thus has come to inform the national agenda both for internal as well as external use; more to the point, collective archaeolatry has been organized as a fundamentally Greek sentiment, inherently Hellenic and profoundly political.[12] Amphipolis is a good example of the inevitable tensions that ensued between, so to speak, archaeology as an academic discipline and discipline as an archaeology of sorts, that is the systematic manufacture of a state control mechanism running on archaeological clichés and the subliminal understanding that the truths of the nation are spoken through the materiality of its antiquities.[13]

Archaeology is thus deployed as the Nation's constituent force, defender of its past and guarantor of its future. Samaras himself said as much that day in Amphipolis: 'The land of *our* Macedonia keeps thrilling and surprising us, revealing extraordinary treasures, which compose, weave all together this unique mosaic that is *our* History, something which makes Greeks very proud' (my emphases).[14] With his talk of national pride over Greece's extraordinary history, about to be revealed yet again in front of our impatient eyes, Samaras is of course hinting at the problem with that 'other Macedonia', the Republic that emerged from the dissolution of Yugoslavia back in the 1990s, a nation often challenging Greece over ownership of the Macedonian legacy, including ancestral claims to Alexander himself. The political dispute between Greece and the newly emerged Republic of Macedonia which had been brewing for decades, was however reignited after the breakup of Yugoslavia and the subsequent independence of its former Socialist Republic of Macedonia in 1991. Since then, it has developed into a bitter dispute marring bilateral and international relations. As modern Greece occupies most of what in antiquity constituted the Kingdom of Macedon (whose most renowned king was Alexander the Great), the rekindling of its northern neighbours' early twentieth-century aspirations to a Slavic Macedonia reaching all the way south to Greece's Aegean shores was seen as a direct threat, even if the newly founded state never quite seriously suggested it was prepared to wage a territorial war against its neighbours. Even though the 'name dispute' became emblematic of the conflict between the new states – with Greece claiming that the newly founded Republic could not assume its historical name because it was actually part of Greece's even *older* history – archaeology was also accorded a significant role in it. The spectacular discovery of a series of 'royal' tombs in Greek Macedonia in the 1970s and later, one of which was attributed to Alexander's father, Philip II, was seen by many in Greece as definite proof of Macedonia's 'Greekness'.[15] At the same time, one guesses, the same discoveries, and their persistent promotion by the Greek state, must have inspired to at least some of its neighbours the idea that northern Greece was, in fact, 'Macedonian'. The conviction that archaeology speaks not only of a land's past but also of its present, and that archaeological finds can decide who has the right to the territory in which they were discovered, is one of nationalism's constituent principles, therefore it is not surprising to find Greece and Macedonia in disagreement over things, bones, and the symbolisms they carry. The dispute over Macedonia's name soon became a fight over archaeological motifs such as the 'star of Macedon' (an ancient image that, in strict archaeological sense, is neither Macedonian nor does it depict a star) and a fierce debate over the significance of archaeological discovery itself, even though the differences between the two states had nothing to do with the glory that was ancient Macedon. More importantly, the 'name dispute' intensified Greece's archaeological hold over its past (something that seems to have also happened in Macedonia); 'archaeological correctness' was thus elevated into a matter of national significance, and lawful subjects soon became expected to abide with the official line regarding matters scientific – such as the dating of one tomb or the attribution of another to a particular historical figure. In Greece, specifically, scholarly views on the matter are subject to strict public scrutiny, sometimes state- or media-controlled but most often generated directly from sectors of the wider public such as the country's multifarious internet-based nationalist and archaeolatric groups. This is what the veteran Greek archaeologist Antonis Zois had dubbed, back in 1987, 'the Vergina Syndrome': that is the privileging of spectacular finds over other, humbler ones, and the way this affects historical studies.[16] Since then, however, the syndrome developed some even more malignant symptoms: the almost self-evident fetishization of politics and, in strictly symmetrical fashion, the relentless politicization of the archaeological project.

On 10 October 2011, Theodoros Pagkalos, acting as Deputy Prime Minister, was present at the inauguration of an archaeological exhibition at the Louvre titled 'In the Kingdom of Alexander the Great: Ancient Macedonia'.[17] The official blurb of the exhibition suggested its aim was to 'retrace the history of ancient Macedonia from the fifteenth century BC until Imperial Roman times', and Pagkalos claimed this was 'a landmark in the history of archaeology'.[18] Oddly enough, a very similar exhibition titled 'Herakles to Alexander the Great' had opened at the Ashmolean Museum in Oxford only a few months earlier.[19] Co-organized by the Greek Ministry of Culture, and subtitled 'A Hellenic Kingdom in the Age of Democracy', the exhibition made no effort at all to conceal its political subtexts against any unwarranted claims to Macedonia's name and heritage. The Greek press anticipated the exhibition as a 'poignant step for the promotion of Greek scientific knowledge in such a renowned international institution',[20] and the exhibition's curator, Oxford history don Robin Lane Fox, remarked that 'though not part of the Greek propaganda, the exhibition shows the truth. Macedonia is Greek. This is proven by the names, the art, the social life, the burials. This is proven by the exhibition'.[21] Referring to the people of the modern Republic of Macedonia as 'those in Skopje' (the country's capital), and branding them as 'ignorant' and 'outrageous', Lane Fox subscribes to Greece's hegemonic truth about Macedonia's past and present implying precisely that archaeology may be the answer to a territorial dispute going back only as far as the nineteenth century. Macedonian archaeology as a 'regime of truth' has long featured in Greek politics where even the faintest murmur of dissent from the accepted canon is bound to bring charges of historical forgery and national treason.[22] In the words of a Greek politician of the populist right, 'Macedonia is one, and only, and Hellenic, and Vergina is the capital of the Macedonians, where the Greekness of the Greek soil is documented'.[23] The two exhibitions need therefore to be seen as systematic attempts by the Greek state (and its friends) to consolidate this regime of truth at home and at the same time export it abroad for anyone who cares to listen.

Owing to archaeology's inherent nationalist agendas – the apparent necessity to tie a nation's present to those 'names', 'art', and 'burials' in what it imagines to have been its past – and the way twenty-first-century politics seem to be following, rather uncomfortably, nineteenth-century ideologies, a certain infatuation over the nation's dead fathers seems to have affected particular branches of mainstream archaeology in Greece. This is particularly evident in Vergina, where the official view (according to which the unlooted Tomb II belonged to King Philip II, Alexander's father murdered by one of his generals in 336 BC) has been challenged by several scholars who maintain different attributions (most convincingly: Philip III Arrhidaeus, Alexander's half-brother and successor).[24] Although archaeologically and historically the down-dating of the tomb by 20 years or so (Arrhidaeus died in 317 BC) would not affect the significance of the find nor that of Vergina as an extremely important site, the counter-attack of the excavators has been rather fierce and unnecessarily ongoing. It is, I find, quite indicative, that *Brill's Companion to Ancient Macedon*, published in 2011, devotes its entire introduction to a point-by-point rebuttal of the Arrhidaeus hypothesis by the volume's editor, Lane Fox again.[25] While the reasons for this are never quite explained in the text, it seems obvious that, at least for this particular scholar, the matter of the tomb's attribution is enough to overshadow a historical range which, according to the book itself, spans from 650 BC to AD 300. A great part of Lane Fox's argument is devoted to the forensic study of the two sets of skeletal remains found in the tomb (a man and a woman), as is the case with one of the contributions in the Ashmolean Museum's Macedonian catalogue, somewhat bizarrely titled 'The occupants of Tomb II at Vergina: why Arrhidaios and Eurydice must be excluded'.[26] Introducing arguments on 'bone pathology and taphonomy' the paper's authors proceed to reject the counter-arguments of fellow forensic archaeologists that had been published before and have been repeated since.[27] When, in August 2015, a new paper attempting to attribute the bones from Tomb II to Arrhidaeus based on forensics appeared in an American scientific journal, the Greek Ministry of Culture, in an unprecedented move, felt the need to retaliate: in a long, unsigned reply, drafted in the Archaeological Service's meticulous, jargon-laden archaeological idiom, it is explained why the tomb *must* be Philip's.[28] With the state interfering in an academic dispute in so blunt a way, attempting to reiterate the hegemonic 'truth' on the matter, against a scientific text published in an international, peer-reviewed journal, it becomes evident that the identification of those old bones is the least of the Ministry's worries. What seems to be at stake here is the standing of Macedonian archaeology as a regime of truth in itself, as a disciplinary mechanism demanding the unqualified compliance of its subjects – be they scholars or their audience. In a sense, the question posed by this debate between forensic experts (is he or isn't he?) is becoming irrelevant through state interference: Macedonian archaeology has to retain its unbreakable authority at all costs.

Hoping that the Amphipolis tomb was bound to reveal a chunk of Macedonian gold and silver that would catch the attention of the international media, Samaras was thus prompting his fellow Greeks to stick to national archaeology as a way of resolving Greece's modern tribulations. This is the sort of archaeology Tasoulas, as the Greek Minister for Culture, was promoting in his statements I mentioned in the beginning of this chapter, adding that the Amphipolis excavation was going to 'emphasize, once again, the historicity of the country, and of Macedonia in particular'.[29] As the spectacular find was not forthcoming, however, new statements had to be made: Samaras was going to repeat, in September of the same year, that 'a Macedonian tomb of such dimensions is something big, and yet another confirmation of the Greekness of Macedonia',[30] whereas Evangelos Venizelos, Deputy Prime Minister at the time, was adding that in Amphipolis lay 'the force of Greek culture and Hellenism as a whole'.[31]

Suddenly, and as if no further proof were needed, the imminent discovery of an ancestral corpse seemed to confirm Greek exception as well as vindicate Greek international politics. In the words of a radio producer, 'if it is actually confirmed that the tomb belongs to the King of Kings (i.e.: Alexander), this discovery alone will "finish" once and for all the propaganda of the Skopjans and will of course bring a large wave of tourists to the country in the next years'.[32] Archaeology in Greece is therefore used to suggest cultural and racial continuity with the classical past as well as promote national exception, while at the same time contribute significantly to the country's finances. To achieve this, it has to be endowed with a biopolitical apparatus, a technology through which to mobilize social groups according to certain political and ideological agendas rehearsing a standardized archaeological ethos.[33] In the next section, I will argue that this sort of archaeology is being employed in Greece not only in order to organize the way its citizens live, but also as a means to effect the death of others.

National archaeology as an exercise in thanatopolitics

'Whoever may be buried in the tomb, he (*sic*) is bound to be Greek' stated Bishop Anthimos of Thessaloniki during his Sunday sermon of 17 August 2014.[34] The Greekness of the land and the nation's racial continuity emerge as incontestable truths from the official rhetoric regarding Amphipolis. By constructing itself as a metaphysical entity of primordial origins, contemporary Greece is thus indulging in what could be termed 'reverse archaeology': using, that is, the material remains of the past in order to write the history of the present. In the years of the crisis this seemed particularly necessary, since criticism against Greece's perceived inability to balance its books, or even look as if it were trying to achieve some sort of sustainable economic growth, is invariably accompanied with images of Greece's classical past.[35] Crippled temples and dismembered statues are employed, time and again, as metaphors of Greece's chronic inefficiencies, thus turning what used to be the country's most obvious advantage to its weakest spot. Orientalist and neo-colonialist as this attitude may be, it nevertheless hits a most delicate nerve with modern Greeks, who are rather getting tired of being accused, persistently, of the 'incomplete', 'belated', or 'inadequate' state of their modernity.[36] Broadcasting the unquestionable Greekness of an archaeological discovery yet to happen was, therefore, a necessary move in Greece's effort to save face against its harsh critics.

At the same time, however, the Amphipolis tomb was deployed as a racist apparatus within Greece – suggesting who, in the country itself, had the right to its glory-bound soil and who did not. Special emphasis was placed, for example, on the toes featured by the two Caryatids found in the tomb, allegedly suggesting their Greek origin and thus proving Modern Greece's racial purity (Figure 2.2). According to Anna Panagiotarea, the journalist appointed by the Ministry as the spokesperson for the Amphipolis excavation team, the two statues featured the so-called 'Greek toe', supposedly an anatomical particularity exclusive to the Greek race.[37] Moreover, Panagiotarea was one of several publicists in Greece at the time who claimed that this discovery 'shuts the mouths of the Skopjans', as it rendered their claims over Macedon void of any historical meaning.[38] In fact, 'Greek toe' has been long diagnosed as a disorder of the metatarsal bones (whereby each foot exhibits a shortened first metatarsal in relation to the second one), and

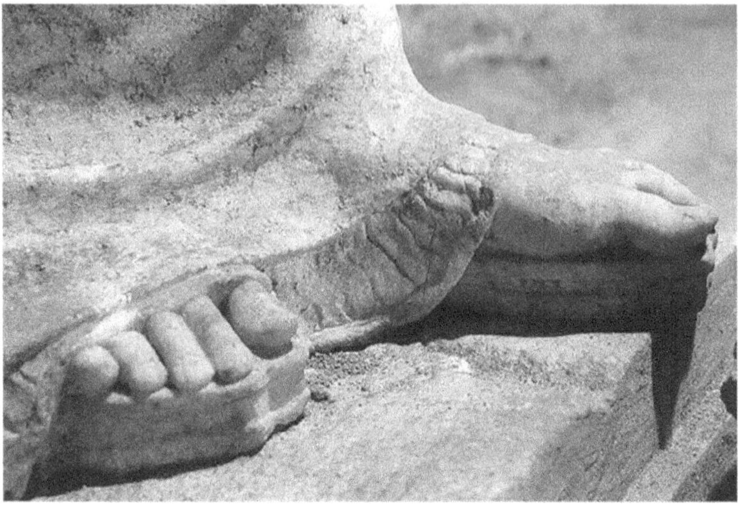

Figure 2.2 The feet of one of the Amphipolis Caryatids as featured in a government press release upon their discovery

has been known to affect 10 per cent of the world population. Known to scientists as 'Morton's toe', from the name of the orthopaedic specialist who first described it,[39] this benign anomaly is common in Africa and other 'un-Greek' parts of the globe; moreover, it can be seen in much of Roman art, and, more crucially perhaps, is missing from many ancient Greek depictions of men and women. Since, however, Greek popular imagination, assisted by the country's persistent clan of pseudo-scientists, has attached a particular element of 'Greekness' to this anatomical oddity,[40] the Amphipolis Caryatids were seen as solid proof of the monument's biological bonds with the Greek race. Deployed as a template of racial identity, the Amphipolis tomb was thus used to suggest that the monument itself, as well as the land in which it lay, belonged only to those who could be identified as genetically associated with it.

The Amphipolis saga was only the culmination of a series of systematic efforts on behalf of the Greek state, especially in the years of the economic crisis, to suggest that the nation's antiquity was the defining force of its modernity and that archaeology could be used to articulate its relations with friends and foes alike. Crucially, this was a period where classical antiquity was systematically used in order to disguise policies and actions that seemed to fly in the teeth of standard human rights regulations and even humanist tradition itself. *Xenios Zeus* ('Hospitable Zeus') is a case in point, a police crackdown against undocumented immigrants carried out between 2012 and 2014 (when it was replaced by a similar project, called 'Theseus').[41] Thousands of random controls and arrests of anyone looking suspicious (which in fact meant 'looking black') spotted in the streets of Athens or other major Greek cities were carried out. The massive enterprise led to only a six per cent rate of actual criminal charges brought, most for illegal entry into the country. Those arrested were incarcerated in concentration camps euphemistically named 'hospitality centres' where they were deprived of any legal representation. Similarly, a parallel operation of 'sweeping' the city centre of drug addicts or homeless people was named 'Operation Thetis', from the name of a Greek sea-nymph who eventually became the mother of Achilles.[42] Much more than a mere 'appeal to classical authority', or 'part of an attempt to assert a perceived difference between "western civilization" and "oriental barbarity" going all the way back to Ancient Greece',[43] these classically made-up police operations deploy ancient Greece's patriarchal ethos in order to suggest which contemporary bodies are acceptable and which are not. Drawing their authority from the classical archive – Zeus was the Greek god of hospitality and protector of visitors to a Greek city and Theseus was thought to be the ancient founder of Athens – such projects in fact reverse the very models they wish to promote: they are deployed as weapons *against* humans, not as pledges for their protection; their cynical use of those ancient names seems to rehabilitate racism as the 'Greek' thing to do.

The refugee crisis that followed the civil war in Syria and its subsequent invasion by Islamist forces since 2014 generated new immigration controls in Greece and the rest of Europe. 'Fortress Europe', an idea born in Nazi Germany but revived through present-day European anti-immigration policies, presupposes that an indefinite number of bodies will be sacrificed in the otherwise quite friendly Mediterranean waters.[44] These people, as non-Europeans, as trespassers, are also considered quasi dead, already before they leave their homelands in search for a better fortune. A poignant example of this deeply racist ideology is the drawing by Ilias Makris published in *Kathimerini* on 29 January 2016 (Figure 2.3): as the Greek islands were inundated by Syrian refugees risking their lives in order to flee the terrors of war, Makris shows Greece as a human drowning in a 'sea' of bearded men and hijab-wearing women. Quite appropriately, only the hand of 'Greece' is

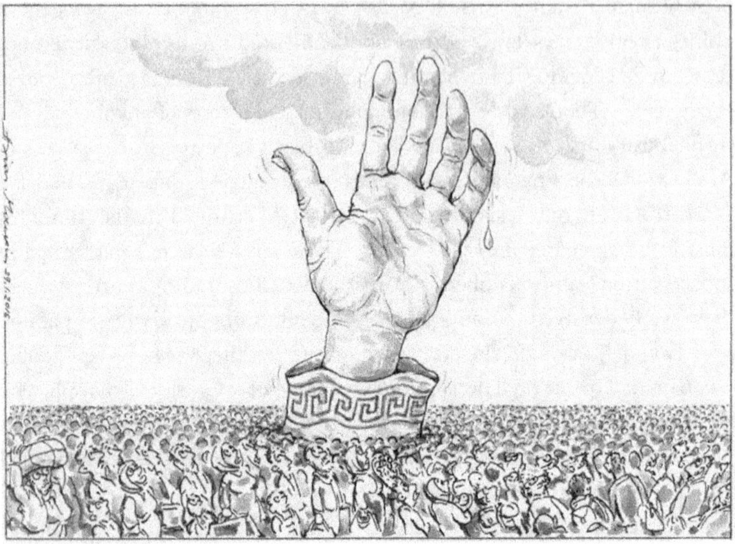

Figure 2.3 Ilias Makris, Untitled. *Kathimerini*, 29 January 2016

visible, barely surfacing amidst the barbaric crowd – a hand clad in the antique meander motif nonetheless. Makris' cynicism – suggesting a metaphorical (cultural? national? racial?) drowning of Greece at a time when Syrian refugees are *actually* drowned by their numbers on the Greek shores – is clearly employing Greece's much-advertised classical ancestry in order to argue that its soil and people have to remain pure from any alien intruders (even if some of the latter must lose their lives in the process). In Greece, therefore, this kind of newly emerging thanatopolitical agenda is facilitated through the racial identification of its present inhabitants with the 'land of their ancestors', an identification systematically illustrated with images borrowed from the classical archive. The nation's antiquity, and its material remains, are thus employed as 'part of a broader tactic to neutralize the rule of law in the name of security'.[45] Even though this kind of systematic 'remaking of state and subject' has been extensively observed across the West in the last decade or so as part of the persistent neoliberalization of public life,[46] in Greece it follows a markedly archaeological agenda.

Michel Foucault laconically defined *thanatopolitique* as the opposite of biopolitics – a politics of, as well as through, death rather than life.[47]

According to Giorgio Agamben, however, current political agendas in the West have turned exclusively thanatopolitical, thus leaving us, its own people, as well those crossing the borders of our states, more and more exposed to both death and operations of power.[48] In order to manage the lives of the people in its care, Modern Greece exposes them to death as 'bare lives';[49] to achieve this, its state apparatus employs a suitably adapted version of the classical ideal as a way to render its thanatopolitical strategies more palatable. These strategies depend on the sort of exceptionalist, introvert, and ultimately xenophobic archaeology practiced in Amphipolis and elsewhere across the country: in the hands of the Greek media and the internet, and with the abundant encouragement of the country's administration, the excavation – always in progress, always *about* to yield magnificent finds – is used to redefine a particular temporality of Greekness where the non-Greek is simply not an issue.

Even if the skeletal remains of the 'occupant of the Amphipolis tomb' were not forthcoming, they could still be imagined by the press or some scholars, as in a drawing published in the newspaper *Ta Nea*, before it could be scientifically shown that the human remains found in the tomb belonged to five different individuals, some of whom were actually women (Figure 2.4).[50] Imagining the 'occupant' as a blond

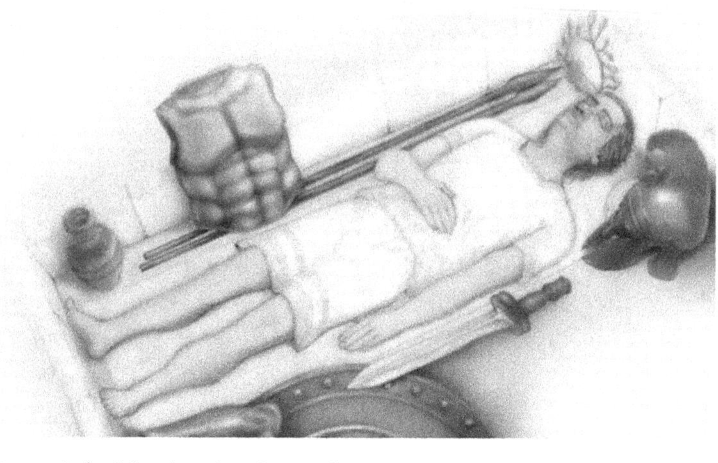

Figure 2.4 The Amphipolis tomb occupant as imagined by the Greek press in 2014

soldier, accoutred with oddly matched burial gifts that looked too early for the supposed date of the tomb, the paper tried to satisfy a widespread need to see, at long last, the nation's hitherto elusive forefather, the man whose bones suddenly became the focus of Greece's cultural life. In my final section, I will define 'Amphipolitics' as a special form of Greek *necropolitics*.[51]

Amphipolitics

Greece's bailout programme was supposed to end in late 2014. Since 2010, when the country was placed under the joint custody of the European Union (EU), the ECB (European Central Bank) and the IMF (International Monetary Fund), the percentage of the country's population on the verge of poverty or social exclusion increased from 28.1 per cent in 2008 to 35.7 per cent in 2013, while serious deprivation of basic goods increased from 11.2 per cent in 2008 to 20.3 per cent in 2013.[52] With unemployment across the nation reaching an unprecedented 28 per cent in September 2013, and unemployment for the young (18–24-year-olds) calculated at an overwhelming 60.8 per cent in February of that same year (which meant that almost 1.5 million Greeks found themselves out of a job), over 44 per cent of the Greek population was calculated as living at an income below the poverty line, as a result of a long series of austerity laws.

Still, for the Minister for Culture, all the Nation had to or could do in the meantime was to wait for a particular 'tomb'.[53] In fact, Tasoulas was not the only member of the Greek government at the time who had not excluded the possibility that the tomb might actually belong to Alexander himself; a possibility most welcome, needless to add, by Bishop Anthimos, who stated at about the same time that, if ever discovered, 'the bones of Alexander will serve as spiritual and national legacy for our country and our land.'[54] So whereas the minister is suggesting that Amphipolis brings national time to its long-awaited climax, the bishop preaches for a new breed of sensory archaeology, enlisted to the service of national indigenism. This sort of archaeologically informed ethos imposed from above, naive and makeshift as it may appear, is nonetheless sharply emphasized and deeply biopolitical. As the Greek crisis has systematically been turned by authorities both at home and abroad into a veritable 'state of exception', in the sense that it consents to the enforcement of the law by means of its own suspension,[55] austerity measures on the one hand and neoliberal rhetoric on the other have been employed in order to manage and regulate the country's population(s). The Amphipolis saga was perhaps seen by the government at the time as a welcome opportunity to divert public focus from the crisis and its predicament to something morally uplifting and therefore politically innocuous if not beneficial for its own goals; the way it developed, however, into a discourse on the materiality of the nation's past, exceptional as well as exclusionary, Amphipolitics became something much more menacing than simply a misconstrued archaeological find: a particular way of assessing Greek archaeology through the abolition of both its disciplinary as well as humanist tradition.

The official rhetoric surrounding Amphipolis re-introduces archaeology as a national discipline, performed through the translation of ancestral relics, an 'authentication ritual' in the terminology used by Nandia Seremetakis, during which the remains of the nation's ancestors are transformed into the stuff national temporalities are made of.[56] Accordingly, if necropolitics are technologies through which life is strategically subjugated to the power of death, operating alongside technologies of discipline for an increasingly authoritarian politics (social, economic, or ideological), in the case of Amphipolis actual skeletal remains are substantiated into living agents of national identity and cultural as well as racial exception designed to organize the country's population into bodies that deserve to occupy its land and bodies that may be treated as quasi lifeless, or dead. Amphipolitics thus rejuvenates a somewhat old and outdated narrative for the cultural and racial primordiality of the Greek nation combined with the biopolitics of the Greek crisis; this way, the country's political and religious leadership wishes to organize a population susceptible to the state of exception implemented by the crisis itself.

Notes

I am grateful to Dimitris Tziovas and Dimitris Papanikolaou for their invitation to participate in the 'Greece in Crisis: Culture and the Politics of Austerity' workshop in May 2015 and their help while preparing my chapter for publication. I am also grateful to the audience on the day for many helpful remarks and encouragement. All reasonable effort has been made to contact the holders of copyright of Figures 1–4. Any omissions will be rectified in future printings if notice is given to the publisher.

1. Anon., 'Μοναδικό μνημείο σε όλη τη Βαλκανική ο τάφος της Αμφίπολης' [The Amphipolis tomb is unique in the entire Balkan Peninsula], *Skai.gr*/ 12 August 2014 (http://goo.gl/FfvWv8; accessed 2 February 2016).
2. For a first critical account on the matter, see Dimitris Plantzos, 'Των Ελλήνων τα ιερά' [On the Sacred Bones of the Greeks], *Unfollow* 33, 2014 (Sept.) pp. 114–9 and id., 'Amphipolitics', *The Athens Review of Books* 55, 2014 (Oct.), p. 10, both available on line, https://goo.gl/br3x10 and http://goo.gl/ohHvP0 respectively (accessed 2 February 2016); see also id., *Το Πρόσφατο Μέλλον* [The Recent Future] (Athens, 2016), pp. 157–217. Also, Yannis Hamilakis, 'Εθνική θησαυροθηρία ή κριτική αρχαιολογία' [National Treasure-hunting or critical archaeology], *I Avgi*, 24 August 2014 (http://goo.gl/7956c2; accessed 24 October 2015) and Dimitris Papanikolaou, 'Πεθαίνω σαν χώρα (στην Αμφίπολη) [I'm dying as a country (in Amphipolis)], *I Avgi*, 7 September 2014 (https://goo.gl/mx0XfS; accessed 24 October 2015). Hamilakis had pointed out the farcical aspects of the endeavour when the anticipated discovery was first announced in the summer of 2013: Yannis Hamilakis, 'Από τη Βεργίνα στην Αμφίπολη: πρώτα ως τραγωδία μετά ως φάρσα' [From Vergina to Amphipolis: first as a tragedy, then as a farce], *I Avgi*, 1 September 2013 (https://goo.gl/sdoxlK; accessed 24 October 2015) and now id., 'Some debts can never be repaid: the archaeo-politics of the crisis', *Journal of Modern Greek Studies* 34/2 (2016), pp. 227–264. See also Leonidas Vournelis, 'Alexander's great treasure: wonder and mistrust in neoliberal Greece', *History and Anthropology* 27/1 (2016), pp. 121–133.
3. See Olga Sella, 'Αρχαιολογικό θρίλερ στην Αμφίπολη' [An archaeological thriller at Amphipolis], *I Kathimerini*, 12 August 2014 (http://goo.gl/gBAVxf; accessed 28 October 2015).
4. Ibid.
5. Ninetta Kontrarou-Rassia, 'Ένας τάφος που κόβει την ανάσα' [A breath-taking tomb], *Eleftherotypia*, 12 August 2014 (http://goo.gl/P4yEKW; accessed 28 October 2015).
6. For an overview, see footnote 2 above.
7. Cf. repeated television appearances of controversial nationalist historian Sarantos Kargakos who insisted on his 'premonition' that the tomb belonged to Alexander: e.g. http://goo.gl/J3sysS from September 13 and http://goo.gl/npc7kL from October 7 of that year (both accessed 2 February 2016).
8. After his premature death in Babylon, in the year 323 BC, Alexander has been known to have been buried in Alexandria in Egypt, where his tomb was seen until the early Imperial period; it was destroyed at some point in the later second or third century AD, but its remains were reported visible as late as the fifteenth century AD.
9. See the reports in *I Avgi*, 10 August 2015 (http://goo.gl/vnh5lS; accessed 2 February 2016). Also, Yannis Hamilakis, 'Archaeo-politics in Macedonia', *LRB blog*, 22 January 2015 (http://goo.gl/Zeu8BY; accessed 2 February 2016).

10. Cf., among many, the reportage from 12 August 2014 in http://goo.gl/x7bkiZ (accessed 2 February 2016).
11. Available on YouTube; see https://goo.gl/1X1xLj (accessed 2 February 2016).
12. Archaeology in Greece, and its role in the formation of contemporary culture, was more or less neglected as a topic for academic research until the late twentieth century but has now become the subject of major rethinking: see chiefly, Artemis Leontis, *Topographies of Hellenism: Mapping the Homeland* (Ithaca and London, 1995), pp. 40–66; Yannis Hamilakis, *The Nation and its Ruins: Antiquity, Archaeology, and National Imagination in Greece* (Oxford, 2007), pp. 57–123; Dimitris Plantzos, 'Archaeology and Hellenic identity, 1896–2004: the frustrated vision', in D. Damaskos and D. Plantzos (eds), *A Singular Antiquity: Archaeology and Hellenic Identity in Twentieth-Century Greece* (Athens, 2008), pp. 10–30.
13. Cf. Dimitris Plantzos, 'The *kouros* of Keratea: constructing subaltern pasts in contemporary Greece', *Journal of Social Archaeology* 12 (2012), pp. 220–44 and id., 'The glory that was not: embodying the classical in contemporary Greece', *Interactions* 3/2 (2012), pp. 147–171 for two case-studies in national identity-forging through archaeology.
14. Widely reported; e.g. Anon., 'Ποιο μυστικό κρύβει το μοναδικό μνημείο της Αμφίπολης;' {Which secret is hidden inside the unique monument of Amphipolis?}, *Lifo*, 12 August 2014 (http://goo.gl/RLUsyx; accessed 3 February 2016).
15. See Hamilakis, *The Nation and its Ruins*, pp. 125–67; on the 'archaeology' of the Macedonian conflict, see Kostas Kotsakis, 'The past is ours: images of Greek Macedonia', in L. Meskell (ed.), *Archaeology under fire: Nationalism, Politics and Heritage in the Eastern Mediterranean and Middle East* (London and New York, 1998), pp. 44–67.
16. Antonis Zois, *Η Αρχαιολογία στην Ελλάδα* {*Archaeology in Greece*} (Athens, 1990), pp. 105–10. On the matter, see Hamilakis, *The Nation and its Ruins*, pp. 125–167, and Dimitris Plantzos, 'Τα ορφανά του Αλέξανδρου' {Alexander's orphans}, *The Athens Review of Books* 30, 2012 (Jun.), pp. 51–54.
17. See here for the official presentation of the exhibition, as hosted at the museum's site: http://goo.gl/XGq8TL (accessed 4 February 2016).
18. Anon., 'Εκθεση για την Αρχαία Μακεδονία στο Λούβρο' {An exhibition on Ancient Macedonia in the Louvre}, *I Kathimerini*, 10 October 2011 (http://goo.gl/jdZn0p; accessed 4 February 2016).
19. See the museum's site: http://goo.gl/9q7ahR (accessed 4 February 2016).
20. Anon., 'Το ελληνικό βασίλειο του Μ. Αλεξάνδρου στην Οξφόρδη' {The Hellenic kingdom of Alexander the Great at Oxford}, 14 October 2010 (http://goo.gl/DDN6Wz; accessed 4 February 2016).
21. Ioanna Kleftogianni, 'Ωδή στην ελληνικότητα της Μακεδονίας' {An Ode to Macedonia's Greekness}, *Eleftherotypia*, 7 April 2011 (http://goo.gl/ubjdcl;

accessed 4 February 2016). See here for a television statement made to the same effect: https://goo.gl/E9hnvU (accessed 4 February 2016).

22. I use the term as introduced by Michel Foucault in the 1970s, that is as a 'general politics [. . .] centred on the form of scientific discourse and the institutions which produce it' and 'in a circular relation with systems of power which produce and sustain it': see Michel Foucault, *Power / Knowledge. Selected Interviews and Other Writings 1972–1977* (New York, 1980), pp. 131–133.
23. Aftodioikisi.gr, 21 March 2011 (http://goo.gl/AWYFqq; accessed 4 February 2016).
24. Summarized in Eugene N. Borza and Olga Palagia, 'The chronology of the Macedonian royal tombs at Vergina', *Jahrbuch des Deutschen Archaeologischen Instituts* 122 (2007), pp. 81–125.
25. Robin J. Lane Fox (ed.), *Brill's Companion to Ancient Macedon. Studies in the Archaeology and History of Macedon, 650 BC – 300 AD* (Leiden and Boston, 2011), pp. 1–34.
26. *Heracles to Alexander the Great. Treasures from the Royal Capital of Macedon, a Hellenic Kingdom in the Age of Democracy* (Oxford, 2011), pp. 127–130.
27. See Antonios Bartsiokas and Elizabeth Carney, 'The Royal skeletal remains from Tomb I at Vergina', *Deltos. Journal of the History of Hellenic Medicine*, 36 (2008), pp. 15–19 and Antonios Bartsiokas and Juan-Luis Arsuaga, 'The lameness of King Philip II and Royal Tomb I at Vergina, Macedonia', *Proceedings of the National Academy of Sciences of the United States of America* 112:32 (2015), pp. 9844–9848.
28. See Anon., 'Διευκρινίσεις του ΥΠΠΟ για τη μελέτη του τάφου του Φιλίππου του Β΄' [Clarifications by the Ministry of Culture on the study on the tomb of Philip II], *SKAI*, 22 July 2015 (http://goo.gl/CXW4MS; accessed 8 February 2016).
29. See note 1 above.
30. Anon., 'Αντώνης Σαμαρά από τη ΔΕΘ' [Antonis Sanaras at the Thessaloniki International Fair] *Ta Nea*, 6 September 2014 (http://goo.gl/cqy6Ac; accessed 12 February 2016).
31. Anon., 'Βενιζέλος: στην Αμφίπολη η δύναμη του Ελληνισμού' [Venizelos: at Amphipolis [lies] the force of Greek culture], *I Kathimerini*, 7 September 2014 (http://goo.gl/V5MsFj; accessed 12 February 2016).
32. Anon., 'Βρέθηκε το ιερό "δισκοπότηρο"'; [Has the "Holy Grail" of the archaeologists been discovered?], *Radio Florina*, 12 August 2014 (http://goo.gl/OSk3Pi; accessed 12 February 2016).
33. On biopolitics as a mechanism through which to effect a top-down arrangement of social and political life, see Michel Foucault, *Security, Territory, Population. Lectures at the Collège de France 1977–1978* (New York, 2007), pp. 1–27 and id., *The Birth of Biopolitics. Lectures at the Collège de France 1978–1979* (New York, 2008).
34. Anon., 'Τα οστά του Μεγαλέξανδρου '[The bones of Alexander the Great], *Ethnos*, 24 August 2014 (http://goo.gl/iO3J9x; accessed 16 February 2016).

35. For an overview, Lauren E. Talalay, 'Drawing conclusions: Greek antiquity, the €conomic (*sic*) crisis, and political cartoons', *Journal of Modern Greek Studies* 31 (2013), pp. 249–276; also Dimitris Tziovas, 'Decolonizing antiquity, heritage politics, and performing the past', in D. Tziovas (ed.), *Re-imagining the Past. Antiquity and Modern Greek Culture* (Oxford, 2014), pp. 1–26, esp. 13–16. For an early account on the politics of the Greek crisis, see Penelope Papailias, *Beyond the 'Greek Crisis': Histories, Rhetorics, Politics*, Hot Spots, Cultural Anthropology website, October 10 (2011); http://goo.gl/1V8SRM (accessed 16 February 2016) and Plantzos, 'The *kouros* of Keratea', pp. 220–244 on the colonization of archaeological images in the framework of the Greek crisis.
36. See Antonis Liakos, 'Greek narratives of crisis', *Humaniora. Czasopismo Internetowe*, 3:3 (2013), pp. 79–86 (http://goo.gl/hqILcL; accessed 17 February 2016). Also Anna Triandafyllidou, Ruby Gropas, and Hara Kouki (eds), *The Greek Crisis and European Modernity* (Basingstoke, 2013).
37. See Anon., 'Η Παναγιωταρέα επιβεβαιώνει το ελληνικό δάχτυλο των Καρυάτιδων' [Panagiotarea confirms the Greek toe of the Caryatids], *TVXS*, 3 October 2014 (http://goo.gl/lEzJ6E; accessed 16 February 2016).
38. See Anon, 'Γιατί η Παναγιωταρέα κατέβασε από το facebook το σχόλιο για τα πόδια των Καρυάτιδων' [Why did Panagiotarea deleted from Facebook her comment on the Caryatids' feet], *Amfipoli News*, 3 October 2014 (http://goo.gl/eHU4i9; accessed 16 February 2016). Accused of racism by members of the public, Panagiotarea deleted the comment on the 'Greek foot' and her statement about the 'Skopjans' a few days later.
39. Dudley J. Morton, 'Metatarsus atavicus: the identification of a distinct type of foot disorder', *The Journal of Bone and Joint Surgery* 9 (1927), pp. 531–544.
40. Cf. Tina Sgouropoulou, 'Το ελληνικό πόδι' [The Greek foot], *Eleftheri Zoni*, no publication date (http://goo.gl/YNKVoO; accessed 16 February 2016).
41. See Dionysis Vythoulkas, 'Ξεκίνησε η επιχείρηση Ξένιος Ζευς' [Operation Xenios Zeus is launched], *To Vima*, 4 August 2012 (http://goo.gl/X3tQlw; accessed 16 February 2016).
42. Cf. Anon., 'Επιθεώρηση Θέτις' [Operation Thetis], *News 247*, 5 April 2013 (http://goo.gl/vldXUY; accessed 16 February 2016).
43. As argued by Yannis Hamilakis, 'Hospitable Zeus', *LRB blog*, 8 August 2012 (http://goo.gl/DdmU7z; accessed 16 February 2016).
44. See Amnesty International, *The Human Cost of Fortress Europe. Human Rights Violations Against Immigrants and Refugees at Europe's Borders* (London, 2014). Available at http://goo.gl/G3uF7Y (accessed 17 February 2016).
45. Judith Butler, *Precarious Life. The Powers of Mourning and Violence* (London and New York, 2004), p. 66.
46. See Wendy Brown, *Undoing the Demos. Neoliberalism's Stealth Revolution* (Cambridge MA and London, 2015), pp. 17–46.
47. Michel Foucault, *Power. The Essential Works of Foucault, 1954–1984*, vol. 3 (London, 2010), p. 416.

48. Giorgio Agamben, *Homo Sacer: Sovereign Power and Bare Life* (Stanford, 1998), pp. 119–125; 136–143.
49. Ibid., pp. 119–188.
50. http://goo.gl/WuA3ol (accessed 23 November 2014); today removed. The illustration was extensively reproduced, though, cf. Anon., 'Αυτός είναι ο νεκρός της Αμφίπολης' [This is the dead man of Amphipolis], *Akous.gr*, 16 November 2014 (http://goo.gl/hzyp6E; accessed 17 February 2016).
51. I am using the term as defined by Achille Mbembe, 'Necropolitics', *Public Culture* 15:1 (2003), pp. 11–40, that is as an advanced form of 'more anatomical and sensorial' biopolitics.
52. All statistics by Eurostat, available at http://goo.gl/LwkFwt (accessed 17 February 2016).
53. See above, n. 1.
54. See above, n. 34.
55. Giorgio Agamben, *State of Exception* (Chicago and London, 2003), pp. 1–31. For the Greek case in particular, see above n. 36.
56. C. Nadia Seremetakis, 'Implications', in C.N. Seremetakis (ed.), *The Senses Still. Perception and Memory as Material Culture in Modernity* (Chicago and London, 1994), pp. 123–145.

PART II

CRISIS BRAIN DRAIN AND DIASPORA

CHAPTER 3

CRISIS BRAIN DRAIN: SHORT-TERM PAIN/LONG-TERM GAIN?

Lois Labrianidis and Manolis Pratsinakis

Introduction

In the context of the debt crisis, recession, austerity and socio-political consequences, Greece is experiencing a new major wave of out-migration. Emigration has become a survival strategy for many people who are finding it hard to make ends meet, while, at the same time, it has also emerged as an increasingly appealing option for others in less pressing need, who see their chances of a career severely reduced.[1] A large part of the outflow comprises young graduates, thus raising concerns about the negative impact of the ongoing brain drain on the country's economy and society. The crisis-driven emigration of professionals that accounts for approximately two-thirds of the outflow has turned Greece into a major exporter of highly skilled labour to the countries of Northern Europe, thus replicating older 'core – periphery' relations within the EU.

While most of the pre-crisis emigrants saw their migration as a significant career move and many planned eventually to return to Greece, only a minority of the post-2010 migrants view their emigration in that way. Most of them emigrate because they feel they lack any prospects in their home country and due to their overall disappointment in the socioeconomic situation in Greece, feelings which often go hand-in-hand with a deep disillusionment with the Greek political establishment and with state institutions. They make use of the right of freedom of movement, seeking a better future in other countries in the European Union, whose institutions they also blame for the socioeconomic condition their country currently finds itself in due to the extreme austerity policies imposed by the Institutions.[2]

In this chapter we explore the magnitude, dynamics and impact of the current emigration flow of young graduates. Placing the phenomenon of the Greek brain drain in a historical continuum, we argue that its structural preconditions predate the crisis. In historical terms it is a phenomenon that can be primarily attributed to the low demand for highly skilled work in the Greek labour market and to related weaknesses in Greece's developmental plan, a situation that has led to an accumulated loss of competitiveness over time. Yet it is only now that the brain drain has reached critical proportions, raising concerns about the prospects of recovery of a country that is being increasingly deprived of its young, educated workforce, an indispensible part of any attempt to ameliorate its production model. The combined effect of the emigration of a highly educated labour force on the one hand and recession and austerity on the other and their mutually exacerbating relationship thus risks imposing a cycle of underdevelopment on the Greek economy.[3]

Taking into account the experiences and aspirations of the emigrants themselves as well as critical voices from the literature that warn against overly optimistic views of highly skilled migrants as agents of development, we conclude this chapter by suggesting concrete policies that could be implemented in the shorter and medium term. These are proposed as a means of alleviating the negative consequences of the phenomenon, and potentially turning the situation into an opportunity for the restructuring of the country in the future, provided that a viable and realistic agreement is reached in respect of Greek debt and that austerity policies are abandoned. It is suggested that, in the current circumstances, this could not be done by focusing on a repatriation policy, since return in the short term is neither part of the plan nor an aspiration for most of the emigrants.[4] Instead it could be done through establishing different means of cooperation, leading to the development of viable and sustained transnational ties between the expatriates and the Greek society and economy.

Development, the migration of professionals and the knowledge economy

Around the year 2000, levels of emigration among highly skilled people worldwide exceeded the rate of emigration of people with lower educational qualifications.[5] Apart from the self-selectivity of migration, i.e. the fact that the highly skilled are among those most likely to move and indeed most capable of doing so, global competition for highly skilled professionals has increased in the past few decades triggered by neoliberal deregulation and encouraged by selective migration management schemes in many destination countries of the North.[6] This competition is related to an increased demand for highly specialized skills and to the rise of the so-called 'knowledge economy' in which human capital is seen as a vital factor in the economic development process.

The concept of the 'knowledge economy' was introduced in the mid-1990s to account for the role of knowledge and innovation in economic development, especially in areas such as IT or biotechnology.[7] Others proposed instead the term 'learning economy' to emphasize the fact that 'the most important feature of modern economies is not only very intense use of knowledge, but rather that the existing knowledge depreciates very fast'.[8] In this context, expanding and upgrading their knowledge-base and human capital resources has become a central feature of the development strategy for countries (as well as cities and regions) either through training of the labour force, or by attracting highly educated people and people working in the creative industries.[9]

By contrast, the international migration of professionals presents a major challenge for sending countries, which are commonly also among the less highly developed ones. These countries see their position further weakened in this global competition,[10] whereas receiving countries are able to reap the benefits of a skilled labour force in which they have not invested.[11] Negative repercussions include a decrease in the average educational levels,[12] loss of public funds invested in the formation of this human capital[13] as well as, in many cases, loss of incoming physical capital, given that physical capital often follows human capital flows.[14] Most crucially the international migration of professionals may be detrimental for the longer term development potential of countries of origin. Yet this is an issue on which views have been divided in the literature. On the one hand, there are those who argue that international migration of professionals massively erodes the human capital and fiscal revenues of sending countries, driving them into a spiral of underdevelopment. On the other, there are those that argue that international migration of professionals may act as a potent force for developing the economy of sending countries through remittances, trade, direct foreign investment, and knowledge transfer.

Following broader ideological and paradigm shifts one may see variations in terms of the predominance of one or the other viewpoint over time.[15] For instance, in the 1970s and 1980s scholars influenced by dependency theory rightly criticized earlier ideas anchored to the modernization paradigm that linked migration with development through a supposed optimal equilibrium between capital and labour, something that was expected to follow flows of remittances and human capital between developed and less developed countries. Reversing the causality of the equation, they argued that it is underdevelopment in the periphery (caused by dependency on and exploitation by the countries of the core) that leads to the emigration of the highly skilled, which in turn feeds further underdevelopment in the periphery and contributes to sustaining inequalities on a global scale. In this context, the brain drain was seen as one of the ways through which migration acts as an exploitation mechanism for countries of the periphery.

More recently such views are once again being questioned. On the one hand, this is done by reasserting arguments based on neoclassical economics, presenting migration as a means towards the better allocation of production factors, higher productivity and the win–win situation envisaged to follow. Migration, it is argued, enables people to increase the returns on their skills and their 'human capital', which is to their own advantage as well as to the benefit of the economies of the sending and receiving states. Yet, the 'triple-win' potential it supposedly entails (for countries of origin and destination, and for the migrants themselves), is based on functionalist, competition-driven and economically deterministic views that are rarely confirmed in practice.[16]

On the other hand, views about the detrimental consequences of international migration of professionals on the development potential of the countries of origin are also challenged by diaspora scholars and those studying processes of transnationalism, who conceive the presence of a highly educated labour force abroad as a mobilized asset for sending countries.[17] Those scholars highlight the importance of expatriate networks, which can potentially form a significant resource when they are connected to countries of origin. They also stress that the negative aspects of the brain drain phenomenon can be – under certain circumstances – reversed. There are two ways for a country to benefit from its professionals working abroad. One is to focus on their return ('return option') and the other is to try to utilize this human capital, taking for granted that it will remain abroad ('diaspora option').[18] Until the 1980s, national and international policies focused on controlling the loss of professionals or on mitigating the negative impact by tax incentives for those who returned. However, the results were in most cases unsatisfactory.[19] More recently most of the initiatives have focused on the so-called diaspora option. The aim is to capitalize on the networks, recourses and knowledge of the nationals abroad through remittances, investments and 'brain exchange and circulation'.[20]

However, despite the need to recognize the day-to-day contributions migrants make to improve the well-being, living standards and economic conditions of countries of origin and related empirical evidence indicating that migrants can potentially accelerate development, there is also a need to acknowledge that they cannot set in motion broader processes of human and economic development all by themselves. Warning against overly optimistic views, de Haas[21] argues that the recent policy focus on the role of diasporas fits into neoliberal development paradigms that tend to overemphasize the power of markets and individuals to bring about political-economic change and social transformation.[22] Such views risk neglecting broader structural constraints such as ingrained socioeconomic and power inequalities. Moreover, they also underplay the significant role that may continue to be played by emigration states on the one hand – by creating favourable conditions for human development – and by immigration states on the other – through policies that empower (rather than exploit) migrants and thus maximize their social, human and economic capacity to contribute to development in their countries of origin.[23]

The structural preconditions to the Greek brain drain

In the postwar era up until the 1970s emigration flows almost uniformly comprised people with little formal education who left the country to fill the gaps in the booming industrial sectors of Western countries, especially in Europe. Highly skilled migration was, to a large extent, a matter of choice for the upper classes, and many emigrants left the country for reasons other than employment.[24] However, labour market restructuring led to the deterioration of employment opportunities for those born from the 1970s onwards and to ongoing relatively high unemployment, underemployment and employment precariousness in the 2000s.[25]

This was *not* mainly due to Greeks being 'over educated', as conventionally assumed.[26] While the numbers of those with a university degree have increased substantially in past decades, they are not among the highest in Europe or, in more general terms, in the developed world. In particular, in the period 2006–2015 Greece ranked 21st in the EU-28 with 29.3 per cent of the population aged 25–44 having completed tertiary education, which is lower than the EU-28 average (31.7 per cent), as are the percentages for graduates in the 25–34 and 25–64 age brackets. In fact, the rapid expansion in the take-up of tertiary education in Greece was not matched by a corresponding increase in demand for high-skilled human capital by businesses in Greece. Indicatively, Greece had one of the lowest rates of employment in high-technology sectors in 2008–2015 in the EU, while Research and Development expenditure in Greece is much lower than the EU-28 average and the comparison is even more unfavourable when it comes to the contribution of the private sector (54.6 per cent EU, 32 per cent GR). Thus the explanation for the unfavourable conditions for graduates in Greece in past decades lies not in the supply side of a supposedly excessively highly skilled workforce, but rather in the demand side of a labour market failing to absorb this workforce.[27]

Greek firms, mostly due to their small size and several other related weaknesses, have been mainly focused on the production of low-cost products and services and have avoided any attempts at upgrading, including the infusion of technology and innovation. These characteristics have hindered the utilization of a highly educated labour force that could act as an intermediary between universities/research centres and the private sector. Combined with the fact that the Greek Research and Development system is not able to attract and retain the growing number of qualified scientists, this has led a significant share of these graduates to migrate abroad, in order to seek employment with better prospects elsewhere.[28] Moreover, the 'informality' of the national economy as well as nepotism have affected the relative significance of graduates in the Greek labour market. The migration of professionals to specific countries was also influenced by the average wages of graduates in those countries. As our 2009–2010 survey showed,[29] outside Greece there is a clear correlation between levels of education and salaries, but when migrants returned to Greece they tended to have lower wages that did not increase in tandem with their academic qualifications.

As a result, even before the outbreak of the crisis a considerable number of highly skilled young Greeks had been emigrating for better career prospects, better chances of finding a job related to their specialization, a satisfactory income and increased opportunities for further training. Yet, the outmigration of graduates intensified significantly as job opportunities shrank in the shadow of the crisis and once public sector employment was no longer an option as a result of cuts and restrictions in new recruitments.[30] A comparative presentation of unemployment rates in Greece and the EU over the past ten years provides a graphic depiction of Greece's exceptionalism as regards the position of the highly skilled in the labour market and explains the sharp increase in emigration among these workers in the period of the crisis.

As seen in Chart 3.1, in the years directly preceding the onset of the global financial crisis and up to 2010 unemployment rates among the

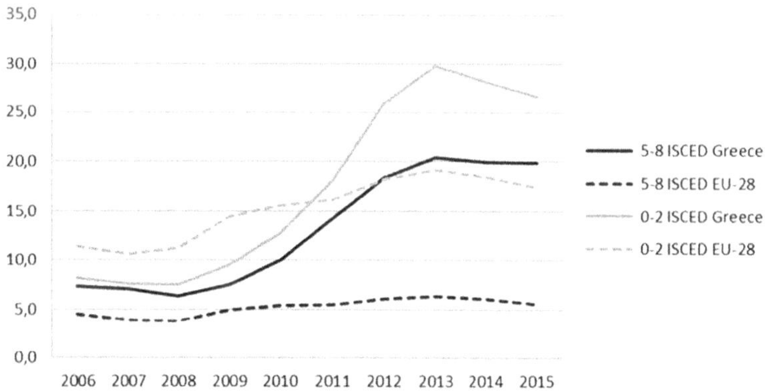

Chart 3.1 Unemployment levels in Greece by educational attainment. International Standard Classification of Education (ISCED). Source: Eurostat (http://appsso.eurostat.ec.europa.eu/nui/show.do?dataset=lfsa_urgaed&lang=en)

poorly educated (0–2 ISCED) were significantly lower in Greece than the EU-28 mean. In fact from 2006 to 2008 they were on a par with those of graduates, indicating that education did not provide significant advantages in terms of access to the labour market in Greece. This changed with the crisis, which had a direct and much more acute impact on the less privileged. In Greece, as elsewhere in Europe, unemployment rates for less well educated people became higher than for those with higher education. Yet, while in most European countries the unemployment rates of more highly educated people increased only marginally, if at all, in Greece they skyrocketed, being almost four times higher those of the EU-28 mean, making the push-pull factors for Greeks with higher education particularly strong.

Greek emigration in times of crisis

In the context of a contraction in GDP of more than a quarter between 2008–2014, the crisis in Greece severely undermined the employment prospects of the entire workforce and also brought about steep decreases in earnings, welfare provision and allowances. The combined effects of recession, extreme austerity, and a concomitant generalized mistrust of institutions and the political system changed mobility intentions drastically. While until recently Greek citizens were amongst those Europeans who least favoured long distance mobility, many people have been forced by circumstances to change their views in a very short period of time.[31] According to EUROSTAT, in a four-year period, from 2010 to 2013, approximately 208,000 Greek citizens left Greece and to that number we should add an approximately equal number of foreign nationals, who returned to their countries of origin or were forced to migrate again due to the crisis. In a recent study we conducted,[32] which included a nationwide representative survey of 1,237 households in Greece (Hellenic Observatory survey, HO survey from here on), we estimated that the total emigration outflow of Greek citizens from 2010 until the end of 2015 ranged between 280,000 and 350,000 people. Given our findings on return migration in that period, which was recorded as 15 per cent of the total outflow, we can estimate that by the end of 2015 240,000 to 300,000 post-2010 Greek emigrants were living abroad.

The magnitude of the outflow has attracted considerable media attention and has triggered a public debate on the ongoing Greek brain drain. Yet the discussion is often characterized by two misconceptions.[33] First, the emigration of the highly skilled is presented as a new phenomenon resulting from the crisis, while the underlying structural causes of the phenomenon are not addressed. Second, the crisis-driven emigration is presented as exclusively pertaining to the young and the educated and the emigration of older people, the less well educated, or minority groups is often neglected.[34] The crisis has amplified push factors that already existed in Greece for the highly skilled, intensifying their emigration patterns. But it has also impacted on the mobility aspirations and practices of people of other socioeconomic backgrounds. Even though they form a minority of emigrants, the crisis seems once again to be pushing people of lower educational backgrounds out of the country.

Thus, the emigration of the highly educated in the post-2010 period should be understood as a continuation of an earlier ongoing phenomenon and a part, albeit a very significant one, of the new crisis-driven emigration. According to the findings of the HO survey approximately 190,000 graduates live outside Greece, of whom more than half emigrated after 2010. Two out of three of the post-2010 emigrants are university graduates and one fourth of the total outflow represents people with postgraduate degrees or who are graduates of medical schools and

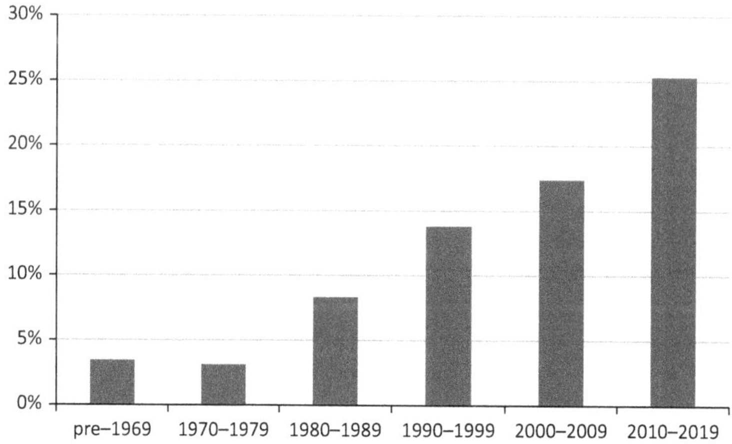

Chart 3.2 Percentage of postgraduate emigrants by decade of emigration (including graduates of 6-year medicine and 5-year engineering degree programmes). Source: HO Survey data

polytechnics. As seen in Chart 3.2, the percentage of those emigrants as part of the total emigration outflow has risen considerably since 2010. Thus it is not only the sheer numbers of professionals emigrating that has vastly increased but also the percentage of those with the most years in education, thus constituting a double drain on the country.

The new emigrants are heading to a variety of destinations from the Middle East to the Far East and from Eastern Europe and the Balkans to Canada and Australia. The vast majority, however, seem to be heading to EU countries. Germany and the UK in particular attract by far the largest share of the outflows, accounting for more than half of the post-2010 emigration. Our HO survey data indicates that there are differences in terms of the educational background of the emigrants according to the country of destination. Those who immigrate to Britain are almost exclusively people with high educational qualifications, while Germany attracts a considerable number of people with low to medium levels of education (43 per cent of the total inflow) in addition to the highly educated.

According to the HO survey data, those with low to medium levels of education commonly find jobs abroad via their social networks, while highly educated emigrants find jobs mostly through applications for (publicly advertised) vacancies based on their own attainments. It thus seems that more poorly educated people migrate to Germany and other former guestworker destinations because they can make use of social networks that are available to them from earlier emigrations.

Concerning the economic background of the emigrants, our findings indicate that, after the year 2000, the households with very high incomes are the ones that are the most likely to 'send' emigrants abroad; a trend that has persisted in the crisis period. In particular, for the period 2010–2015, emigrants from households with very high incomes comprise 9 per cent of the total outflow, even though those households form only 2 per cent of the total survey sample. Emigration is a costly project and thus more easily undertaken by those with means. However, the adverse socioeconomic position in which many people have found themselves as a result of years of austerity politics in Greece has led to a sharp increase in the rate of emigration of people from 'low to very low' income households. While before the crisis this category used to be the least prone to emigrate, they now constitute 28 per cent of the post-2010 emigration outflow, a percentage that is on a par with their share in the total sample (26 per cent).

Change is also observed in the breakdown by age of the emigrant population. According to the HO survey data, the average age of emigrants is 30.5 years in the post-2010 period, which is 6 years higher than in the 1990–1999 period (24.3). As regards remittance flows, according to the HO survey findings, the vast majority of migrants neither send nor receive money (68 per cent). It thus appears that emigration contributes mainly to the subsistence and/or the socio-economic progress of the emigrants themselves and not of the household as a whole. Only 19 per cent of emigrants, who come, as might be anticipated, mainly from low and very low income households, send money to Greece. The low volume of remittances is further corroborated by data from the World Bank according to which their value has been progressively decreasing from 2008 onward.[35]

Feelings of attachment and prospects of mutual assistance and knowledge transfer

As noted above, since the early 2000s the diaspora option has become the most popular policy response by governments facing considerable outflows of highly educated people. Yet such policies are often driven by a narrow definition of the communities they recognize as their diasporas. In so doing they overlook the multiplicity of the aspirations of nationals abroad, while restricting their attention to a certain segment of the diaspora whose practices they try to channel towards a certain predefined developmental plan.[36] Such an approach limits the potential for cooperation and can alienate people and organizations that are already engaging in all kinds of development activities in the broader sense of the term and not necessarily equated with economic growth. In addition, interconnected questions concerning on the one hand the ability and on the other hand the willingness of nationals abroad to help should be central to any policy approach that reaches out to them. Below, drawing on 21 in-depth interviews that were conducted with highly skilled emigrants in the city of Amsterdam and the Greater London area in the context of the EUMIGRE project,[37] we provide some evidence about the aspirations of Greek expatriates and the potential for knowledge exchange and cooperation with institutions, professionals and businesses in Greece.

Analysing the accounts of our informants on how they relate to Greece, we can see that, in some cases, the crisis and the grim socioeconomic situation in Greece had triggered the urge to act and 'do something', especially among those most settled abroad (the majority of whom had left before the crisis).[38] It should be noted that in the two cities in which we conducted the research there were already a number of new initiatives in place with very diverse aims, such as trying to organize and mobilize the diaspora, providing orientation to newcomers, channelling economic support to Greece, debunking negative representations about Greece abroad, informing and supporting potential investors in Greece, assisting emigrants in developing new innovative businesses, etc.[39]

Most of our informants told us that they felt very close to family and friends in Greece and were deeply concerned about their conditions and the gloomy prospects back home. The vast majority of them also expressed strong feelings of attachment to Greece as a place and physical environment and constructed a positive image of contemporary 'Greekness' with reference to an extrovert way of life and the more caring attitude in social terms that they felt characterized everyday culture in Greece. They contrasted this image positively with what they identified as the individualistic life of western Europe. Several of our informants also told us that they came to feel more Greek outside Greece than they did when living there. The experience of migration made them re-evaluate positively certain aspects of what they identified as Greek culture. Equally important for some of them was the emphasis on Greekness as a quality stemming from the ancient heritage in which they felt they had a part and which was a source of pride to them and a way of boosting their self-esteem in their interpersonal interactions with non-Greeks abroad. It was this quality, however, that they deplored as absent from present-day Greece.

To our question about their willingness to develop transnational professional collaborations with institutions and businesses in Greece, several of our informants claimed that they would like to do so and some described concrete plans they had already implemented or were about to. Development of transnational activities and transfer of knowledge between Greece and the countries of settlement of the new emigrants is already a reality. Yet our material also highlights a number of barriers that the emigrants perceived to exist or experienced in their attempts to engage in partnerships or transnational activities with Greece. Some of our informants, for instance, expressed reservations about pursuing any such plans in the light of what they described as a typically Greek narrow-minded attitude of suspicion towards new ideas and envy of success. At the same time, many of our respondents were very critical about Greek state institutions, bureaucracy and the business culture in Greece and made reference to a lack of transparency in employment conditions, onerous bureaucracy in dealings with the state and insufficient support by institutions.[40]

It should be noted that the more recent emigrants were the least inclined to engage in any sort of transnational activity with Greece. That was for two reasons. First, many of them felt betrayed by the Greek state and some of them told us that they felt that they were pushed out of their country. Their bitterness made them negative about trying to reconnect with Greece. They considered it quite reasonable to focus their energy on building their life abroad and felt that any engagement with Greece would be a backward step. Moreover, and not unrelated to this, it should be noted that several of the more recent emigrants are still struggling to build lives for themselves in Amsterdam and London and in that context developing relations with institutions and people in Greece was not currently a priority to them.

This was particularly the case for people seeking work in fields not highly valued in the labour market of their destination cities and, in the case of Amsterdam, in jobs for which fluency in the local language was essential.[41] Unlike those specialized in fields such as IT and engineering, who could easily secure employment abroad, others, usually graduates in the humanities and social sciences, found it much more difficult to find employment that matched their qualifications. If they lacked the necessary economic resources to invest further in their training and education or to support themselves until they had built up their social networks in the receiving country and improved their language skills, in many cases they ended up working for extended periods in jobs below their skill levels. Such difficulties in adapting to their destination countries obviously weakened their capacity and willingness to seek any transnational ties with Greece.

Policy recommendations

Greece has long postponed the move from a low-cost to a knowledge-based economy, despite the fact that since the 1990s a significant upward trend in higher education studies was observed in the country. As a result, the Greek economy has been unable to take advantage of the presence of a highly educated workforce and even before the crisis many highly educated people left the country in search of employment that corresponded to their qualifications and career ambitions. In the past few years, in times of crisis and austerity politics, the ongoing brain drain has acquired alarming proportions, triggered by a sudden aggravation of the unfavourable conditions in the national labour market that were already acting as push factors.

In this context, the need for a state policy aimed at alleviating the negative consequences of this phenomenon is acute. In the current circumstances focusing on a repatriation policy will not do, since return to Greece in the short term is not something most emigrants are planning or indeed dreaming of. Instead the focus should be on helping to develop means of cooperation which could lead to the development of viable and sustained transnational ties between them and the Greek society and economy.

Our findings in Amsterdam and London highlight the considerable willingness on the part of settled members of the Greek diaspora to develop transnational economic relations with Greece and indeed many people have already taken steps in this direction. Yet we also recorded considerable reservations towards state institutions, suggesting that any policy towards the diaspora should first concentrate on restoring the state's credibility in the eyes of expatriates. Policy aims should be framed in such a way as neither to appear patronizing nor to be treating Greeks abroad as owners of resources that can 'be tapped',[42] but rather as collaborators in a common mission. The approach needs to be as inclusive as possible and the measures aimed at the highly skilled recent emigrants needs to be part of a broader strategy addressing the diaspora as a whole. That means that the policy should also address older expatriate communities but also lower skilled migrants living abroad, recognizing their existing contributions and support, starting from the fact that they are the ones most likely to be sending remittances back home. Such an approach should thus also include interventions and measures that support initiatives or structures abroad that empower low skilled emigrants as well as those better educated Greeks abroad who are facing difficulties. The smoother the adjustment of the emigrants to their new homes, the greater their willingness and ability to contribute to Greece is likely to be and the consulates could play a much more active role in that respect.

In relation to the group that forms our focus here, namely the more highly educated migrants and particularly the most settled among them, it is suggested that state policies should actively support existing bottom-up initiatives not only as a means of recognizing their contributions but also as a way of identifying the areas in which expatriates perceive opportunities or the need for action and as an optimal way of connecting and expanding relations with them. As Brinkerhoff argues, the aim should be to target interventions to those members of the diaspora who are already mobilized, willing, and able to contribute; that is 'governments should primarily target the mobilized, and not seek to mobilize the targeted'.[43] At the same time, Greek professionals working abroad should be considered as a significant 'pipeline' connection between the Greek economy and productive and innovative international centres. Every Greek professional working abroad should be seen not only as a unit, but as a 'node' in a system with many connections that can link the Greek economy with this system.

Thus, state policy needs to be coordinated by a comprehensive structure operating on different levels and promoting the interconnection of expatriate professionals with the Greek society and economy in a systematic and sustained way. The broad strategy could be devised by an executive body in the Ministry of Economy and Development, advised by a steering committee consisting of Greek professionals, entrepreneurs, academics, researchers and artists who live and work abroad. Policy goals need to be informed by research findings and regular research into the brain drain phenomenon should be supported. At the same time, monitoring and evaluating policy goals and instruments should be a continuous process. On the public sector side, a lean and flexible operational team should also be set up to solve practical issues. A number of actions could be promoted by such a policy structure in the short term such as (a) the creation of a website that will provide constantly updated information for those wishing to return to or to cooperate with Greece while working abroad, (b) the organization of events in Greece and abroad, in cooperation with charitable organizations, private donors, Greek communities, and Greek professional associations abroad, (c) the designation of liaison offices at Greek consulates in countries with a significant concentration of Greek academics, (d) the provision of incentives to build networks developing relations with Greece as well as rewards for all notable initiatives, (e) the promotion of schemes enabling collaboration between both the public and private sector and those networks abroad, e.g. by creating opportunities for expatriate Greek academics to participate in research projects in Greece or by offering Greek professors abroad the chance of dual appointments, or by promoting cooperation in the private sector in the form of educational and training seminars taught by invited professionals and (f) by encouraging alumni associations to establish effective links between graduates who are either continuing their studies or working abroad.

Such actions could provide a platform allowing emigrants to transfer their ideas and knowledge through collaborations with universities, research centres and private companies, by working intermittently in their country of origin or by establishing their own businesses, a 'bridge' that might later bring them back. That said, while the issue of return may be seen as a longer term aim, the containment or at least moderation of the ongoing outflow is critical at present. The emigration of professionals has currently acquired momentum and through a process of cumulative causation threatens to alter the demographic make-up of the country and to bring about significant labour shortages in certain fields of the economy, thus further limiting their potential not only for advancement but sustainability.[44] Thus small-scale actions with immediate results are necessary to retain young graduates.

A number of such actions are being put into practice with the aim of: (a) promoting self-employment among graduates, (b) allowing the recruitment of people with doctorates to universities and technical colleges, so that they can acquire academic teaching experience and (c) promoting positive discrimination for young postdocs to be recruited as teaching staff in the Open University. Yet further action is needed to create a more challenging and attractive working and business environment through incentives provided by the incentives law, structural funds or the Juncker Plan. Moreover, further unravelling of bureaucracy and better coordination among public institutions are also required, as is the creation of an institutional framework that monitors and ensures the quality of employment conditions. Finally, the setting up of policies that enable people to take the first steps in starting their own companies is critical, especially given the current high social security/tax costs for freelancers in Greece. As a means to that end it is suggested that NSRF funds would be better employed if allocated to subsidizing the social security contributions of start-up companies and freelancers rather than as one-off grants.

These policy measures are a necessary part of the process of altering the mode of economic development of the country and steering the economy towards the production of products and services with a higher knowledge content. To that end the Greek state must publicly and formally recognize the fundamental value of this human capital and constantly encourage the creation of a more meritocratic labour market, in order to ensure that the highly educated labour force is not only employed as befits its skills and knowledge, but also occupies a central role in the Greek administrative/political system and the decision-making centres. Even though highly skilled expatriates cannot steer the process of changing the developmental model of a country all by themselves, they can be extremely valuable partners in such a process. In Greece's case, that could eventually help address the reasons that led to their leaving in the first place, hence also enabling the return of some of them with positive outcomes for the Greek economy, society and culture.

Notes

The chapter is an outcome of the EUMIGRE project, which is funded by the EU's Horizon 2020 research and innovation programme under the Marie Skłodowska-Curie grant agreement No 658694.

1. Lois Labrianidis and Manolis Pratsinakis, 'Greece's New Emigration at Times of Crisis,' *GreeSE: Hellenic Observatory Papers on Greece and Southeast Europe* paper 99 (2016), pp. 1–38.
2. 'Insitutions', formerly 'Troika', is the term used for the triumvirate representing Greece's creditors.
3. Lois Labrianidis and Nikos Vogiatzis, 'The Mutually Reinforcing Relation between International Migration of Highly Educated Labour Force and

Economic Crisis: The Case of Greece,' *Southeast European and Black Sea Studies* 13/4 (2013), pp. 525–551.

4. Labrianidis and Pratsinakis, 'Greece's New Emigration at Times of Crisis'.
5. Jean-Christophe Dumont, Gilles Spielvogel and Sarah Widmaier, *International Migrants in Developed, Emerging and Developing Countries: An Extended Profile* OECD Social, Employment and Migration Working Papers, 2010.
6. Triadafilos Triadafilopoulos (ed.), *Wanted and Welcome?: Policies for Highly Skilled Immigrants in Comparative Perspective* (New York, 2013); Devesh Kapur and John McHale, *Give Us Your Best and Brightest: The Global Hunt for Talent and its Impact on the Developing World* (Washington DC, 2005).
7. Aimee Kuvik, 'The Race for Global Talent, EU Enlargement and the Implications for Migration Policies and Processes in European Labour Markets,' in Brigit Glorius, Izabela Grabowska-Lusinka and Aimee Kuvik (eds), *Mobility in Transition: Migration Patterns After EU Enlargement* (Amsterdam, 2014), pp. 113–132; Anna Lee Saxenian, *Silicon Valley's New Immigrant Entrepreneurs*, Vol. 32 (San Francisco, 1999).
8. Peter Nielsen and Bengt-Åke Lundvall, 'Innovation, Learning Organizations and Industrial Relations', DRUID Working Paper, 2003.
9. Ibid.; Organisation for Economic Co-operation and Development, *Better Skills, Better Jobs, Better Lives: A Strategic Approach to Skills Policies* OECD, 2012.
10. Bogdan Glăvan, 'Brain Drain: A Management or a Property Problem?', *American Journal of Economics and Sociology* 67/4 (2008), pp. 719–737; Ronald Skeldon, 'International Migration as a Tool in Development Policy: A Passing Phase?', *Population and Development Review* 34/1 (2008), pp. 1–18.
11. Allan Williams and Vladimír Baláž, *International Migration and Knowledge* (London, 2014).
12. Robert J. Barro and Xavier Sala-i-Martin, *Economic Growth* (New York, 1995).
13. Richard Raymond, 'The Interregional Brain Drain and Public Education,' *Growth and Change* 4/3 (1973), pp. 28–34.
14. Thomas Straubhaar, 'International Mobility of the Highly Skilled: Brain Gain, Brain Drain Or Brain Exchange' *Hamburgisches Welt-Wirtschafts-Archiv (HWWA)* Discussion Paper 88 (2000), pp. 1–23.
15. Hein de Haas, 'The Migration and Development Pendulum: A Critical View on Research and Policy,' *International Migration* 50/3 (2012), pp. 8–25; Thomas Faist, 'Migrants as Transnational Development Agents: An Inquiry into the Newest Round of the Migration–Development Nexus,' *Population, Space and Place* 14/1 (2008), pp. 21–42.
16. Triadafilopoulos, *Wanted and Welcome?*
17. Jean-Baptiste Meyer, 'Network Approach Versus Brain Drain: Lessons from the Diaspora', *International Migration* 39/5 (2001), pp. 91–110.
18. Jean-Baptiste Meyer and Mercy Brown, *Scientific Diasporas. World Conference on Science*, UNESCO – ICSU, Budapest, 26 June–1 July 1999.

Available at http://digital-library.unesco.org/shs/most/gsdl/cgi-bin/library?e=d-000-00---0most--00-0-0--0prompt-10--4------0-1l--1-en-50---20-about---00031-001-1-0utfZz-8-00&a=d&c=most&cl=CL4.1&d=HASH018238f95602a0dbde930783.

19. There have been some successes for repatriation policies but they were either in newly industrialized countries, such as Singapore and the Republic of Korea, or in large countries, such as China and India, where the robust repatriation programmes of the 1980s were followed by the creation of significant R&D structures and high development rates.
20. Elizabeth Mavroudi, 'Helping the Homeland? Diasporic Greeks in Australia and the Potential for Homeland-Oriented Development at a Time of Economic Crisis' in Anastasia Christou and Elizabeth Mavroudi (eds), *Dismantling Diasporas: Rethinking the Geographies of Diasporic Identity, Connection and Development* (New York, 2015), pp. 175–187.
21. Hein de Haas, 'Migration and Development: A Theoretical Perspective', *International Migration Review* 44/1 (2010), pp. 227–264; de Haas, 'The Migration and Development Pendulum', pp. 8–25.
22. Hélène Pellerin and Beverley Mullings, 'The "Diaspora Option", Migration and the Changing Political Economy of Development,' *Review of International Political Economy* 20/1 (2013), pp. 89–120.
23. De Haas, 'The Migration and Development Pendulum', p. 21.
24. Lois Labrianidis, *Επενδύοντας στη φυγή: Η διαρροή επιστημόνων από την Ελλάδα την εποχή της παγκοσμιοποίησης* {Investing in Leaving: The Greek Case of International Migration of Professionals in the Globalization Era} (Athens, 2011).
25. Maria Karamessini, 'Life Stage Transitions and the Still-Critical Role of the Family in Greece' in Dominique Anxo, Gerhard Bosch, and Jill Rubery (eds), *The Welfare State and Life Transitions. A European Perspective*, (Cheltenham, 2010), pp. 257–283.
26. With the exception of certain disciplines, such as medicine and law, in which a growing demand during past years resulted indeed in saturated job market prospects.
27. Lois Labrianidis, 'Investing in Leaving: The Greek Case of International Migration of Professionals', *Mobilities* 9/2 (2014), pp. 314–335.
28. Ibid.
29. Labrianidis, *Επενδύοντας στη φυγή: Η διαρροή επιστημόνων από την Ελλάδα την εποχή της παγκοσμιοποίησης*.
30. Labrianidis and Pratsinakis, 'Greece's New Emigration at Times of Crisis'.
31. Ibid.
32. Ibid.
33. Manolis Pratsinakis, Panos Hatziprokopiou, Dimitris Grammatikas, Lois Labrianidis, 'Crisis and the Resurgence of Emigration from Greece: Trends, Representations, and the Multiplicity of Migrant Trajectories' in Brigit Glorius, and Josefina Domínguez-Mujica (eds), *European Mobility in Times*

of Crisis. The New Context of European South-North Migration (Bielefeld, 2017), pp. 75–102.

34. The outflow of immigrants which, as mentioned above, amounts to half the post-2010 wave of emigration, has also been overlooked. In relative terms foreign nationals were more likely to leave Greece as a result of the crisis than were Greek citizens.
35. http://data.worldbank.org/indicator/BX.TRF.PWKR.CD.DT.
36. Hein de Haas, 'Engaging Diasporas: How Governments and Development Agencies can Support Diaspora Involvement in the Development of their Origin Countries,' International Migration Institute (IMI), University of Oxford, for OXFAM NOVIB (2006); Giulia Sinatti and Cindy Horst, 'Migrants as Agents of Development: Diaspora Engagement Discourse and Practice in Europe', *Ethnicities* 15/1 (2015), pp. 134–152.
37. The interviews were conducted between January and August 2016. The informants were aged from 26 to 38 years and they had emigrated to the Netherlands and England respectively from 2006 onward.
38. As mentioned above, many people were equally disillusioned and angry with EU institutions whose policies they blamed for driving their country into a downward spiral.
39. Examples of such organizations include: the Help Children in Greece foundation, the Neoafixthentes stin Ollandia, the New Diaspora and the Nederlands-Griekse Mediacirkel in Amsterdam and reloadGreece, The Greek Energy Forum and Hellenic Hope in London.
40. Similar viewpoints were also recorded among member of the Greek Diaspora in Australia by Mavroudi, 'Helping the Homeland?'.
41. It should be noted that overall the Greeks in London had considerably more favourable experiences.
42. De Haas, *Engaging Diasporas.*
43. Jennifer M. Brinkerhoff, 'Creating an Enabling Environment for Diasporas' Participation in Homeland Development', *International Migration* 50/1 (2012), p. 90.
44. Douglas S. Massey, Joaquin Arango, Graeme Hugo, Ali Kouaouci, Adela Pellegrino, and J. Edward Taylor, 'Theories of International Migration: A Review and Appraisal', *Population and Development Review* 19/3 (1993), pp. 451–454.

CHAPTER 4

CITIZENSHIP AND ENTREPRENEURSHIP: GREEK AMERICA AS DIASPORA AT A TIME OF CRISIS

Yiorgos Anagnostou

Since the early 2010s, when the Greek debt crisis was inflicting an acute humanitarian emergency on the most vulnerable sectors of the population, Greek America has been activating a wide range of institutional, grassroots and private relief initiatives. The engagement ranges from philanthropy – supporting Greek charities and food distribution networks – to campaigns advocating heritage tourism, to establishing endowed scholarships at American universities for the purpose of fostering entrepreneurialism among Greece's youth; and from launching funds for children in need, to awareness campaigns to inform the American public about the extent of the human suffering. Providing material aid, boosting the economy and generating hope are deemed essential to sustaining a nation under duress. This extensive mobilization of resources underscored the operation of a diaspora identity in Greek America. The grim realities of the historical homeland-in-crisis set in motion diaspora's empathy and solidarity, rendering visible the emotional and material links between a diaspora and its country of origins.[1]

Greek America's connections with Greece in this context extend beyond mere financial flows. The engagement enters the realm of cultural representation, as grassroots initiatives, organizations and diplomatic agencies produce narratives defining Greek American identity. This in an era where the media, political debates, experts and popular culture across the globe, including in Greece itself, frequently point to national culture as the root cause for the crisis. This culturalist explanation associates Greece's economic upheaval with the question of identity. It pressingly asks, isn't it that the country's bankruptcy is due to a fundamental flaw in the 'national character'? In fact, to a cultural pathology? The internationalization of a nation-in-economic crisis generates a nation-in-cultural crisis. The question surfaces repeatedly: Who are the Greeks? A litmus test of the effects of neoliberal capitalism, or perpetrators of their own demise? The answer is often unflattering for the nation; the Greek image is tarnished.

The questioning of Greek identity inevitably entangles the diaspora into the cultural crisis. If the world asks who are the Greeks, who are, then, the Greeks in the United States? This question is addressed by a multitude of texts – documentary films, journalistic investigations, books, and organizational reports – as well as economic initiatives specifically launched to address the crisis. They are produced in multiple geographical locations and institutional sites, ranging from Chicago to Los Angeles to Greece, and they originate from sources such as international solidarity campaigns, Greek and Greek American media outlets, the Greek American public and the US Embassy in Athens. Their production may initially utilize local contexts – a US cultural diversity festival for example – and draw upon national discourses, such as American multiculturalism or Greek nationalism. The texts may subsequently circulate transnationally – a Greek American documentary shown on Greek television for instance – and be consumed internationally through the internet. This multifaceted terrain features both online and offline dimensions that interrelate with each other, including transnational flows of capital and knowledge, which generate, as I will show, specific modes of identity. The resulting constellation of images, ideas and practices performs a number of functions: it produces citizen-subjects, construes images of the homeland and regulates the nature of transnational affinities.

How do these narratives produce Greek America? In this chapter I probe the construction of Greek America as a diaspora in the context of the Greek debt crisis and the ensuing international contestation over the nature of Greek identity. I ask who defines diaspora, how, and for what purpose? This angle of inquiry shifts the emphasis beyond the conventional analysis of diasporas as typologies of dispersed populations, or as *descriptions* of lived experiences, social networks, population movements and cultural forms which are documented to subsequently theorize transnational identities. Instead, I draw from scholarship which places the making of diaspora in the context of political economy, particularly as a 'governmental category',[2] and which accords analytical premium on how political and economic structures *regulate* the content, nature of exchanges and boundaries of transnational connections. I examine the ways in which these structures constitute diaspora and I discuss the purposes these constructions serve. I analyse texts (documentaries, promotional trailers, reports, essays) and the subjectivities these texts produce in *relation* to state discourses and global structures of power. Diaspora is constructed at the juncture of particular political and economic interests that regulate its meaning and material expressions.

I focus my discussion on how institutions, specifically the US government, the Greek State and global financial corporations, deploy their respective policies on diaspora to shape national and transnational citizenship and belonging. I discuss the ideas and ideals these modalities of power produce to define a 'diaspora subject', as well as a diaspora subject's relation to the host and the sending nation. When I link power with the making of subjectivity I draw from scholarship that addresses the ways in which modern liberal democracies regulate the conduct, morals and beliefs of populations in alignment with a set of political and economic calculations.[3] Instilling values and virtues to individuals offers a social technology to govern not by coercion or authoritative imposition, but by hailing subjects to identify with specific ways of thinking, judging and acting upon the world. In other words, power in this case does not repress individuals; it seeks to shape human beings as subjects in ways it deems desirable. Power, as Nicholas Rose puts it, 'works through, and not against, subjects'.[4]

This operation is inherently political because it is instrumental in the regulation of subjects as members of the polity; of turning them into citizen-subjects. Citizenship in this formulation is more than a legal status and its associated rights. It entails a definition of what is meaningful in life, what must be aspired to and desired by subjects, of what the self is and must be in order to function as a productive member of society. In governance-through-regulation, the subject is hailed to internalize those ideals and contribute through the aspiration to enact those values it is being asked to consent.

Along these lines I further build on scholarship that connects governance-through-regulation with transnationalism, the bourgeois ideal of the American citizen and the market logic of neoliberal capitalism.[5] The ideal of the middle-class American citizen underwrites a specific constellation of values, namely self-reliance, freedom, calculation, individualism, innovation and flexibility. Notably, these are consistent with the logic of the free market. Because neoliberal capitalism fosters profitability, it interfaces with the ideal of the entrepreneurial citizen to promote those values that foremost produce profits at the expense of those citizen-subjects who pursue alternative modes of civic engagement such as civic duties and obligations. The specific question I address is how neoliberal principles and ideals of American citizenship regulate Greek American transnational affinities, and I place this in the context of my wider discussion of the construction of Greek Americans as American and Greek transnational citizen-subjects. To which values do these narratives ask subjects to consent, and to what end? What is at stake in these constructions?

The crux of my argument is as follows: cultural representations of diaspora at the time of Greek crisis connect with at least three discourses, namely Greek nationalism, middle-class American citizenship and economic growth in global capitalism. I show how these three seemingly disparate narratives intersect at a particular juncture: they intertwine identity with entrepreneurship. The ideal of a model citizen-subject as a self-reliant, entrepreneurial self provides the common thread in the definition of Greek Americans as ideal American and transnational citizens. Good citizens according to this narrative contribute to economic growth and social order. They, whether immigrant, expatriate, or American-born, embody values – such as innovation, risk-taking and entrepreneurial flexibility in the marketplace – that not only structure the ideal citizen-subject but also express the logic of late capitalism.

The making of Greek Americans as national and transnational citizen-subjects also intersects at yet another juncture: embracing ideals such as civil society based on the rule of law, participatory democracy, gender equity and philanthropy. The universality of these values across the Western world enables a shared identity among citizen-subjects that transcends the particularities and possibly conflicting elements engendered in the tension between national, ethnic and diaspora loyalties.

Contexts and circulations

The crisis unfolds at a time when Greek America in the United States enjoys premium cultural capital. The analysis of the latest US Census figures illuminates this phenomenon. The statistics register a 20 per cent increase in the Greek American population between 1980 and 2000, and a further 11 per cent growth between 2000 and 2010, a development that points to intermarriage as the 'most likely explanation' for this demographic growth.[6] The 'non-Greek' spouse is drawn to Greek ethnicity, exemplifying a cultural pull of historical significance: it is not merely that Greek America lacks social stigma. It is that, in fact, it enjoys great cultural cachet. Greek ethnicity's popularity is seen as 'the emerging victory of the twenty-first-century Greek American world'.[7] It is culturally triumphant, embraced by 'non-Greeks' as well as individuals of mixed ancestries. In interethnic marriages and among bicultural children, Greek ethnicity works 'as a sort of "trump" identity in which Greek plus non-Greek equals Greek'.[8] The competition over cultural affiliation benefits those ethnic groups, like Greeks or Italians, that have established themselves as most desirable in the American multicultural agora.

Negative publicity over the Greek crisis threatens to tarnish this image. In fact, it creates a deep anxiety among sectors of Greek America.[9] Although US media paid limited attention to Greece compared to that paid by European media,[10] there has been a spillover of negative images and stereotypes: the 'lazy ouzo-sipping irresponsible' Greek (*Greek American Girl*, 2015); the unworthy descendants of glorious ancestors; the uncivil abuser of the system. Political satire in cartoons, including in the US press, crystallize 'a negative view of Greek behaviour; subverting the past glory of the culture; or eliciting a sense of dismay, disgust, or, at times, sympathy'.[11] The *New York Times*'s reporting of the crisis frequently paints the country as corrupt and inefficient. In some instances Greece metaphorically stands as an example of dysfunctionality.[12] When a Philadelphia judge presiding over a child support case equated a person's Greek background with corruption, the Greek American media registered the toxic effects of totalizing representations, calling for the debunking of negative stereotypes whenever one encounters them:

> A broad brush has been used, however, since day one of this crisis, to paint *all* Greeks as the lazy, tax-evading leeches of Europe . . . .

> [I]t is our duty as members of the Hellenic diaspora to counter such stereotypes whenever we hear them, be it in a courthouse or a coffeehouse.[13]

Contesting misrepresentation offers a strategy of reclaiming a measure of control over self-representation.

The making of Greek America under conditions of the crisis takes place within yet another context, an international one that renders diasporas as political, economic and social capital,[14] and therefore vital agents for global development and stability. The term diaspora now pervades the vocabulary of governments, policy agencies, developmental experts and global financial institutions. International development and human rights organizations such as the World Bank, the United Nations (UN), the International Organization for Migration (IOM), the Global Forum for Migration and Development (GFMD), the European Union, and a plethora of nation-states utilize the concept of diaspora in a flexible manner that encompasses populations with various forms of connectivity with a historical homeland. Institutions have adopted '"diaspora" as a positive link between migration and development'.[15]

The aforementioned institutions mobilize and employ networks of academics, scientists, policy experts, think tanks and agencies to design policies and subsequently 'strongly advise' their implementation by states 'aiming at embracing them more efficiently into the space of the nation'.[16] Policies that incorporate 'diaspora engagement' have become an essential component of state 'best practices' to advance foreign policy and national economic interests.

In this politico-economic appropriation of diaspora the criteria for diaspora belonging have expanded to include populations exhibiting multiple national loyalties, assimilated populations who nurture affect for the historical place of origins, immigrants in technical fields, or scientists, professionals and entrepreneurs who connect with the homeland but have no intention of returning. The spacious definition maximizes the scale of the diaspora potential for transnational development at a time of expanding global capitalism and blurs cultural categories often demarcating different degrees of difference within the host nation, such as 'ethnicity' and 'diaspora'.

In this context, narratives shaping the meaning of Greek America move beyond the local or national sites of their production to transverse across the transnational field of United States–Greek America–Greece and elsewhere, as I mentioned earlier. Communication technologies such as Youtube and Vimeo, as well as various other social media outlets on the internet, enable and intensify this circulation.[17] The short documentary *What It Means to Be Greek* for instance, interfaces the local, the national, the transnational and the global.[18] Featuring interviews of Chicago's Greeks, conducted to highlight Greek culture, the film was initially created to promote an event entitled *Coming Together in Skokie* (2013), an annual festival that aims to promote ethnic diversity in the town of Skokie, Illinois. The documentary was subsequently shown on Greek television, specifically on *Skai* channel, in a programme which also included interviews with the producers, and touted the diaspora as empowering for Greece. Now it is available on Youtube (*What It Means to Be Greek*, 2013). Two other examples of transnational flows are *Greeks Gone West* (2014) and *Greeks Gone West Reloaded* (2015), an annual series of short biographical profiles of professional and entrepreneurial Greek Americans. Produced by the US Embassy in Athens in collaboration with the Greek newspaper *Kathimerini* and *Huffington Post Greece*, and available on Youtube and Vimeo respectively, the series features the accomplishments of Greek Americans who have professionally distinguished themselves in the United States and globally. New information technologies, employed by a dense network of Greek and Greek American media, contribute to transnational flows of Greek American images, mediating their meaning. The discussion below illuminates the production of these meanings and the purposes they serve.

The global Greek nation: Nationalism and diaspora's currency

To maintain the identification of diaspora populations with the historical homeland, nationalism instills a sense of oneness with the nation via tropes of affective kinship and organic unity. The cultivation of deep belonging in this manner advances national interests that range from diaspora remittances to investments to political and social solidarity. Not surprisingly, several identity narratives in the context of the crisis construe the global Greek nation as a family to which Greek America is an integral component; as a seamless entity bound together by blood and affective ties for Greece. In the promotional campaign *I Am One Greece* (2013), for instance, global Hellenism is seen as a community of belonging based on shared descent: 'We are family; we have the same blood running in our veins for thousands of years'. And in the documentary *USA: Made in Hellas* (2014), actress Nia Vardalos also employs the language of biology to link identity with the future of US Greek ethnicity: 'our blood is Greek and we want to preserve our culture and heritage'.[19] Greek Americans internalize biological criteria of belonging, inherent in the discourse of the American category of 'ethnicity' as descent, and the Greek definition of the 'diaspora' as *omogeneia* (same lineage), to subsequently declare their commitment to a Greek identity.

Greek Americans position themselves as diaspora subjects when they register their emotional attachment to Greece, their intense longing for its sounds and sights, and their appreciation for the natural products of the land. Organic metaphors of belonging abound. A Greek-born marathon runner interviewed for *What It Means to Be Greek* likens Greek identity as a tree that 'spreads its branches' all over, being 'thirsty for ... more'. This arborescent metaphor, common in nationalist discourse, promotes a natural link between the scattered Greeks, the diaspora (the branches) and the nation (the tree).[20] It places the diaspora as an organic extension of the homeland nation, which is seen as the diaspora's foundational roots. In this image, Greece figures as the national centre, an ideology that historically anchors the Greek state's diaspora policy.[21]

Narratives produced in the context of the crisis reproduce the widely held notion of Greece as an idea that transcends territory. In *Greek Reporter*'s cultural vision, for instance, 'Greece is not a confined physical space with borders, but an idea that lives in people's hearts.' Interviewees in *What It Means to Be Greek* speak about it in aesthetic and transcendental terms: 'Greece is a light. Immortal'. The course of Greek people has produced a 'collective wisdom' to which Greeks everywhere partake and hold the responsibility to preserve and pass on. The making of diaspora as a spatially and temporally seamless entity, unique and organic, connected with bonds of blood and affect represents the ideology of romantic nationalism. Greek identity is articulated as a discrete and coherent identity of inherent value. Under the crisis, however, it is the diaspora identity that carries cultural capital by virtue of its own socioeconomic success, in dire contrast to Greece as a 'falling and failing nation'. The diaspora occupies a privileged position within the organic nation as the repository and therefore spokesperson of Hellenism's diachronic value. Let me elaborate.

At one level, Greek America is conventionally narrated as an organic extension of the nation, a natural component of the global nation of Greeks. Greece represents a trans-state nation whose space transcends Greek territory. One thread of this narrative imagines the nation as a borderless community with Greece at its centre. In this construction one witnesses the enduring power of the Greek state's discourse on the diaspora. Following the collapse of the Soviet Union, the aim of the state's policy has been to harness the diaspora as a vital political (through advocacy) and economic (through remittances and investment) resource that serves national interests from afar. To foster and revitalize the diaspora–homeland ties, the diaspora is reincorporated into the nation as an organic component of a global collective – frequently invoked as 'worldwide' or 'Ecumenical' Hellenism. These terms, as Lina Venturas notes, 'reinforced the desired emphasis on the supraterritorial nature of the nation,' with 'common descent and a common heritage as extra-territorial connective links'.[22] Diaspora citizen-subjects, regardless of their official citizenship, owe allegiance to Greece from afar.

In the historical juncture of the crisis, however, another thread in this narrative portrays diaspora as *the* component of the nation that possesses a legitimate claim as the heir of continuing Greek achievement. This positioning reframes the ways in which diaspora is discussed in relation to Greece. Greek America's role shifts from a peripheral extension of the nation to a centre. This is evident in the reception of the documentary *What It Means to Be Greek* (2013) during its airing in Greece on *Skai* channel. The show's hostess reads the narratives featured in the documentary as examples of national unity across borders, and Greek Americans as spokespersons who advocate a positive meaning of 'ελληνικότητα' (Greekness) in the English-speaking world, a position which reproduces the ideology of Greece as a supraterritorial essence, as I pointed out previously. The hostess's reading, however, reframes the historical role of the diaspora from the national periphery to the centre. Now that Greece has 'fallen into a black hole', as she put it, diaspora's narratives about the enduring value of Greek culture serve as a 'source of inspiration' and empowerment for the nation. They spark its will to revitalize itself. If in the past it was Greece that was nourishing the diaspora (έδινε δύναμη), now it is the diaspora that contributes to the reclaiming of the dejected national self: the documentary's 'optimistic message ... explains to others but also helps us, Greeks, to understand and rediscover what it really means to be Greek'. The fallen nation has its diaspora to look up to as a guardian and cultural ambassador of the 'true meaning' of identity. Greek Americans are positioned at the global forefront as authentic bearers of Greek distinction.

The regulation of diaspora as an extension of the nation constructs diaspora citizen-subjects as owing solidarity to Greece-in-crisis. Affective kinship with the national community, a hallmark in the discourse of nationalist belonging, determines empathy for the suffering nation. The late Chris Tomaras, an investor and philanthropist, aptly captures this connection: 'The facts are sad, the way things evolved saddens us all, whenever we are, since we are Greeks'.[23]

Imagining the Self as an organic extension of the transterritorial collective offers itself as a strategy to harness diaspora and mobilize collective action on behalf of Greece. This is evident in *The Hellenic Initiative* (2012), a 'global movement of the Greek Diaspora'. This initiative, with headquarters in the United States and Australia, was founded 'by members of the global Greek and philhellene communities who were compelled to respond to the worsening economic crisis and inspired to help shape Greece's long-term recovery'. Its Board of Directors features presidents, directors, chairpersons and executives of international corporations and banking and investment firms. It includes The Coca-Cola Company, The Dow Chemical Company, Fortress Investment Group, LLC, Admirals Bank and Capital Resources. It makes the revitalization of Greece through philanthropy and economic growth its principal investment.

Its campaign, *I Am One Greece* (2013), harnesses diaspora solidarity to 'empower people to provide crisis relief, encourage entrepreneurs, and create jobs'. *I Am One Greece* hails the individual to imagine herself as a national citizen-subject who invests and acts (as 'donors and doers') to revitalize the nation: 'I am one person but together – μαζί – we are an idea no walls, no borders, no limits. ... We are one Greece. I am one Greece. We are one Greece'. Exemplifying distinction, as I will show, Greeks abroad are called to identify as part of the national whole to empower the nation-in-crisis.

The Hellenic Initiative brings together Greek nationalism and the utilization of the Greece/United States transnational space as one that generates capital and mobilizes humanitarian aid. Often in collaboration with the US Embassy in Greece, it infuses capital to foster an environment of transnational entrepreneurship. It supports 'a new generation of creative and innovative business', including educating high school students to transform 'a business idea from concept to reality', and finances Greek startups, including those competing in the United States. It promotes philanthropy, too, funding projects like *Together for Children*, an association that provides medical assistance to children, including special training for those with disabilities. In this project then nationalism's diaspora citizenship as solidarity with Greece intersects with the economic and humanitarian transnational space inhabited by entrepreneurial and humanitarian selves.

Diaspora's success and ethnic pride

One answer to cultural devaluation is revaluation. A wide range of cultural producers – filmmakers, cultural activists, expatriate experts who market culture, institutions, think tanks and media associated with Greek America – produce narratives construing Greek identity as value. They call upon the public to recognize 'Greek' as a positive heritage, a distinguished culture, a beautiful idea, a compelling landscape, a fertile land. 'Greek' stands for accomplishments and success. National branding nurtures ethnic pride.

The purpose for this positive valuation is transparent. If the crisis raises doubt about the value of the Greeks, the global nation offers a living testament of the Greeks' worth. Lives associated with civic, scientific and entrepreneurial contributions refute negative stereotypes. *USA: Made in Hellas* (2014), a documentary trailer, for instance, aims to counteract the Greeks' 'negative image around the world' by pointing to 'countless examples of Greeks who are changing the world in their respective fields and contribute greatly to the American and global society'. In fact, the very title of this documentary, *USA: Made in Hellas*, locates Greeks as agents in the making of the United States. Greek America is construed as a distinguished component of the transterritorial Greek nation: 'There is another Greece outside of Greece.' Politician Michael Dukakis, actress Nia Vardalos, professor of Astrophysics Vicky Kalogera, investor John Calamos and film director Alexander Payne inhabit this space, among others. In affirming their Greek identity their professional record speaks back to the international devaluation of the Greeks. 'Hellenism's greatest treasure' then, according to the documentary, 'is its people. The members of the Greek diaspora in the US prove[s] this quietly everyday'.[24]

Diaspora narratives then amplify emphasis on Greek identity as an uncompromising pride. The narration and consumption of the documentaries consistently return to this trope. 'Greek pride will never die!' a viewer of *What It Means to Be Greek* asserts. A child featured in that same documentary exclaims: 'Greek makes me proud!' Similarly, in *USA: Made in Hellas*: 'All around the world Greeks are everywhere. All of them proud of their origin, of their legacy. They pass on their love for Greece'. And further, 'Greeks have lost a lot; but not our pride, our honor, our nature, our Hellenic spirit, our identity'.[25] Pride, strongly expressed, it is announced and possessed; it is enduring, intrinsically connected to identity, which it nurtures.

Identity-as-pride based on socioeconomic distinction constitutes a Greek American answer to the global devaluation of the Greeks in the context of the crisis. It testifies to the worth of a people and in doing so it challenges negative stereotypes. It functions as a corrective to devaluation and reframes the ways in which the world speaks of and thinks about modern Greeks. It also fosters ethnic identification among the Greek American youth. An ethnic group's positive image buttresses the individual from the potential stigma associated with cultural difference in the United States. It positions identity in relation to what is acclaimed, distinguished, desirable, lauded and enjoyed, affirming the value and thus empowering that identity. Hence, pride works to entice diaspora youth to the orbit of ethnic identity. What is at stake is cultural preservation. For its emergence as the dominant trope takes place against a history of shaming ethnicity. In multiculturalism pride functions as a powerful mechanism of reproducing difference selectively. Distinction and socially sanctioned achievement are privileged as sources of identification; non-normative experiences and ideas are displaced.

Greek Americans as national and transnational citizens

While a host of Greek American narratives produce identity via romantic nationalism, the US Government construes Greek America via middle-class ideals of American citizenship. This is evident in *Greeks Gone West* (2014 and 2015), an initiative sponsored by the US Embassy in Athens, which focuses on Greek American civic and professional achievements. In a two-part series of short biographical profiles of a total of 43 individuals – professionals, scientists, journalists, athletes, artists, filmmakers, museum curators and other cultural producers, entrepreneurs and a priest – Greek Americans are portrayed as anchored in the

American nation, contributing to global development, and cultivating transnational economic and philanthropic networks. This configuration links the self who strives for professional and personal fulfillment with US foreign policy that promotes diaspora as an engine for transnational economic growth and social stability. In other words, it forges a connection between a certain construction of the self with a specific political and economic rationality.

All this at a moment, as I mentioned earlier, when the United States values diasporas as engaged agents for development and diplomacy. Connections with a multitude of diaspora countries of origin position the country as a central hub of political and economic networks globally. Diaspora populations, specifically highly skilled professionals and entrepreneurs, represent a valuable human and economic capital, one which mutually benefits various interests in the country of settlement and origins. As a result, diaspora pervades the vocabulary and practices employed by governments, global financial institutions, policy agencies and developmental experts throughout the world. The International diaspora Engagement Alliance (IdEA), a 'non-partisan, non-profit organization managed via a public-private partnership between the US Department of State, the US Agency for international Development (USAID), and Calvert Foundation' exemplifies how the diaspora intertwines with both government and corporations. In IdEA's short video, a range of individuals proclaim an American hyphenated identity, including a Greek American one, to subsequently affirm an array of multiple affiliations: 'We are all Americans and we are global citizens. We stay connected to our roots, identities. We are the diaspora, and we connect through IdEA' (*IdEA Introductory Video*). Harnessing diaspora communities to promote multilateral economic development and social order recognizes the operation of multiple identities within a subject, inevitably making diaspora identity visible, in fact, marking it in endorsement.

A subject's multiple identities, of course, may raise a political problem. How to reconcile, for instance, the tension between national and diaspora commitments when the former requires singular loyalty to the host nation, while the latter, in contrast, underlines a centrifugal loyalty, one toward the nation of origins? US national interests therefore require the containment of multiple, potentially conflicting, identities. The imperative to promote diaspora under conditions of global capitalism makes the regulation of diaspora necessary. Demarcating citizen-subjects as simultaneously

American, American ethnic, diaspora and transnational raises the issue of governing the commitments and actions of disparate populations in alignment with national interest. As I explained in my introduction, the making of a person's subjectivity is a function of power that holds in check and shapes the values and practices of subjects; it channels their loyalties and aspirations. This operation renders subjectivity, conventionally seen as an affair of private life, inherently political.[26] An analysis of identity narratives must take into account therefore a larger process, the regulative mechanisms that seek the installation of a certain model of citizenship in Greek America. This discussion in turn helps us understand how this identity construction works within the global discourse of diaspora as 'best practice' to regulate the ways in which Greek America intervenes on behalf of Greece to alleviate the severe crisis.

Citizenship, the national (American) space

A US initiative within the context of diaspora policy, *Greeks Gone West*, undertakes the making of Greek American citizen-subjects in an era of expanding global capitalism. The documentaries portray individuals from the perspective of their respective professional achievements. It features Greek Americans who have left a mark in the worlds of fashion, art, advertisement, political activism, journalism, lifestyle, research, science, philanthropy, sports and the food industry. Some of the interviewees enjoy national or local limelight.[27] Others are distinguished professionals.[28] Though not every interviewee touches upon Greek identity and heritage, *all* showcase professional achievement. Some directly address the crisis, others mention it only in passing, while some bypass it entirely. Together, they compose an aggregate of individuals whose commonality lies in their Greek ancestry and socioeconomic distinction.

The interview questions in the series frame biographical mini-profiles in terms of personal challenges faced, risks taken, rewards experienced, and potential of professional partnerships in Greece practised or considered. The majority of the interviewees, particularly in the first series, condense their biographical trajectories via the trope of struggle and success. Some emphasize humble beginnings, starting life poor or disadvantaged. Many identify the personal and professional risks they have taken. The narratives point to false starts and the determination to start all over again, the flexibility and daring to reinvent oneself anew. They plot lives uniformly as a quest for professional and personal fulfillment, which often intersect. They centre on virtues such as hard work, resilience, independence, persistence, boldness, courage, risk-taking, innovation, experimentation and entrepreneurialism. All in all, these are Greek Americans who have fulfilled the 'Greek Dream in America' and who in turn both exalt the United States as a place that rewards effort, innovation and entrepreneurship and underline how this ultimately enables deeply fulfilled lives. Ted Maglaris, a restauranteur, effectively captures the series' underlying ideology of bootstrap mobility and the nation as opportunity: 'if you want to work [in America] you can always find a way to become successful'.

In this telling of success, *Greeks Gone West* recirculates a vital identity narrative in Greek America, namely the view of United States as a place of redemption for the Greek people. Specifically, it reiterates the storyline of the documentary *The Greek Americans* (1998), in which America serves as a homecoming to a restless and wandering diaspora, which reaches its fullest potential in the host country. In the words of the documentary's narrator:

> We've made our impact on the world over the centuries, but we've only been in America since the 1800s. [...] We've always been searching for new challenges since the time of Alexander the Great. We found it in America.

Travelling *West* across the Atlantic then enables the culmination of a people's potential. If political and social flaws in Greek society – the people's exploitative relation to the state, and 'clientelist and personal patronage' – are stereotypically attributed to the Ottoman legacy's frustrating efforts for improvement; if in fact this Eastern-derived political culture is seen as the cause of the crisis, a Western society like the United States enables Greeks to distinguish themselves.[29] The narrative constitutes Greek Americans as ideal American citizen-subjects who embody self-reliance, choice-making, and the flexibility of the innovative, ever self-reinventing entrepreneur.

In the construction of 'Greek' in *Greeks Gone West*, a professional and business class of individuals of predominantly Greek descent makes up and speaks for the collective.[30] This class is selected because it embodies a set of rules for one's self-conduct in the workplace, and more generally, in life: aspiring to betterment and taking the initiative and investing energies to achieve self-fulfillment, as well as making it one's personal responsibility to overcome limitations, take control of career, and transform the self, often through high risks. These are ethical presuppositions – what is considered true and desirable – that inspire the self to aspire and empower itself to achieve happiness. They underwrite the autonomous self to control its life and destiny. This narrative posits that to successfully inhabit the workplace, whether national or transnational, requires that subjects embrace and act upon these principles that turn them into productive and happy citizens.[31]

The making of this 'enterprising self' links with a specific political rationality because the notion of the self-reliant individual, a central ideal of middle-class American citizenship, connects with a particular political philosophy, that of neoliberalism. Nicholas Rose aptly delineates this association:

> [T]he wellbeing of both political and social existence is to be ensured not by centralized planning and bureaucracy, but through the 'enterprising' activities and choices of autonomous entities–businesses organizations, persons – each striving to maximize its own advantage by inventing and promoting new projects by means of individual and local calculations of strategies, tactics, costs and benefits.[32]

This positioning of Greek American selves in the market is pervasive in *Greeks Gone West*. Petros Benekos, an entrepreneur in the food and clothing industry, offers a telling example when he celebrates the enterprising self as created by an insatiable drive to expand across diverse domains of industry: 'A career is the excitement of changing things. [...] That's why I am in clothing and in restaurant. That's why I can be in the movie [industry] tomorrow or somewhere else'. Seemingly unencumbered by any constraints, the autonomous entrepreneur celebrates the freedom and pleasures of flexible economic investment to tap the seemingly unlimited potential of the market.

Notably, the making of neoliberal subjectivity in Greek American narratives bears a remarkable ideological resonance with a host of narratives in the Greek public sphere which locate the answer to the crisis in reshaping Greek identity along cultural lines: the transformation of the national Self into a Western identity characterized by entrepreneurialism, economic rationality and competitiveness.[33] Thus neoliberal principles create a transnational alignment between certain Greek American and

Greek identity narratives. If nationalism posits descent and culture as the unifying link of the nation and its diaspora, neoliberalism continues capitalism's emphasis on the entrepreneurial self to forge a Greek transnational commonality around this enterprising figure.

A critical note is necessary: the neoliberal rationale for success deflects attention from the structural conditions contributing to poverty, and in doing so it obscures the way in which policies and labour practices actually contribute to inequality and the uneven distribution of 'choices', mediating, in turn, mobility. What is more, the making of neoliberal citizen-subjects equates economic rationality for self-betterment and profitability with moral responsibility. The locus of these narratives is an individual's potential and its value in the market. This brackets, as a result, questions of civic participation, democracy and citizenship as duties and obligations to the collective.

In *Greeks Gone West* the perspectives of the working and the lower middle class, as well as those who embrace alternative visions of citizenship, are absent, as is any academic perspective explaining the structural causes of poverty and the conditions for Greek American mobility. Thus the making of citizen-subjects is regulated by selective inclusion of voices consenting to dominant interests and the concomitant exclusion of dissenting voices. As a result, what constitutes legitimate identity is defined by a professional and political elite, which construes diaspora as a unitary collective.

Citizenship: The transnational space

If the enhancement of the United States' position in global networks depends on collaborations across geographical, political and cultural boundaries, it is necessary for the state to mediate the transnational spaces where these links materialize. This is to say that it is of national interest to regulate the meaning, boundaries and direction of human flows, as well as the nature of interactions and exchanges that may unfold within this space. Transnationalism in this framework is seen as structured flows 'in terms of the tensions between movements and social orders'.[34] It is subjected, in other words, to techniques of governance in order to shape activities and beliefs within the transnational space.

Consistent with the notion of diaspora as a developmental policy, *Greeks Gone West* positions Greek Americans as key players for bilateral economic growth. It features, for instance, Evie Zambetakis, a Greek American energy security specialist, who works for the University of Nicosia, Cyprus, to 'build [collaborative] relationships with North American Universities' and also to create 'a centre with the University for the study of Mediterranean energy security'.[35] Similarly, John Pyrolovakis, founder of the company Innovation Accelerator which advances 'American competiveness in the global economy by promoting American innovation', and in this capacity manages Federal Government-funded startups, taps into 'Greek American circles' to partner with a Greece-based team:

> When I talk to people about [this partnership] I got, you know, 'don't work with Greeks, Greeks are lazy [. . .] My experience with the [Greek team] has been the exact opposite. The quality of their work has been extraordinary. [. . .] This is getting the best of the green talent by US standards.

Greek American professionals inhabit the space of knowledge of the global economy, a fluid, non-territorial 'networked space'.[36] In this context, transnational spaces are animated through business and scientific connections. Their diaspora affinities – social circles and friends – in Greece function as resources to set in place transnational networks operating through principles shared across this domain: professional integrity and skill, technological know-how and hard work, all leading to high productivity. Diaspora's solidarity with the Greek nation does not, by default, constitute this space; rather, the diaspora functions as available social capital within the wider project of bilateral economic growth based on principles of sound entrepreneurialism. To draw from the previous example, Innovation Accelerator does business with Greece not necessarily because of diaspora effect and solidarity, but primarily because of economic rationality. In this configuration, *Greeks Gone West* recentres Greece from a national centre for the diaspora to a pole within the transnational space of Greece–United States, a domain that governmental policies and economic institutions are in the business of shaping. Construed in this manner, this terrain accommodates commitments to and affect toward both nations. It aligns national, hyphenated and diaspora identities under the principle of profit-generating business practices.

Diaspora engagement extends beyond strictly economic relations. Unlike romantic nationalism, which idealizes the nation as beautiful, eternal and pure, *Greeks Gone West* directs attention to the nation's problems and situates the diaspora as an agent for social transformation. It showcases individuals who channel diaspora affinity towards alleviating humanitarian crises and generating activism to correct social ills. Good diaspora citizenship entails philanthropy, which Nick Politakis, an executive director of a law firm, enacts transnationally. He was granted a leave of absence to volunteer in Greece with *μπορούμε* (we can), a non-profit organization that manages the distribution of surplus food for charity purposes across Greece, a project he subsequently supports from afar by undertaking fundraising on its behalf in the United States. In regards to initiating activism, on the other hand, Kristina Tremonti, founder and director of the initiative *EdosaFakelaki* (I bribed) employs the internet to promote participatory democracy and combat corruption in Greece, specifically bribing.

Narratives in this series then bring to focus diaspora as situated civic engagement. There is neither idealization nor nostalgia but action toward a goal. Diaspora professional networks act as agents to transform civil society. This is consistent with the enhanced role of transnational communities for development in the context of globalization 'from below'. As Thomas Faist notes, this political repositioning of grassroots transnationalism is concomitant with the transformed 'role of the state as a principle of social order in development'.[37] The state, he writes, 'is now a service provider for markets and partly for communities, creating the very conditions for market exchange through non-corrupt rule-making, a stable bureaucracy and the guarantee of minimum human, civil and political rights' in the interest of the rule of law.[38] Social order is in turn considered indispensable for economic development. Diaspora citizenship advances transnationally 'ideas and practices which are "good" and to which nobody in his or her right moral mind would object: human rights, gender equity and democracy'.[39]

Conclusion: The stakes in the making of Greek transnational citizenship

Greek America has historically been linking identity with material and social prominence to place itself as equal within the American polity. As this analysis illustrates, this narrative acquires poignant application in two interrelated contemporary contexts, namely the Greek debt crisis – and the attendant identity crisis that it generates – and the ideology of diaspora as best practice. First, the making of Greek America as a socioeconomic powerhouse solidly refutes the global devaluation of the Greeks. It decisively undermines any stereotype that may malign the Greeks as inherently unworthy people. The English-speaking public is invited instead to recognize diaspora 'Greek' as a sign of distinction.

Second, it places Greek Americans as exemplary US national and transnational citizens at a time in which the US government and financial institutions embrace diaspora as best practice for economic development and social stability. The public is presented with a paradigm of an ideal transnational citizen-subject as entrepreneurial, a highly mediated image, which Greek Americans and Greeks, among other audiences, are hailed to emulate. The diaspora figures as an agent invested in transforming Greek society in a manner that alleviates the crisis. It is called to display solidarity with and mobilize on behalf of the suffering nation within a transnational space regulated by the principles of economic growth, social order, gender equality and humanitarianism.

Diaspora initiatives stress transnational partnerships to counterbalance the massive exodus of Greece's educated youth, a flight abroad of human capital commonly referred to as 'brain drain'.[40] The economic (re)connection of Greek American professionals with Greece via transnational collaborations provides a route to direct diaspora resources towards the development of the historical homeland. New information and communication technologies dispense with the necessity of accomplished professionals actually returning 'home', enabling diaspora's function to transfer human capital – and thus 'return dividends' – from afar, a brain *gain.*[41] Brain gain slows down brain drain by transnational investments that aim to sustain and create an entrepreneurial class of Greek youth. Once again, diaspora functions as an agent for growth and stability.[42]

The narrative of Greek Americans as self-made citizen-subjects aligns, as I have shown, with the dominant figure of the US middle-class ideal citizenship which touts the autonomous subject willing itself to self-realization. In this construction national (American), ethnic (hyphenated Greek) and diaspora (Greek) identities coalesce around a common set of culturally specific values – entrepreneurship, determination, creativity, originality, boldness and risk taking – which a Greek American transnational identity encapsulates. The power of this narrative rests on its ultimate promise as a route for fulfillment in work and life. This strikes as compelling and its truth as self-evident. Why should anyone raise objections to this vision of the world where individuals strive for assuming control over life and self-realization, for improving their circumstances? The narrative is hailing viewers to aspire along similar lines. If happiness was realized by those featured in *Greeks Gone West*, why not us, the viewers? Scientists devote their lives in advancing the public good and citizen-activists in battling corruption, ensuring gender equity, and restoring fairness in the workplace. This paradigm enjoys the status of the national (American) norm, and is in a position to further shape the ways Greek American citizen-subjects but also Greeks and other viewers place themselves in and act upon the world. Power exercised not by the state but by seemingly 'neutral' narratives is indeed productive.

Because it presents a powerful ideal that is touted as a model for Greek identity and a *solution* out of the crisis one must render visible this narrative's ideology; make visible those facets of social processes that it hides. Though it is empowering for the self, the narrative of citizenship as 'enterprising self' engenders elements of oppression. I have discussed elsewhere how this ideology of 'struggle and success' directs attention away from the ways in which social and racial structures of inequality perpetuate poverty and may limit or preclude mobility.[43] By making individuals responsible for their own socioeconomic ascent, it blames the poor for their condition. Citizenship that celebrates the self-realization of the entrepreneurial self deflects reflection from and political action toward addressing inequality structurally. It does so by displacing that mode of citizenship that envisions the self in terms of civic duties and obligations, values such as combating labour exploitation, displaying political commitment against *structural* poverty and racism, investing in social justice and exhibiting historical consciousness. The cultural production of Greek America under crisis stifles this latter paradigm of citizenship, advancing instead, an *ahistorical* model of citizenship.

The proposed ideal of the self-propelling individual encourages policies that foster entrepreneurialism and economic investments, but it does not address the crisis in Greece in terms of structural reforms that aim to alleviate inequality. How then to shift attention to alternative ways of being a citizen-subject? The focus on diaspora lives for identifying civic commitments offers an analytical angle to narrate the complexity of diaspora engagements and potentially locate other modes of citizenship. The micronarratives featured in *Greek Gone West*, for instance, may raise several issues when examined closely. For example, when Matthew Bogdanos, Assistant District Attorney for NYC, fleetingly cites Sophocles to define the ethical life, no further probing of this association is present. The broader question comes about regarding the role of classics, or perhaps, a limited, selected appropriation of classics, in shaping civic identities.

My work in this chapter registers the ongoing acceleration of flows of knowledge and capital across the transnational field comprised by the United Sates, Greek America and Greece in response to the Greek crisis. It brings attention to a range of institutional and personal initiatives aiming to direct cultural and financial resources to Greece, to identity narratives, and to business partnerships between the US public/private sector with Greek companies as well as to volunteerism, and activism. The discussion illuminates the ways in which US governmental agencies and a sector of Greek American and Greek media, economic elites, and the public produce a version of transnational identity which aims at cultivating ethnic pride, mobilizing the diaspora on behalf of the historical homeland, and addressing ways to redress the Greek debt crisis. This analysis explores only a fraction of a larger, vastly complex terrain, which is crisscrossed by various constructions and practices of the Greek diaspora as citizen-subjects in transnational political activism, journalism, autobiography, documentary and literature.[44] This landscape includes interfaces between Greek American economic initiatives and the Greek public and private sector, narratives proposing *filotimo* as a key value in Greek America but also in global Greek identity, and projects aiming to reach the diaspora youth and shape the next generation's vision of the public good in relation to Greek heritage. To the ongoing scholarly interest in the topic of the Greek debt crisis this chapter brings attention to the transnational aspect of the crisis.

The privileging of diaspora discourse in the United States and the role of Greek America as a player in shaping Greece underline the importance of situating the crisis in a transnational perspective. An interdisciplinary conversation is necessary to explore how the political economy of diaspora connects with the making of citizen-subjects in specific transnational contexts (United States, Canada, Australia, Europe, Greece) and in relation to global capitalism. The profound political implications of these transnational flows confront scholarship, including Modern Greek studies, with the responsibility of not only understanding the making of transnational Greek identities and their impact on Greece, but also of identifying modes of citizenship that exhibit consciousness of the structural conditions producing inequality. The global valence of the diaspora as it emerges during the unfolding economic, political and cultural crisis renews this academic critical mission, for a great deal on how we imagine Greek citizenship in the future is at stake.

Notes

1. For examples of philanthropic activism in Greek America see Pappas Gregory, 'Four months of action: New York's Hellenic Relief Foundation active in aiding Greeks in need', *The Pappas Post* 18 August (2015), available at http://www.pappaspost.com/four-months-of-action-new-yorks-hellenic-relief-foundation-active-in-aiding-greeks-in-need/, 'Chicago's Greek American Foundation distributes $30,000 to Greek charities', *The Pappas Post* 7 May (2014a), available at http://www.pappaspost.com/chicagos-greek-america-foundation-distributes-30000-charities-assisting-communities-impacted-financial-crisis-greece/ and 'Venetia Kontogouris '$1m gift to Northeastern to benefit Greek students', *The Pappas Post* 29 March (2014b), available at http://www.pappaspost.com/venetia-kontogouris-1m-gift-to-northeastern-to-benefit-greek-students/ (accessed 15 February 2016); and Luce Jim, 'Fund launch for kids in Greece characterized by ancient Hellenic ideals', *The Huffington Post*, 21 December 2015, available at http://www.huffingtonpost.com/jim-luce/fund-launch-for-kids-in-g_b_8845712.html (accessed 1 July 2016). Notably, Elizabeth Mavroudi shows that many Greek Australians feel no obligation to help the nation-in-crisis beyond supporting family and kin. She writes in this context, 'those in diaspora cannot be relied upon to help even in times of crisis, even if they have strong socio-cultural connection to the homeland, which they still feel they belong to' (Elizabeth Mavroudi, 'Helping the homeland? Diasporic Greeks in Australia and the potential for homeland-oriented development as a time of economic crisis', in Anastasia Christou and Elizabeth Mavroudi (eds), *Dismantling Diasporas: Rethinking the Geographies of Diasporic Identity, Connection and Development* (New York, 2015), p. 183. The breadth of Greek American support to Greece in 2012 was the subject of public debate in the popular media (Leonidas V. Vournelis, *Living the Crisis: Identities and Materialities in a Transnational Greek Setting*. Diss., Southern Illinois University Carbondale, 2013). Further research would illuminate the range and scale of US diaspora's solidarity with Greece-in-crisis.
2. Wendy Larner, 'Expatriate experts and globalising governmentabilities: The New Zealand strategy', *Transactions of the Institute of British Geographers* NS 32 (2007), p. 333.
3. Michel Foucault, 'The subject in power' in H. Dreyfus and P. Rabinow (eds), *Michel Foucault: Beyond Structuralism and Hermeneutics* (Chicago, 1982).
4. Nikolas Rose, 'Governing the enterprising self' in Paul Heelas, Paul Morris, and Paul M. Morris (eds), *Values of the Enterprise Culture: The Moral Debate* (New York, 1992), p. 142.
5. Aihwa Ong, *Buddha Is Hiding: Refugees, Citizenship, the New America* (Berkeley, 2003).
6. Peter C. Moskos and Charles C. Moskos, *Greek Americans: Struggle and Success* 3rd ed. (New Brunswick, NJ, 2014), pp. 191, 193.

7. Kostis Karpozilos, Review of Peter C. Moskos and Charles C. Moskos, *Greek Americans: Struggle and Success* 3rd ed. (New Brunswick, NJ, 2014), pp. xxii +234. 9 illustrations, Foreword by Michael Dukakis, *Journal of Modern Greek Studies* 33/1 (2015), p. 202.
8. Peter C. Moskos and Charles C. Moskos, *Greek Americans: Struggle and Success*, p. 193.
9. Leonidas V. Vournelis, *Living the Crisis: Identities and Materialities in a Transnational Greek Setting*.
10. George Tzogopoulos, *The Greek Crisis in the Media: Stereotyping in the International Press* (Burlington, VT, 2013), p. 67.
11. Lauren E. Talalay, 'Drawing conclusions: Greek antiquity, The €conomic crisis, and political cartoons', *Journal of Modern Greek Studies* 31/2 (2013), p. 268.
12. Andreas Antoniades, 'At the eye of the cyclone: The Greek crisis in global media' (Athens, 2012), p. 14.
13. Georgia Logothetis, 'Anti-Greek comments at courthouse are a reminder of the need to fight stereotypes', 20 August 2015. Available at http://hellenicleaders.com/blog/anti-greek-comments-courthouse-reminder-need-fight-stereotypes/#.VspB15MrLVq (accessed 25 August 2015). I have personally experienced references to lazy, untrustworthy and irresponsible Greeks both in the classroom and in everyday interactions in the United States.
14. As Faist notes, social capital 'constitutes resources, such as reciprocity and solidarity, which are available to groups and thus enable cooperation' ('Migrants as transnational development agents: An inquiry into the newest round of the migration–development nexus', *Population, Space and Place* 14/1 (2008), p. 39fn4.
15. Stéphane Dufoix, 'From nationals abroad to "diaspora": The rise and progress of extra-territorial and over-state nations', *Diaspora Studies* 4/1 (2011), p. 12.
16. Ibid.
17. This as a component of a dramatic proliferation of 'new' media practices on the crisis. As Maria Kakavoulia (2014) notes, 'YouTube video production emerged, websites, social network pages or online video platforms (e.g. vimeo) flourished as a significant part of everyday media and commentary'.
18. Ivan Silvenberg and Georgia Taxaki, 'What it means to be Greek' (23 September 2013). Available at https://www.youtube.com/watch?v=8sLILU3Maa0 (accessed 15 February 2016).
19. Anastasios Papapostolou, 'USA: Made in Hellas – Watch the Trailer of our New Documentary on Greek Life in America', *Greek Reporter* (January 12 2014). Available at http://greekreporter.com/usa-made-in-hellas-watch-the-trailer-of-our-new-documentary-on-greek-life-in-america/ (accessed 1 January 2016).
20. Liisa H. Malkki, '*National Geographic*: The rooting of peoples and the territorialization of national identity among scholars and refugees', in Akhil Gupta and James Ferguson (eds), *Culture, Power, Place: Explorations in Critical Anthropology* (Durham, NC, 1997).
21. Elpida Vogli, 'The making of Greece abroad: Continuity and change in the modern diaspora politics of a "historical" irredentist homeland', *Nationalism and Ethnic Politics* 17 (2011), pp. 14–33.

22. Lina Venturas, '"Deterritorializing" the nation: The Greek state and "ecumenical hellenism"' in Dimitris Tziovas (ed.), *Greek Diaspora and Migration since 1700: Society, Politics and Culture* (Farnham, England; Burlington, VT, 2009), p. 135.
23. Chris Tomaras, *USA: Made in Hellas*, documentary, 2014.
24. Anastasios Papapostolou, 'USA: Made in Hellas – watch the trailer of our new documentary on Greek life in America'.
25. The Hellenic Initiative, I Am One Greece, 2013, https://www.youtube.com/watch?v=O_o_UOUmaEs.
26. Michel Foucault, *History of Sexuality, Vol. 1: An Introduction* (London, 1979); Rose, 'Governing the enterprising self'.
27. For example, designer George Lois professes himself as 'the master of mass communications in America and possibly the world'; Emmy Award winner Greg Yatanes, television director and producer, is noted for the show *Banshee*; and George Kotsiopoulos is a style expert and host of E!'s *Fashion Police*. Several among those featured have been instrumental in shaping the meaning of Greek America: Greg Pappas, founder and president of *The Pappas Media Group*, blogger and founder of the Greek American Foundation; John Aravosis, political activist, consultant and journalist; and George Veras, television producer and event manager, maker of the documentary *The Greek Americans* (1998).
28. Such as Matthew Bogdanos, Assistant District Attorney for NYC and US Marine Corps Cornell; Patricia Field, a fashion designer and entrepreneur; and music supervisor Alexandra Patsavas.
29. Thomas W. Gallant, 'Greece and Germany: The last tango?', *Chronos* 27, July 2015. Available at http://chronosmag.eu/index.php/tw-gallant-greece-and-germany-the-last-tango.html (accessed 1 August 2015).
30. There in an instance where *I Am One Greece* claims a person of non-Greek descent as a member of the global Greek community. For a discussion of this inclusion and its implications see, Yiorgos Anagnostou, 'Beyond Greek as biology: What Giannis Antetokounmpo and Tom Hanks have to do with it?' (November 4 2016). Available at http://immigrations-ethnicities-racial.blogspot.com/2016/11/beyond-greek-as-biology-what-giannis.html (accessed 4 November 2016).
31. Michel Foucault, 'Technologies of the self', in L.H. Martin, H. Gutman and P.H. Hutton (eds), *Technologies of the Self* (London, 1988), pp. 16–49.
32. Nikolas Rose, 'Governing the enterprising self', p. 145.
33. Yiannis Mylonas and Panos Kompatsiaris, 'Pathologizing politics: The making of the neoliberal subject during the Greek crisis', *Academia.edu* 2016. https://www.academia.edu/6202916/Pathologizing_Politics_The_Making_of_the_Neoliberal_Subject_during_the_Greek_Crisis_co-authored_with_Panos_Kompatsiaris_ (accessed 1 July 2016).
34. Aihwa Ong, *Buddha Is Hiding*, p. 6.
35. Institutions further utilise diaspora academic communities to cultivate transnational collaborations with Greek universities. The Stavros Niarchos Foundation has launched the *Greek Diaspora Fellowship Programme* to support 'US- and Canadian-based Greek-born academics' to visit Greek universities and 'create collaborative, mutually beneficial engagements between students,

academics and universities' (http://www.ekathimerini.com/206611/article/ekathimerini/community/snf-to-fund-scholarships-for-greek-diaspora).

36. Wendy Larner, 'Expatriate experts and globalising governmentabilities: The New Zealand strategy', p. 340.
37. Thomas Faist, 'Migrants as transnational development agents: An inquiry into the newest round of the migration–development nexus', p. 25.
38. Ibid.
39. Ibid., p. 22. *Greeks Gone West Reloaded* (2015) features a critique of ongoing sexism in the American workplace, in the narrative of journalist Alexia Tsotsis. For an example of Greek–German diaspora civic engagement to strengthen Greek civil society, see the *vouliwatch* initiative (http://www.greeknewsagenda.gr/index.php/features-interviews/interviews/5993-parliament-watch-antonis-schwarz-on-the-vouliwatch-project-and-citizen-engagement-in-greece).
40. The Bank of Greece reports that '[n]early half a million Greeks have left the country in search of better opportunities abroad since 2008 due to the financial crisis', mostly educated professionals, Stratis Karakasidis, 'Nearly half a million Greeks have left, Bank of Greece report finds,' *I Kathimerini*, English edition (2 July 2016). Available at http://www.ekathimerini.com/210072/article/ekathimerini/news/nearly-half-a-million-greeks-have-left-bank-of-greece-report-finds (accessed 29 July 2016).
41. Thomas Faist, p. 22.
42. Organizations promoting interconnections among Greek identity, youth entrepreneurism, innovation and globality are becoming increasingly visible, both in the United States and Europe. See for example the London-based group *Reload Greece*, a 'hub of youth entrepreneurship [...] aiming to inspire & educate young people with a global outlook' (https://www.facebook.com/ReloadGreece/info/?tab=page_info). And in the United States *The Next Generation Initiative* (https://www.hellenext.org/about-us/got-greek/). These projects invite cultural studies and ethnographic research.
43. Yiorgos Anagnostou, 'Re/collecting Greek America: Reflections on ethnic struggle, success and survival', *Journal of Modern Hellenism* 31/ Fall (2015), pp. 148–175.
44. This includes the formation of left groups (AKNY, Syriza NY, Antarsia NY) and their political activism within the context of transnational solidarity actions for Greece, pro-democracy and anti-austerity movements globally. See Despina Lalaki, 'First we take Manhattan ...: Global cities and diasporic networks in the aftermath of Syriza's victory', 24 March 2015, available at http://newpol.org/content/first-we-take-manhattan%E2%80%A6 (accessed 25 March 2015), and Maria Kousis, 'The transnational dimension of the Greek protest campaign against troika memoranda and austerity policies, 2010–2012' in Donatella della Porta and Alice Mattoni (eds), *Spreading Protest: Social Movements in Times of Crisis* (Colchester, UK, 2014) pp. 137–169. I have elsewhere discussed how Greek American history has been deployed transnationally to critique austerity in Greece (Yiorgos Anagnostou, 'The diaspora as a usable past for a nation-in-crisis: Media readings of *Palikari: Louis Tikas and the Ludlow Massacre*', *Filmicon: Journal of Greek Film Studies*, Occasional Papers, November 5 [2014]).

PART III

CULTURAL ECONOMIES AND INSTITUTIONS

CHAPTER 5

THE ECONOMY AND ECOLOGY OF GREEK CINEMA SINCE THE CRISIS: PRODUCTION, CIRCULATION, RECEPTION

Lydia Papadimitriou

Since the advent of the financial crisis Greek cinema has met with unprecedented international recognition. Greek films have been awarded and shown in a number of prestigious film festivals, such as Cannes, Berlin, Venice, Rotterdam, San Sebastian, Busan and Shanghai, while one of them, Yorgos Lanthimos' *Κυνόδοντας* [*Dogtooth*] (2009), reached the Oscars for the first time after 34 years. Such success was matched by the rapid adoption of the term 'Weird Wave of Greek cinema' among audiences and critics – a term that suggests the distinctively troubled, eccentric, but also seductive quality to be found in many Greek films produced since the financial crisis.[1] Paradoxically, in other words, the crisis seems to have benefited Greek cinema. By bringing the country at the centre of debates about the perils of globalization, the future of Europe and the changing world order, it has also thrown the international limelight on its cinema.

However, despite such positive publicity and a number of creative and critical hits since the crisis, cinema in Greece has been facing multiple challenges – some ingrained, others new – with variable degrees of success. The aim of this chapter is to map out the landscape of post-crisis Greek cinema in order to highlight conflicting forces of creativity and stagnation, progress and regression, growth and contraction, in its recent trajectory. The emphasis is on contexts (of production, circulation and reception), while Syllas Tzoumerkas' film *Η Έκρηξη* [*A Blast*] (2014) will be used as a case study to illustrate some of the impacts of, and responses to, financial, institutional and cultural changes since the crisis. In exploring these issues, the chapter draws on the concepts of economy and ecology, two different but complementary modes of understanding systems of interrelation and exchange – in human society, nature and the technologically mediated environment. While economy foregrounds monetarily mediated exchanges, ecology highlights interactions and effects as part of processes of change and adaptation in natural and/or cultural contexts.

An etymological analysis of the two words highlights their complementarity and appropriateness in the context of the discussion that follows. Both are compound words that start with the prefix 'eco-' (from the Greek *οίκος*), which means house or household, and are followed by suffixes originating in two other key Greek words: -nomy, from *νόμος*, distribution or law; and -logy, from *λόγος*, speech or discourse. In its original Greek meaning, the word economy (*οικονομία*) meant the adminstration of a household. In its modern, post-industrial use it refers to questions of money – wealth and scarcity – and its distribution in society. Coined much later in the West, ecology refers to the study of habitats of different biological species in the natural world.[2] In the context of the contemporary technologically mediated environment and its study, both terms have developed specific meanings: media economics focuses on the operation of firms and industries that produce and circulate media content;[3] while media ecology explores the effects and impact of media technologies on culture.[4] Cinema represents one aspect of this broader media environment, and as Stephen Rust and Salma Monani argue, it is ideally positioned to be examined from an 'ecocritical' perspective – a dimension of media ecologies that situates the analysis of media in the context of their circulation and consumption, while relating them to issues around the (natural) environment.

> From an ecocritical perspective, environment is not just the organic world [. . .]: it is the whole habitat which encircles us, the

> physical world entangled with the cultural. It is an *ecology of connections* [my emphasis] that we negotiate to make our meanings and our livings. In this habitat, cinema is a form of negotiation, a mediation that is itself ecologically placed as it consumes the entangled world around it, and in turn, is itself consumed.[5]

The analysis that follows will situate aspects of contemporary Greek cinema within such 'ecology of connections'. While some of these are located within a formal framework of industrial organization and economic exchange that are meaningfully discussed in the context of film *economy*, others are more fluid, informal, shifting, contingent and precarious and are therefore best addressed as part of a more loosely conceived *ecology* of interactions, exchanges and interdependencies. The concept of ecology will be therefore used in this broad and metaphorical sense here, rather than more literally with respect to the natural environment. More specifically, in what follows I will explore the production, circulation and reception of Greek films in the years since the crisis. I will position the critical success of some flagship films in context, highlighting both the state of the national film industry, and aspects of the broader film culture in relation to Greek cinema in the period 2010–2015. And finally I will use one case study to illustrate the pathways that enabled a film *about* the crisis to be made, bringing together aspects of contextual and textual analysis.

The approach is informed by both quantitative and qualitative methods, involving data and discourse analysis. The first section – on economy – will explore the ways in which the crisis affected Greek cinema financially and the immediate consequences of the drop of the public's disposable income on the national film industry. Focusing on the years 2010–2015, it will show how the financial crisis affected theatrical box office receipts and other ancillary sources of income, and how this impacted on the commercial exhibition and distribution sector. It will then examine production by highlighting historically available funding routes and exploring the options currently available to filmmakers. The second section – on ecology – will consider some of the practical and creative responses to the intensified challenges of how to bring a film to fruition during the crisis. After identifying some patterns in the broader context of post-crisis cinematic exchanges in Greece, the section will focus on a film produced and released during the crisis that also tells a story about the crisis, Tzoumerkas' *A Blast*. The analysis will illustrate the conditions of its possibility – in other words the national and transnational links that enabled its production, circulation, and reception – while also exploring some of the film's thematic links to crisis – financial, familial, existential and even ecological. By adopting a combined quantitative and a qualitative approach, this chapter challenges both exalting and condemnatory accounts of the recent state of Greek cinema, and presents a documented and analytical view of the effects of the cultural politics of austerity on the production, circulation and reception of Greek films.

The financial state of Greek cinema since 2010: Production, distribution and exhibition

An examination of the overall box office receipts in Greece since the crisis shows a very significant 45 per cent drop of income from theatrical admissions between 2010 and 2014 (from 99.4 to 58 million euros), and a 10 per cent recovery (63 million euros) in 2015 (see Table 5.1). However, a comparison with the number of admissions (measured as tickets sold) indicates a less radical drop of about 25 per cent (from 11.7 to almost 9 million). This discrepancy reflects the fact that, in order to counter the drop in audience attendance, exhibitors reduced the price of admission since 2012, while also introducing a number of special offers (such as 'two for the price of one'). Until then admission prices in Greece were among the most expensive in Europe, only exceeded by Switzerland, Finland and Sweden, thus – arguably – disproportionately reflecting the country's overall economy.[6] The drop of ticket price (from an average of 9 euros to 6.5) helped stimulate cinema-going, especially among younger audiences who were keener to engage with special offers provided via mobile phone companies, while also being more readily available to attend mid-week screenings in multiplexes.

The sector affected most immediately by this significant drop in box office returns was exhibition, as theatres are the first to collect box office receipts. During the first week of a film's release exhibitors in Greece usually keep 55 per cent of the box office. This goes up to 60 per cent for the second week and 65 per cent if a film continues to be screened for a third week or longer.[7] As admissions are normally higher during the opening week (or weekend) of a film, and exhibitors are often keen to

Table 5.1 Overall box office takings in Greece. Data: Greek Film Centre.[8]

	2009	2010	2011	2012	2013	2014	2015
Box office takings (in euros)	100,240,000	99,440,000	92,990,000	70,180,000	59,310,000	58,000,000	63,386,600
Admissions	N/A	11,720,000	10,850,000	10,100,000	9,210,000	8,973,000	9,806,141

change titles, the percentage increase in their cut offers an incentive for keeping a film on show for longer, should initial admissions prove promising enough. Irrespective of the specific financial arrangements, the fact that the theatres' income is based almost exclusively on admissions underlines how quickly they were hit by the downturn.

Returning to the allocation of the admissions income, the remaining 45 per cent, 40 per cent or 35 per cent, accordingly, goes to the distribution company. How the money is shared afterwards depends on the specific deals struck between distributors and studios or sales agents (for non-Greek films), or distributors and producers (for Greek films). In the case of US studio films, Greek distributors only keep a small percentage of the receipts, while the rest goes to the studio. In the case of independent films – in other words, non-Greek films acquired by Greek distributors via sales agents in markets or festivals – the distributor collects the entire amount until it covers the 'minimum guarantee' (or 'MG' in industry speak), in other words the price that they paid to buy the rights for a particular film's exploitation in a given territory (in this case, Greece and Cyprus). Once the MG is reached (which is usually after the film has also circulated on video and television), the distributor returns a percentage of the income to the sales agent (who then pays the producers). In the case of Greek films, the distributors make direct deals with the producers (that is, *not* through sales agent) and the financial terms they agree on are highly variable; on average, however, in these cases, the distribution company keeps about 25–35 per cent of the box office receipts after the exhibitor's cut, and returns the rest to the producer.

The above discussion of the profits allocations shows that producers receive their cut well after other intermediaries who have more direct contact with audiences are paid. Having been most immediately hit, it was also exhibitors who first responded to the crisis, not only by reducing the ticket price, as already noted, but also by streamlining their operations – in other words, reducing staff working in cinemas,[9] negotiating lower rents for the real estate and, in some cases, closing certain sites.[10] Distributors proved more resilient, largely because they can take advantage of more exploitation windows, as theatrical admissions are only part of their income, as will be shown below. Therefore, neither the number of films they released in the Greek market (Table 5.2), nor the overall structure of the distribution industry in

Table 5.2 Comparison between overall admissions and Greek film admissions. Data: Greek Film Centre

	2010	2011	2012	2013	2014	2015
Overall admissions	11,720,000 (Films: 263)	10,850,000 (Films: 302)	10,100,000 (Films: 224)	9,210,000 (Films: 272)	8,973,000 (Films: 286)	9,806,141 (Films: 308)
Greek film admissions	1,400,000 (Films: 27)	1,160,000 (Films: 39)	1,145,000 (Films: 32)	758,000 (Films: 40)	310,000 (Films: 46)	826,024 (Films: 45)

Greece, changed dramatically in the years following the advent of financial crisis.[11] Where some companies closed or reduced operations (such as the distribution arms of Audiovisual and, more recently, Village), some newcomers (such as Feelgood) established themselves dynamically, suggesting that possibilities for business were still ripe.

While the data examined so far refer to all films theatrically shown in Greece, the effects of the crisis on Greek film producers becomes clearer if we examine the admissions for Greek films. A comparison with the overall admissions data (Table 5.2) shows that receipts from Greek films dropped disproportionately after 2013, and especially in 2014. While between 2010 and 2012 the percentage of national films in relation to the overall box office was 12 per cent and 11 per cent, this dropped to 8 per cent in 2013, only to fall further to a critical 3 per cent in 2014 before recovering to a more comfortable 8 per cent in 2015. Whether such a disproportionate drop was an *effect* of the crisis, or not, is difficult to assert; what is beyond doubt is that it represents *in itself* a financial crisis for the sector as returns, let alone profits, from Greek films were all but eliminated.

Theatrical box office receipts, however, represent only one source of income deriving from a film's exploitation. Ancillary markets provide more – often more profitable – exploitation windows. These markets include DVD/Blu-Ray, Video-on-Demand (VOD – transaction and subscription) and television (pay and free TV) sales. In Greece, the DVD market in the 2000s developed mainly through rentals from video-stores (an extension of the VHS stores) rather than direct sales of official DVD copies. Throughout the 2000s, DVDs were also extensively used as 'cover mounts', in other words, they were given away for free with the purchase of a newspaper or magazine. To obtain the rights for the reproduction and circulation of DVDs as cover mounts, publishers paid generous amounts to distributors, thus providing them with a major source of income. Greek films – although mostly older classics rather than recent productions – were also circulated in this way. However, the advent of the financial crisis and the exponential growth of technology, led to the collapse in the early 2010s of both the rental market and the practice of cover mounts. The latter was also the consequence of widespread problems in the newspaper industry, as a result, on the one hand, of the dramatic drop in the advertising income that followed the financial crisis, and, on the other, of the increasing adoption of (free) online platforms for newspapers, instead of print copies.

The DVD market was globally hit in the late 2000s as technological changes, such as internet streaming and downloading, started to rapidly replace physical forms of circulating media. While, by late 2016, formal VOD options remain relatively limited in Greece, the years since the crisis have seen an exponential increase in the use of 'piracy' – the unlicensed copying and sharing of files with audiovisual material – which has arguably intensified the downward trend in theatrical admissions, and worsened the economic outlook of the Greek film industry.[12]

Sales to television offer another ancillary market for films, both in the form of the relatively new pay TV channels, like NOVA and OTE TV, and free TV. The latter, however, has faced major problems since the financial crisis: on the one hand, the state-owned Ελληνική Ραδιοφωνία Τηλεόραση [Greek Radio and Television] (ERT) was forced to shut down for almost two years (2013–2015) as part of the then government's attempts to meet its austerity targets;[13] on the other, private television channels struggled financially due to the significant loss of advertising income, a situation that has led to the (controversial) reduction, via auctioning, of the number of licences for private channels to only four in September 2016.[14] So while sales to television remain a significant ancillary market, the crisis has affected both the regularity of such sales and the prices of the transactions (although such financial details are rarely disclosed in public).

The above discussion of box-office returns and ancillary markets highlights the means through which a film can recoup (some of) its costs through the market. It would be deceptive, however, to suggest that contemporary Greek film production relies on such a cycle of supply and demand based exclusively on the market. While the economic growth of the 2000s boosted the commercial strength of the Greek film industry and introduced a number of new players – mostly large distributors and exhibitors – into the film-financing arena, the film production landscape in Greece (as elsewhere) is much more varied, and relies on a mix of state and private funding, as well as on unpaid labour, and, most recently, crowdfunding.[15]

A brief account of the funding options historically available for Greek cinema will provide some necessary background for the discussion of the post-crisis situation, and help identify continuities and breaks with past practices. The postwar growth of the Greek film industry was based on a private and commercial basis, as all film-related activity was seen as a business. The broader postwar economic growth and the national audience's growing appetite for cinema enabled a number of producers-entrepreneurs, such as Filopoimin Finos, to build successful filmmaking (and distributing) businesses. With the first signs of a drop in audience attendance that were due primarily to the advent of television in Greece in the mid 1960s, calls for the introduction of protectionist measures for Greek cinema intensified. While some efforts were made to support Greek cinema as an industry in the 1970s, it was only with the election of a socialist government in 1981 that the state's policy towards cinema significantly changed, as cinema was now seen as art and culture and deemed worthy of state support. Adopting policies similar to those established in many (western) European countries since the 1970s, support mostly took the form of state subsidies for production via the newly established Greek Film Centre (funded and under the auspices of the Greek Ministry of Culture).

By the 1990s, however, a number of factors, including the low popularity of most Greek state-funded films, broader changes of policy in the now unified Europe that started favouring co-productions, as well as economic growth in the country, led to the gradual introduction of hybrid modes of film funding that often involved a combination of state and private sources. The deregulation of Greek broadcasting in the early 1990s that led to the establishment and growth of private television channels also contributed significantly to the changing landscape of cinema funding in Greece.[16] By the end of the decade, the unprecedented commercial success of *Safe Sex* (Thanassis Papathanasiou and Michalis Reppas, 1999), a film funded by a private television channel (Mega) and a distributor (Papandreou AE), made it clear that Greek cinema was ripe for new commercial possibilities. Indeed, the continuing economic growth in Greece during the 2000s brought more commercial players willing to invest in Greek films, including the new multiplex owners and large distributors Village, Odeon and Audiovisual.[17] Throughout this period state funding (via the Greek Film Centre and ERT) continued – albeit increasingly as part of co-productions with both national and international partners.

The advent of the financial crisis in the late 2000s found Greek cinema in a relatively good shape. Not only was the business side flourishing, but, most importantly, during almost two decades of affluence, many young filmmakers had found the opportunity to work in the industry in various capacities, thus gaining valuable experience that soon enabled them to produce mature work. Argyris Papadimitropoulos was one of them. His low-budget, guerrilla-style co-directed film *Wasted Youth* (2011), that is loosely based on the real-life story of the killing of 17-year-old Alexandros Grigoropoulos by a policeman in December 2008, launched its international career at the Rotterdam Film Festival. However, prior to this, Papadimitropoulos had shot his first feature film, a gangster comedy, *Bank Bang* (2008), during the years of affluence; not only had he secured private funds to make it (from exhibitor-distributor Village), but the film was both a commercial and critical success, reaching the fifth position in the overall box office in Greece with over 4 million dollars grossed, while also winning him the Best First Director Award at the then newly established Hellenic Film Awards.[18] Another notable example is Yorgos Lanthimos, a well-established director of advertisements in the 1990s and 2000s, who managed to finance and produce independently his first film *Κινέττα* [*Kinetta*] (2005), and later – through a combination of state and private funds – *Dogtooth*, the film that paved the way for the 'Weird Wave of Greek cinema'. Seen from this perspective, the international recognition of Lanthimos' film emerged right at the moment of transition in Greek cinema, when the material possibilities offered by the pre-crisis period met with the sudden and radical collapse of a number of presumed certainties that had supported it until then. The Greek Weird Wave, in this sense, was possible precisely *because* the crisis in Greece was preceded by rapid, unsustainable, and debt-inflated affluence.[19]

After 2010, and despite the crisis, state funding for film production in Greece has not stopped. While the overall budget allocated to the Greek Film Centre reduced, and some of the sources of its funding were annulled,[20] it was mostly internal dysfunctions and political changes that resulted in significant delays in filmmakers receiving allocated funds for their films.[21] Furthermore, the abrupt closure of ERT in June 2013 left a number of film projects awaiting funding financially exposed and threatened co-production arrangements. While the state broadcaster eventually and gradually resumed its film-funding activity, especially after the restoration of ERT in June 2015, the closure and funding disruption caused significant upheaval.[22]

Frustrations related to the dysfunctions of a slow and often inefficient state funding system in Greece have not been new. Their aggravation by the crisis, however, gave extra impetus to a generation of filmmakers who were now ready to make their first or second films, to change their approach towards working and looking for funds. As will be illustrated in the next section, this often consisted of increased 'extroversion' and the search for collaborations and funding from outside Greece; but it also ushered in a new ethos of mutual support, solidarity and collaboration among filmmakers that helped cement critical perceptions about the emergence of a new – Weird or not – wave of Greek cinema since the crisis.

The ecology of Greek cinema since the crisis: *A Blast*

In contrast to the above analysis which explored post-crisis Greek cinema from an economic perspective and in its width of manifestations – production, circulation, reception – what follows will focus on Tzoumerkas' work and especially on his second film *A Blast*. The discussion posits him as representative of the generation of Greek film directors who emerged with their first or second feature-length film around the start of the crisis, and who make films with hard-hitting subjects that aim to challenge and provoke their audiences by triggering thought through discomfort. While the work of this generation is often critically referred to with the suggestive term 'Weird Wave', Tzoumerkas' cinematic language does not fully conform to this characterization, which is more accurately applied to the films of the directors Yorgos Lanthimos, Athina Rachel Tsangari and Babis Makridis (which are often co-scripted with Efhtymis Filippou). In their films, the characters' unconventional ways of acting and talking, as well as the overall visual and acting stylization shatter verisimilitude and conventions of realism – thus fittingly being referred to as 'weird'; Tzoumerkas' work, on the other hand, is characterized by an excessive and heightened realism, punctuated by a mobile and jarring camera, rapid jump cuts, and parallel editing, in which characters take their – otherwise recognizable – actions to extreme, while the stories are told in a fragmented way, with numerous flashbacks that create an often frantic visual and narrative energy.

Stylistic discrepancies with the Weird Wave aside, Tzoumerkas' films and the way they have come to fruition, offer an illuminating case study of the funding and working options available to Greek filmmakers since the crisis – and by extension, of some of the national and transnational 'ecologies of connections' in which the filmmakers and their films function. In order to situate the films of this new generation of Greek filmmakers within the broader context of the post-crisis film culture in Greece, and before zooming in on Tzoumerkas, it is useful to throw some light on the reception of these films in Greece. In order to do this I will briefly return to an account of theatrical admissions, which, while not covering the full extent and contexts in which these films can be seen (given the ever increasing options for home-viewing), it nonetheless offers a good indication of what Greek films Greek audiences prefer to watch. Thus, for example, *Dogtooth* reached 40,000 admissions in Greek cinemas, *Attenberg* 11,000, *Άδικος Κόσμος* [*Unfair World*] (Filippos Tsitos, 2011) 10,000, *Wasted Youth* (Argyris Papadimitropoulos and Jan Vogel, 2011) 8,000. The genre-orientated (but equally hard-hitting), more recent, *Ξενία* [*Xenia*] (Panos H.Koutras, 2014), *Το Μικρό Ψάρι* [*Stratos*] (Yannis Economides, 2014) and *Τετάρτη 4:45* [*Wednesday 4:45*] (Alexis Alexiou, 2015) ranged from 14,000 to 16,000 admissions, which represent rather disappointing returns given their significantly higher budget, critical acclaim and international festival career. Compared with the 700,000 admissions of star-director Christopher Papakaliatis' crisis-themed puzzle film *Ενας Άλλος Κόσμος* [*Another World*] (2015), or with 350,000 of veteran Pandelis Voulgaris' heritage melodrama *Μικρά Αγγλία* [*Little England*] (2013), it is clear that the often formally experimental and 'feel-bad' movies of the New/Weird Wave generation that expose societal problems and turn an accusatory mirror against Greek society, cannot be sustained by a commercial mode of production and financing from within Greece.[23]

For reasons both textual (that is, related to subject matter and style) and contextual (that is, concerning funding origin, mode of circulation and assumed audiences), many of the films of this new generation of filmmakers, are more meaningfully situated in the context of a tradition of a European art/quality cinema than within a closer ecosystem of a national cinema that is made for, and speaks to a (predominantly) national audience. While the 'national' still matters as a framing discourse for locating the films in the context of European (and global) cinema, and as a label of differentiation for their circulation and identification in film festivals,[24] the relationship of many of these films with the national audience is often more ambivalent, as an exploration of both reviews and box office suggests.[25] The films' international trajectory and recognition, therefore, is not just a desired extra, but a fundamental condition of possibility for many these films to be made and seen both within Greece and beyond. Whether produced with the participation of international (usually European) financial partners or not, in the broader ecology of cinematic interactions, these films, in other words, are crucially dependent on international circulation in order to exist. They are, in this sense, often, transnational projects whose cinematic language aims (and often succeeds) to communicate as much with an international, than a national, audience of cinephiles and art-film aficionados.

The above characteristics are particularly evident in Tzoumerkas' *A Blast*, as the film is a European co-production with Greece as the majority partner. Since 2011 the number of co-productions with international partners has doubled from the previous decade to an average of twelve annually.[26] While this number includes both majority and minority co-productions, it does, however, clearly indicate an upward trend in the search for funding and creative collaborations beyond Greece.[27] Such transnational connections are not only valuable for a film's production, but they open up pathways for its circulation and promotion too. Film festivals play a very significant role in this regard, especially through their talent development and market activities. The filmmakers' participation in co-production forums, pitching labs and works-in-progress programmes not only helps them find co-producing partners, but it also enhances a particular project's exposure that can lead to festival premieres, distribution deals and even awards. International film festivals, in other words, are increasingly central in the ecosystem that can help the creation of a film as well as its circulation and visibility.

To place the average number of annual co-productions cited above in context, it is also important to refer to another seemingly paradoxical phenomenon, namely the increase in the number of Greek films released in cinemas in Greece in the last three years, despite the otherwise deepening of the crisis. According to the box office tables provided by both the Greek Film Centre and the publications of the Union of Greek Film Critics (PEKK),[28] the number of films produced annually in the last five years has increased from an average of 30 in the early years of the crisis (2010–2012), to almost 45 since 2013 (see Table 5.2).

This phenomenon can be explained in part because of the inclusion in the lists of a number of films that have had very limited releases (for example, documentaries or double bills of medium length films, that have had less than a handful of screenings). It also reflects the fact that the advances in digital technology (such as affordable high-definition cameras and post-production packages) have enabled certain films to be made with very low budgets. Examples of cheaply made films that managed to reach cinema screens include: the fantasy adventure film *Ο Αδάμαστος: Τα Χρονικά του Δρακοφοίνικα* [*Indomitable: The Dragonpheonix Chronicles*] (Thanos Kermitsis, 2013); the experimental art film *Αλφα* [*Alpha*] (Stathis Athanasiou, 2014); and the observational documentary *100* (Gerasimos Rigas, 2012). It is also worth noting that the first two films mentioned above complemented their private resources with crowdfunding campaigns that directly appealed to the public for financial contributions – an approach to funding enabled by web-based tools, which has as yet met with limited (although critical for the completion of the films) success in the Greek context.[29]

One of the most celebrated aspects of the post-crisis 'behind-the-scenes' culture is that limited budgets have often been complemented by creative collaborations and labour exchanges among filmmakers. Aware of the fact that in order to make films they had to take matters in their own hands, as they could not afford to wait for a dysfunctional state or elusive sponsors to give them money, filmmakers started working in each other's projects with no pay – or with small percentage returns should a film enter into profit – sharing experience, expertise and simple labour. Tsangari has often highlighted this new ethos of solidarity in post-crisis Greece.[30] In her own film *Attenberg*, for example, Lanthimos played one of the main parts, while she produced his film *Alps* the following year. Such collaborations are evident among other filmmakers too: for example, Alexandros Voulgaris appears in *Dogtooth*, Tzoumerkas and Economides perform in Papadimitropoulos' *Suntan*, Papadimitropoulos produced Karanikolas' *Στο Σπίτι* [*At Home*] (2014), Tzoumerkas co-authored Papadimitropoulos' *Suntan* – and so on.

While this new attitude among filmmakers was a major factor in mobilizing and enhancing creativity at a time of crisis, the need to put together a sustainable production package and secure viable distribution pathways has all but rescinded. In fact, as digital technologies have dropped the cost of making and circulating a film, globally the number of films that vie for attention has significantly increased. For a film to be noticed, therefore, it requires the support of an ecosystem of institutions, networks and agents that will enable it to survive in this extremely competitive landscape. Tzoumerkas' successful Greek, German and Dutch coproduction for *A Blast*, and the film's international circulation, illustrates some of the interactions and processes necessary for finding production funds, entering into distribution networks, and inhabiting exhibition spaces – in other words, some of the ecologies of connections that enable a film to be made and seen.

Tzoumerkas studied theatre and cinema in Athens and then Utrecht and New York, in the late 1990s/early 2000s. His first international breakthrough took place in 2001, when his short film *Τα Μάτια που Τρώνε* [*The Devouring Eyes*] participated at the Cannes Film Festival Cinefondation section, and later won the jury award at the Karlovy Vary International Film Festival.[31] During the 2000s, he directed television documentaries and performed on stage, while in 2010 he released his first feature film, *Χώρα Προέλευσης* [*Homeland*]. Juxtaposing documentary footage from recent riots in Greece, 1970s family photos and scenes from three generations of a family's present and past, the film is a frenetic indictment of the self-destructive dysfunction at the heart of the fictional family, and by extension, the nation. This was a 'small', low-budget, film (250,000 euros) financed, according to Tzoumerkas, in the 'old way';[32] that is, through state funds (Greek Film Centre, ERT and the Ministry of Macedonia/Thrace), and with the involvement of three Greek-based production companies (Fantasia Optikoakoustiki, PanEntertainment, Homemade films). An ambitious production given its budget (it included '15 main parts and 150 locations'), it involved significant amounts of unpaid work to be made. Despite not being made with international distribution in mind, the film premiered at the International Film Critics' week section of the Venice Film Festival (September 2010). When it opened theatrically in two screens in Athens about a month later, it became a surprise hit, becoming sold out for four weeks and selling 12,000 tickets (entering in the top five Greek films that year). The film was shot while Greece was, in Tzoumerkas' words, a 'riot country, not a debt country', referring to the events of December 2008 that triggered extensive public eruptions of anger against the state and its dysfunctions. By the time *Homeland* opened in Athens in autumn 2010, the debt crisis had clearly reached Greece; the predominant national feeling, however, was still anger at the sense of betrayal by the political class, rather than personal hardship, as many of the austerity measures that would affect people's livelihoods had not, yet been decided and/or implemented. The film's critical look on a family falling apart at the seams, and the implicit indictment of the older generation, felt very topical for the Greek urban youth that the film mostly addressed, even though critics were split over its virtues.

Tzoumerkas and Yula Boudali, who had previously written *Homeland* together, started working on the script for *A Blast* in 2011. Conceived, written, financed, produced and released well after Greeks had started feeling the consequences of the financial crisis and the austerity measures, this was, from the start, an 'extrovert' project; targeting as much an international as a national audience with a story about Greece in crisis, the filmmakers sought European collaborations and funding from the start. The film tells the story of mother-of-three Maria (Angeliki Papoulia) who chooses to break away from her present and past in an incendiary and explosive manner, as the film's title suggests. Considering her life 'ridiculous', 'painful' and 'pointless', as she explains in an introspective monologue, Maria abandons her children to her unreliable sister and her dangerous husband, cuts off contact with the father of her children who travels at sea, violently confronts her disabled mother for hiding debts, and after the latter commits suicide, convinces her pusillanimous father to set fire to a forest. Morally dubious and deeply troubling, the central character's actions reject all sense of community, and selfishly prioritize individuality. This is a profoundly angry film, whereby survival is equated with destruction and escape – ethically problematic, but emotionally plausible. The film posits Maria's actions in the context of the declaration of human rights, as in a flashback sequence situated at the start of the film, she ironically and playfully teaches her sister the principles of equality, the right to life, freedom and personal security, while mockingly undercutting the 'spirit of brotherhood'.

With evident stylistic and thematic similarities with *Homeland* in its fragmented presentation of the story through multiple flashbacks, its harsh indictment of the institution of the family and its focus on characters pushed to the edge, *A Blast*'s topicality, namely its crisis-related subject matter, had potential to appeal to European co-producers interested in contemporary Greece. In order to capitalize on such possibilities, Tzoumerkas, Boudali and producer Maria Drandaki (Homemade films) participated at the CineLink co-production market at the Sarajevo Film Festival in August 2012 with a short sample of the film and the script. Winning the top prize, the Eurimages co-production development award that includes 30,000 euros, enabled them to hire a German script editor, Franz Rodernkirchen. But even more importantly, in Sarajevo they started developing the co-production team, as they found the German co-producer Titus Kreyenberg (Unafilm), who was soon followed by the Dutch producers Ellen Havenith (PRPL) and Jeroen Beker (EFP).

With the film's main co-production partners in place, the team started applying to different national and regional funds, including the Greek Film Centre, the Netherlands Filmfonds, and two regional funds from Germany – Film und Medien Stiftung NRW, and Filmförderung Hamburg Schleswig-Holstein – all of which agreed to finance them. Gradually more producers were added to the team, providing further support and specialisms: four from Greece (Graal, Marni Films, Proseggisi and PanEntertainment), and one from Italy (Movimento Film). It is worth noting that while ERT had also agreed to finance the film, the broadcaster's closure in June 2013 placed the co-production at risk, not only because of the loss of the allocated money, but also because the participation of a television channel in the co-production was a necessary precondition for the release of the other funds. The solution eventually came through the German channel ZDF/ARTE, which replaced ERT as the television partner for the co-production.

A Blast's budget was 800,000 euros – more than three times that of *Homeland*. It was shot predominantly in Greece, with only few scenes in Germany as required by the script. Following the usual co-production practice, the creative team roughly reflected the funding: the director of photography, production and costume designers were from Greece; the editor, sound designer and mixer, and stuntmen were from Holland; while camera operators and other technicians were from Germany.

The film premiered at the Locarno International Film Festival in August 2014. This offered a very important launchpad for the film's international career, as its selection for the festival's main competition programme resulted in reviews in all the main trade journals, while the designated industry screenings led to distribution deals for three territories

(Poland, Italy, Holland). As a result of this initial sales success, the production team took the relatively unconventional decision of not engaging a sales agent, but chose to sell the rights for the film in different territories directly.[33] Despite involving extra work, this approach paid off as the film managed to find distribution in at least 16 territories – a considerable number for such a thematically and emotionally challenging Greek film. The film was also shown widely at over 35 international film festivals, thus reaching further audiences and receiving some income as smaller festivals often pay for the rights to screen films.[34] Its reception within Greece, however, was lukewarm, reaching 4,300 theatrical admissions – a third of those of *Homeland* – and generating mixed reviews.

Aside from attracting the attention of producers and audiences, the crisis marks the film thematically in different ways too: the financial crisis inhabits both the broader social space of the narrative – for example, news about the closures of small businesses are heard on the car radio – and the characters' lives, especially Maria's as she struggles with exuberant debts, accumulated unpaid tax bills, and unhelpful bank employees. The crisis in the film is familial too, as it portrays Maria's radical break with all members of her family, as she unforgivingly confronts her parents, and abandons husband, children and sister. The familial crisis is an existential one too, as questions about the meaning (lessness) of her life motivate Maria's actions and push her to extremes. Finally, and no less significantly, the film also points to an ecological crisis as Maria gets her father to burn out the forest by his family village – an event first presented in an enigmatic manner in the pre-credit sequence. However, the depiction of nature and its crisis is more ambivalent: while ecological destruction is literally depicted through the narrative, the film's visuals reinstate nature as a site of hope and escape. Such connotations are conveyed especially through the identical static long shot of green pine trees against the sea that punctuates the film twice. The shot first appears after the title card *A Blast* (which follows the opening sequence with the forest fires), and introduces the pivotal scene where Maria teaches her sister the declaration of human rights. The exact same shot recurs in the last sequence, establishing the scene for Maria's final (and hopeful) escape away from 'civilization', and towards nature and the sea. The film's *mise-en-scene*, in other words, posits nature as a renovator via attributing some subtle and ambiguous hope to what is otherwise a very bleak story. For despite the fact that she is running away with a bag full of money, Maria's post-escape options are rather uncertain.

The multiple crises explored in the film that culminate in a metaphoric explosion and a literal fire, are succeeded – if not resolved – by the promise of nature. Ecology thus provides a 'condition of possibility' for the character and, by extension, perhaps, for the troubled nation, to exist. Textual interpretations aside, however, the main focus of this section was on a different kind of ecology: on the transnational and cross-institutional sets of exchange which enabled the production, circulation and reception of Tzoumerkas' film – and which, by extension, represents broader conditions of possibility for cinema in post-crisis Greece.

This chapter has mapped out the varied landscape of post-crisis Greek cinema that contains conflicting forces of creativity and stagnation, progress and regression, growth and contraction. The dynamism, extroversion and solidarity evident in the films of the generation of filmmakers that emerged in the late 2000s has offered strong impetus to Greek art cinema, and hope for renewed (national and) international presence. Furthermore, while the number of popular Greek films produced since the crisis has significantly dropped, the few that appealed to audiences and became commercial successes were quality productions, that also achieved critical approval, thus suggesting that commercial production has prospects too. However, despite the cheaper and more easily accessible technology required for making a film and distributing it digitally, obtaining production funds and accessing the networks that will enable a film to access audiences is becoming increasingly harder. But these are global challenges, faced by filmmakers from Greece as much as from anywhere else. Indeed, the forces of globalization that triggered the crisis in Greece (and elsewhere) are radically changing the dynamics of cultural exchange at both national and transnational levels, and they are themselves constantly shifting. Whether, as the final scene of *A Blast* suggests, after the fire there is hope, and whether the economy and ecology of post-crisis Greek cinema will find ways of continuing to renew itself, remains to be seen.

Notes

I would like to thank the Onassis Foundation for providing me with a scholarship that allowed me to spend time conducting interviews with members of the Greek film industry and collecting relevant data. Among my interviewees, I would also like to thank in particular Syllas Tzoumerkas who provided me with invaluable information for the completion of this chapter.

1. For the initial uses of the term 'weird' in relation to Greek films, see A.O. Scott, 'Dogtooth: A sanctuary and a prison', *New York Times*, 24 June 2010. Available at http://www.nytimes.com/2010/06/25/movies/25dog.html?_r=1& (accessed 28 October 2016); and Steve Rose, 'Attenberg, Dogtooth and the Weird Wave of Greek cinema', *Guardian*, 27 August 2011. Available at http://www.theguardian.com/film/2011/aug/27/attenberg-dogtooth-greece-cinema (accessed 28 October 2016).
2. Many thanks to Professor Peter Mackridge for etymological advice.
3. Gillian Doyle, *Understanding Media Economics*, second edition (London, 2013).
4. See the website of Media Ecology Association. Available at http://www.media-ecology.org/index.html (accessed 28 October 2016).
5. Stephen Rust, Salma Monani and Sean Cubitt, *Ecocinema Theory and Practice* (London, 2013), p. 1.
6. Data from Unesco Institute of Statistics. Available at http://www.uis.unesco.org/culture/Pages/movie-statistics.aspx (accessed 9 October 2016).
7. The data cited here and below based on information from interviewees, rather than published figures.
8. The Greek Film Centre provides data (on request) only after 2010. The data is compiled from the information provided to it by the Greek distribution companies. Any data prior to this date is not deemed reliable.
9. Information from interview with Akis Voilas (2015), theatrical sales and programming manager at Village Cinemas.
10. See Dimitris Develengos, Dimitris, 'Γιατί "έριξε" τίτλους τέλους το Kosmopolis Park' [Why did [Odeon's multiplex] Kosmopolis Park close?], *Capital.gr*, 22 September 2015. Available at http://www.capital.gr/story/3065350/giati-erixe-titlous-telous-to-kosmopolis-park (accessed 9 October 2016).
11. For more detail on the distribution landscape in Greece, see Lydia Papadimitriou, 'Film Distribution in Greece: Formal and Informal Networks of Exchange since the crisis', *Screen* 59/4 (2018).
12. Ibid.
13. See BBC, 'Greece suspends state broadcaster ERT to save money' (12 June 2013). Available at http://www.bbc.co.uk/news/world-europe-22861577 (accessed 28 October 2016); and BBC 'Greece's state broadcaster ERT back on air after two years' (11 June 2015). Available at http://www.bbc.co.uk/news/world-europe-33090373 (accessed 28 October 2016).
14. See BBC, 'Auction halves number of Greek private TV stations' (2 September 2016). Available at http://www.bbc.co.uk/news/business-37259277 (accessed 28 October 2016).
15. See Lydia Papadimitriou, 'Transitions in the periphery: Funding film production in Greece since the financial crisis', *International Journal on Media Management* 19/2 (2017).

16. Stelios Papathanassopoulos, 'The politics and the effects of the deregulation of Greek television, *European Journal of Communication* 12/3 (1997), pp. 351–368.
17. For more on popular Greek films of the 2000s, see Lydia Papadimitriou, 'The national and the transnational in contemporary Greek cinema', *New Review of Film and Television Studies*, 9/4 (2011), pp. 493–512; and Michalis Kokonis, 'Is there such a thing as a Greek Blockbuster? The revival of contemporary Greek cinema' in Lydia Papadimitriou and Yannis Tzioumakis (eds), *Greek Cinema: Texts, Histories, Identities* (Bristol, 2011), pp. 37–54.
18. Data from Box Office Mojo. Available at http://www.boxofficemojo.com/intl/greece/yearly/?yr=2008&sort=gross&order=DESC&pagenum=1&p=.htm (accessed 10 October 2016).
19. Maria Chalkou, 'A New Cinema of "emancipation": Tendencies of independence in Greek cinema of the 2000s', *Interactions* 3/2 (2012), pp. 243–261; Lydia Papadimitriou, 'Locating contemporary Greek film cultures: Past, present, future and the crisis', *Filmicon* 2 (2014), pp. 1–19.
20. Most notably, since August 2015, the special tax on cinema tickets that was dedicated to film production was cancelled as a result of the latest memorandum agreement. See, among others 'Τι αλλάζει στα εισιτήρια κινηματογράφου με το νέο Μνημόνιο' [What changes with cinema tickets with the new memorandum], *Financial Press.gr* (30.9.2015). Available at http://www.fpress.gr/oikonomia/forologia/item/36893-ti-allazei-sta-eisitiria-kinimatografoy-me-to-neo-mnimonio (accessed on 28 October 2016); and 'Για την κατάργηση του φόρου στα κινηματογραφικά εισητήρια' [On the abolition of tax in the cinema tickets] (20.8.2015). Available at http://www.lifo.gr/team/u46465/59823 (accessed 28 October 2016).
21. Indicative reports about some of the dysfunctions: Vena Georgakopoulou, 'Αργεί η άνοιξη του σινεμά' [The Spring of cinema is late], *Enet.gr*, 22 June 2011. Available at http://www.enet.gr/?i=news.el.article&id=286661 (accessed 28 October 2016); Evanna Vernardou, 'Αρχισαν τα όργανα στο Κέντρο Κινηματογράφου' [The instruments have began at the Film Centre], *Enet.gr*, 4 August 2014. Available at http://www.enet.gr/?i=news.el.article&id=442111 (accessed 28 October 2016); *Ελληνικό Κέντρο Κινηματογράφου* [*Greek Film Centre*] (various dates). Available at http://www.huffingtonpost.gr/news/elleniko-kentro-kinematoyrafoe/ (accessed 28 October 2016).
22. Some film productions received funding while the broadcaster functioned under the interim name Δημόσια Τηλεόραση (DT) [Public Television] (from July 2013 to May 2014); and then as Νέα Ελληνική Ραδιοφωνία, Ιντερνετ και Τηλεόραση (NERIT) [New Greek Radio, Internet and Television] (from May 2014 to June 2015), but these consisted mostly of release of frozen funds followed by the closure of ERT in June 2013. In May 2016, the reopened/renamed ERT (since June 2015) announced a new round of funding for Greek films. See Manolis Kranakis, 'Μετά από τέσσερα χρόνια απουσίας, η ΕΡΤ στηρίζει έμπρακτα το Ελληνικό σινεμά' [After four years of absence, ERT

supports Greek cinema in practice]. Available at http://flix.gr/news/ert-supports-greek-cinema-again.html (accessed 28 October 2016).

23. Rounded up data from the Greek Film Centre.
24. See Thomas Elsaesser, *European Cinema: Face to Face with Hollywood* (Amsterdam, 2005), p. 83, on the role of film festivals in 'reinstating [the national] as a second-order category'.
25. See Papadimitriou, 'Locating contemporary Greek film cultures', p. 5.
26. Data based on Eurimages and Lumiere databases. For more details, see Papadimitriou, 'Transitions in the Periphery'.
27. As international and European co-productions are increasingly blurring the boundaries of a film's national identity, specific criteria are applied to allocate a film's nationality in different countries. For the criteria currently assigned in the Greek context, see Law 3905/2010, entitled 'Ενίσχυση και ανάπτυξη κινηματογραφικής τέχνης και άλλες διατάξεις' ['Strenghtening and development of cinematic art and other provisions']. Available at http://www.eetep.gr/wp-content/uploads/2016/06/%CE%A6%CE%95%CE%9A-%CE%91-219-2010.pdf (accessed 20 October 2016).
28. PEKK, *Κινηματογράφος 2011* [*Cinema 2011*] (Athens, 2012), p. 27; PEKK, *Κινηματογράφος 2012* [*Cinema 2012*] (Athens, 2013), p. 33; PEKK, *Κινηματογράφος 2013* [*Cinema 2013*] (Athens, 2014), p. 36; PEKK, *Κινηματογράφος 2014* [*Cinema 2014*] (Athens, 2015), pp. 41–42; PEKK, *Κινηματογράφος 2015* [*Cinema 2015*] (Athens, 2016), pp. 44–45. Both lists consist of all Greek films that have had a theatrical release in Greece – even a very limited one. They do not normally include minority Greek co-productions – although inconsistencies occasionally emerge (for example the inclusion of the Lithuanian/Greek 2015 film *Modris* in *Kinimatografos* 2015, p. 45).
29. See Papadimitriou, 'Transitions in the periphery'.
30. Athina Tsangari, 'On solidarity, collaboration and independence: Athina Rachel Tsangari discusses her films and Greek cinema with Vangelis Calotychos, Lydia Papadimitriou and Yannis Tzioumakis' *Journal of Greek Media and Culture* 2/2 (2016), pp. 237–253; Lydia Papadimitriou, 'In the Shadow of the Studios, the State and the Multiplexes: Independent Filmmaking in Greece', in M. Erickson and D. Baltruschat (eds), *The Meaning of Independence: Independent Filmmaking around the Globe* (Toronto, 2014), pp. 113–130.
31. For biographical details, see Tzioumerkas' site, available at http://syllastzoumerkas.com/ (accessed 28 October 2016).
32. Unless indicated otherwise all quotes by the director that follow are based on a personal interview with Tzoumerkas in Athens (26.3.2015).
33. Sales agents act as intermediaries between producers and distributors, buying the rights from the producers to sell a particular film in different territories.
34. For details about the film's distribution career and festival screenings, see http://syllastzoumerkas.com/films/a-blast/ (accessed 28 October 2016).

CHAPTER 6

GREEK MUSEUMS IN TIMES OF CRISIS

Andromache Gazi

Introduction

The financial crisis that has swept Europe since 2009 has had severe and far-reaching effects on the cultural sector. In many countries, including Greece, where cultural institutions depend heavily on state funding and support, large-scale budget cuts and strict restructuring measures have led to uncertainty and distress. As a result of these changing circumstances, cultural organizations have been revising their policies and experimenting with alternative ways of funding. In many cases, however, the crisis brought to light and accentuated already existing deficiencies in cultural policy models in force. As a rule, rigid policies and centralized administrative structures have not facilitated change and readjustment. This applies especially to Greece, a country with a traditionally narrow model of cultural policy (focusing on heritage and monuments), a centralized structure of cultural administration controlled by a powerful Ministry of Culture and a very high percentage of state-run museums.

This chapter attempts to chart the situation of Greek museums since the onset of the economic crisis. The emphasis will be on state archaeological museums not only because they form the largest category of museums in the country, but also – and more importantly – because they still enjoy a privileged position in perpetuating deeply-rooted notions of Greek identity. The discussion is by no means exhaustive;

rather, it is an attempt at outlining key issues in the museum field in Greece, such as official policies and strategies, funding and museum visiting, and highlighting topics for further research. It will be argued that, despite vanishing budgets and reductions in staff that have led most Greek museums to the verge of stagnation, one of the main problems facing the sector is the lack of a culture of openness and sharing that would facilitate synergies and bring about enhanced support at various levels. In order to provide a general introduction to the state of the Greek museum sector before the crisis, the chapter begins with an outline of cultural policy and cultural management along with a brief discussion of the public museum landscape in the country.

Cultural policy, administrative structure, operational framework

Cultural policy in Greece has historically been geared towards the preservation and protection of cultural heritage – primarily *archaeological* and specifically *classical* – as this has provided the political and ideological backbone for the formation of a distinctive national identity from 1830 (when the Modern Greek State was established) onwards. Notions of national identity based on Greek antiquity are deeply rooted in the Greek collective consciousness and continue to pervade social and political life.[1] As a consequence, archaeology's privileged position as an arena for playing out various battles – at a political, ideological, scientific and financial level – is perpetuated, while a strong predisposition towards archaeology permeates legislation, policies and management structures relating to culture. For example, it is revealing that legislation providing for cultural matters *other* than archaeology was only passed in the 1990s;[2] while an all-encompassing notion of 'cultural heritage', which broadened the scope of protection to all cultural traditions and historical periods, was endorsed for the first time in 2002 by Law 3828 'On the protection of antiquities and cultural heritage in general'.[3] Cultural sponsorship was regulated as late as 2007,[4] while contemporary culture and creative industries have been specifically addressed only recently.

Jurisdiction for cultural heritage and the arts lies exclusively with the Ministry of Culture (henceforth the Ministry) established in 1971. The Ministry has absolute authority over archaeological heritage, in particular, since, according to the Greek Constitution, all antiquities in the country are state property. At central level, museum issues are regulated by the Directorate of Museums, which has a bureaucratic role with limited possibilities for proposing comprehensive museum policies and strategies. At regional level, all archaeological and museum work is undertaken by regional services, the Ephorates of Antiquities (henceforth Ephorates), which are responsible for excavation, research, conservation, protection and management of monuments, as well as sites, collections and regional museums. The Ephorates are predominantly staffed by archaeologists. Given this and the fact that, with the exception of some major museums which function as semi-autonomous units, all state archaeological museums operate under the relevant regional Ephorates, it is easy to understand why museum work is just one of the myriad tasks entrusted to archaeologists working in the Archaeological Service. The shortcomings of this system are obvious and have often been criticized.[5]

Following the well-established and deeply embedded notion of a tripartite continuum of Greek history (Antiquity – Byzantium – Modern Greece), the Ephorates were traditionally divided into Prehistoric and Classical Antiquities, Byzantine and Post-Byzantine Antiquities and Contemporary and Modern Monuments respectively. With the Ministry's new Statute of 2014 the government merged the Prehistoric and Classical Ephorates with the Byzantine ones, in an attempt to downsize the public sector.[6] There were also mergers within the departments of the regional Ephorates: the former Department of Museum, Exhibitions and Educational Programmes merged with the Departments of Monuments, Sites and Research. As a result, museums lost even the very small degree of self-regulation they had enjoyed within the previous organizational structure, while no alternative model for the development of their various activities and outreach work was proposed.

The Ministry is assisted by consultative bodies, such as the Central Archaeological Council, the Council of Modern Monuments and by arm's-length agencies, such as the Archaeological Receipts Fund. Of specific interest for the discussion in this chapter is the National Council of Museums, which was introduced in 2002 and became operational after 2006. The Council functions as an advisory body to the Minister of Culture with an emphasis on providing informed opinion on the establishment of new museums and exhibitions. Yet, although the Council's activity has led to a systematization of procedures, it has yet to play a key role in setting specific museum policies with realistic priorities and strategic objectives.[7]

To sum up, the protection of cultural heritage continues to be an absolute priority in state policy, funding and organizational support.[8] The government has an all-embracing and interventionist role in drafting and enforcing policies with very limited powers being delegated to regional/local authorities or other stakeholders. Because of this centralized state control, the effects of the financial crisis on all services dealing with heritage, including museums, are felt more deeply, a trend that is observed in many other European countries. Moreover, this strong statist approach implicitly restricts the interest in heritage to trained specialists and does not allow the development of a dynamic public archaeology, despite the plethora of educational programmes in museums and at archaeological sites.[9] Finally, the frequent reshuffles of organizational structures that characterize public administration, as a result of fluctuating political priorities, have a negative effect on cultural policy and make long-term provision and programming hard.

Before focusing on the repercussions of the crisis on the Greek museum sector, it is necessary to outline the sector's main structural and operational features. As the discussion later in this chapter will show, these core features, along with an outdated organizational culture and constant changes in political priorities affecting heritage management, as outlined above, have rendered most public museums totally unequipped to face any – financial or other – disturbances.[10]

The (public) museum landscape

Museums in Greece are either public (owned by the state, local authorities, the Church or universities) or private (owned by individuals, cultural foundations, scientific or professional associations or local cultural bodies/ groups). The total numbers are difficult to assess with any precision due to fluctuating official data coupled with the lack of accreditation.[11]

State museums are predominantly archaeological. In 2004 these were found to represent 66 per cent of the museums in the country.[12] Currently, the best estimate for their overall number is 219.[13] With very few exceptions, they come under the jurisdiction of the Ministry and are part of the regional Ephorates. Thus, museums share financial and human resources with all other departments within each particular

Ephorate and have very limited autonomy. Only a few major museums (the National Archaeological, the Epigraphical-Numismatic, and the Byzantine and Christian museums in Athens, the Museum of Byzantine Culture in Thessaloniki and the Archaeological Museums of Thessaloniki and Herakleion)[14] have been given special regional service status, which allows them to do their own planning.[15]

Exceptions to the scheme described above are the Benaki Museum (an independent museum established in 1930, which functions as a private-law legal entity, but is still partially subsidised by the state) and two state archaeological museums that function as public-law legal entities: the Kanellopoulos Museum (established in 1976 to house a private collection of antiquities donated to the state) and the new Acropolis Museum (inaugurated in 2009). The Acropolis Museum, in particular, is an exceptional case: endowed with an autonomous status, it enjoys a significant degree of independence, sets its own strategies and manages its own funds (derived mainly from sales, fees and ticketing revenues). However, the Museum's unique management model has been strongly challenged (see below).

Another type of museum functions at arm's length from the Ministry (operating as a private-law legal entity), but traditionally depends on central government for funding. Examples of such museums include the National Gallery and the National Museum of Contemporary Art in Athens, and the State Museum of Contemporary Art in Thessaloniki. Finally, a plethora of independent museums of all sorts (folk art, applied arts, local history etc.) are supervised by the Ministry.[16]

Within the strict structure outlined above, delegation to regional museums is minimal. Attempts to relax the statist approach have generally been met with a negative reaction, usually from members of the State Archaeological Service. In 2005, for example, a government plan to transform eleven archaeological museums into special services of the Ministry, separated from the local Ephorates, was met with strong opposition,[17] while the administrative separation of the new Acropolis Museum from the relevant Ephorate and its subsequent autonomy was objected to by the majority of the archaeological profession and, especially, the Association of Greek Archaeologists.[18]

The rigid administrative structure and the lack of self-regulation have discouraged change and new approaches in museums and have led to a long period of stagnation. For decades a visit to any archaeological museum in the country would present almost the same picture, since they all followed the same display model in which collections were arranged according to a linear chronological and typological progression. Even today public archaeological museums follow a virtually identical narrative, which is in line with the official approach to Greek civilization.

In view of all the above, it is clear that good museum practices have not been the result of specific policies and strategies; rather, they have emerged as a result of the vision, motivation and innovative practices that were initiated by some museums under the guidance of talented directors.[19] Prominent examples include the Byzantine and Christian Museum in Athens,[20] the Museum of Byzantine Civilisation in Thessaloniki and the Archaeological Museum of Thessaloniki.[21] It is true, however, that such practices can flourish primarily thanks to the semi-autonomous status enjoyed by a minority of museums, whereas the majority, structurally entangled as they are with the Ephorates, are ill placed to follow suit. The few exceptions just confirm the rule.

In brief, despite a centralized administration and the existence of several advisory bodies, a clear, feasible, national strategic planning for museums, free from political interventions and shifts in central government and administration, is still lacking. With very few exceptions, the same management model is universally followed: public museums operate within a strict and bureaucratic institutional framework, which obstructs flexibility and allows limited self-governance. Specific policies and practices are usually restricted to each museum's micro-environment without considering the museum's macro-environment, e.g. at European and international level.[22]

Funding

Traditionally, the Ministry has been allocated a tiny part of the state budget, rarely exceeding 0.50 per cent. During the last decade, for example, only 0.37 per cent of the overall public budget of the Greek state was allocated to culture.[23] Ironically, this trifling percentage sharply contrasts with the official – stereotypical – rhetoric in which culture is the country's 'heavy industry' and qualitative advantage. Most importantly, this budget is thinly spread, being used to cover a plethora of different needs (from excavations, conservation and site protection to contemporary culture and subsidies), with the main part going on salaries, recruitment of temporary staff, and operational and maintenance costs.[24] It includes funding for museums, but the exact amounts are almost impossible to assess, as this represents only a share of the total budget allocated to the Ephorates. However, during the years of the current economic crisis state funding has decreased dramatically, leading to a series of austerity measures, as discussed below.

It is a peculiarity of the Greek system that museum revenues (from tickets, shops, photography and filming fees etc.) are managed neither by the museums themselves nor by the Ministry. Instead, they are managed by the Archaeological Receipts Fund (henceforth ARF), an arms-length body that supports the work of the Archaeological Service mainly through management of revenues, publications of archaeological work and expropriation of land for archaeological purposes. Only about 40 per cent of all proceeds collected by the ARF are earmarked for the Ministry, to be redistributed to the regional services according to priorities decided centrally.[25] Consequently, museums have no control over their revenues, while the legal framework in force does not encourage other means of fundraising.

Since 1994, the funding of culture has largely depended on EU support, initially through the EU Community Support Frameworks (CSF) and later through EU Regional Programmes.[26] Within a decade, for example, and through CSF II (1994–2000) and III (2000–2006), the cultural sector was granted a total of 1.7 billion euros.[27] This was by far the highest amount of funding the Ministry had ever enjoyed.

Recent research has shown that before CSF III the majority of Greek archaeological museums, even large and internationally acclaimed ones, had limited services.[28] Through the programme 'Culture', CSF III gave museums the opportunity to develop mainly hard infrastructures and improve existing buildings. Thanks to a financial package of approximately 469 million euros, it became possible to provide museums of national importance with vital technical improvements, to construct many new museums or expand existing ones, and to organize major redisplays throughout the country.[29] However, it has been suggested that the priorities in allocating funding within the above-described EU programmes continued to support the traditional political view of culture. The political choice was made to maintain the stereotypical interpretation of national prestige, based largely on archaeological heritage, at the expense of new forms of cultural expression. Accordingly, and despite the priority given in CSF III to the construction of some large prestigious cultural centres (such as the Concert Hall in Thessaloniki), there was a marked contrast between the portion of funds spent on the protection and display of archaeological heritage and the one allocated to contemporary culture.[30]

The National Strategic Reference Programme (NSRP) 2007–2013, did not specifically include a cultural programme; nevertheless, the Ministry managed to implement 653 projects,[31] including 46 public archaeological museum projects which cost nearly 112 million euros.[32] A large proportion of the funds was allocated to the operation of museums constructed during the previous period, including the hiring of temporary personnel, enhancement of public accessibility and promotion of digitization projects. The implementation of the NSRP 2007–2013 coincided with the harshest period of austerity in Greece. In 2011 and 2012 a considerable number of experienced members of the Ministry's hierarchy were forced into early retirement as a result of a measure described as 'labour reserve'. In 2013 the Fund for the Management of Resources for the Implementation of Archaeological Projects, a specialized service dealing with the implementation of EU projects, was abolished. In 2014 the restructuring of the Ministry's services caused considerable disruption to the work flow. Despite these problems, to which the imposition of capital controls in 2015 should also be added, the programme was concluded successfully.[33] The current NSRP 2014–2020 funding programme does not make specific provision for cultural heritage in the narrow sense. So far very few museum projects have been put forward for inclusion.

Occasionally, museum funding may be secured through collateral agreements between the Ministry and the regions or municipalities, which are usually eager to enhance the cultural identity of their district. Finally, another source of revenue for museums is the various 'Friends of the Museum' associations, which often provide financial support for specific aspects of museums (e.g. educational programmes).

To sum up, ample EU funding gave the Greek Ministry of Culture a unique opportunity to gradually complete an ambitious programme of constructing new museums and improve the infrastructure and services of existing ones;[34] according to the terms of agreement, however, this money could not be used for operational costs. This has led to the paradox of ongoing construction of new facilities that cannot be fully operated and maintained.[35] The next section looks more specifically at the effects of the recession on the Greek museum sector, records recent trends and discusses some data on museum visiting.

Museums within, despite and beyond the crisis

From 2009 onwards, efforts to consolidate public finances and reduce public spending have led to substantial cuts in funds allocated to the cultural sector. Consequently, the smooth funding and operation of all related activities were severely hampered. The first results of the financial crisis were evident in 2010 when a series of measures, including reduction of the Public Investment Programme, salary and pension cuts and suspension of recruitment in the public sector, were implemented.

From 2009 to 2012 the Ministry's budget dropped by 30 per cent. This was felt across the public and private cultural sector, with museums reducing their opening hours or temporarily closing parts of their collections.[36] In 2010 budget cuts and a shortage of attendants forced more than 40 archaeological museums and sites to close parts of their collections, or even shut down altogether, for periods of a few weeks up to a couple of months. These were mostly small museums in the provinces but also included major institutions like the National Archaeological Museum in Athens (which had to close an entire floor temporarily). In 2013, in an effort to restructure several overstaffed state organizations and to resolve the problems caused by the lack of personnel (mostly guards) in museums, the government moved staff from the Hellenic Railways Organization (OSE) to museums as attendants. Yet, this did not solve the problem: in 2013 and 2014 some museums still kept important sections of their exhibitions closed to the public or shut altogether.

Similar effects have been recorded in the private cultural sector, the most prominent example being the Benaki Museum, the country's oldest, biggest and most prestigious private museum. The museum, which is run by a board of trustees and operates under private law, has attracted significant donations, bequests and private funds over the years; yet, its operational costs and salaries have been covered, in part, by the state. In recent years the massive drop in state funding has forced the museum to dismiss a large number of staff members, reduce the salaries of the remaining workforce by 20 to 40 per cent, and their working hours by 20 per cent. As a result, the museum can no longer afford to remain open on a daily basis and some of its branches are open to the public only four days a week.[37] In 2012, however, the museum launched a wide-reaching 'Support Campaign for the Benaki Museum' as well as an 'Adoption' programme, which enables donors to 'adopt' and support a specific activity from within the museum's departments financially.[38] Through this scheme the Benaki has been able to finance nine curatorial and other positions to date. In a similar vein, the Goulandris Museum of Cycladic and Ancient Greek Art in Athens introduced a series of measures in order to attract visitors, including reduced prices, free entrance to temporary exhibitions on specific days, special offers to tourists, etc.[39]

As a reaction to huge cuts in their budgets and the reluctance of potential sponsors to commit themselves, many public museums are now introducing 'networks of museums'. In June 2010 five museums in Thessaloniki, including two archeological and three contemporary art museums, formed the 'Initiative of the five museums of Thessaloniki', which aims to give mutual support to their various activities and to organize major exhibitions and educational or research activities collectively.[40] Another network was established earlier by the small museums and non-profit cultural institutions of the historical centre of Athens.[41] These initiatives mark 'a new era for cultural matters in Greece, initiating a new collaborative understanding of museum responsibility and action'.[42]

Indeed, several public museum directors seem to have realized the advantages of alliances and synergies and are trying to make the best possible use of all resources at their disposal, in spite of the stringent financial conditions.[43] An interesting trend in this respect has been the recycling of material from past exhibitions and the compensation of overtime with extra days leave.[44] A further example is co-operation with local authorities in order to sponsor specific museum activities such as the very successful *Sleepover* programme which has been running since 2011 in several museums in Thessaloniki thanks to sponsorship by the city's Municipality.

In brief, faced with the need to completely revamp their operational mode without the necessary resources, many public museums found themselves in deadlock.

But, as a result of an emerging change in attitude, quite a few are now determined to upgrade their services to the public, strengthen relationships with local communities and offer a wide range of activities ranging from workshops, music events and exhibitions to innovative projects such as the radio broadcast 'Evening coffee at the Archaeological

Museum of Thessaloniki' launched in 2015.[45] Further research would reveal if such efforts are starting to have real effects (i.e. increased participation among the locals).

Museum visiting

Informal discussions on museum visiting in Greece often refer to declining audiences. But careful reading of official data on museum ticket sales, as gathered by the ARF and analysed by the Hellenic Statistical Authority (ELSTAT), present a rather different picture.[46] As shown in Chart 6.1, between 2008 and 2010 museum visitors were on the rise. There followed a period of decline, but numbers were rising again from 2012 to 2015.

In reality, this picture is misleading, as it incorporates a factor that significantly affects the data: namely, the opening in 2009 and subsequent operation of the new Acropolis Museum. Thus, the growth observed between 2008 and 2010 is due to the masses of visitors attracted to the Acropolis Museum during the first year of its operation. If studied separately, the number of visitors to all other archaeological museums during the same period dropped by 5 per cent a year

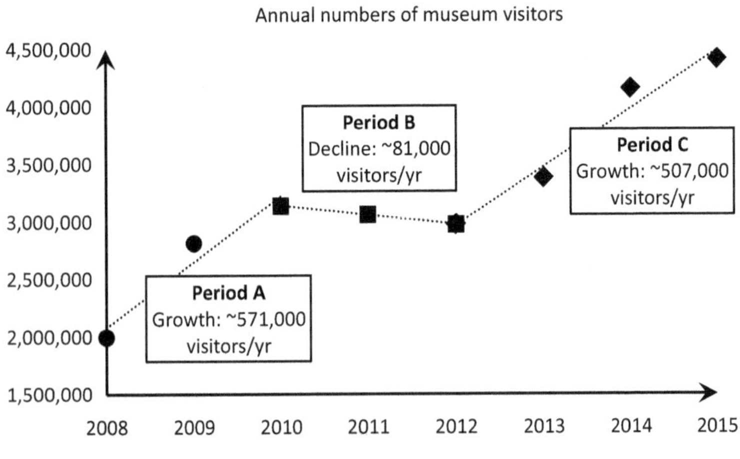

Chart 6.1 Annual numbers of museum visitors, 2008–2015. Data adapted from: ARF 2016, *personal communication*; ELSTAT, *Greece in Figures 2016*, (http://www.statistics.gr/documents/20181/1515741/GreeceInFigures_2016Q2_GR.pdf/b5554738-1829-4d4e-8b75-53b631b016fc)

(Chart 6.2). A similar rise (5 per cent/year) is seen until 2013, when numbers started rising significantly (21 per cent/year). On the other hand, in the Acropolis Museum, after peaking at just under 1.4 million tickets in 2010, visits declined by 12 per cent a year until 2012, growing thereafter by 7 per cent a year.

How should we interpret the data depicted in Charts 6.1 and 6.2? Firstly, it would be tempting to attribute the declining or relatively stagnant trends observed between 2008 and 2012 to the financial crisis. This seems to be in line with findings in other European countries. For example, according to a 2013 Eurobarometer report, there has been a marked decline in cultural participation across Europe, compared to figures recorded before the economic downturn.[47] This may reflect an overall reduction in the amount of money EU citizens spend on cultural activities within the current difficult economic circumstances. Interestingly, however, recent research on the demand for museums in Athens concluded that the reasons for not visiting are not primarily economic.[48] Ticket prices, for example, do not seem to affect visitors seriously.

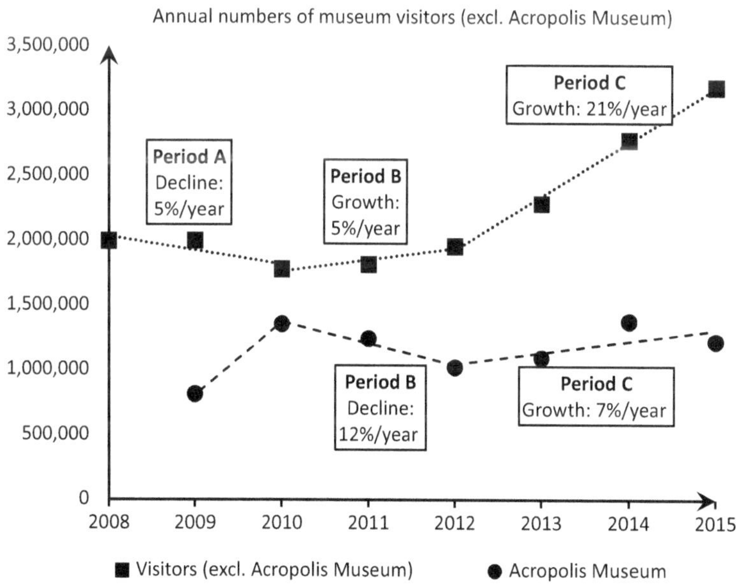

Chart 6.2 Visitors to archaeological museums (excl. Acropolis museum), 2008–2015. Data adapted from: ARF 2016, *personal communication*

What does seem to affect decisions about visiting are opening hours, time constraints, difficulty in understanding the content and lack of interest. Indeed, as discussed above, until very recently many Greek museums presented a picture which was unattractive to potential visitors. When this picture starts to change, a renewed interest in museums may be observed (see below).

Secondly, museum visiting has to be examined within the larger context of tourism in Greece, as any variation in tourist flow has a direct impact on museum visits. As shown in Chart 6.3, there is a strong correlation between the two lines. Indeed, between 2011 and 2015, museum visitors as a percentage of non-resident arrivals was, on average, 18.8 per cent with a remarkably low deviation.

In addition, the period 2012–2015 saw the re-opening after reorganization of major museums with high levels of recognizability such as the Herakleion Archaeological Museum (2014) and the organization of important large exhibitions such as 'The Antikythera Shipwreck: the Ship, the Treasures, the Mechanism' at the National

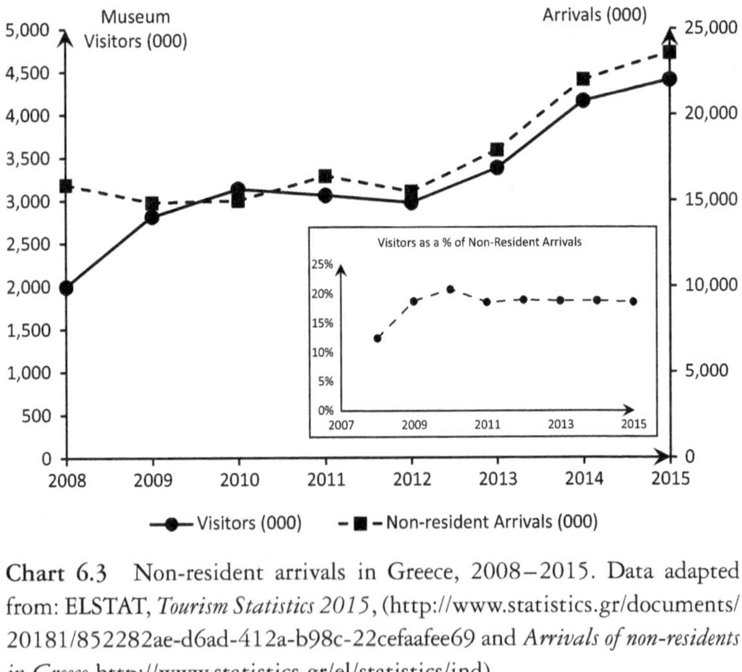

Chart 6.3 Non-resident arrivals in Greece, 2008–2015. Data adapted from: ELSTAT, *Tourism Statistics 2015*, (http://www.statistics.gr/documents/20181/852282ae-d6ad-412a-b98c-22cefaafee69 and *Arrivals of non-residents in Greece* http://www.statistics.gr/el/statistics/ind)

Archaeological Museum (2012–2014), which acted as magnets for Greek and international audiences alike.[49]

Finally, within the course of the last five or six years several museums, such as the Archaeological Museum of Thessaloniki, have renovated their services and launched a more vigorous public involvement. Other factors influencing museum visiting numbers could include the impact of industrial action and the predisposal of locals and tourists towards such an activity during the period under observation (2008–2015). This, though, should be the subject of further research.

Discussion

When the economic crisis hit Greece in 2009 the museum sector had a wide network of newly constructed or newly opened museums along with an admirable new infrastructure, made possible mainly through EU funding; the problem was that this infrastructure could not be sustained due to severe cuts in both financial and human resources. But, as will be suggested below, this was only one aspect of the problem.

Although the results of the financial crisis have had devastating effects on the country and Greek society at large, Greece was not the only country affected. In many European countries museums have traditionally relied on government funding; but, as state subsidies and corporate donations have been sinking steadily, new revenue sources are looked for. As can be witnessed everywhere, museums that depend entirely on state subsidies, or on a small number of alternative income sources, were more badly hit by the recession. It seems that the more autonomous institutions are, the more adaptable they are likely to be; while the less flexible ones are the most vulnerable.[50] Similarities with other European countries can also be observed in the merging of cultural institutions and the tendency of museum professionals to concentrate on internal museum functions instead of looking for networking opportunities and cooperation at a macro-level.[51]

In the Greek case, beyond its severe repercussions on museum finances and administration, the crisis has accentuated long-standing structural deficiencies relating to heritage management as a whole. The inner causes of these deficiencies must be traced to the monolithic view of national identity, based largely on archaeological heritage, and an unchanging approach to the past as a *legacy* which has to be protected through a rigid, centrally controlled, mechanism, instead of a *cultural resource*, which could be more openly shared and further exploited in a socially meaningful way. Apart from preventing the formation of an all-inclusive cultural policy, which would embrace all aspects of cultural expression equally, this attitude alienates the public from its heritage, making it hard for museums to seek local support.[52] This is particularly important, as it has been argued – at least in Europe – that in order to survive, museums should become increasingly dependent on local support. For that reason, this crisis may be viewed as an opportunity for museums to become more socially beneficial, particularly at the local level, and generate positive change in terms of more demand-oriented attitudes toward the various parts of society.[53]

The difficulty the Greek museum sector has experienced in adapting to the crisis in innovative ways also results from the emphasis traditionally given to the *social value* of heritage as opposed to any other value (e.g. financial). According to this view, any investment in culture (museums included) can only be repaid in social terms (e.g. education, quality of life). In practice, however, although nobody would challenge such an ideal, this notion of social value is rather vaguely expressed and rarely translated into truly inclusive strategies engaging communities, groups and individuals. The general lack of a participatory culture is reflected in the fact that the majority of public museums insist, even in the midst of the crisis, on providing old-style activities (such as educational programmes in the narrow sense), instead of investing in innovative ways to encourage genuine and long-term co-creation, cooperation and social inclusion. It should moreover be noted that, for reasons of cultural diplomacy, the central policy of both the Ministry and museums in general focuses on organizing exhibitions; these may attract large audiences and enhance a museum's overall profile, but they do not serve the cause of long-lasting public engagement well.

As shown above, heritage management in Greece is standardized, inflexible and does not support a culture of openness and sharing. This outdated mentality permeates the entire system and is to a large extent due to archaeologists' total control over the management of the country's museums. Because of their academic training (which neither equips them with cultural management skills[54] or with a real understanding of a museum's social impact) and their reluctance to delegate authority to other specialists or interested parties, archaeologists are generally not happy with change.[55] Consequently, irrespective of the current financial crisis, there is an urgent need for a complete paradigm shift.

Going back to the financial problem, this is also a question of attitude and policy. Things might have gone better if private cultural sponsorship and professional fundraising were more widespread (as is already the case in other European countries).[56] Unless this situation changes, the future for many museums is uncertain. In fact, research has shown that income diversification coupled with more focused management increases the financial stability and long-term sustainability of non-profit cultural organizations such as museums. It has further been suggested that the financial challenges facing museums are related more to structural and political issues than to fluctuating economic cycles.[57] Therefore, firm yet adjustable and diversified, strategic management can help reduce the vulnerability related to financial difficulties.

Dealing with the economic crisis and the changes in the world of museums requires complex competencies. Museums should be flexible, promote social participation, concentrate on strategic activities, develop networks, partnerships and cooperation, improve the competence of museum professionals and promote interdisciplinary and inter-professional networks.[58] We must consider the long-term sustainability of the sector, which goes beyond the purely financial. This applies especially to Greek state museums, which also need to redesign the entire range of future policies and operating conditions, and adopt a culture of sharing with larger segments of society.

Notes

1. The issue has been exhaustively discussed. For background see Yannis Hamilakis, *The Nation and its Ruins* (Oxford, 2007); Dimitris Damaskos and Dimitris Plantzos (eds), *A Singular Antiquity. Archaeology and Hellenic Identity in twentieth century Greece* (Athens, 2008). See also Andromache Gazi, 'National Museums in Greece; history, ideology, narratives' in P. Aronsson & G. Elgenius (eds), EuNaMus, *European National Museums: Identity Politics, the Uses of the Past and the European Citizen*, Report No. 1 (WP2) (Linköping, 2011), pp. 365–370. Available at www.ep.liu.se/ecp_article/index.en.aspx?issue=064;article=016 (accessed 30 July 2016).

2. Law 2121/1993 on 'Copyright, family rights and cultural matters' (available at: www.wipo.int/wipolex/en/text.jsp?file_id=127562) and Law 2557/1997 on 'Institutions, measures and actions for cultural development' (available at www.yppo.gr/files/g_1940.pdf).
3. Available at www.eui.eu/Projects/InternationalArtHeritageLaw/Documents/NationalLegislation/Greece/3028eng.pdf.
4. Law 3525/2007 on 'Cultural sponsorship'.
5. Daphne Voudouri, *Κράτος και μουσεία. Το θεσμικό πλαίσιο των αρχαιολογικών μουσείων* [State and Museums. The institutional framework of archaeological museums] (Athens, 2003): passim; Ester Solomon, Εισήγηση σε Στρογγυλή Τράπεζα, Διημερίδα του Συλλόγου Ελλήνων Αρχαιολόγων [Introduction to the round table. Conference of the Association of Greek Archaeologists] (Athens, 2016). Available at www.youtube.com/watch?v=ttRtdgODagU (accessed 30 August 2016).
6. 'Organization of the Ministry of Culture and Sports' (28 August 2014, article 10).
7. Marlen Mouliou, 'Το μουσείο ως ποιότητα, εμπειρία, αστικό σύμβολο και ήπια δύναμη. Παραδείγματα από τη διεθνή και εγχώρια μουσειακή πρακτική' [The museum as quality, experience, civic symbol and soft power. Examples from international and Greek museum practice] in I. Poulios et al. (eds) *Πολιτισμική διαχείριση, τοπική κοινωνία και βιώσιμη ανάπτυξη* [Cultural Management, Local Communities and Sustainable Development] (Athens, 2015), pp. 74–79.
8. Compendium 2013, *Cultural Policies and Trends in Europe*, Country profile GREECE, edited by C. Dallas. Available at www.culturalpolicies.net/down/greece_102013.pdf (accessed 27 August 2016), p. 8.
9. Yorgos Vavouranakis, 'The Greek economic crisis and its reverberations upon antiquities', *Predella* 36 (2013). Available at www.predella.it/index.php/current-issue/2-non-categorizzato/31-32-8-the-greek-economic-crisis-and-its-reverberations-upon-antiquities (accessed 30 August 2016).
10. The state's ambivalent approach to culture is clearly – and symbolically – reflected in the Ministry's changing structure. In 2009 it merged with the Ministry of Tourism; in 2012 it was downgraded to a General Secretariat within the then newly created Ministry of Education and Religious Affairs, Culture and Sports; in 2013 it was separated from Education to be established as Ministry of Culture and Sports; in early 2015 it was unified again with the Ministry of Education only to be renamed Ministry of Culture and Sports a few months later (Myrsini Zorba, 'Πολιτική του πολιτισμού στην Ελλάδα της κρίσης: Όροι και συνθήκες της αλλαγής παραδείγματος' [Cultural policy in Greece in times of crisis: terms and conditions of the paradigm shift], in D. Voudouri (ed.) *Διαχείριση πολιτιστικών οργανισμών σε περίοδο κρίσης*, Πρακτικά διημερίδας [The management of cultural institutions in a period of crisis. Conference proceedings] (Athens, 2013), pp. 13–19. Available at www.cl.ly/0Y191s0l3w41# (accessed 25 July 2016); Myrsini

Zorba, 'Cultural policy under conditions of economic crisis', *International Conference on Public Policy* (Milan, 2015). Available at www.icpublicpolicy.org/conference/.../1433832974.pdf (accessed 25 August 2016). Obviously, this lack of clear orientation renders long-term strategic planning almost impossible.

11. The notion of museum accreditation was introduced in 2002 and ratified in 2011. An interdisciplinary working group was set up to draft relevant documents, which were then made available online for public consultation in 2014. In March 2016 the Ministry organized a conference to present the scheme and discuss it with interested stakeholders (Teti Hadjinicolaou, Το ελληνικό σύστημα αναγνώρισης μουσείων [The Greek system of museum accreditation], Ημερίδα *Αναγνώριση μουσείων*, Υπουργείο Πολιτισμού (Athens, 2016). Available at www.blod.gr/lectures/Pages/viewlecture.aspx?LectureID=2674 (accessed 11July 2016). The details are still being formulated. Although in reality the scheme pertains to museums which are not owned by the state, its implementation will mark a major breakthrough in the Greek museum sector.
12. Sofia Tsilidou, 'Greece' in M. Hagedorn-Saupe and A. Ermert (eds), *A Guide to European Museum Statistics* (Berlin, 2004), p. 60. Available at: www.egmus.eu/fileadmin/statistics/Dokumente/A_guide_to-European_Museum_Statistics.pdf (accessed 25 August 2016).
13. Ministry of Culture, Directorate of Museums, Unit of Public Archaeological Museums and Collections; September 2016, personal communication.
14. This list also includes the Museum of Asiatic Art (Corfu) and the Museum of Greek Folk Art (Athens).
15. See 'Organization of the Ministry of Culture' (13 May 2003, article 2). In 2014 they acquired the rather confusing status of 'Public Museums'.
16. Alexandra Bounia, 'Cultural Policy in Greece, the Case of the National Museums (1990–2010): an Overview' in L. Eilersten and A. Bugge Amundsen (eds), *Museum Policies in Europe 1990–2010: Negotiating Professional and Political Utopia* (Linköping, 2012), pp. 127–156.
17. Ibid., p. 132. The issue of separating museums from their respective regional Ephorates has been repeatedly discussed on various occasions, most recently at the 2016 Conference of the Association of Greek Archaeologists (see, inter alia, the final round table, available at www.youtube.com/watch?v=ttRtdgODagU, accessed 6 September 2016).
18. See, inter alia, Association of Greek Archaeologists, 'Ο ρόλος των δημόσιων μουσείων' [The role of public museums], Εισαγωγική εισήγηση στη στρογγυλή τράπεζα *Ο ρόλος των δημόσιων μουσείων σήμερα*, Σύλλογος Ελλήνων Αρχαιολόγων [Introduction to the round table: The role of public museums today. Association of Greek Archaeologists] (Athens, 2008). Available at www.sea.org.gr/details.php?id=248 (accessed 1 July 2016).
19. Mouliou, Το μουσείο ως ποιότητα, [The museum as quality] p. 78.

20. Exploiting the administrative autonomy of the museum to the full, the late Dimitris Konstantios managed to bypass the rigid management structure and ventured into areas previously unexplored by state museums (Dimitris Konstantios, 'Μια άλλη πολιτική είναι εφικτή' [Another policy is feasible], *ILISSIA* 1, pp. 4–13; Gazi, National Museums, pp. 383–384.
21. Over the last decade the museum has been turned into a lively hub of cultural activity for the city; see Polyxeni Adam-Veleni, 'Εκπαιδεύοντας τη Ρίτα: η επικοινωνιακή και εκθεσιακή πολιτική του Αρχαιολογικού Μουσείου Θεσσαλονίκης 2007–2009' [Educating Rita: the communication and exhibition policy of the Archaeological Museum of Thessaloniki 2007–2009] in *Το Αρχαιολογικό Έργο στη Μακεδονία και τη Θράκη* 23 (Thessaloniki, 2013), pp. 303–318.
22. Theodore Metaxas and Alexis Deffner, 'Marketing, management and promotion policies of city image: defining the role and the contribution of public museums in Greece' (pp. 125–26), in A. Bounia, N. Nikonanou and M. Economou (eds) *Technology in the Service of Cultural Heritage: Management, Education, Communication* (Athens, 2008), pp. 117–129.
23. Compendium, *Greece*, p. 34.
24. See, for instance, the Ministry of Finance Analytical Report for the fiscal year 2011, available at www.minfin.gr/sites/default/files/financial_files/proypol2011_eis_ektesh.pdf, pp. 83–84.
25. Archaeological Receipts Fund, September 2016, *personal communication*.
26. Zorba, Cultural policy, pp. 359–378; Vassilis Avdikos, *Οι πολιτιστικές και δημιουργικές βιομηχανίες στην Ελλάδα* [*Cultural and Creative Industries in Greece*] (Athens, 2014), pp. 173–187.
27. Lila Mendoni, 'Πολιτισμός και ανάπτυξη: Η ανταποδοτικότητα των δημοσίων επενδύσεων σε περίοδο οικονομικής κρίσης' [Culture and development: The benefit of public investments in times of economic crisis], Εισήγηση στην Ημερίδα *Η κοινωνική και οικονομική διάσταση των έργων του τομέα πολιτισμού* [Introduction to the colloquium The social and economic dimensions of the work of the cultural sector] (Athens, 2014). Available at www.ep.culture.gr/Lists/Custom_Announcements/Attachments/174/Politismos.kai.Anaptyksi_Mendwni.Aug.2014.ppt (accessed 5 September 2016).
28. Angeliki Petrou, *Balancing Preservation and Utilization in Greek Museum Policy: the case of EU regional policy investments in state regional archaeological museums*, PhD dissertation, National Graduate Institute for Policy Studies (Tokyo, 2015), p. 118. Available at www.grips.repo.nii.ac.jp/?action=repository_action_common_download&item_id=1339&item_no=1&attribute_id=25&file_no=3 (accessed 25 August 2016).
29. Final report, *Τελική έκθεση εφαρμογής του προγράμματος ΠΟΛΙΤΙΣ ΜΟΣ 2000–2006* [Final report on the implementation of the POLITISMOS 2000–20006 programme]. Available at: www.ep.culture.gr/el/Documents/%CE%95%CE%A0%20%CE%A0%CE%9F%CE%9B%CE%99%CE%A4%CE%99%CE%A3%CE%9C%CE%9F%CE%A3%202000-2006/Teliki.Ekthesi.

2000_2006.zip (accessed 1 September 2016); Konstantinos Moussouroulis, 'Αποτελέσματα των παρεμβάσεων στον πολιτισμό από τα ΚΠΣ' (Results of CSF interventions in the field of culture), *Tetradia Politismou* 1 (2007), pp. 141–155. Available at www.new.culture.gr/DocLib/g_30885.pdf (accessed 20 July 2016).

30. Zorba, Conceptualizing Greek cultural policy, p. 255.
31. Maria Vlazaki, Ομιλία Γενικής Γραμματέως [Speech of the Ministry of Culture's General Secretary], Ημερίδα *Η μετάβαση από το ΕΣΠΑ 2007–2013 στο ΕΣΠΑ 2014–2020: Απολογισμός δράσεων, επιτεύγματα, προβλήματα και σχεδιασμός νέου προγράμματος*, Υπουργείο Πολιτισμού [Colloquium *The transition from NSRP 2007 – 2013 to NSRP 2014 – 2020: an account of activities, achievements, problems and drafting of the new programme*, Ministry of Culture] (Athens, 2016). Available at www.ep.culture.gr/Lists/Custom_Announcements/Attachments/189/2016.04.20.Omilia.Vlazaki.doc (accessed 15 September 2016).
32. Ministry of Culture, *Special Service of the Sector for Culture* (EYTOP), September 2016, personal communication.
33. Vlazaki, ibid.
34. For an overall picture, see the video 'The contribution of NSRF to the Greek culture', available at: www.youtu.be/BUz50hZTI28 (accessed 15 September 2016).
35. Cherkea Howery, 'The effects of the economic crisis on archaeology in Greece', *Journal of Eastern Mediterranean Archaeology and Heritage Studies* 1/3 (2013), p. 231.
36. Sofia Tsilidou, 'Rethinking museum value in times of crisis: a European perspective' (2014), pp. 3–4. Available at www.ne-mo.org/news/article/nemo/article-rethinking-museum-value-in-times-of-crisis-a-european-perspective.html (accessed 17 July2016); Howery, *The effects of the economic crisis*, p. 229.
37. Ioannes Georganas, 'The effects of the economic crisis on Greek heritage: A view from the private cultural sector', *Journal of Eastern Mediterranean Archaeology and Heritage Studies* 1/3 (2013), p. 242.
38. See www.benaki.gr/index.asp?id=7&sid=0&cat=0&lang=en and www.benaki.gr/index.asp?lang=en&id=701 respectively.
39. Ninetta Kontrarou-Rassia, 'Ένα μουσείο επιτίθεται στην κρίση' [A museum attacks the crisis], *Ελευθεροτυπία*, 7 July 2010. Available at: www.enet.gr/?i=news.el.article&id=180920.
40. www.5museums.gr/.
41. www.athensmuseums.net/index.php?lang=en.
42. Bounia, Cultural Policy in Greece, p. 141.
43. See, for example, Agathoniki Tsilipakou, interviewed by N. Pappas, *Elliniki Gnomi*. Kultur/Geschichte, 14 December 2013. Available at www.elliniki-gnomi.eu/ (accessed 2 August 2016).
44. Anastassia Lazaridou, 'Μουσεία σε κρίση;' [Museums in crisis?] in Voudouri, *Διαχείριση πολιτιστικών οργανισμών* [Management of cultural organizations], pp. 72–75.

45. The same tendency to re-evaluate priorities and practices and move in the direction of resilience and self-management is also observed in the field of art museums and contemporary culture in general (Syrago Tsiara, 'Contemporary Greek Art in Times of Crisis: Cuts and Changes', *Journal of Visual Culture* 14/2 (2015), pp. 176–181.
46. It should be noted that only the overall number of visitors is recorded, without reference to their demographic or other profile.
47. Eurobarometer, *Cultural Access and Participation*, Special Report 399, European Commission, Directorate General for Education and Culture (2013). Available at www.ec.europa.eu/public_opinion/archives/ebs/ebs_399_en.pdf (accessed 27 August 2016).
48. Anastasia Doxanaki, 'Τα αρχαιολογικά μουσεία και η επικοινωνία τους με το κοινό: Ανασταλτικοί παράγοντες επιρροής στο μοτίβο της επισκεψιμότητας των αρχαιολογικών μουσείων της Αθήνας' (Archaeological museums and their communication with the public: inhibiting factors influencing the pattern of archaeological museum visiting in Athens), *Mouseio* 8 & 9, (2013) pp. 60–71.
49. Initially intended to run from April 2012 to April 2013, this exhibition, which was made possible thanks to courageous sponsorship, attracted vast audiences and was extended until June 2014 (www.namuseum.gr/exhibitions/temporary/%CE%91ntikythera/mechanism_ant-gr.html).
50. Ilde Rizzo, 'Museums facing the crisis: challenge or opportunity?' in European Museum Academy (ed.), *Proceedings of The Kenneth Hudson Seminars* 2009–2010 (Pisa, 2010), pp. 47–59. Available at www.europeanmuseumacademy.eu/4/upload/kh_seminar_proceedings.pdf (accessed 5 September 2016).
51. Clara Frayão-Camaho, 'Restructuring governmental organizations on museums in European countries: A change of paradigm for a better management?' in *Public Policies Toward Museums in Times of Crisis*, ICOM Portugal and ICOM Europe Joint Conference (Lisbon, 2013), pp. 27–32. Available at www.issuu.com/mapadasideiaspt/docs/icom_view_final (accessed 15 September 2016).
52. Vavouranakis, The Greek economic crisis.
53. Michelle Stefano, 'Responding to change: the economic crisis, museums and ecomuseological opportunities' in European Museum Academy (ed.), *Proceedings of The Kenneth Hudson Seminars* 2009–2010 (Pisa, 2010), pp. 47–59. Available at www.europeanmuseumacademy.eu/4/upload/kh_seminar_proceedings.pdf (accessed 5 September 2016); Rizzo, Museums facing the crisis, pp. 47–59.
54. See, for instance, DISCO, 'Discovering the Archaeologists of Greece 2012–14', Report published as part of the *Discovering the Archaeologists of Europe 2012–14* (York, 2014). Available at www.discovering-archaeologists.eu/greece.html (accessed 30 July 2016).
55. Although this is being repeatedly noted and discussed (see, among others, Hamilakis, *The Nation and its Ruins*; Voudouri, *Κράτος και μουσεία* [State and museums]), reluctance to change lingers on. The public round table

organized as part of the 2016 Conference of the Association of Greek Archaeologists is revealing (see, for example, Yorgos Vavouranakis, Εισήγηση στη Στρογγυλή Τράπεζα που οργανώθηκε στο πλαίσιο της Διημερίδας του Συλλόγου Ελλήνων Αρχαιολόγων (Athens, 2016). Available at www.youtube.com/watch?v=ttRtdgODagU (accessed 30 August 2016); Solomon, Εισήγηση [Introduction].

56. Georganas, The effects of the economic crisis, p. 245.
57. Katja Lindqvist, 'Museum finances: challenges beyond economic crises', *Museum Management and Curatorship* 27/1 (2012), 1–15.
58. Alberto Garlandini, 'Museums in a changing world: Eight key points to defy the global crisis', in *Public Policies toward Museums in Times of Crisis*, ICOM Portugal and ICOM Europe Joint Conference (Lisbon, 2013), pp. 33–38. Available at www.issuu.com/mapadasideiaspt/docs/icom_view_final (accessed 15 September 2016).

CHAPTER 7

FEASTS IN TIME OF 'PLAGUE': FESTIVALS OF WESTERN ART MUSIC IN GREECE DURING THE CRISIS

Katerina Levidou

The paradox

Who needs classical music? The question was posed by Julian Johnson in his polemic of 2002, long before the outbreak of the economic and socio-cultural crisis that has affected the entire Western world in recent years.[1] The answer to it might seem straightforward for those that have first-hand experience of the perils with which contemporary Greece specifically has been faced since the outbreak of the crisis.[2] And yet, the country's cultural reality disproves what might seem the obvious reply through one area of musical activity specifically: the paradoxical and unprecedented blossoming of festivals of Western art music.[3] Indeed, nowadays festivals of Western art music map the contemporary Greek landscape in their own, singular way, with most Greek towns and islands – certainly the major ones – hosting at least one such festival, which usually takes place during the summer. The case of the recently-founded 'Koufonissia Classical', for instance, which ran for the second year in the summer of 2016, reveals the astonishing vitality of such festival activity, as it reaches the most unexpected destinations, even as the crisis shows hardly any sign of retreating.[4] And all this, despite the severe challenges with which the field of Western art music is currently faced, namely, the funding cuts in culture due to the economic crisis, the shrinking of the audience of Western art music (the so-called 'classical' music) worldwide, as well as the limited popularity of this art form in a country with no strong tradition in this area, such as Greece.[5]

What do such 'feasts in time of plague',[6] to paraphrase the title of Alexander Pushkin's play, have to tell us about contemporary Greece, its culture, its musical life more specifically, and the crisis itself? To start with, it should be noted that the condition of crisis has traditionally been associated with artistic creativity in multiple ways. The perception that crises, personal or otherwise, are fruitful for the arts, triggering inspiration as well as innovation, giving birth to masterpieces or just boosting artists' productivity, is a Romantic conception, that survives, to a lesser degree, up to the present day. More broadly speaking, a sense of crisis in historical, social and cultural terms can give rise to artistic movements, as the case of modernism reveals, which broadly took the shape of an artistic response to a sense of crisis of the modern world.

The current, global financial recession has also been discussed with respect to the way it has stimulated artistic production, notably even giving birth to crisis-specific genres.[7] The case of Greece itself, and Greek literature, more specifically, has come into focus in recent research.[8] However, as regards Western art music, by no means does the thriving festival activity outlined earlier reflect the broader picture. Indeed, most orchestras, music ensembles and cultural organizations associated with Western art music in Greece have been faced with severe difficulties, some of them struggling to survive, sometimes to no avail – for instance the Orchestra of Colours, founded by Manos Hatzidakis in 1989 – due to the recession.[9] At the same time, music education has felt the repercussions of the crisis even more deeply due to shortage of manpower and infrastructure and long-term deficient government planning.[10]

While examining the explosion of festivals of Western art music in contemporary Greece, we are faced with the complete absence of previous research on the matter. Indeed, no study of Greek festivals of Western art music before the outbreak of the crisis exists, which would have facilitated the comparison between the pre- and post-2008 circumstances; not to mention the overall lacuna, more broadly, in research on Western art music festivals at the international level.[11]

This is, therefore, the first study to focus on festivals of Western art music in Greece. It offers, firstly, an overview of the relevant festival activity in recent years, and, subsequently, an analysis of the key factors that have enabled the blossoming of such festivals under the unfavourable conditions of the crisis.[12] Drawing both on historiographical as well as ethnomusicological methods, I examine festivals not with respect to their repertoire and participating musicians – an approach dictated by traditional music historiography – neither from the perspective of cultural management, as is often the case in the bibliography. Instead, music festivals are considered as 'cultural performances' – namely performances that communicate and express the gist of a specific culture, in other words, a means through which a culture performs itself.[13] In analysing the factors that have facilitated the blossoming of such festivals in recent years, I shall focus on specific practices, and changes in practices, by looking at the broader picture, while at the same time referring to distinctive examples from particular festivals.[14]

The presence of Western art music festivals in Greece

Although the human need for public celebration of various landmarks in the circle of life dates back to the ancient times and has assumed multiple forms,[15] the beginning of modern urban festivals as we know them in contemporary times may be traced in the nineteenth century and is interlinked with city development as well as the consolidation of the bourgeoisie, and more particularly with urban elites.[16] At about the same time, though, rural music and drama summer festivals, which took place in ancient theatres, flourished in the south of France, aspiring to revive the ancient Greek civilization.[17] In a similar spirit, the exploitation of the Greek landscape and archaeological sites lies at the heart of the emergence of festivals in modern Greece in the twentieth century; the Delphic Festivals (organized in 1927 and 1930), organized by Angelos Sikelianos and Eva Palmer-Sikelianou, is an early exponent of this trend.

The systematic promotion of festivals in Modern Greece, though, is a postwar phenomenon and is closely associated with state and private efforts to boost tourism specifically – see especially the Athens and Epidaurus Festivals, founded in 1955.[18] The institution of festivals spread in Greece thanks to state funding provided to local authorities since the 1980s for the organization of festivals in particular, in the context of the Greek accession to the EU, as a means of aligning the country with European models.[19] Numerous festivals were founded, many of which faded away in the end due to organizational, administrative and financial difficulties. The overall sense of prosperity that surrounded the organization of the 2004 Athens Olympic Games, and the funding that was made available for cultural projects, gave a boost to culture more generally, and festival activity more specifically, laying the foundations for the present picture.[20]

My survey of festivals of Western art music in Greece since 2008, undertaken between April 2014 and July 2015, brought to the fore the infeasibility of the task of compiling a complete record of such events. Indeed, spotting some of them is challenging, particularly the local, smaller ones, that is, those with less visibility and limited means of advertising (for example, in the press and through the internet).[21] Elsewhere I have published an indicative list of 91 such festivals, which took place at least once between 2008 and 2015 and included in their programme at least one concert of Western art music (even though very few involved just one such concert).[22] The term 'Western art music' has deliberately been selected over 'classical' music for embracing music that belongs to the extended respective musical tradition stretching from the Middle Ages up to contemporary exponents and recent experimentations. Such festivals are usually organized in the form of a series of concerts (81.3 per cent). Among the most renowned ones dedicated to Western art music exclusively are the Nafplio Festival, inaugurated in 1991, and the more recent International Music Festival of Cyclades, founded in 2004 on the basis of the very same idea, namely, promoting Western art music at an idyllic summer destination with a prominent bourgeois profile. Sometimes, the element of competition is included as well, particularly in the case of choir festivals. Less frequently, festivals combine concerts with music masterclasses (18.7 per cent), as happens with the numerous guitar festivals that take place throughout Greece, some of them organized by the same artistic director. Competition is a feature of some festivals belonging to this category too, such as the International Piano Festival – Poros (established in 2009). In both cases, festivals at times also comprise events that involve the other arts, arts exhibitions, talks and so on – see, for instance, the Aegean Arts International Festival, founded in 2014. As for their geographical distribution within the country, the festivals in question are held primarily on the mainland (58.24 per cent), although a significant number of them are organized on islands (36.3 per cent) and just 5.5 per cent take place on both.

The explosion of festivals of Western art music in contemporary Greece, as well as their persistence under unfavourable circumstances over the last few years, should undoubtedly be viewed in association with the main functions such festivals serve. Indeed, in a country where familiarity with this musical tradition, and its popularity, are even lower than in most other European countries, the blossoming of such festivals is less a matter of satisfying an existing large demand for this repertoire than a question of increasing the supply in order to facilitate the key purposes such festivals serve, namely, networking, education and tourism. As regards networking, it involves primarily artistic networking both on the national and the international level. Hence, an invitation to participate in a festival extended by its artistic director to a musician who runs another festival, either in Greece or abroad, will be reciprocated by an invitation by the latter to the former to perform at their own event. Such artistic exchanges occur frequently in the Greek milieu in particular; for instance, the artistic directors of the Nafplio Festival, the International Music Festival of Cyclades, the International Music Festival of Aegina (inaugurated in 2006) and the Piraeus Sinfonia Festival (the latter founded in 2012, in response to a funding call of the National Strategic Reference Network (ESPA)) have performed at each other's festival, while often their programmes share certain musicians, or ensembles, or thematic concerts. At the same time, festivals may facilitate political networking and public relations as well. The distribution of concert invitations to a cycle of the few 'privileged' has been a popular means towards this end. This has been a long-standing practice, among others, at the Nafplio Festival, and its suspension at the 23rd edition (in 2014), owing to shortage of funding due to the crisis, triggered widespread discontent, despite the low ticket price (5 euros per concert, 25 for a full pass to the festival).

The second major purpose festivals of Western art music serve, education, becomes quite explicit when it comes to festivals that include the element of seminars or masterclasses on a particular instrument, or on music more generally. The *Μουσικό Χωριό* [Music Village] (inaugurated in 2006), offering music seminars not strictly on a specific instrument, but on musical genres and ensembles more broadly, is a renowned exemplar and, actually, a pioneering exponent.[23] Yet, the organizers' objective to use festivals for educational purposes is not restricted to structured music lessons. For festivals, thanks to the concentration of musical activity in a short period of time and, sometimes, their thematic orientation, have been aiming to cultivate their audience, primarily the local society, more broadly speaking, to acquaint it with Western art music and initiate it into the ritual of Western art music concerts and practices associated with this musical tradition, such as the culture of applauding only at the end of a musical work rather than between its movements. This has been the vision of the founders of the Nafplio Festival as well as the International Music Festival of Cyclades; and, in fact, the choice of place for those events was based on the conviction that bourgeois societies, such as that of Nafplio and Syros, are more receptive to the musical tradition of Western art music, hence those festivals stood better chances of flourishing. However, even in cases where no such fertile ground existed, 'taming' the local society has been a challenge festival organizers have decided to take on at certain occasions, and under difficult circumstances. Crete is a case in point, and the festivals Serenata Kriti and the Aegean Arts International Festival, founded (both notably during the crisis, in 2013 and 2014 respectively) and run by foreigners who have settled in Greece, have had as their primary aim to introduce Western art music to the local community.

Last but not least, tourism is a major motive for most organizers of festivals of Western art music, particularly those that take place over the summer and beyond the large urban centres.[24] Tourism, for instance, often serves as enticement at choir festivals, especially those that involve amateur musicians. Events such as the established International Choral Festival of Preveza (which ran its 34th edition in 2016) and the Festival of the Aegean, organized in Syros since 2005, aim to provide an exceptional tourist experience to members of the participating choirs shaped by the uniqueness of the local landscape and the feeling of community, membership and participation emanating from living the festival experience. The opportunity to have a paid holiday in Greece has a lure for many professional musicians from abroad as well, even if no additional reward is offered, as in the case of Serenata Kriti, which has managed to recruit in this way members of some distinguished British orchestras. Finally, festivals of Western art music, contributing to the enrichment of the local cultural life overall, improve a place's potential to attract tourists from elsewhere in the country as well as from abroad.[25] It should be noted, though, that choir festivals have admittedly invested more in their potential to appeal to tourists – since participation involves mainly visiting choristers – than have festivals consisting primarily of concerts, which have tended to concentrate to a greater extent on the event's capacity to integrate into the local community. The following discussion illuminates the latter tendency, and the role it has played in the survival of festivals of Western art music during the period of the economic and socio-cultural crisis, with an emphasis on the case of the Nafplio Festival.

Tuning into the local community

Traditionally, festivals have relied heavily on the local community, which would take the leading role in organizing them, as well as participating in the events in question. Yet, the part played by the local community in a festival's success has also been acknowledged in the case of contemporary events, even when they are organized externally; in fact, as mentioned already, the local society has been the primary concern of certain festivals of Western art music, such as Serenata Kriti and the Aegean Arts International Festival, whose main objective has been to educate it. As one of the organizers declared, 'I feel, how should I put it, that I'm introducing classical music to Crete. I wanted some old ladies, some older people, some small children whose parents do not even know what this is, to see this; I wanted to show them that this music also exists. This is a thing foreigners do.'[26]

The different kind of relationship each of those festivals – which otherwise share some striking common characteristics – has developed with the local community, and its impact on the event's success, are telling for the importance of a festival's integration into a specific place. Indeed, both of those events were founded during the crisis by foreigners, female in both cases, who settled in Crete: Serenata Kriti, by a Briton and an Australian former inhabitant of Britain, who moved to the island after retirement; the Aegean Arts International Festival, by a Briton married to a Cretan man. Both events are non-profitable enterprises, the former offering their earnings to charity, the latter providing free entry concerts. Although in both cases the organizers share the common vision of initiating Cretans to Western art music, thus making a substantial contribution to the island and its people, in practice the Aegean Arts International Festival has accomplished a much greater degree of acceptance by the locals and integration than Serenata Kriti, which in effect has ended up with a very limited audience comprising almost exclusively of British expatriates in Crete, the very community its organizers belong to. Such alienation has no doubt resulted from specific practices that have discouraged the Greek population from attending in the case of Serenata Kriti. The language barrier is certainly a significant factor, since the organizers of Serenata Kriti, in contradistinction to that of the Aegean Arts International Festival, do not speak Greek, and demonstrate no intention of learning it, an issue that creates some distance from the locals. At the same time, the decision of the Serenata Kriti organizers to discourage concert attendance by young children has surely put off locals, especially in a country where the institution of family still holds such a prominent place. Finally, the Aegean Arts International Festival has been more successful in getting the local community involved through voluntarism, thus building bridges of communication with the local people. By encouraging locals to contribute through unpaid work, for instance by distributing concert programmes, welcoming the audience, taking care of the piano (polishing it, covering it in order to protect it from the sun), and offering dinner to the artists after the concerts, the local community has eventually felt that the event is theirs, that they are proud of it and wish to help promote it.[27] Consequently, the practices each festival has employed have resulted in different kinds of relationship with the locals and, by extension, different degrees of success, affecting the event's viability.

The challenges which some festivals have faced in the period of the economic and socio-cultural crisis, have on certain occasions urged the organizers to review their policy and proceed to changes in long-established practices, thus facilitating the event's adjustment to the new circumstances and improvement of its chances of outliving the crisis. Such changes were evident, for example, in the 23rd edition of the Nafplio Festival, which took place in June 2014, and are, in fact, reflective of recent tendencies witnessed in the realm of Western art music in Greece more broadly. There are three main areas in which such changes in practices have occurred, which have facilitated the survival of festivals by improving their relationship with the local community: (a) the festival target group, where practices have been modified in order to enable the broadening of the audience; (b) the choice of venue, which relates to modes of concert attendance; and (c) the choice of 'product', namely, changes in musical choices with respect to the repertoire.

Founded in 1991 by the respectable Greek pianist (now resident in Paris), Yannis Vakarelis, the Nafplio Festival managed to establish itself in the town through his successful directorship, and the generosity of sponsors such as Ballantine's whiskey and later Rolex – both factors enabling the inclusion in the festival programme of top quality artists in the past. In fact, the festival has become an institution nowadays, and is identified as a central component of the town's very identity, having been fervently embraced by the locals. This is not to say, though, that it has addressed everyone. Its identity has been closely intertwined with an 'elite' of a select few belonging to the local as well as the Athenian middle class (who would often travel to the town just to enjoy a concert). For many of those festival fans, attending the festival is a status symbol, since some reportedly show up merely so as to be seen there, an act of enhancing their sense of belonging to that group. As one of my interlocutors put it 'There is the audience of the foyer and the audience of the inside hall. Many people just go in order to be seen and to see who else is going. [...] Some have to go because it is part of who they are.'[28]

Members of the board of the Municipal Organisation of Sports, Culture, Tourism and Environment of Nafplio (known as DOPPAT) have clearly sensed the perils posed by the crisis – which has, admittedly, given them the upper hand over the last few years, since the shortage of private funding has made this organization the festival's main sponsor. At the same time, they have grasped the disappointment of part of the local community, which feels excluded from the Nafplio Festival.[29] Thus, in my discussions with representatives of DOPPAT, the need for change and of opening up the festival to a wider audience surfaced. Moreover, issues such as building relations with the local conservatories throughout the year, working on the festival's connection with tourism, or even more radical ideas, such as using venues in the broader Nafplio area, which would encourage more people to attend, emerged.

Although Vakarelis has taken pains to develop over many years, and in fact to cultivate, the festival's dedicated audience, while at the same time, shaping the festival as an elitist and prestigious event, in recent years he has proved open to taking Western art music outside its 'habitat', the concert hall, as reflected, for instance by his suggestion to hold a free entry concert on Nafplio's main square, Syntagma Square, in the festival's 2014 edition. Open air venues have been employed in the past by the Nafplio Festival, for instance St George's square; yet the spaces were protected by using barriers, in order to prohibit vehicles entering the area, thus aiming to restrict the noise, but also allowing attendance only to ticket holders. The practice of organizing open air events of classical music in Greece had been controversial, especially during the years of prosperity before the crisis, the period when concert attendance at the Athens Concert Hall became a status symbol and open air concerts were frowned upon. Yet, with the outbreak of the crisis, and the precarious place Western art music has acquired in contemporary culture, concert and festival organizers have found this a useful means of broadening their target group.[30] Therefore, by proposing a free entry concert on Syntagma Square in Nafplio, a decision that would mark a radical change to audience access to the festival, Vakarelis was aligning himself with the latest trends in the realm of Western art music in Greece.

Finally, another area in which the festival artistic director has traced fertile ground in appealing to a greater audience is the repertoire, by introducing one concert of lighter music (a high-brow popular musical genre known in Greece as the popular 'art' genre, the *entehno*). The inclusion of lighter choices – very often the opera being considered as such – is another wide-spreading practice among Greek institutions of classical music. The International Music Festival of Cyclades, which is devoted to the challenging, for many, repertoire of chamber music, specifically, has embraced over the last few years the opera as a secondary theme, in an attempt to attract a broader audience through a more accessible repertoire. The 23rd edition of the Nafplio Festival followed this lead by including a concert (on 25 June 2014) which merged the genre of opera with a string ensemble of mandolins.

The case of Nafplio, therefore, is a most interesting example of negotiating practices through the interaction of two institutions, the festival itself and the local authorities (DOPPAT), and at the same time the interaction of private and public initiatives. And notably the practices that encourage innovation and further integration of the festival into the local community have come from both directions, in investing in its relevance for the people and, by extension, its survival in the years to come.

Tuning into the crisis: Changes on the artistic and economic level

> KL: What has been the effect of the crisis?
>
> X: It has affected us to an incredible extent. Because you cannot make a single move for the next year. [. . .] [Y]ou cannot produce a programme in time. Then again, you have to be ready at any point to face [the issue of] an agreement breach on your behalf, which you will be forced to do, that is taken for granted. How will you fill the gap with as little cost for the institution as possible? [. . .] Our problem is a financial one, not a problem of ideas.
>
> [. . .]
>
> KL: Are there cases of musicians who perform without payment?
>
> X: Of course there are. First and foremost, at my own festival. And if someone asks me to help somehow because there is no payment involved, I will go, so that my own festival can survive too.
>
> (Excerpt from my interview with a festival artistic director)[31]

A map of Western art music festivals in Greece over the years of the crisis would suggest that this is an area of unprecedented cultural prosperity. Yet, by no means should the difficulties with which the organizers of such events are faced be overlooked. In truth, the circumstances of the crisis have called for many compromises, from various parties, on the artistic as well as the economic level. To start with, the crisis has affected festivals as regards the artistic quality of their concert programmes, due to funding shortage. Although in the past certain events had figured some celebrated names in their programmes, the Nafplio Festival being renowned in that respect, the crisis has made the inclusion of expensive productions in the festivals' programme prohibitive; neither is there a question of costly invitations of musicians and ensembles from abroad. The festival duration and frequency have also been reduced, in response to lack of funds. Finally, organizers have developed a more relaxed attitude towards the repertoire, as mentioned already, and are advancing a more inclusive approach towards lighter choices or even popular music, aiming to render their event attractive to a wider audience.

On the economic plane, a factor that has facilitated festival activity despite the recession is their flexibility as regards modes of funding. Actually, the crisis has brought about major changes in the roles of private initiative and the public sector with respect to the organization of festivals. Municipalities are no longer the main driving force behind those events, or, indeed, their sponsors, as they used to be since the 1980s. Nowadays, local authorities are frequently involved in festival organization merely as supporters, and this entails providing venues for free or waiving taxation. The Nafplio Festival, which has been relying heavily on sponsorship by the local municipality in the period of crisis, is, in fact, one of the very few exceptions. Therefore, compared to other cultural areas, festivals have been affected less because they depend, to a great extent, on private initiative and funding, and much less on public funds. Private initiative usually involves fundraising on the part of artistic directors and production companies, often drawing on the artistic director's own personal acquaintances. It may also entail applications made for state or EU-funding, as in the case of the Piraeus Sinfonia Festival, as already indicated.

The connection with tourism has most certainly contributed greatly to the survival and blossoming of festivals of Western art music, particularly those that take place in the summer. In this context, festivals figure as an appealing investment, despite the broader grim economic situation, although they rarely manage to lure independent tourists. Yet, as already indicated, participation in a festival, primarily with respect to choir festivals, involves tourism, and that also applies to foreign musicians who agree to perform at a festival by being rewarded merely with a paid holiday in Greece. Foreign consulates often play an important role as well, since they appear as festival sponsors by funding travel of foreign musicians to Greece in order to perform at festivals. Thanks to this connection with tourism, individuals, and whenever possible the state (that is, municipalities), are encouraged to invest in festivals. It is telling that, as one of my interlocutors pointed out, in July the island of Syros practically lives on the Festival of the Aegean, which manages to attract a vast number of participants from all around the world.[32] Actually, this is one of the reasons why this festival is more popular with the locals than the other renowned festival of the island, the International Music Festival of Cyclades – the repertoire being the second major factor, since the former festival focuses on the opera, while the latter on chamber music.

Festivals of classical music in Greece also benefit from one of the positive repercussions of the economic recession, namely the advancement of the culture of volunteering and charity, an increasing willingness to contribute for free for the common good. One of my interlocutors, a British organizer of a festival in Greece, has in fact stressed the connection between this sense of offering one's services for a common purpose with the crisis; she even drew a parallel between the emergence of a culture of volunteering in Britain as a result of the financial crises in which the country had found itself in the past with the development of such an attitude in contemporary Greece.[33] The existence of a growing corpus of volunteers reflects not only the increasing bonds of a certain festival with the local community, but also, importantly, a change of attitude with respect to volunteering on the part of the Greek people in general, that is, a change in values.

Finally, an important factor that has contributed to the survival of festivals in Greece during the crisis has been that of artistic networks. Artistic networks are anything but a new feature in the musical world.[34] However, it appears that the shortage of funding has strengthened and broadened their function especially as regards festivals of Western art music. As indicated earlier, networking has always been a major objective of festivals, particularly for artistic directors who would extend invitations to artists from abroad with the expectation that this invitation will be returned. This practice has been slightly modified due to the financial difficulties brought about by the crisis. Thus, a system of relations of exchange and reciprocity through artistic networks has blossomed, which is based not on financial reward, but on the exchange of services. This may entail payment of travel expenses and accommodation to have a holiday at the same time as performing at the festival. Yet, more frequently, artists, particularly festival artistic directors, participate in such events without (or for very little) payment because they anticipate that this favour will be returned to them in the future.

It is evident, therefore, that although the festivals of classical music themselves are blossoming, musicians, artistic directors and production companies do not benefit financially in any significant way. So, the question that naturally arises is: why do they insist on organising festivals and participating in others' events? This is clearly an investment in the future. Even though at the moment festivals cannot bring substantial financial profit, individuals and institutions support them hoping that one day they may start paying back. Moreover, one should not overlook the importance of artistic networks, since by investing in relations of exchange and reciprocity musicians can profit beyond festivals too, that is, at independent concerts taking place throughout the year. After all, participating in such events is one way of remaining in the spotlight of musical life in Greece.

Conclusion

The study of festivals of Western art music in Greece is uncharted territory; yet in effect festivals occupy a crucial place in musical life associated with this repertoire, not only due to their increased presence, but also thanks to their contribution to the operation of artistic networks. On the one hand, the intensity of festival activity in recent years reveals that those events have functioned as potent outlets of creativity for musicians at a trying time for this repertoire, and culture more broadly. On the other hand, such festivals flourish because they have served, even before the crisis, multiple purposes: networking, education and tourism. Of course, not all events that made their appearance in the period of crisis have survived; but this is not a crisis-specific feature, since that was the case even during the years of prosperity. However, as some festivals disappear, others spring up, and thus the overall momentum is maintained. Precarious as this situation might appear, such recycling of creative energy and the incredible impetus in this field of musical activity, demonstrate that no matter how severe the difficulties imposed by the financial circumstances are, the forces that feed into this cultural area are strong enough to keep things going.

Notes

Research for this chapter was mostly conducted as part of the research project 'Western Art Music at the Time of Crisis: An Interdisciplinary Study of Contemporary Greek

Culture and European Integration' (Faculty of Music Studies, National and Kapodistrian University of Athens), which was realized in 2014–2015 in the context of the programme 'Aristeia II' (NSRF 2007–2013) and co-funded by the EU (European Social Fund) and National Resources.

1. Julian Johnson, *Who Needs Classical Music?* (Oxford and New York, 2002).
2. The exact starting point of the economic and socio-cultural crisis in Greece is anything but a clear and uncontested question. For the purposes of this research, the period under consideration reaches back to the year 2008. This is earlier than the point at which the Greek government officially resorted to the IMF for financial aid, yet the first repercussions on the social and cultural level were already felt.
3. On the use of the term 'Western art music' to describe the so-called 'classical' music, as well as the ideological connotations surrounding it, see Laudan Nooshin, 'Introduction to the Special Issue: The Ethnomusicology of Western Art Music', *Ethnomusicology Forum* xx/3 (2011), pp. 285–300.
4. On the 2016 edition of this small-scale and little-known festival see http://www.specsnarts.gr/festivals/item/202-koufonissia-classical-music-festival (accessed 17 August 2016).
5. For an insightful and provocative account of the place of Western art music in Greece during the period of the economic and socio-political crisis, see Kaiti Romanou, 'Ορφέας στον Άδη [Orpheus in Hades]' in Pavlos Kavouras (ed.), *Η έντεχνη δυτική μουσική στην περίοδο της κρίσης: Μία διεπιστημονική μελέτη του σύγχρονου ελληνικού πολιτισμού και της ευρωπαϊκής ολοκλήρωσης* [Western Art Music at the Time of Crisis: An Interdisciplinary Study of Contemporary Greek Culture and European Integration] (Athens, 2015). Available at http://westartmusinenglish.weebly.com/uploads/4/2/1/4/42143431/westartmusvolume.pdf (accessed 17 August 2016).
6. The term festival is closely intertwined with the concept of festivity, feast, as it derives from the Latin *festum*, which meant 'public joy, merriment, revelry'. Alessandro Falassi's definition of the festival as 'a constellation of very different events, sacred and profane, private and public, sanctioning tradition and introducing innovation, proposing nostalgic revivals, providing the expressive means for the survival of the most archaic folk customs, and celebrating the highly speculative and experimental avant-gardes of the elite fine arts' has been well-established in the humanities and social sciences, and is embraced by the present research. Alessandro Falassi, 'Festival: Definition and Morphology' in Alessandro Falassi (ed.), *Time out of Time: Essays on the Festival* (Albuquerque, 1987), pp. 1–2.
7. See Natasha Lemos and Eleni Yannakakis, 'Introduction', in Natasha Lemos and Eleni Yannakakis (eds), *Critical Times, Critical Thoughts: Contemporary Greek Writers Discuss Facts and Fiction* (Newcastle upon Tyne, 2015), pp. 9–10.
8. Ibid.

9. See Nikos Poulakis, 'Θεσμοί σε κρίση; Μουσικά σύνολα και πολιτιστικοί οργανισμοί στην Ελλάδα του 21ου αιώνα' [Institutions in Crisis? Music Ensembles and Cultural Organisations in Greece of the 21st century], *Polyphonia* 26 (Spring 2015), pp. 96–123.
10. See Anastasios Hapsoulas, 'Έντεχνη δυτική μουσική και ελληνική μουσική εκπαίδευση: Κρίση και προοπτικές' [Western Art Music and Greek Music Education: Crisis and Prospects], *Polyphonia* 26 (Spring 2015), pp. 82–95.
11. A recent report on the academic and cultural policy/'grey' literature about music festivals recommends undertaking '[f]urther research on festivals as events from within the fields of classical music and opera, which seem relatively under-represented'. See Emma Webster and George McKay, *From Glyndebourne to Glastonbury: The Impact of British Music Festivals. An Arts and Humanities Research Council-Funded Literature Review.* Available at https://impactoffestivals.files.wordpress.com/2016/01/the-impact-of-british-music-festivals-large-print-version.pdf (accessed 17 August 2016), p. 15.
12. In terms of theory, the crisis is conceptualized as an 'event', after Alain Badiou, that is, as an out-of-the-ordinary rupture to the status quo, which occurs when the prevailing principles and values are neutralized, even if temporarily. Thus, the flow of events is interrupted and in the void that emerges – the so-called 'eventual site' – new directions and alternative visions may appear, directed by human agency. For the employment of Badiou's concept of 'event' in this context, see Pavlos Kavouras, 'Η έντεχνη δυτική μουσική στην περίοδο της κρίσης: Μία διεπιστημονική μελέτη του σύγχρονου ελληνικού πολιτισμού και της ευρωπαϊκής ολοκλήρωσης [Western Art Music at the Time of Crisis: An Interdisciplinary Study of Contemporary Greek Culture and European Integration]', *Polyphonia* 26 (Spring 2015), 46–47 and Jim Samson, 'Music in Crisis: Fundamental Terms and Concepts' in Pavlos Kavouras (ed.), Η έντεχνη δυτική μουσική στην περίοδο της κρίσης, pp. 47–48.
13. The term 'cultural performance' was coined by the anthropologist Milton Singer in his seminal study of aspects of Indian culture. See Milton Singer, *When a Great Tradition Modernizes: An Anthropological Approach to Modern Civilization* (New York, 1972).
14. The term 'practice', that is the capacity of individuals to act according to specific rules, attempts to combine the terms 'structure' and 'agency', 'objectivity' and 'subjectivity'. See Kavouras, 'Η έντεχνη δυτική μουσική στην περίοδο της κρίσης', p. 42.
15. Liana Giorgi and Monica Sassatelli, 'Introduction', in Liana Giorgi, Monica Sassatelli and Gerard Delanty (eds), *Festivals and the Cultural Public Sphere* (London and New York, 2011), p. 1.
16. Bernadette Quinn, 'Arts Festivals and the City', *Urban Studies* 42/5–6 (2005), p. 6.
17. See Giorgos Vlastos, *Η πρόσληψη της ελληνικής αρχαιότητας στη γαλλική μουσική του 20ου αιώνα: 1900–1918* [The Reception of Greek

Antiquity in French Music of the Early Twentieth Century: 1900–1918]. PhD dissertation (Athens, 2005), pp. 158–171.

18. Kaiti Romanou, *Έντεχνη ελληνική μουσική στους νεότερους χρόνους* [Greek Art Music in Modern Times] (Athens, 2006), pp. 236–237, 249–252.
19. Maria Psarrou, *Φεστιβάλ: Ζητήματα διοργάνωσης, χρήσεις και προεκτάσεις για την τοπική αυτοδιοίκηση* [The Festival: Issues of Organisation, Uses and Reverberations for Local Self-Government]. Available at http://festival.culture.gr/wp-content/uploads/2012/10/topikh_autodioikhsh_kai_festival1.doc (accessed 17 August 2016), 19.
20. The explosion of festivals, for over a decade now, is actually a global phenomenon. It may be accounted for, partly, by migration, cultural globalization and the erosion of distinctions between high and low culture, changes in the nature of the public, and the wider democratization and internationalization of culture. Gerard Delanty, 'Conclusion: On the cultural significance of arts festivals' in Liana Giorgi, Monica Sassatelli and Gerard Delanty (eds), *Festivals and the Cultural Public Sphere* (London and New York, 2011), p. 191. See also Bruno S. Frey, 'The rise and fall of festivals: Reflections on the Salzburg Festival', *Working Paper/Institute for Empirical Research in Economics* 48 (Zurich, 2000), p. 2. Available at https://papers.ssrn.com/sol3/papers.cfm?abstract_id=236016 (accessed 17 August 2016). And Webster and George McKay, *From Glyndebourne to Glastonbury*, 3, for Britain specifically.
21. Data collection involved fieldwork at the Nafplio Festival, the International Music Festival of Cyclades, the festival Manni-Sonnenlink and Serenata Kriti (autumn/summer 2014), as well as interviews, internet, advertisement and press research and analysis in Athens (winter 2015).
22. Katerina Levidou and Georgia Vavva, 'Παράρτημα: Φεστιβάλ με έντεχνη δυτική μουσική στην Ελλάδα, από το 2008 έως σήμερα (ενδεικτικός κατάλογος)' [Appendix: Festivals with Western art music in Greece, from 2008 up to the present (indicative catalogue)], *Polyphonia* 26 (Spring 2015), pp. 224–245.
23. On the 'Music Village', see Georgia Vavva, 'Η έντεχνη δυτική μουσική στην «κοινότητα»: Η περίπτωση του Μουσικού Χωριού', *Polyphonia* 26 (Spring 2015), pp. 209–223.
24. The connection of festivals of Western art music with tourism is not a Greek phenomenon. See, for instance, the cases of a chamber music festival held on Washington's Olympic Peninsula (Vicki L. Brennan, 'Chamber music in the barn: Tourism, nostalgia, and the reproduction of social class', *The World of Music* 41/3 (1999), pp. 11–29) and the Wexford Festival Opera in the Republic of Ireland (Bernadatte Quinn, 'Symbols, Practices and Myth-Making: Cultural Perspectives on the Wexford – Festival Opera', *Tourism Geographies* 5/3 (2003), 329–349). See also Webster and George McKay, *From Glyndebourne to Glastonbury*, pp. 10–11.
25. See, however, the case of the Wexford-Festival Opera, and the controversial role tourism has played for the local community. Quinn, 'Symbols, Practices and Myth-Making'.

26. Interview conducted on 5 February 2015.
27. For an example of a festival of Western art music that treated the local community in the completely opposite way, disdaining the locals while placing the emphasis on tourists who visited from a nearby urban centre, thus also building social hierarchies, see Brennan, 'Chamber music in the barn'.
28. Interview conducted on 24 June 2014.
29. This information surfaced, among others, during an interview with a resident of the broader Nafplio area on 24 June 2016.
30. For the embrace of this practice by the Greek National Opera, see Poulakis, 'Θεσμοί σε κρίση;', 109–118.
31. Interview conducted on 16 June 2014. In the transcription of this interview excerpt, KL refers to my name while my interlocutor has been marked as X.
32. Interview (conducted on 4 February 2015) with a musician that comes from the island of Syros that had volunteered as an usher at the International Music Festival of Cyclades, who had also participated in the International Festival of the Aegean as a chorister.
33. Interview conducted on 5 February 2015.
34. The importance of artistic networks in the realm of Western art music specifically surfaces in Stephen Cottrell, *Professional Music-Making in London: Ethnography and Experience* (London, 2004).

PART IV

STREET ART AND NOSTALGIA

CHAPTER 8

VISUAL ENCOUNTERS WITH CRISIS AND AUSTERITY: REFLECTIONS ON THE CULTURAL POLITICS OF STREET ART IN CONTEMPORARY ATHENS

Julia Tulke

> And through all this crisis I think we should all actually feel lucky – in quotation marks – because it makes us more creative. I was talking with another artist yesterday exactly about that. We are creative now because if we were in a period where everything is calm and nothing really happens, we wouldn't have the motivation to express ourselves. It's not a good situation to be in, I'm not saying that; but I think it makes you creative.[1]

In contemporary Athens, emerging from an urban landscape deeply transformed by crisis and austerity, street art has gained enormous significance as an unsanctioned medium of public expression, rendering the city 'one of the most "stained" and "saturated" [. . .] in the world'.[2] During the past few years the walls of the city have come alive with poetic scribbles and political slogans, with portraits of protest and struggle, and expressive depictions of everyday life in the city. Due to a lack of municipal funding, street art is only sporadically removed from the walls of the city, allowing it to sprawl unhindered and, even on highly emblematic public buildings, to remain visible for long periods of time.[3] The so-called trilogy, a neoclassical architectural ensemble consisting of the National Library, the National University of Athens and the Academy of Athens, is a telling example. The facades of the buildings, which are located along one of the main roads in the centre of Athens, tend to be covered in combative political slogans, which often remain there for months at a time (Figure 8.1). As they are seldom bothered by the authorities, artists can work on their pieces freely, often in broad daylight. The resulting dense accumulation and elongated lifespan of public artworks has allowed for elaborate dialogues and interactions to unfold on the walls of the city over time. Here, the ruptures created in urban space by disinvestment, austerity and years of political struggle constantly produce new surfaces and spaces – boarded-up urban ruins, unfinished buildings, vacant shop windows, and decaying billboards with nothing left to advertise – that become highly significant sites for creative appropriation. Moreover the proliferation of street art is catalyzed by the un- and underemployment of large parts of the

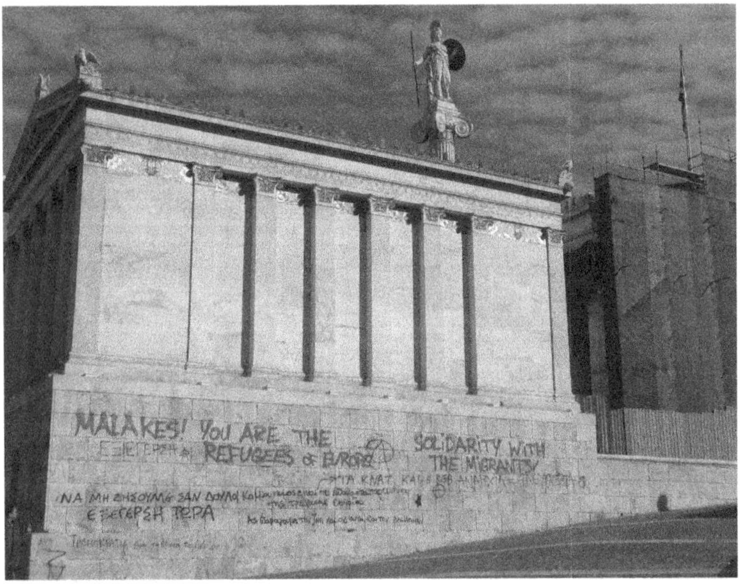

Figure 8.1 The Academy of Athens covered in political slogans, 2013. Photo: Julia Tulke/aestheticsofcrisis.org

productive population, particularly the young and highly educated, which has freed-up a vast amount of creative potential. This 'renewal and creativity that the financial and socio-political instability has inadvertently helped foster'[4] in both formal and informal cultural production is documented in the contributions to this volume. Simultaneously, as artist Sonke points out, there has been a shift in public attitudes towards the immaterial value of arts and culture:

> I think people are more focused now on the simple things, not so much on cars and style as before. We had a period when lifestyle was really promoted in Greece because the government told us we have a lot of money and we are doing the Olympic Games, so at that time society, the media and the newspapers were very into lifestyle with cars and pools and nice homes. And now people are turning back to the basics. So art [...] is something that [...] people in Athens are more interested in, in art, in music, in the simple things, in the things you don't have to pay to have.[5]

As the context of crisis and austerity profoundly permeates all aspects of everyday life in the city, it also fundamentally shapes the form and content of the artworks that can be found on the walls of Athens.[6] According to sociologist Myrto Tsilimpounidi, 'street art becomes a visual history of nonhegemonic voices [...] that points towards the wider socio-political tensions in the era of austerity and crisis'.[7] The walls of the city are thus transformed into a living archive of the current historical conjuncture, at the same time becoming a site for collectively negotiating grievances. This chapter examines this twofold dynamic and analyses how Athenian street artists encounter, reflect upon and make sense of the ongoing crisis through the cultural practice of street art. Based on a dialectic approach that takes into account street art as *visual artefacts* mediated through historical, political, and affective narratives and iconographies, as well as a *performative practice*, I argue that street art is not merely a static representation of the given socio-cultural context it is embedded in but also has the potential to actively transform urban space and reimagine everyday life by inscribing alternative histories and possibilities into the very surface of the city. In arguing this I follow the approach of the Italian theorist Maurizio Lazzarato who claims that:

> [i]mages, signs and statements are [...] possibilities, possible worlds, which affect souls [...] and must be realized in bodies. Images, signs and statements intervene in both the incorporeal and the corporeal transformations. Their effect is that of the creation and realization of what is possible, not of representation. They contribute to the metamorphoses of subjectivity, not to their representation.[8]

In the context of this chapter the term street art will be used to refer to self-authorized visual and material interventions in public space.[9] This includes a variety of different practices: from slogan writing and graffiti to stencils, paste-ups and murals to conceptual performances in public space. Departing from this broad understanding, my analysis focuses particularly on the political significance of street art as a cultural practice which emerges from three interrelated levels. On the most basic level, all works of street art, regardless of their immediate intentions or messages, represent a *semantic intervention* in the visual configuration of the city that creatively appropriates, reinterprets and transforms urban space. All interventions thus implicitly challenge and contest dominant notions and ideologies of what urban space should be and look like, at the same time questioning public ownership and representational regimes. On a more concrete level, street art and graffiti may become politically significant through their *encrypted messages* and narrative contextualization by the artist. Finally, the performative act of writing and painting on walls generates *alternative channels of communication*, creating new meanings, encounters and possibilities for interaction in urban space.[10] In moments of crisis the political significance of street art is amplified, an observation already made by Lyman G. Chaffee in his influential 1993 monograph *Political Protest and Street Art: Popular Tools for Democratization in Hispanic Countries*. While Chaffee bases his analysis on a number of historical examples, a growing body of empirical work testifies to the continued significance of street art as part of a transnational political aesthetic in the current political conjuncture, be it in the context of the Egyptian Revolution of 2011,[11] Athens at a time of crisis,[12] or the struggle for Gezi Park in Istanbul in 2013.[13]

Street art in Athens: Unwritten histories and contingent present

The current proliferation of street art in Athens is a relatively new phenomenon. It is commonly assumed that graffiti, inspired by North American and Western European traditions identified with urban hip hop culture, only began to appear in Greece in about the early 1990s, finally diversifying into the more complex art forms subsumed under the term 'street art' since the 2000s. Yet, public writing as a politically inclined cultural practice has a much longer and more complex local history, a fact that architect Kostas Avramidis attributes to the city's 'turbulent past and [. . .] tolerant citizens'.[14] Contemporary inscriptions in urban space are, as sociologist Myrto Tsilimpounidi notes, layered over a palimpsest of 'writings on ancient columns, poems on marble signs, and names and quotations of ancient philosophers on marble monuments, with some of the inscriptions going back to the fifth century BCE.'[15] Although such historical lineages of public writing are not consistently documented, they regularly resurface in popular culture as well as in narratives about political struggles and resistance movements of the twentieth century. *Ο Δρόμος* [*The Street*], a popular song by Greek composer Manos Loizos written in 1974, the last year of Greece's military dictatorship, features a line explicitly referencing writings in public space: 'The road had its own story, some said it was written by children'.[16] Some more concrete examples can be found in Alinda Dimitriou's oral history documentary about the role of women in political activism in Greece. As the protagonists tell their stories of disobedience, struggle, and detention they often recall strategically engaging in wall writing as a political practice, either to communicate and coordinate with other underground groups via a sort of encrypted language or to spread subversive messages of encouragement, hope and strength to their fellow people.[17] Public writing as a historical practice – whether politically motivated or not – forms an integral part of Greece's collective memory and continues to reverberate in the streets of present-day Athens through slogans, vocabularies and aesthetic references excavated from history and adapted to the current context.

The dense presence of street art characteristic of contemporary Athens only started to unfold with the events of December 2008 when the murder of 15-year-old anarchist Alexis Grigoropoulos at the hands of two police officers sparked a number of mass demonstrations and riots. Within just a few days the political discontent had also laid claim to the walls of the city: angry political slogans, impromptu memorials to Alexis and symbolic references to the newly emerging protest culture invaded public space all over the centre of Athens. French street artist Oré contrasts this movement and the subsequent politicization of public space with attitudes in his home country:

> In terms of aesthetic and political issues, the big difference is how, since the murder of Alexis by the police in December 2008, graffiti and street art have become like a weapon for the youth to express what they feel about this society. And with the collapse of the economy that matter grows. I think the Greek [street art] scene is much more political than France, definitely.[18]

While the riots of 2008 and 2009 eventually subsided, paving the way for a new anti-austerity movement, street art remained a powerful means of political expression, the shape and content of the artworks evolving in line with changing political circumstances. The urban landscape of Athens, the terrain of everyday life, emerges as a site of documenting past political struggles, thereby keeping them present in the urban landscape. Yet, in moments of heightened political drama the streets also have the capacity to sustain a quick, even immediate, reaction. When in June 2015 Prime Minister Alexis Tsipras announced a referendum regarding the current state of negotiation between Greece and its creditors, it took a mere few hours for the first *όχι* [no] slogans to appear on the streets of the city (Figure 8.2). During the following week, a plethora of slogans and stencils, almost entirely in favour of the anti-austerity No campaign, emerged on the walls of Athens reflecting on and contributing to the immediate political discourse: 'No', 'No to fear', 'No to the blackmail of EU-IMF', 'No more saving', 'With a head held high: say no'.[19]

Street art has long been argued to be a highly masculinized subcultural formation. It is thus not surprising that the contemporary Athenian street-art scene has been found to consist mostly of male artists, hailing from middle-class backgrounds.[20] Yet, the specific contexts and motivations of individual artists differ widely. They include political activists who engage in slogan writing and other creative pursuits as part

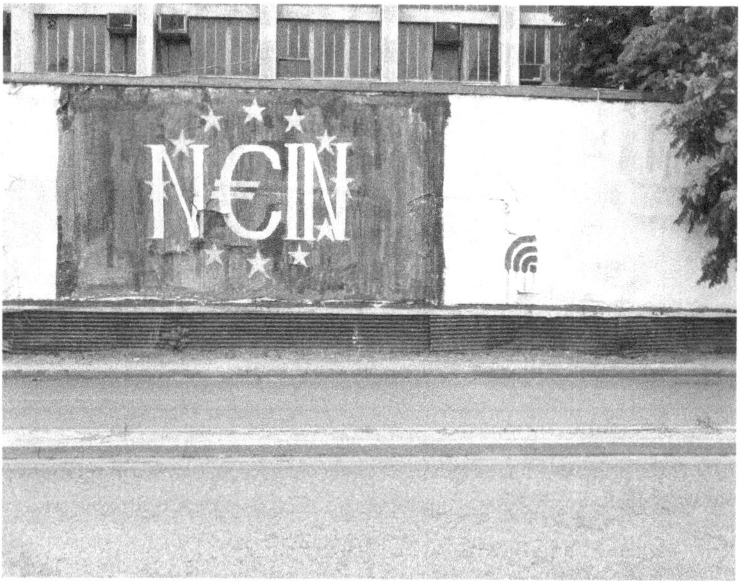

Figure 8.2 *Nein* [No], mural by the artist N-grams in the vicinity of the campus of the Athens School of Fine Arts, 2015. Photo: Julia Tulke/aestheticsofcrisis.org

of their repertoire of political action, without necessarily identifying as artists. They also include self-defined street artists driven by explicitly political motivations and strong affinities to social movements. A number of them, such as the members of the Political Stencil Collective, use stencils to spread what they explicitly label 'political propaganda':

> The 'dominant powers' and the Penal Code look upon us as vandals! In our minds and that of our friends, comrades and all who go along with our standpoint and practices, we are entities beyond the law, we focus our actions beyond the framework of the established esthetics. We inject colour into an otherwise grey and neutral townscape, with one overriding aim: strike a blow to the onlooker, hoping to bring about his awakening, be it momentary.[21]

Furthermore, there are street artists who came to the practice via graffiti writing, studio art, or design practice, most of whom try to remain politically neutral and distance themselves from any political context or institution. In 2013 artist Cacao Rocks described his intervention as being an affective and aesthetic one, rather than explicitly political:

> All graffiti and street art is a political action and an effort for communication. Some artists try to do propaganda with their work and I'm not one of them, I just try to change our environment and the city landscape. I try to do it without the permission of the authorities and, of course, by breaking some rules. My work is more like telling a story without trying to change the ideas of the spectators, if this is possible. I just want to make them feel other things than just walking by a grey wall in the city.[22]

In order to realize their shared goal of affecting the observer and transforming the urban landscape, artists employ references and iconographies that borrow from both Greek history and popular imagination, as well as transnational cultural and political symbols.

Street artists in Athens find themselves in a comparatively favourable legal situation. The practice itself is illegal but potential repercussions are mild and prosecutions are rare. Most artists are able to work in broad daylight – though some prefer the night for symbolic reasons – and almost all the artists I have talked to over the years have shared gleeful stories of being caught red-handed by police and still getting away with it. On the whole, public attitudes towards street art are ambivalent. For some Athenians, especially the young and politically minded ones inhabiting the most densely painted areas of the city, street art is an integral part of the urban geography. Individual artworks may become personal landmarks and focal points for navigating and making sense of one's surrounding. To others, the suburban population in particular, the phenomenon is perceived as undifferentiated visual noise and part of the general physical deterioration of central Athens. Thus reactions to street artists can vary, as artist Cacao Rocks describes: '[s]ome people like it and some people don't. Some people get me something to eat while I'm working and some people call the police. Everything is possible when you are painting out in the streets.'[23]

This ambivalence is echoed in the representation of street art in the Greek media and political discourse, both of which are structured along a static binary antagonism pitting good street art – commissioned murals and the like – against bad vandalism – tags and political slogans.[24] Street art effectively entered the political discourse in 2015 when a group of artists painted the outside walls of the Polytechnic of Athens in a massive, dystopian black-and-white mural (see Figure 1.3). As Artemis Leontis has noted, the momentous appearance of the artwork had a powerful impact on public attitudes towards graffiti and street art:

> People were shocked by its magnitude and darkness. Despite the general unkemptness of the building, with layers of air pollutants, posters, and numerous graffiti tags having accrued for years without sustained public objection, on this occasion a majority of the public (over 60 per cent) identified the graffiti as a defiling event.[25]

The removal of the Polytechnic mural was unusually swift, but as a discursive event this piece of art continues to resonate. It forced political and civic actors in Athens to clearly articulate their position towards street art and graffiti, often for the first time, and, as a test case, it became the basis for consolidating more strategic political approaches towards the uncontrolled spread of graffiti and street art in Athens. An emblematic statement of this new political rhetoric has been formulated by Amalia Zepou, Athens vice mayor for civil society and municipality decentralization, who suggests that 'when a city collapses, and has been tagged everywhere, we have an obligation to stop it. Once graffiti becomes commissioned art, it is a signal of the beginning of the end of the financial or social crisis that the city has gone through'.[26]

Aesthetics of crisis: Of broken bodies and gas masks

The emergence of crisis-related street art in Athens has garnered considerable attention from international media and has been the subject of a number of exhibitions and research projects in Greece and abroad. In such accounts, street art is often perceived as a static representation of subjectivities in crisis, a small glimpse of what the general public *really* feels in this historical moment, put on display on the walls of the city and rendered authentic by virtue of their very location.[27] Individual artworks are selected to be photographed, circulated, listed, catalogued, and interpreted to tell the true story of the crisis, while never revealing more than a fragment of their significance. I take the walls of Athens to be contingent, living entities rather than bearers of authentic truth or representation. One artist may write 'Athens is the New Berlin' on one wall and 'Athens is not Berlin' on another; they may call their work apolitical in one interview and call themselves an activist in another. What lends meaning to an artist's work is not merely the encapsulated intention or message, but rather the continuous performance in the public realm, where individual pieces become part of a continuously unfolding visual body and an ongoing dialogue that is constantly being rewritten. Artworks are animated and imbued with significance only through interaction with one another and with the urban dwellers that make their everyday lives among them. They offer no stable belonging, no concrete truth. Rather, they inscribe a multitude of alternative imageries and positionalities into the urban fabric, thereby claiming public space as a significant site for negotiating the crisis as a context for everyday life. Of course, within the larger body of inscriptions, a number of aesthetic clusters – never more than approximations – can be identified.[28] Much of the street art found in Athens consists of deeply personal accounts of the lived reality of crisis and austerity. Quite often such artworks are paste-ups of drawings or hand-painted murals, suggesting a deeply personal engagement with urban space. The overwhelming majority of them figure realistic and expressive portrayals of human form. The walls of Athens are covered in faces and bodies bruised and broken – worn down from years of enduring a perpetual state of social and affective emergency – pale faces with hollow cheeks and tired eyes set in expressions of fear and despair, emaciated bodies hanging flaccidly in urban space. Such artworks depart from the representations of the crisis as an abstract and disembodied economic dynamic that are characteristic of most mainstream media depictions, framing it instead as a corporeal experience, at times a literal life-and-death struggle. Daniel Knight, an anthropologist who has charted the impact of the crisis in rural Trikala in central Greece, made a related observation in his research, when one of his respondents described herself as feeling 'physically beaten', her 'bones crushed' by the crisis.[29]

Often the bodies and faces (dis)figured on the walls of Athens belong to children, many of them boys, and young adults, symbolically standing in for the precarity of living in expectation of a future that can no longer be anticipated. The artworks of Dimitris Taxis, mostly paintings on paper pasted on the walls of different neighbourhoods, are perhaps the most meaningful representations of this correlation. His paste-ups feature young boys, crouching fearfully, clutching guns in terror or seeking refuge in the hollow log of a tree (Figure 8.3). *I wish you could learn something from the past*, a piece made in 2012 and still in situ at the time of writing, shows a boy sitting motionless in between two oversized stacks of books (See Figure 1.4). 'Socrates', 'Plato' and 'Democracy' is written on the books the boy is sitting on, 'Athens means Luxury', 'No Future' and 'Survival Guide' is written on the ones weighing down on his head. The boy's hunched pose – stuck in time

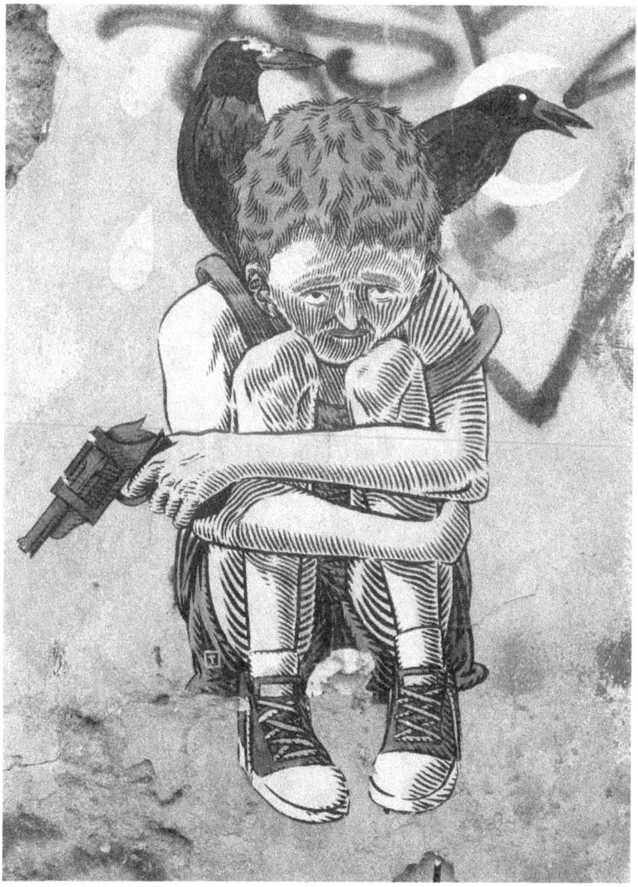

Figure 8.3 Paste-up by Dimitris Taxis in Kerameikos, 2013. Photo: Julia Tulke/aestheticsofcrisis.org

between ancient past and disastrous present with, literally, no future in sight – evokes the displacement of linear temporality so characteristic of the crisis, a condition that Maurizio Lazzarato has described as 'the strange sensation of living in a society without time, without possibility, without foreseeable rupture'.[30] Simultaneously the artwork is haunted by the presence of a romanticized Greek antiquity, echoing an observation made by anthropologist Daniel Knight, who has argued that in this absence of conceivable futures, Greek society is returning to historical moments from the past to make sense of their precarious present subjectivity.[31]

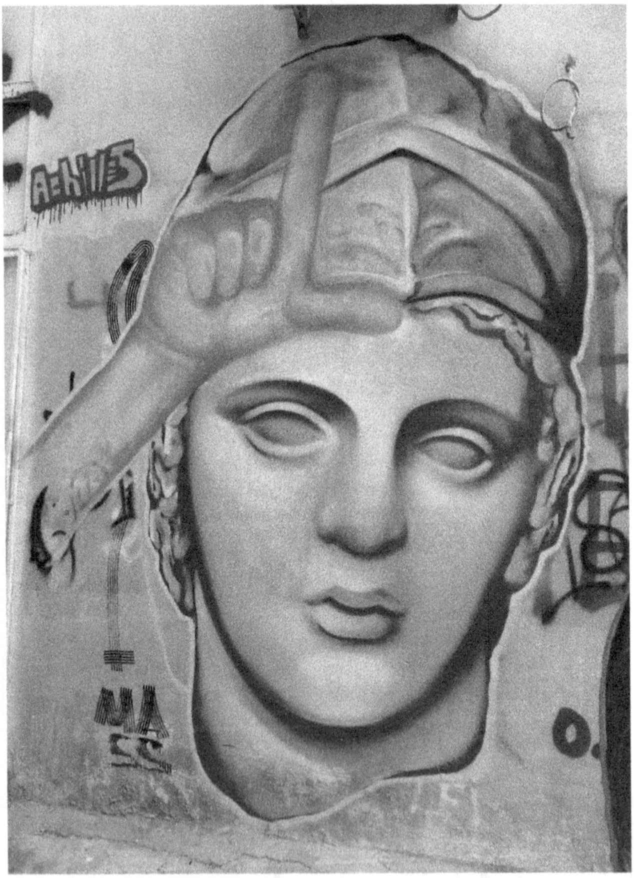

Figure 8.4 *Loser*, mural by artist Achilles in Kerameikos, 2015. Photo: Julia Tulke/aestheticsofcrisis.org

In Athenian street art such engagements with the past are sought through interrogations of the continued symbolic purchase of antiquity. Visual markers of antiquity – statuesque figures or depictions of Greek philosophers – repeatedly surface in banal and absurd contexts far removed from their usual aura of sacred monumentality. One artwork by artist Achilles shows a stereotypical depiction of the head of an ancient statue, the right hand pressed against its forehead gesturing the letter 'L' – international shorthand for 'loser' (Figure 8.4). At the same time neoclassical buildings have become significant material sites of political struggle. As anthropologist Michael Herzfeld has noted, 'young people, clearly unimpressed by the neo-classical pretensions on display in these extravagances, but perhaps with fine historical sensibility associating them with both wealth and Western domination',[32] reappropriate ancient spaces and buildings, covering their walls in political graffiti or tearing off chunks of marble to hurl at the police during riots, thereby renegotiating what the material presence of Greek antiquity in the public space may mean in the ongoing crisis.

The numerous bodies that inhabit the walls of Athens are usually shown in isolation, echoing what art historian Max Haiven has described as the basic imaginative logic of capitalism:

> On a basic level, [the economic system] relies on each of us imagining ourselves as essentially isolated, lonely, competitive economic agents. It relies on us imagining that the system is the natural expression of human nature, or that it is too powerful to be changed, or that no other system could ever be desirable.[33]

By visualizing the embodied realities of an atomized capitalist society in crisis, Athenian street artists do not merely affirm this logic, but rather open it up for interrogation. Depictions of bodies in crisis circulate through the urban everyday as affectively imbued artifacts on display for collective consumption, through which they then acquire meaning. However, such appeals to the collective affective condition of the crisis are not merely enacted through figurative artworks but also through textual interventions. The slogan '*vasanizomai*' ['I am in torment/being tortured'], which has appeared on the walls of Athens in all shapes, sizes and colours imaginable, is one significant example. While its origin is unknown, its omnipresence in public space and circulation through other media has imbued *vasanizomai* with universal significance in the Greek crisis imagination (see Boletsi, Chapter 11). Unlike the mainstream media and political narratives about the crisis that put the blame on certain deviant subjects and behaviours – 'the excessive demands of the governed [. . .] who want nothing more than to laze about, and [. . .] the corruption of the elites'[34] – Athenian street artists make visible how universally the crisis permeates the life of every single inhabitant of the city. Through their realistic portrayals of the corporeal and affective impact of crisis and austerity on everyday life, they claim the walls of the city as a space for emotionally processing the continuous state of exception. The collective vulnerability and melancholia of the everyday that these projects visually interrogate may eventually become meaningful as a basis and resource for political solidarity and community formation.[35]

Another aesthetic cluster that can be found on the walls of central Athens consists of artworks devoted explicitly to politics and protest – political slogans, memorials to fighters killed in the struggle, depictions of protest and portraits of protesters – the majority of them located in the politicized neighbourhood of Exarhia. The techniques most frequently employed are stencilling, slogan writing and freehand graffiti, pointing to a slightly more aggressive spatial politics. Certain iconographic references to protest recur repeatedly – anarchist symbols, petrol bombs, images of the city engulfed in flames; but no image is as omnipresent as the gas mask clad protester, which is symbolically meaningful on two levels. On the one hand, gas masks point to the actual reality of protests in which they have become an obligatory accessory. On the other hand, they are emblematic of the increasing militarization, violence and social polarization of the city in a more general sense (Figure 8.5). Through its visual manifestation in urban space, protest is detached from its usual framing as an exceptional momentary eruption of political sentiments and becomes an integral part of the city's imaginary geography. While in reality protests and occupations are often swiftly broken up, the affective ambience of political discontent remains present on the walls of Athens at all times.

Conclusion: Reimagining the city

As the country arguably most dramatically affected by the ongoing crisis and its material effects, Greece and particularly her capital Athens are implicated in a spectacularized media regime that focuses on images of

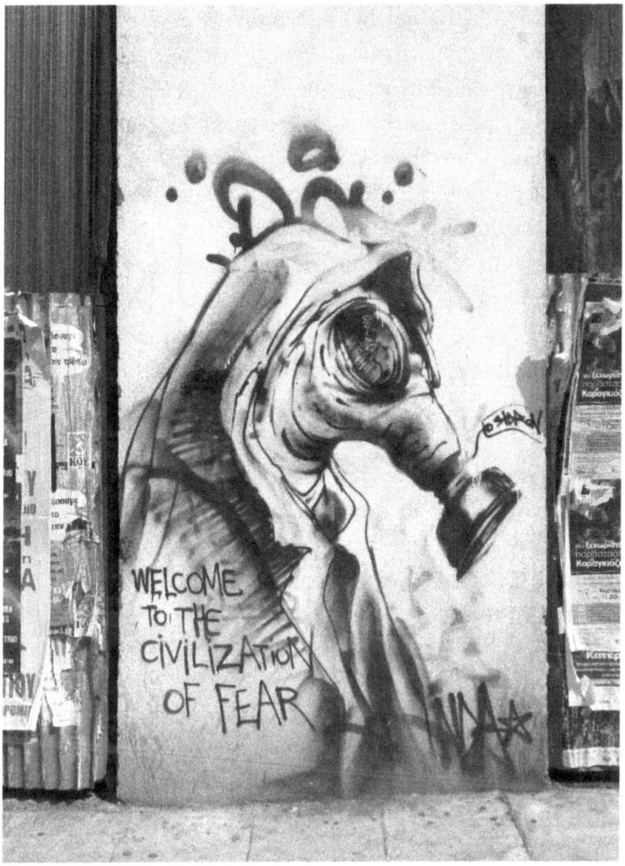

Figure 8.5 *Welcome to the Civilization of Fear*, mural by Sidron and NDA in Omonia. Photo: Julia Tulke/aestheticsofcrisis.org

disorder and precarity or, to borrow the words of architectural theorist Petros Babasikas:

> [a] montage of riots, poverty and failure, talking heads, speculation punditry, noncontextual statistics and disaster narratives, sea-and-antiquity postcards, Photoshop visions, cultural postcards and unlikely success stories [which] dominate the public sphere and eclipse the self-image of its citizens in a strongly moderated, hyper-media stream of spectacle, insolvency and uncertainty: a delirious, anxious, ubiquitous carpet of white noise.[36]

It is this complex visual apparatus that the street art of Athens is set against. The media and political narratives discursively produce the crisis as an exceptional event perpetuating, as Eva Fotiadi argues, the 'psychological pressure of living precariously *and* surrounded by images of violence, misery and disorder',[37] and creating an affective ambiance of 'shame and other moralized negativity.'[38] By contrast, Athenian street art engages with the crisis through its everyday material, symbolic and affective landscapes. The walls of the city are not the site of a directed response and nor do they hold any truths about the current historical moment. Instead they accumulate countless traces of personal and contingent engagements with the body of the city that deeply resonate with the everyday experience of crisis, which Lauren Berlant has described thus:

> The people experience the state of emergency not as an exception but as an embedding in the ordinary in which they are always tipped over, walking ahead while looking around, and feeling around their pockets for something, both focused and distracted and getting by, without assurance.[39]

The task of dealing with this deeply felt precarity is typically relegated to the privacy of the domestic sphere. As affectively imbued artifacts circulating through the body of city, pieces of Athenian street art reframe precarity as the shared condition of the crisis, which may then become politically animated via notions of community and solidarity. As it inhabits the material configurations produced by the crisis, the ruptures, cracks and vacant spaces in between that texture the urban fabric, street art also points to the crisis city as a radically contingent site of emerging possibilities and political imagination.[40] The lack of a linear future, the 'disturbance in the reproduction of life'[41] that structures everyday life in the crisis is here taken seriously as an experience of corporeal and affective precarity, while also providing a symbolic point of departure for the potential reimagining of the collective entities that may emerge from the current moment.

Notes

The analyses presented here are based on material gathered for my MA thesis during eight weeks of ethnographic fieldwork in Athens in 2013: see Julia Tulke, 'Aesthetics of Crisis: Political Street Art in Athens in the Context of the Crisis',

Master's Thesis submitted to the Department of European Ethnology at Humboldt University Berlin (2013). Available at http://aestheticsofcrisis.org/thesis-publications/ (accessed 5 May 2016) as well as observations from various visits in 2015 and 2016. More information on the project, interviews with artists as well as the full-length MA thesis can be accessed at aestheticsofcrisis.org.

1. The artist Refur, interview with the author, 2013. All artist interviews quoted in this article were conducted in English. They are rendered here in their original wording, with only slight modifications for clarity.
2. Orestis Pangalos, 'Testimonies and Appraisals on Athens Graffiti, Before and After the Crisis' in M. Tsilimpounidi and A. Walsh (eds), *Remapping "Crisis": A Guide to Athens* (London, 2014), p. 154.
3. See ibid., p. 162.
4. Olga Kourelou, Mariana Liz, and Belén Vidal, 'Crisis and Creativity: The New Cinemas of Portugal, Greece and Spain', *New Cinemas: Journal of Contemporary Film* 12/1 (2014), p. 13.
5. The artist Sonke, interview with the author, 2013.
6. There is certainly a large number of artworks still present in Athens that were created prior to the current period of crisis. Yet, rather than enforcing a strict division between pre- and post-crisis street art, as other authors have suggested, I treat all artworks present at the time of my research as artifacts of a city at a time of crisis, examining how street art that was not originally crisis-related may acquire new meanings in the new context.
7. Myrto Tsilimpounidi, '"If These Walls Could Talk": Street Art and Urban Belonging', *Laboratorium* 7/2 (2015), p. 72.
8. Maurizio Lazzarato, 'Struggle, Event, Media', *RePUBLICart* (2003). Available at http://republicart.net/disc/representations/lazzarato01_en.htm (accessed 10 August 2016).
9. The term street art is highly contested, lacking a univocal definition and existing alongside a multitude of alternative denominations (urban art, post-graffiti, urban intervention etc.) with slightly diverging connotations, genealogies, and histories. The term street art is chosen precisely because of its broad and inclusive nature in order to accommodate the ethnographic, empirically lead approach of my work. Yet, I maintain a critical stance towards the term, explicitly contesting the popular, linear historical narrative that identifies the 1970s New York graffiti scene as the point of origin for the contemporary global proliferation of street art as professed in Cedar Lewisohn, *Street Art: The Graffiti Revolution* (London, 2008) among others. Instead I aim to investigate the hybrid histories and often undocumented cultural lineages of the practice.
10. My typology of the political significance of street art is influenced by and indebted to a number of transdisciplinary contributions to the emerging field of graffiti and street art studies, most notably Rafael Schacter, *Ornament and Order: Graffiti, Street Art and the Parergon* (Surrey, 2014); Luca M. Visconti et al., 'Street Art, Sweet Art? Reclaiming the "Public" in Public place', *Journal of Consumer Research* 37/3 (2010),

pp. 511–529; Luke Dickens, '"Finders Keepers": Performing the Street, the Gallery and the Spaces In-Between', *Liminalities: A Journal of Performance Studies* 4/1 (2008), pp. 2–30; Lyman G. Chaffee, *Political Protest and Street Art: Popular Tools for Democratization in Hispanic Countries* (Westport, 1993), Rosalyn Deutsche, 'Art and Public Space: Questions of Democracy', *Social Text* 33 (1992), pp. 34–53; and Jean Baudrillard, 'Kool Killer or the Insurrection of Signs' in Jean Baudrillard *Symbolic Exchange and Death* (London, 1993).

11. See Basma Hamdy and Don Karl Stone (eds), *Walls of Freedom: Street Art of the Egyptian Revolution* (Berlin, 2014) and Georgiana Nicoarea, 'Interrogating the Dynamic of Egyptian Graffiti: From Neglected Marginality to Image Politics', *Revista Română de Studii Eurasiatice* X/1–2 (2014), pp. 171–186.
12. See Tsilimpounidi, 'Street Art and Urban Belonging', pp. 71–91; and Panos Leventis, 'Walls of Crisis: Street Art and Urban Fabric in Central Athens, 2000–2012', *Architectural Histories* 1/1 (2012), pp. 1–10.
13. Christiane Gruber, 'The Visual Emergence of the Occupy Gezi Movement', *JADmag* 1/4 (2013), pp. 29–36.
14. Konstantinos Avramidis, '"Live Your Greece in Myths": Reading the Crisis on Athens' Walls', *Professional Dreamers Working Paper No 8*, 2012. Available at http://www.professionaldreamers.net/_prowp/wp-content/uploads/Avramides-Reading-the-Crisis-on-Athens-walls-fld.pdf (accessed 10 July 2016), p. 4.
15. Tsilimpounidi, 'Street Art and Urban Belonging', p. 74.
16. I am indebted to the artist Lebaniz Blonde for bringing this to my attention during a private exchange.
17. See Πουλιά στο βάλτο [*Birds in the mire*] (2008), Η ζωή στους βράχους [*Life among the rocks*] (2009) and Τα κορίτσια της βροχής [*Girls of the rain*] (2012).
18. The artist Oré, interview with the author, 2013.
19. See Julia Tulke, 'Oxi-Nein-No: Some Visual Impressions from the Streets of Athens' (2015). Available at http://aestheticsofcrisis.org/2015/oxi-no-nein-some-visual-impressions-from-the-streets-of-athens/ (accessed 10 August 2016).
20. I have found this to be true in my own research, but it is also confirmed in other accounts of the Athenian street art scene, notably in Tsilimpounidi, 'Street Art and Urban Belonging' and Georgios Stampoulidis, 'Rethinking Athens as Text: The Linguistic Context of Athenian Graffiti During the Crisis', *Journal of Language Works* 1/1 (2016) pp. 10–23.
21. Political Stencil Collective, *Political Stencil in the Streets of Athens* (Athens, 2014). Available at http://www.politicalstencil.com/wp-content/uploads/2014/07/political_stencil_book_web-opt.pdf (accessed 10 June 2016).
22. The artist Cacao Rocks, interview with the author, 2013.
23. Ibid.
24. For a recent example see Naya Kostiani, 'Μήπως έχουμε ξεφύγει λίγο με το tagging στην Αθήνα;' [Is Tagging in Athens Getting out of Hand?], *The Huffington Post Greece*, June 24, 2016. Available at http://www.huffingtonpost.gr/2016/06/23/culture-mhpws-exoume-ksefygei-ligo-me-to-tagging-sthn-athina_n_10589910.html (accessed 10 August 2016).

25. Artemis Leontis, 'Not Another Polytechnic Occupation! Reading the Graffiti on the Athens Polytechneio, March 2015', *Hot Spots Cultural Anthropology* (2016). Available at https://culanth.org/fieldsights/862-not-another-polytechnic-occupation-reading-the-graffiti-on-the-athens-polytechneio-march-2015 (accessed 10 August 2016).
26. Quoted in Tsilimpounidi, 'Street Art and Urban Belonging', p. 85.
27. For an example see Christoph Asche, '19 Pieces of Athens Graffiti That Perfectly Sum up the Attitude of Young Greeks', *Huffington Post*, June 18, 2015. Available at http://www.huffingtonpost.com/2015/06/18/graffiti-in-athens_n_7611580.html (accessed 10 June 2016).
28. I offer a more quantitative assessment in Julia Tulke, 'Aesthetics of Crisis. Political Street Art in Athens in the Context of the Crisis', op.cit., pp. 38–44.
29. Daniel Knight, an anthropologist who has charted the impact of the crisis in rural Trikala in central Greece, made a related observation in his research, when one of his respondents described herself as feeling 'physically beaten', her 'bones crushed' by the crisis. Daniel M. Knight, *History, Time, and Economic Crisis in Central Greece* (London, 2015), p. 2.
30. Maurizio Lazzarato, *The Making of the Indebted Man: An Essay on the Neoliberal Condition* (Los Angeles, 2012), p. 47.
31. Knight, *History, Time, and Economic Crisis*, pp. 3–5.
32. Michael Herzfeld, 'Crisis Attack: Impromptu Ethnography in the Greek Maelstrom', *Anthropology Today* 27/5 (2011), p. 23.
33. Max Haiven, *Crises of Imagination, Crises of Power: Capitalism, Culture and Resistance in a Post-Crash World* (London, 2014), p. 7.
34. Lazzarato, *The Indebted Man*, p. 10.
35. See Judith Butler, *Precarious Life: The Power of Mourning and Violence* (London & New York, 2004), p. 30.
36. Petros Babasikas, 'Crisis Landscapes', 2014. Available at http://depressionera.gr/228010/2556156/texts/petros-babasikas (accessed 7 April 2016).
37. Eva Fotiadi, 'State Interventions in Public Space in Athens and the Mediatization of the Crisis: Sustaining the Unsustainable Using Precarity as a Tool', *European Journal of Cultural Studies* 2015, p. 9.
38. Gesa Helms, Marina Vischmidt, and Lauren Berlant, 'Affect & the Politics of Austerity: An Interview Exchange with Lauren Berlant', *Variant* 39/40, 2010 Available at http://www.variant.org.uk/39_40texts/berlant39_40.html (accessed 10 June 2016).
39. Lauren Berlant, 'Austerity, Precarity, Awkwardness', Paper presented at the Annual Meeting of the American Anthropological Association (Montreal, 2011). Available at https://supervalentthought.files.wordpress.com/2011/12/berlant-aaa-2011final.pdf (accessed 10 June 2016), p. 3.
40. See Fran Tonkiss, 'Austerity Urbanism and the Makeshift City', *City* 17/3 (2013), pp. 312–24.
41. Berlant, 'Austerity, Precarity, Awkwardness', p. 2.

CHAPTER 9

NOSTALGIC VISIONS OF THE GREEK COUNTRYSIDE IN TIMES OF CRISIS: NATIONAL IDYLL, PERSONAL FULFILMENT OR RESCUING THE ECOSYSTEM

Trine Stauning Willert

Introduction

Nostalgia for the countryside and the ideal of an authentic life in harmony with nature as an alternative to urban life is nothing new. It has played a role in human history since classical antiquity, but has acquired even more significance since the early modern period. In the age of nation building, the ideal of the ancestral landscape became a powerful trope for mobilizing people in favour of a national cause, thus replacing the ideal of heavenly 'Paradise' as the longed-for site of redemption. The horrors of World Wars I and II intensified criticism against modern civilization and the 1960s flower-power movements in the West represented a longing for simpler means of production and human relations, laying the foundations for today's ecological movements. The intense globalization of the last few decades has both caused and facilitated a growth in environmental awareness that brings nature back to the core of discussions about 'the good life'.

Greece forms an interesting object of study when examining the new nature discourses that emerge in response to the ever-intensifying patterns of consumerism and debt economies increasingly experienced both in the developed and the developing world. The predominant socio-political situation in Greece over the last seven years is the so-called Greek crisis with its economic, social, political and ideological repercussions. With an ever-increasing unemployment rate, affecting young people especially, it is in the cities that the effects of the crisis are felt the most. The city thus becomes a symbol of decay which does not offer any vision for the future, while the countryside is projected as a hopeful alternative by certain political and cultural actors.

Contrary to most western European countries, a large part of the Greek population has retained a close emotional and practical relationship to an ancestral village or country region. Relations with this place are maintained through holidays and perhaps through the consumption of agricultural goods (oil, vegetables, herbs and so on). Consequently, the countryside in Greece has up until today been represented as something less distant than rural regions in countries like Britain and Denmark, where most people do not experience an attachment to an ancestral village or region. It seems to me that the economic crisis has enforced such representations significantly. I regard the intensified attention to the countryside as an expression of nostalgia, a longing not only for life before the crisis, but for a life before the life style that led to the crisis. Various versions of this countryside discourse embody a longing for a pre-capitalist and pre-urbanization life. In these cases, the nostalgia does not only function as a comforting day-dream about an imagined lost past and home in harmony with nature. The nostalgia for an imagined harmonious pre-urbanization past has the potential to function as a discursive device to enhance a critique of civilization. This is the case in some of the cultural texts that are examined in this chapter.

In the years from 2011 to 2013, newspaper headlines frequently referred to the 'return to the countryside' as an alternative to the crisis.[1] At the same time, leading politicians attempted to project increased employment in the agricultural sphere as a way out of it. Adopting a favourable perspective on these efforts, one might say that there were some good reasons for this strategy, as there is much unexploited potential in Greek agriculture and there is a desperate need for increasing domestic production to avoid importing basic goods. Growth in agriculture would mean a better export–import balance, and it would directly feed more people. However, from a more critical point of view one could interpret the eagerness with which certain politicians promoted a 'return to the countryside' and support for the farming occupations as (1) fishing for votes among people belonging to occupations that were always under pressure, (2) improving unemployment statistics by sending young unemployed people to work in farming and (3) creating an idealized counter-image of the crisis as a way of finding happiness and authenticity through a so-called 'return to the roots'. The latter seems to have been the strategy of PASOK politician Kostas Skandalidis who, as Minister of Agriculture from 2010 to 2012, proclaimed: 'Some years ago the average Greek dreamt of a villa in the northern suburbs, a big car and a weekend cottage [. . .] Now people search for better human relations in smaller communities, greater security and a return to the roots'.[2] Even though some people may find it hard to trust the good intentions of this politician, who has been accused of being part of the abuse of public money that led to the crisis, the quotation does reflect a tendency found in parts of the population, something which can also be seen in the media landscape.

Mass media have played a double role in promoting the countryside as a crisis solution. On the one hand, news media have been thirsty for good stories to tell despite the crisis. Statistics and opinion surveys showing clear tendencies of relocation from urban to rural areas and increasing employment in the agricultural sector have provided substance for media stories about change and hope for a way out of the crisis. On the other hand, the depressing crisis discourse in news media has provided the media entertainment industry with a chance to profit from an increasing need among the population for comforting nostalgic stories and images of a better life, as in the good old days. This can be seen in the sphere of advertising where the countryside has been projected as a guarantee for pure, authentic and robust products providing the consumer not only with the real taste of the good old days, but also with a feeling of being there, of being part of that story, far from the plight of the city and the crisis.

By examining cultural texts such as TV shows and literature, this chapter focuses on how the countryside as an ideal has appeared in Greek cultural discourses since the onset of the economic crisis. The purpose is to show how the countryside, and longing for it, can be made to serve various ends and represent very different proposals for crisis alternatives on three distinct levels, namely the collective national, the individual personal and the universal ecological level. Below, I will briefly refer to some recent theoretical approaches to the concept of nostalgia that have framed my approach to the various popular uses of nostalgia for the countryside. After considering countryside discourses in two TV shows, both of which reflect the political and media interests described above in different ways, I turn to three short novels by Yannis Makridakis which form particular representations of this author's blending of nature nostalgia, political activism and literary expression.

Nostalgia for nation and nature: Restorative, reflective and counter

Nostalgia is usually associated with idealization of what is longed for. Because of this tendency towards idealization, nostalgia is often looked upon with contempt as a not very sophisticated emotion that should preferably be avoided, or at least kept at an ironic distance, in fine art. Lately, however, nostalgia seems to be experiencing a kind of rehabilitation which can be seen in particular among authors and literary scholars. The spark of this new paradigm in nostalgia studies seems to have been Svetlana Boym's *The Future of Nostalgia*.[3] In this seminal work, Boym recovers nostalgia from its bad reputation by pluralising the concept into two different modes: *the restorative*, which aims at restoring an idealized image of the past, and *the reflective*, where the emotion of nostalgia prompts reflection on and engagement with the past in the present. Understanding nostalgia as a double concept highlights its potential as both regressive and progressive.

Boym's research dealt especially with nostalgia related to the experience of exile and to bygone political and social systems in high modernity, not with a yearning for nature. Conversely, in her *Reclaiming Nostalgia: Longing for Nature in American Literature* Jennifer Ladino devotes her research exclusively to projections of nature in literature, introducing the concept of *counter-nostalgia*.[4] Ladino shows how nostalgia for nature can be used in criticism of the paradigm of progress: 'Nostalgia becomes "counter-" when it is strategically deployed to challenge a progressivist ethos. Counter-nostalgia is nostalgia with a critical edge'.[5] Ladino's work points to '[n]ew forms of nostalgia [in literature, which] include longings for authenticity [. . .] for connectivity – to "nature" and to other people – and for intact natural processes'.[6] *Reflective nostalgia*, which is the progressive mode of Boym's typology, emphasizes longing as a transformative emotional state, where nostalgia becomes a creative or life-changing force. Ladino focuses less on the transformative potential in nostalgia and rather on what she calls the 'return home' and 'the ways in which specific literary homes are imagined as sites from which the politics of the present may be renegotiated'.[7] What distinguishes *counter-nostalgia* from the restorative and reflective modes is 'its attitude toward the object of this longing – the home – and the ways in which it envisions a return to this space and time'.[8]

Boym's concept of *restorative nostalgia* is often mobilized in religious and national revival projects with the aim of preserving a cultural or political status quo, while *reflective nostalgia* represents individual or collective reflection on how longing for the past can inform the present and the future. Ladino's concept of *counter-nostalgia* points to even wider trans-national processes of revising human past, present and future. Contrary to nostalgia in collective national settings, 'counter-nostalgia revisits a dynamic past in a way that challenges dominant histories and reflects critically on the present'.[9] I aim to show how the selected Greek cultural texts can be interpreted as representing a mobilization of nostalgia on three different levels: (1) the restorative national, (2) the reflective or transformative personal and (3) the counter-nostalgic universal.

Back to the village

The first example of countryside discourse is the TV show *Επιστροφή στο χωριό* [*Back to the village*], produced and screened by the private channel Alpha. Eleven episodes of 80 minutes each were screened at noon on Sundays from the autumn of 2014 to the spring of 2015, and it received high ratings, especially among the elderly audience.[10] Each episode visits a different Greek province and a particular village which hosts the show in their main square. The show has all the ingredients of a feel-good programme addressing people who long for past epochs but have no real wish to make a life change. On the official website of the show, it is presented as follows:

> Human conversation, dances and songs with a traditional tint, mores and customs that are preserved till our days, magical landscapes and products reminiscent of the good old days, bring us back to our roots, bring us 'back to the village'.[11]

The show intends to provide viewers with 'Fairy-tale images of the past,' but also an invitation to forget the future by living 'as if there is no tomorrow'.[12] The light and entertaining character is underscored by the casting of the hostess, who is a pretty, young and smiling woman.

Each episode adheres to a standard scheme that includes reference to some national historical event displaying heroism and myth, often during what is called 'the dark years of Turkocracy', to an ancient or Byzantine legacy, to a local Orthodox religious tradition, to a local tourist attraction or contemporary sport activities, to local customs including dance and song, and – not least – to a culinary speciality. The soundtrack is traditional Greek music, and the filming is that of a tourism promotion video featuring breathtaking landscapes and traditional costumes. The economic crisis is not mentioned directly, and the show is staged so as to make the audience forget their current troubles and instead remember, and take pride in, a common ideal past which the show claims to be still alive.

The show is a typical example of using nostalgia in the restorative mode promoting, in the words of Boym, 'a sense of a shared past as a "place of sacrifice and glory" by creating a kind of collective belonging that transcends individual memories'.[13] Nostalgia at this national level 'encourages its adherents to return to a celebrated origin to find both comfort and justification for the present'.[14] The TV show exemplifies nostalgia in its non-transformative version: a 'classic' nostalgia, the purpose of which is to comfort and soothe. As the show was produced and screened in the fifth consecutive year of economic crisis, the focus on national history and on the joy of traditional village life can be seen as an attempt to attract an audience that wishes to escape the depressing reality, images and discourses of that crisis. Three years earlier, another show took a more pragmatic and individualistic approach to the prospects of returning to the countryside as an alternative to modern urban life. This older show, presented in the ensuing section, reached out to an audience that was perhaps still optimistic with regard to ways out of the crisis through creative life changes.

Those who took to the mountains

The TV show *Αυτοί που πήραν τα βουνά* [*Those who took to the mountains*] was screened on Saturdays in 2011 on the Greek national broadcasting channel ET1. Thirteen episodes of 50 minutes each were originally broadcast, some of which were repeated on the ERT web-TV channel in the autumn of 2014 in parallel with the screening of the Alpha show. According to the producers, the show 'sheds light on people who even though they were born and grew up – or lived for a long period of time – in an urban centre, decided to leave the city and drastically change their lives and their work'.[15] The show represents a nostalgic countryside discourse that could be called 'nostalgia as an impetus for life change', as expressed in this quote from a young woman who left her academic career in Athens to run a guesthouse in her ancestral village: 'I lived well in Athens, but I always felt that I was missing something' (episode 6). The show's host is a woman whose role is to conduct journalistic research into these people's life choices. Her appearance, with spectacles and a 'serious' look, is that of an intellectual rather than that of the typical beautiful hostess.

This show also features magnificent landscapes and village sceneries that somehow idealize the Greek countryside; but the visual idyll is accompanied by quotations from, for instance, Voltaire, who said that in times of crisis you should 'cultivate your (own) garden' (episode 1), and Victor Hugo, who is cited as saying that 'nothing can prevent an idea for which the time has come' (episode 4). This embeds the show in a wider European tradition, in contrast with the Alpha show which is exclusively focused on the national traditions of Greece. The ERT show's soundtrack is a blend of Greek and Western pop, rock and folk music from the 1960s to 1990s with a preponderance of English-language songs. The show's musical theme, a Greek song written and performed by Stamatis Kraounakis, has an air of alternative Greek rock music; and the animated video that accompanies it indicates alternative life styles and nostalgia for the 1960s and 70s, exemplified by a colourful Citroen 2CV.

The lyrics speak about letting 'minds get some air', going beyond 'the bad luck (γκατεμιά), the imprisonment (εγκλεισμός), the black competition (μαύρος ανταγωνισμός)', ending with the words 'beautiful nature, beautiful crisis' – a rhyme in Greek – which indicate that the crisis is a welcome chance to discover the beauty of nature. Since it was produced as early as 2010, the protagonists' decision to settle in the countryside was made before the long-lasting repercussions of the crisis were recognized. However, their decisions are presented as prompted by a moral and ideological crisis that preceded the economic meltdown. The motives for leaving the city are about finding 'life of a better quality' (episode 4). One person says: 'With the salary in Athens you simply survive, but my goal in life is not only to survive but to do things' (episode 5). The theme of life change is the guiding principle of the show, and this has been carefully reflected in the soundtrack with lyrics such as 'I nullify my life, it means that I begin anew, I do not turn back' (Eleftheria Arvanitaki), and 'change your pace' (Robbie Williams). The will to change as reflected in the soundtrack is associated with a longing for nature, which is the other guiding principle of the episodes: 'I had very much missed being in touch with nature' (episode 8). Nature is also associated with freedom and with a quality of life that the protagonists had missed in their lives in the city: 'being in touch with nature, the warmth in human relations which does not exist in Athens' (episode 4) and 'enjoying the freedom that comes from being in touch with the earth; the earth attracts me' (episode 5). The first episode ends with the lyrics 'There's freedom within, there's freedom without. Get to know the feeling of liberation and release' (Crowded House), while the voice of the hostess says: 'From the madness of work and the buzz of the city to the calmness of a life with plenty of time and energy. So in the end, what are 600 kilometres when at the end of the road you find freedom without restrictions?' For several protagonists, the change, the freedom and the new relationship with nature have existential dimensions: 'I believe that nature opens the mind of man, inspires his personality, his relations and creativity. Here man is confirmed every day' (episode 7) and 'for me it was a matter of coming to terms with some existential issues; I have learned to appreciate the human dimension much more' (episode 5). But nature is also associated with business, because the protagonists make their new living on the basis of nature as a resource, pursuing such activities as ecotourism, organic farming and art work. One protagonist believes that 'local products are our future' (episode 5).

As was mentioned above, the Alpha show was produced in the fifth year of consecutive recession, and it presented the audience with a passive worship of national and folk traditions where traditional gender roles are reproduced and old crafts kept alive. The ERT show, on the contrary, challenges traditions by presenting alternative life courses and untraditional gender roles. Women build up their own businesses bringing development to the countryside, such as Sultana (episode 9) who left her academic career in Germany to develop a tourist enterprise providing culturally and historically inspired walks, and Fotini (episode 10) who left her research job in microbiology to breed animals in a farm. In addition, there are men who give up careers to engage in traditional female spheres, such as Sultana's husband who cooks and takes care of the children and Nontas (episode 8), who left his job as a dental technician in Athens to open a shop with organic products in a small provincial town where he – as the only man – takes artistic ceramics classes in his leisure time. In these narratives, nostalgia for the countryside is mainly presented as an individual personal longing which impels the protagonists to create a different future and revolt against the hegemonic values of urbanism and consumerism, thus illustrating the empowering and transformative potential contained in longing. In these cases, it is the pain of longing, the *algos*, and not the idea of *nostos* that is mobilized to inform the future. Boym's concept of reflective nostalgia, which also refers to playfulness and irony in relation to longing, is perhaps not appropriate in the case of these life choices; but because of the creativity that emerges from the longing, one might say that nostalgia here has a transformative potential, in this case on an individual level. In these individuals, the development of society towards urbanization and commercialization awakened nostalgia for their childhood or for the lives of earlier generations in the countryside. This nostalgia then drove them to take action and create their new conditions, endeavours which turned nostalgia into a creative force rather than a pacifying space of comfort and daydreaming.

The title *Those who took to the mountains* makes a link between these modern rebels and the historical myth about the Christians who, during Ottoman imperial rule, took to the mountains to prepare their fight for freedom. To conclude that the show presents the protagonists as freedom fighters against a new imperialist rule (the EU or capitalism) is probably too farfetched, since they remain 'in the system' and do not fight for a common cause. Fighting for a larger cause is a more fitting label for the author analysed in the latter part of this chapter. His literary work represents a third example of nostalgia discourse, a discourse which tends towards a universal level.

Yannis Makridakis: Natural farmer and author

The expression 'revolutionary spirit' is appropriate when speaking of the natural farmer, activist and author Yannis Makridakis. Through his website [http://yiannismakridakis.gr/], decorated with a red flag, he initiates activities to promote natural farming, the new paradigm of degrowth, and an educative forum called *'Simplicity'*.[16] Even without considering his literary work, we can hence conclude that he belongs to the category of progress sceptics. As in the ERT show, the mountain has a certain symbolic meaning in Makridakis' life course as well as in his literary work. Upon returning to Chios, his native island, from Athens where he studied and worked as a mathematician, he founded a centre for Chiot studies and a local historical magazine named after the Chiot mountain of Pelineo. Makridakis' first novel, *Ανάμιστης ντενεκές* [*One and a Half Tin*],[17] is a tale about a local folk hero from the 1920s who took refuge from the authorities in that mountain. The novel is a deeply nostalgic eulogy to its nature and to the communities that used to live there. The author said in an interview, 'Petikas, the hero of *One and a Half Tin*, is my pretext for describing the nature and the folklore of Chios'.[18]

After a number of novels with a historical focus, nature and farming have become the key themes of several recently published short novels (novellas) by Makridakis. The following discussion will focus on three such novels: *Το ζουμί του πετεινού* [*Cockerel's Soup*][19] (2012), *Του Θεού το μάτι* [*God's Eye*][20] (2013) and *Αντί Στεφάνου* [*Instead of a Wreath*][21] (2015). The action in these three novellas evolves around small-scale cultivation of the land. The protagonists are all men who own a piece of land which they have inherited from their grandfathers. The many references to life as it was in the days of the grandfathers, often symbolized by age-old trees that belonged to them, create the nostalgic mood of these novellas.

In *Cockerel's Soup* (2012), the middle-aged protagonist, Panagís, lives isolated with his wife on his grandfather's farm where he cultivates all sorts of fruits and vegetables, keeps a small livestock and runs a tavern. The plot evolves around a three-day crisis he experienced when he suddenly started watching the Greek news on TV about the economic crisis. Panagís used to watch wildlife TV shows on a foreign channel every night, so his daily life is full of animals – his livestock during the day and wild animals at night. Panagís is described as a true animal lover who stopped killing animals after once killing a calf. The book has detailed descriptions of the acts of killing, acts which engender pity for the slaughtered animal in the reader, too. The novel's starting-point is the three days of crisis which end with Panagís' breaking the TV set by throwing an ashtray at it. He used to watch the wildlife shows with great, almost devout, attention, but the late-night Greek news causes him to scream and shout at the news-speakers as if they could hear him. His wife, fearing that he has gone mad, calls their daughter in Athens to find a doctor to ask for advice. The economic crisis thus sets the scene; but its function is that of providing an occasion to develop a celebration of the richness of the earth which is able to supply man with all sorts of food for survival as well as beauty, creating peace and harmony. Panagís' garden has the best-quality trees. At the time of his great-grandfather, 'people planted in their garden only the best they could find, not whatever the one or the other told them, no, they knew [. . .] that's how the ancestors made their land which we now step on and you want to undo it, to give it all to foreigners who don't have a clue about such things' (42–43). As the novel was published in 2012, this comment refers to the selling of Greek land in the context of the economic crisis.

In *God's Eye* (2013), too, the link to previous generations is essential. The story is narrated in the first person by the hero Peponas, who talks to his scarecrow Diomedes while building it. Peponas, who bears the name of his grandfather, says: 'At the end of the day, Diomedes, I guess I take after my grandfather. [. . .] That's why I love the earth and the creatures. That's why I didn't cut the oak. Because in there lives the soul of my grandfather' (103) and 'when I depart from life I will go and live with my grandfather, Peponas, in the oak [. . .]. My soul will wander here in the farm and watch the next master when he rejoices in cutting an apricot, a fig. I will also become an eye of God' (133). The novel represents (nostalgia for) a pantheistic romantic worldview where God's eye can be the birds, the oak tree or the chameleon living on its branches, or the spirit of the grandfather buried under it. Peponas lives his life in total communion with the surrounding nature, a communion reflected in his talking to plants, trees, birds, insects and animals. The distinction between human beings and other creatures is blurred. He thus names the people surrounding him after animals; his partner is 'Weasel' and the anarchist who takes an interest in old seeds is 'Blackbird', while the animals are given human names.

In *Instead of a Wreath* (2015), the land of the grandfather is also praised: 'This small but fertile land, which his grandfather cared for with devotion as if it had been his third child, turning it into an earthly paradise and a horn of plenty' (28). The central character in this novel is a forty-year-old man who has returned from Athens to his native island to cultivate his grandfather's farm with methods from natural farming. The plot evolves around his taking on the duties of the village gravedigger and the burial of his mother. The philosophy of natural farming that the hero represents is taken to extremes when he attempts to recycle his mother's corpse by establishing a vegetable garden on her grave in the cemetery, an act which is of course seen as blasphemy by the local community and even more so when he also fertilizes the grave with his own stools. As in the two previous novels, Makridakis creates a universe where God is in every seed, tree and creature of the earth, and where human beings are just one material link in the cycle of life.

The novels' avoidance – with a few exceptions – of references to the parental generation can be seen as a dismissal of the generations who built Greek society in the 1960s to 1990s, that is to say, the decades when the average Greek population left the extreme poverty that characterized the first half of the twentieth century, especially in the countryside, behind. Makridakis idealizes the days of the grandfathers as a time before the rapid modernization and commercialization of Greek society, and he steers clear of references to the harsh living conditions of those years, with poverty and restricted access to healthcare. The argument seems to be that if you cultivate your own products, nature will provide you with everything you need – something that cannot be realized in the cities. The thinly veiled message in Makridakis' novels is that modern means of production and exploitation of natural resources are, along with consumerism, to blame for the contemporary dire conditions.

The heroes of the first two novels are middle-aged to elderly men with a long life experience. The hero of the last novel is the same age as the author, and his life resembles the author's in many respects. In an interview, Makridakis stated: 'Stefanos is me. His life is almost the life that I lead. Sparse with regard to the use of natural resources and my material life evolves around the life cycle of the soil. In the past I have very much felt society's hesitation, doubt but also aggressiveness towards my different view of life. Now things are much better. Of course, literature and the reception of my works among people helped towards this change'.[22]

This quotation indicates that Makridakis finds literature a suitable medium for communicating his convictions about the need for societal change. Like the TV shows discussed above, he also imparts a feel-good atmosphere to past ways of life in the countryside, more specifically on a small farm [μούρκι]. But in Makridakis' writings, the level of nostalgia for the past as a way out of the crisis is neither national nor individual. In the Alpha show, the common harmonious cultivation of the national tradition is essential; in the ERT production, the protagonists succeed on an individual level as they supposedly return to qualities of life associated with the pre-urban past. The characters in Makridakis' fiction are lonely fighters in the service of a larger purpose, and they are guided by a longing for an imagined primordial harmony in the ecosystem. Therefore, the novels do not idealize the village and local communities as the TV shows do. The aggressiveness or suspicion on the part of the surrounding community is reflected in the stories, which do not picture an idyllic village community with music, dance, pure food and honesty. Whereas the protagonists are pictured as authentic through their connections to their grandfathers, the local village people surrounding them are, for the most part, characterized by narrow-mindedness and gossip. The majority of fellow villagers are corrupt – either politically, as in *God's Eye* where Peponas owes a vote to the local party representative because she secured his son a job in the public sector, or economically, as in *Instead of a Wreath* where the rich Greek American uncle buys himself permission to build a mausoleum and otherwise flaunts his wealth and influence. Another kind of corruption is also seen in *Instead of a Wreath*, where people's health is threatened by 'pesticides with which they themselves sprayed their plants, from chemical fertilisers [. . .] and from the preservatives in the food they buy' (120), which is 'mass-produced and industrially processed food' (108). The village people have thus been corrupted; but the novels highlight the example of a few who have refused to give in and therefore keep the old connection to the earth alive, men like Panagís in *Cockerel's Soup* and Peponas in *God's Eye*. However, Makridakis' fiction also contains representatives of younger generations who return to discover and live from the earth and connect with the local folk history and wisdom, people like the historian-ethnographer in *One and a Half Tin*, the political activist/anarchist Blackbird in *God's Eye* and Stefanos in *Instead of a Wreath*.

A problem in Makridakis' nostalgic representations of age-old values is that they refer exclusively to patriarchal traditions. All protagonists are male, and they refer to their male ancestors. Female characters are at best companions, at worst gossips and consumers. In this author's work, nostalgia for a return to the countryside is hence portrayed as a male longing with male role models. This aspect may render Makridakis' literary project more conservative and essentialist and less counter-nostalgic than it may appear at first sight. However, the novels' insistence on the return to a model where man is an integrated part of nature's cycle on a universal level does represent what Ladino has termed counter-nostalgia, which 'inverts the idea of progress'. This is perhaps even better reflected in the author's political activism for 'welfare without growth', as expressed in the statement of intent for the institution of '*Simplicity*':

> So, in order to discontinue this blind course we believe that we have to 'un-develop', to 'minimize', to simplify our lives and our relations, to reduce our egos; to take up *responsibility* for our living, our food and the use of the natural resources of the life of the whole planet; we must learn to live with respect towards Nature, to reconnect with it and to draw from it a different system of life and values in line with natural unity, balance and harmony. (Italics in original)[23]

Makridakis' novels, despite their shortcomings with regard to gender equality and realism, do live up to Ladino's definition of the counter-nostalgic as nostalgia with a critical edge which challenges the 'progressivist ethos' and exhibits longings for authenticity and intact natural processes. The idea of return, of 'coming home' to an aboriginal time and space (associated with childhood and the ancestors), challenges dominant narratives on the national level, criticising contemporary Greek history and politics. The novels written in Greek are addressed to a Greek audience with awareness of Greek politics, but the (imagined) home to which a return is envisaged is neither national nor personal; it is universal, and any modern man may find it in the soil.

Conclusion

In the cultural texts presented above, I see the use of nostalgia discourse as a response to crisis discourse. Representing a classic type of national nostalgia, the Alpha show is like a museum unifying the nation in satisfying a common longing for the good old days when folklore, national pride and culinary well-being were supposedly common denominators of the imagined community of the Greek people. The Alpha show provides an escape from the present crisis through worship of the nationally defined past and the countryside. Viewers receive nostalgia-driven collective crisis therapy without leaving their sofas! In the ERT show, individual life projects driven by modern man's nostalgia for nature or childhood experiences lead to non-urban businesses where nature is employed as a resource for a more balanced life, whereby the effects of the crisis are reduced. The large community of the nation is replaced by local communities gathered around care for local natural resources, for example a mountain or a lake. The ERT show represents an individualist nostalgia that prompts action. Viewers are inspired to find their personal nostalgia for the countryside and make changes in their own lives. In Makridakis' ideological and literary project, the crisis cannot be overcome through escapist nostalgic visions of national pride or through nature-based business activities and an individual return to the countryside. The novels are driven by nostalgia for something more universal, namely nature at large and the idea of a natural cycle of production, a cycle in which man is just one link. The contemporary Greek crisis is present as the backdrop of the novels' stories, but they refer to the universal narrative of a harmonious relationship between man and nature. Makridakis' characters seem to be provided as role models for change, and thus the nostalgia that drives them is in a sense removed from the individual to a universal level, which is also what distinguishes the medium of fiction from the TV (reality) shows exhibiting real people in more or less idealized and staged versions. Whereas the protagonists of the ERT show search for harmony in their own lives, also on a family and community level, the characters in Makridakis' fiction are lonely male figures who are somehow in the service of a larger cause, namely that of bringing the world back into balance.

The reader is invited to reflect on the meaning of nature and perhaps share the author's almost religious vision of nature as a panacea for the crisis not only of Greece, but of the whole world.

Indeed, the nostalgic visions of nature and the good life presented in this chapter contain a large amount of utopia, and one might point out that they are reserved for the select few whose circumstances permit a move to the countryside. As such, they cannot be regarded as realistic vehicles of change and ways out of the crisis. People living in Greek villages are still a minority; no working-class families were represented in the intellectually stimulating ERT show; and Makridakis himself as well as his characters represent a masculine life-style independent of the duties and demands that come with family and children. Therefore, on the one hand, we might dismiss these nostalgic voices proclaiming change and revolution against consumerism and urbanization, especially since they are themselves, as TV shows and books, part of the cultural market. On the other hand, however, we can also see them as simply the tip of the iceberg under which we find a plethora of alternative post-national, post-consumerist, post-capitalist initiatives in Greece at the time of crisis, initiatives such as exchange economy, organic farming, seed banks and other local activities. Paraphrasing Margomenou and Papavasiliou, the debt crisis could consequently become 'a national turning point, not of trauma, but of new possibilities'.[24] The comparatively low degree of mental urbanization in Greece, which has kept nostalgic dreaming of the countryside alive as a feasible option, may be what makes this turn possible. And even if the remembered past is flawed or never existed, framing it within nostalgic discourse – especially in the reflective/transformative or counter-nostalgic mode – may inspire new directions in the midst of crisis depression.

Notes

1. Some headlines: 'Young people return to the countryside to become farmers: Not only a way out of unemployment but also a life choice' (*To Vima*, 16/8 2011), 'The young return to the countryside for a better quality of life: 1–1.5 million people are expected to return to the countryside' (*To Vima*/*KAPA research*, 27/3 2012), 'The solution to the crisis is to return to our villages' (*Galaktokomika*, 4/7 2013).
2. http://www.agronews.gr/business/fakeloi/arthro/79043/i-epistrofi-stin-upaithro-kai-o-fovos-tis-georgias-/ (accessed 17 May 2016). The full interview

is no longer available online. For the full quotation, see Vamiedakis, 'Επιστροφή στο χωριό' [Return to the village], p. 4. Available at https://issuu.com/levga/docs/levga7?viewMode=doublePage&e=3506162/2973984 (accessed 1 September 2016).

3. Svetlana Boym, *The Future of Nostalgia* (New York, 2001).
4. Jennifer K. Ladino, *Reclaiming Nostalgia: Longing for Nature in American Literature* (Charlottesville and London, 2012).
5. Ibid., pp. 14–15
6. Ibid., p. 226.
7. Ibid., p. 15.
8. Ibid.
9. Ibid., p. 16.
10. A rating analysis for 11 January 2015 indicates that the show was viewed by 21.4 per cent of all viewers and 13.2 per cent of young (15 to 44 years) viewers, which are some of the highest numbers on that specific day. Available at http://www.tvnea.com/2015/01/t-15-44-11-2015.html (accessed 17 May 2016).
11. http://www.alphatv.gr/shows/entertainment/epistrofistohorio (accessed 17 May 2016).
12. Episode 1, quotes from the speaker's voice.
13. Boym, *The Future*, p. 15.
14. Ladino, *Reclaiming*, p. 16.
15. http://webtv.ert.gr/katigories/psixagogia/30noe2014-afti-pou-piran-ta-vouna/ (accessed 21 April 2016).
16. The term in Greek is *Απλεπιστήμιο*, a neologism that resembles the word for university (πανεπιστήμιο) replacing 'universal knowledge' with 'simple knowledge'.
17. Yannis Makridakis, *Ανάμισης ντενεκές* (Athens, 2008).
18. Maria Stella Papageorgiou, ''Ενας «ασκούμενος» συγγραφέας στα χνάρια του Παπαδιαμάντη'. [An author 'trainee' in the footsteps of Papadiamantis], *Νέος Κόσμος* 15 June 2009. Available at http://neoskosmos.com/news/el/node/1558 (accessed 12 August 2015).
19. Yannis Makridakis, *Το ζουμί του πετεινού* (Athens, 2012).
20. Yannis Makridakis, *Του Θεού το μάτι* (Athens, 2013).
21. Yannis Makridakis, *Αντί Στεφάνου* (Athens, 2015).
22. Interview published 25 March 2015. Available at http://www.athensvoice.gr/the-paper/article/519/%CE%B3%CE%B9%CE%AC%CE%BD%CE%BD%CE%B7%CF%82-%CE%BC%CE%B1%CE%BA%CF%81%CE%B9%CE%B4%CE%AC%CE%BA%CE%B7%CF%82 (accessed 17 May 2016).
23. http://aplepistimio.gr/%cf%80%ce%bf%ce%b9%ce%bf%ce%af%ce%b5%ce%af%ce%bc%ce%b1%cf%83%cf%84%ce%b5/ (accessed 17 May 2016).
24. Despina Margomenou and Faidra Papavasiliou, 'Times of Crisis and Seeds of New Intimacies on a North Aegean Island: Activism, Alternative Exchange Networks, and Re-Imagined Communities', *Studies in Ethnicity and Nationalism* 13/3 (2013), p. 527.

PART V

LITERATURE AND THE DISCOURSES OF CRISIS

CHAPTER 10

UNDOING HIS/STORY: ON FATHERS, DOMESTICITY AND AGENCY IN PETROS MARKARIS' CRISIS TRILOGY

Patricia Felisa Barbeito

The fourth and presumably final volume of Petros Markaris' Crisis Trilogy novels titled *Τίτλοι Τέλους: Ο Επίλογος* (*Closing Credits: The Epilogue* (2014))[1] opens with a disturbing scene: Katerina, the daughter of Inspector Costas Haritos, the unlikely protagonist of this popular crime series, is sprawled on the ground outside the court buildings in Athens, unresponsive after a brutal beating with brass knuckles by *Hrisavgites* (members of the neo-fascist Golden Dawn Party). Katerina, who works as a lawyer, usually *pro bono*, is targeted because she is representing an African client whose shop was vandalized by members of this same neo-Nazi group. Although paralysed by pain, she is most shocked by the fact that despite the many witnesses to the beating, no one does anything to help her. The sense of social paralysis and disintegration in this scene is palpable: young, idealistic, socially conscious Katerina is cut down in front of the blind eyes of justice while an impassive citizenry looks on. The scene is typical of the openings of the Crisis Trilogy novels, a mix of *tableau vivant* and topical social commentary, it acts as a foil to the 'real' crime (soon thereafter Haritos is beset by a steady stream of corpses) and introduces the main issue at the heart of the novels: a failed social collectivity and public sphere, the type of 'social breakdown' and mood of existential pessimism and despair that have long been the domain of the noir crime novel.[2]

Indeed, the novel's opening scene indexes the political and social turmoil caused by events taking place in Greece at what was presumably the time of the novel's final revisions: despite the fact that the coalition government headed by the centre-right New Democracy's Antonis Samaras had consistently turned a blind eye to Golden Dawn's increasing violence against immigrants, in September 2013 over a dozen of their members were finally taken into custody after the targeted assassination of popular hip-hop artist and anti-fascist figure, Pavlos Fyssas. It is not surprising, then, that *Closing Credits*, like Markaris' other crisis novels, posits itself as a narrative of history in the making, a social history of sorts that provides 'a timely portrait of the issues of our time,' a description that has been applied to the contemporary crime novel more broadly.[3] These complex, contemporary, all-too-real plots have garnered much praise for Markaris, primarily from critics who hail him as an extraordinarily successful chronicler of Greece's current trials and tribulations: Markaris is the 'only writer who can really talk about what is going on in the country' writes Lakis Fourouklas, or, as Mark Mazower writes in his article for the *Nation* titled 'No Exit? Greece's Ongoing Crisis,' 'with social and political disintegration reaching extremes not seen since World War II, it is not longer easy to separate fact from fiction'.[4] Markaris has abetted this kind of reading in his own statements about the novels: in a *Guardian* article appropriately titled 'Markaris channels Greek rage into fiction', he describes his novels as correctives to strictly economic or political narratives; instead, his novels try to holistically capture the story of the crisis as a lived, multifaceted experience and 'tell the real story of how this crisis has developed and how it affects ordinary people'. He goes on to attribute even his choice of genre to the dictates of the situation he describes: 'crime writing provides the best form of social and political commentary available, because so much of what was going on in Greece now is criminal'.[5]

While these assessments of Markaris' novels are, of course, accurate – no one reading the Crisis Trilogy can fail to be struck by Markaris' keen eye for the impact of the crisis on the grain of daily life in Athens (even on its traffic flow) – they fail to take into account the literariness of his work. Yet the Crisis Trilogy's social commentary cannot properly be understood without a consideration of Markaris' resistance to narrative conventions and his interweaving of a number of popular literary, television and film tropes in a way that both parodies and *creatively rethinks* them. This playful experimentation is broadly evident in his resistance to the logic of numbers and genre in his most recent novel, the fourth of a trilogy, whose title – 'closing credits' – indexes film rather than literature. As Markaris maintains in his discussion of the role of Brechtian theatre in the student movements of the early 1970s in Greece, cultural subversion can often function as an important catalyst to political resistance, at first by providing an outlet for what he describes as 'quiet resistance', a 'feeling of satisfaction and hope that comes from the idea "something is happening,"' then by creating a space that powers political reimagining and intervention.[6] Indeed, it seems that Markaris draws on his own Brechtian pedigree to re-function the crime genre in order to model new forms of social identity, engagement, and collectivity.[7]

Given the multitude of commentaries of all ilks – economic, political, social, etc. – that the crisis has spawned, how exactly does the Crisis Trilogy 'tell the real story of ... [the] crisis' and 'how it affects ordinary people'? And how is Markaris' experimentation with the noir crime genre central to negotiating the telling of this crisis story? The main argument of this essay is that Markaris engages noir conventions in order to address and rethink the tension between individual and collective conceptions of agency and responsibility that have bedeviled not only the crime genre but also narratives of the crisis itself. Indeed, popular hegemonic narratives of the crisis tend to reinforce two, equally paralyzing yet polarized versions of responsibility and agency: on the one hand, Greek people are depicted as lazy, corrupt, self-indulgent and entirely responsible for their fate; on the other, as victims of (global) powers and market fluctuations beyond their control.[8] This dynamic is neatly encapsulated in the novel's opening scene of a beaten Katerina stymied by the absurd figure of Greek neo-Nazis, characters whose actions are conceptually linked to the country's systemic punishment, and are symptomatic of what Judith Butler has described as the 'peculiar turning of a subject against itself,' the psychic process by which we accede to and desire our own subjection.[9] Uli, Katerina's German friend acknowledges as much when he says, 'Greek neo-Nazis target Greeks. Everything you do here is wrong,' only to have Haritos angrily respond,

'You've settled in just fine, but you're still German at heart ... [p]lease tell us where German neo-Nazis hold their seminars so that we might send ours to learn how to do it properly.'[10] As Robin Truth Goodman has written of contemporary detective novels and policing narratives, then, Markaris' Crisis Trilogy 'make[s] transparent the transitions, conflicts, and movements between public and private spheres of political power', in the new neoliberal world order.[11] Part of the relatively recent resurgence of neo-noir crime writers around the globe, primarily at the margins of Anglo-US cultural hegemony, who recycle the sense of disillusionment and anti-institutional worldview found in canonical American noir while parodying many of its conventions, Markaris' Crisis Trilogy 'explor[es] the social effects of globalization' while at the same time 'examining the revolutionary possibilities of literature and popular culture'.[12] Along with those of his contemporaries', Markaris' novels are shaped by the legacy of the failed utopian leftist project of the 1960s; as such, they eschew predictable political polarizations between left and right, and instead focus on dismantling the discursive mechanisms – particularly the notion of an autonomous subject shaped by the logic of market forces – behind neoliberal narratives of globalization through their use of a particularly popular, accessible and commodified literary form – the contemporary noir crime novel.

The noir dilemma: Agency and collectivity

Noir, as many scholars of its fictional and filmic forms have pointed out, emerged in the early twentieth century in response to the advent of corporate capitalism and its laws of rational calculability. As, in Christopher Breu's words, a 'negative cultural fantasy',[13] it 'unleashed demons bottled up in the [...] psyche'[14] on both social and individual levels. On the one hand, in its focus on urban misery and squalor, it exposed the sordid, hidden underbelly of the dream of economic progress, modernization and development; on the other, its obsession with sexual and racial transgression spoke to the psycho-sexual anxieties buried under the ideal of bourgeois heteronormativity based on what Kristin Ross has described as the 'disciplining of everyday life' organized by three foundational concepts: hygiene, privatization, and consumption.[15] The traditional noir dyad – the square-shouldered, trench-coat wearing, morally ambiguous, disaffected, anti-social and independent hyper-male, along with his ritually sacrificed, sexually transgressive femme fatale foil and counterpart – and their haunts became the ultimate articulations of these cultural 'demons'. However, because of the noir form's 'inability to imagine a collective politics' – its persistent silence in the face of capitalist alienation,[16] as well as its ultimate fetishization of a radically autonomous, hard-boiled masculinity – it eventually came to reinforce the very system it set out to critique: as Christopher Breu puts it, noir:

> represented an adaptation to, as well as a reaction, against, the workings of corporate capitalism [...] hard-boiled masculinity represents an aggressive reformulation of male hegemony as much as a defensive reaction to what might have been perceived as a set of economic and social threats to this hegemony.[17]

Indeed, this resistant, autonomous masculinity rather than a symbol of resistance becomes one of reification, the ultimate expression of notions of agency and subjecthood shaped by capitalism. Novels like Jim Thompson's *The Killer Inside Me* (1952) with its psychopathic sheriff protagonist, the representative of law and order during the era of postwar economic boom and cold war tensions in the US, or Brett Easton Ellis's *American Psycho* (1991), with its serial killer investment banker narrator during the Wall Street boom of the 1980s, take this notion to an extreme. Both protagonists are pillars of society, apparently exemplary young men, whose dehumanizing brutality and violence is depicted as the necessary counterpart to their disciplining and monetizing ethos. In these novels, then, the noir masculinist ethos becomes, to echo Robert Polito's words, a clichéd figure of commercialized language and ideological deception, that must be 'detonated' and 'flipped on its head'.[18]

It is not surprising, then, that one of the hallmarks of contemporary neo-noir novels that try to reinvigorate socially engaged literature by reversing classic noir's trajectory towards an isolated, privatized subjectivity is a wholesale dismantling of its gender dynamics.[19] Indeed, one of the widely acknowledged trends in these neo-noir revisions is the supplantation of the noir detective by a younger generation of female sleuths or sleuth-like characters, as in Stieg Larsson's enormously popular Millennium Trilogy.[20] Even more importantly, however, this passing of the mantle is conceptually linked to the abandonment of models of negativity and resistant despair found in classic noir and an exploration of new forms of social alliance and active resistance, as in the brilliant, collaborative and aptly subtitled 'novel by four hands', *The Uncomfortable Dead*, in which Mexican crime writer Ignacio Paco Taibo's well-known, classic detective Hector Belascoarán Shayne is joined by his co-author, Subcomandante Marcos' delightfully unconventional rural investigator, who operates under the principles of the Chiapas *caracoles*, based on indigenous forms of self-government and community organization. While explicitly identifying themselves as the inheritors of the mantle of classic noir, these writers also thereby challenge the traditional, unitary cynicism and disaffection of the classic noir male protagonist. They replace or complement this character with a collectivity of perspectives and voices who, in unison, are able to form small pockets of resistance to the overwhelming social chaos that surrounds them.

Markaris' Crisis Trilogy takes its place among this new wave of neo-noir novels in its performance of a type of symbolic patricide. This patricide occurs on a variety of different levels: on the one hand, there is, as Lakis Dolgeras has pointed out in a recent analysis of the trilogy, the literal 'murder of the old Polytechnic generation' by the younger generation in *Ψωμί, Παιδεία, Ελευθερία* [*Bread, Education, Freedom*] (2012);[21] on the other, there is the wholesale transformation, as I have argued in detail elsewhere, of the staunchly antisocial, whisky-slugging detective into a parfait ice-cream eating, decidedly family-minded and community-orientated figure.[22] This concerted and gradual subversion of an autonomous, resistant masculinity and its legacy are also, significantly, linked to a complication of the neat polarizations between individual and collective, perpetrator and victim, active and passive subjects. Indeed, Markaris plays with the moral ambiguity characteristic of the noir form in particularly interesting ways. In his novels, we are urged to sympathize, and even at times empathize, with the perpetrators of the crimes, who are 'not driven by personal motives ... but rather take on the responsibility of punishment for their entire society'; they are 'intelligent and, on the whole, honest citizens'[23] whose actions are both shockingly brutal yet also somehow admirable. These murderers often take the law into their own hands, compensate for an inefficient and corrupt state – as with the self-declared 'National Tax Collector' in *Περαίωση* [*Settling Accounts*] (2011) – or, as with the murderers in *Closing Credits* who didn't know whether to 'cry or to kill,' and did what they did out of the desire to 'react',

act out valiantly against decidedly overwhelming odds and thus give voice to a seething collective frustration.[24] Instead, it is the victims of the crimes that the reader spurns: all male, they are clichéd, Citizen-Kane-like caricatures of a rapacious, self-interested, anti-social (almost all are alienated from their families) and power-hungry masculinity, who are clearly complicit in the causes of the crisis and are among the few to profit from it. Their deaths (deserved, to some extent, we are made to feel) function as a form of phantasmatic catharsis – the overwhelming 'crisis' is embodied in problematic and recognizable characters who are ritually sacrificed. However, while the moral ambiguity of the crimes simply affirms the function of noir as 'negative cultural fantasy', an imaginative outlet for what is forbidden or impossible, the process by which they are solved – Haritos' process of detection and the social and family ties that enable it – becomes a positive social praxis that models forms of collective empathy, connection and survival left out of the classic noir novel. The novels thus strategically flip the neoliberal mantra of privatizing gains and socializing losses – the much commented upon growing wealth gap between the rich, who have continued to get richer despite the crisis, and the rest of the population. Instead, they conceptually privatize loss – by ritually exorcising or marginalizing characters who embody the autonomous neoliberal subject – and socialize gains – the institution of a non-sovereign, collective forms of agency for change. Similar to the way in which the crime story is interwoven with a narrative about indigenous community governance in Taibo and Subcomandante Marcos, then, Markaris ultimately turns the crime novel (social chaos and disintegration) into a domestic family novel of sorts (social cohesion and reintegration). The Crisis novels thus posit themselves not only as a corrective to the traditional crime novel, but also to the trope of the broken or dysfunctional family, especially centred on the notion of a broken masculinity – evident, most saliently, in Yorgos Lanthimos' *Dogtooth* (2009) and Yiannis Economides' equally neo-noir *Little Fish* (2012) – that has become such a staple of contemporary crisis culture in Greece.

Instrumentalized bodies: A biopolitics of globalization

The opening scene of *Closing Credits* is not unique to the Crisis Trilogy novels, which are, in fact, replete with violated and broken bodies. Like the traffic stoppages that punctuate these novels and serve as symbols of the contradictions of progress that resonate, of course, with the importance of car as trope of modernity in the classic noir novel, these bodies similarly function as sign and symptom of the alienated and instrumentalized individual, reduced to an inert, voiceless number or statistic under an economic logic of rational calculation that infiltrates all aspects of social life. The opening scene of *Settling Accounts* describes a group of elderly women retirees who have committed suicide in their shared apartment:

> They sit across from each other on two armchairs with low backs and wooden arm rests. Still playing on a side table facing them is a television the size of an old computer, but they aren't watching the screen. Their eyes are shut and their heads droop to the side. Outside, an immigrant's accordion is playing the type of waltz they used to play long ago for the first wedding dance.
>
> The other two are lying down in the neighbouring room, on a double bed, their eyes glued to the ceiling. All four are dressed simply [. . .] Three of them are wearing black, woolen cardigans, because outside it is cold and a light rain is falling; the fourth, an old-fashioned dress, covered in wildflowers. The two in the front room wear thick socks and black flat shoes. Like the good housewives they are, the others have left their slippers next to the bed and have lain down in their socks.[25]

The focus on the materiality and vitality of objects – their texture, immutability (an old-fashioned dress covered in wildflowers), and perseverance (the still-playing television) in the face of the women's inertness – is truly uncanny and emblematic of the way characters are often distilled into, or pitted against, their function as cliché in the novels. The women are defined (housewives) and quite literally given shape by the objects they've consumed, and like these objects they are discarded when useless. As elderly widows and retirees in the noir economy of capitalist and heteronormative instrumentalization they have been rendered completely worthless – a fact they acknowledge in the suicide note they leave behind: 'We realize that we're a burden on the state, on the doctors, on the pharmacies and on our entire society. We're leaving: with four fewer pensions to worry about, you'll be better off'.[26] The irony of the last sentence merely heightens the dissonance and false logic of a social and economic system that demands punishing sacrifice of its citizens/victims. This sense of a vampiric system of austerity that feeds off its most vulnerable members and turns them either into corpses or ghostly shells, is everywhere present in the trilogy and its many jobless, hopeless, displaced, drug-addicted characters. The group of silent women who gather to bear witness to the ambulances that are carrying the retirees' bodies, akin to the chorus in ancient tragedy, reinforces this sense of feminized vulnerability. One of the women responds to the sight by shouting: 'my son sits all day with his computer searching the internet like a madman to find work. When I see him like this I wonder what he'll do when they cut off our phone, because we can no longer pay the bill'.[27]

Markaris' Crisis Trilogy thus reframes the notion of crisis to emphasize its biopolitics and the human, environmental and ethical toll it exacts in a way that consistently targets the core values at the heart of neoliberal globalization and turns some of its most salient clichés on their head (in the passage quoted above for example, the internet is not a pathway to freedom and independence, but a highly tenuous conduit to fruitless information). The very first novel in the trilogy, *Ληξιπρόθεσμα Δάνεια* [*Expiring Loans*], sets the stage for this project in its characterization of both the victims and the two characters who commit murder collaboratively. One of the murderers is a wealthy, horribly crippled ex-Olympic athlete, confined to a wheelchair because of the steroids he used at the urging of sponsors and trainers who summarily write him off once he is no longer competitive. His prosthetic 'right hand', the one who beheads the victims at his behest, is another ex-athlete, an African immigrant to Greece, and the crippled athlete's butler, who had to leave his homeland after the spread of GMO crops and big farming rendered his own family farm obsolete. Their targets are all important figures in the world of finance: a former central banker, a Dutch credit ratings executive, and the CEO of a small Athenian debt collection agency. In the depiction of this crime, then, Markaris simultaneously embodies and critiques the effects of the hierarchies implicit in the international flow of capital and resulting transnational migrations of people, as well as deregulation, privatization and the complete commodification of forms of cultural production, along with additional neo-noir themes present in all the Crisis Trilogy novels that include urban segregation, gentrification and the marginalization of the poor and immigrants, the uses of mass media communications and the manipulation of information.[28] This environment of systemic inequity, exploitation and petty corruption of every type – from the workings of the educational system to the power of pharmaceutical companies[29] – fundamentally shapes Markaris' characters. The killers and their victims in particular represent the uncanny, constitutive contradictions in hegemonic, masculinized narratives of agency, autonomy and progress. They are either stereotypical embodiments of masculine power and success (athletes, bankers, inventors) that are literally beheaded and shot in the head in the novels (a symbolic countering of their particular brand of rationality), or their abjected counterparts.

In this context, the repetition of the theme of suicide in these novels is important as it becomes the apogee or culmination of the noir gesture of resistance to characters' enslavement to circumstances – the ultimate, solitary gesture of negativity and an escape from/submission to cliché (or a dire statistic) through self-erasure. Interestingly, suicide threatens Haritos' own family at the very beginning of the trilogy when Andriani, Haritos' wife, is so traumatized by the sight of the man who leaps to his death out of the window of an apartment above theirs, that she almost loses her mind. Again at the very end of the series, suicide is the catalyst to the central crimes in *Closing Credits*: an expatriate German-Greek who returns to his long-yearned for homeland to establish a green energy wind farm on an island near Turkey is driven to hang himself by the slow frustration and final rejection of his plans once he gets there. The shattering of his starry-eyed, naive dreams of valiantly saving his suffering homeland is depicted as an especially harsh blow given the man's attachment to the image of his dead father, which he uses as a screen saver on his computer and which greets him each time he turns to it with the imagined reproof: 'well, look here, I managed to succeed'.[30] In all cases, suicide in these novels is associated with both an incapacitating isolation (an inability to imagine and implement collective solutions and actions that in typical social realist style are hinted at in the group of silent, waiting, watching women at the beginning of *Settling Accounts*) and the haunting absence of a father figure and his impossible memory.

'The system which has run the country since the fall of the junta is dead,' Markaris has said. 'The austerity measures have destroyed the political landscape. The question is if Greece gets through the austerity measures and survives, and if Europe can survive a Greek collapse. I don't know what the answers are'.[31] Deaths, survival strategies – both individual and collective – and potential rebirth: Markaris' Crisis Trilogy consistently and cumulatively articulates the depletion of a particular discourse of identity and agency, in order to counterpose it to discourses that breathe new life into (paralyzed) subjects by reconstituting practices of active and enabling collectivity. The uncanny domesticity of the opening scene of *Settling Accounts* – the elderly women suicides – is juxtaposed with the nostalgic evocation of a long-gone domestic promise symbolized by the immigrant's accordion playing a bygone wedding waltz. Like all noir novels, Markaris' exhibit the 'ache of temporal distance and displacement' constitutive of the fundamental noir theme of nostalgia.[32] But if nostalgia, as Svetlana Boym has argued, is often driven by a 'restorative' impulse, the longing for the long-lost home and the impossible fantasy of the happy family, the trilogy, in its consistent exorcism of the father – punitive, disapproving, and delinquent fathers and the models of masculinity and individuality they entail – suggests instead a 'reflective' nostalgia that weds 'longing to critical thinking' and represents a 'strategy of survival, a way of making sense of the impossibility of homecoming'.[33]

'Grab the ram by the horns':[34] Impossible homecomings

In *Closing Credits*, when Haritos finally tracks down the group that signs its internet announcements *'Οι Έλληνες του 50'* [The Greeks of the 1950s] after each murder, he realizes that they are actually second-generation Albanians, who execute their victims with one bullet to the head in symbolic retaliation not only for their own marginalization and exploitation but also as a reminder of Greece's history of poverty and emigration, an uncanny evocation of a conveniently forgotten past: 'We are the Greeks of the '50s, Mr. Policeman. We'll take any job we're offered; we work non-stop and we can accomplish anything. Our only fear is not having work and seeing our family suffer. Ask your grandfathers, they'll tell you the same thing'.[35] Given the opening scene of the novel, it is both ironic and appropriate that the Albanians, when interrogated by Haritos about who actually pulled the trigger, insist on – often preemptively – answering in unison: 'the Greeks of the

1950s'. While Haritos warns the Albanians that their strategy will 'lead nowhere',[36] he is haunted by the legacy of the very decade that the Albanians conjure: the conflict between right and left, the history of dictatorship, repression and torture, cycles of economic boom and decline; and a 'Greece that never dies and also never changes'.[37] Haritos, the representative of the noir crime novel, is driven by a rueful lingering on both the lost potential of the past and its traumatic repetitions – he is, as Nichols writes of Spanish crime writer, Vazquez Montalban's, detective Pepe Carvalho, 'a man of memory',[38] who, like the Albanians, 'resist[s] cultural amnesia often perceived (and advocated by the dominant classes) as a requisite step for the assimilation of a "modern" identity'.[39] He thus insists on and models an investigation of the relationship between individual and collective or official memories, the past and present that speaks to the need for a different his/storical trajectory and engagement.[40] Haritos is consistently outdone, frustrated, preempted by the crimes he solves and the contemplated punishment of its perpetrators: a model of surveillance and disciplining that becomes increasingly problematic and even dissonant, given the novels' genre.

While Haritos is ultimately relegated to the past on which he dwells, he is increasingly complemented, if not outright supplanted, by a coterie of women characters who are decidedly future-minded. Indeed, Markaris' main engagement with the classic noir sense of time is his *rejection of its lack of future orientation*.[41] There is, on the one hand, Koula, his hyper-efficient, computer-savvy, and deeply empathetic colleague, whose gesture at the end of the Albanians' interrogation is to refuse the language of rational systematization and replace it with empathetic identification: 'I see Koula raise her hands from the keyboard, cover her face, and run out of her room. "Why is she crying?" I ask myself'.[42] On the other hand, there is the collaboration between Katerina, the lawyer, and her friend Mania the psychotherapist, emblematizing the union between psychopolitics and the rule of law, that increasingly accompanies and complicates Haritos's narrative of law and order, and to which he attributes a carefully muted, yet more hopeful vision for the future: 'It's not clear whether my daughter and Mania will encounter happier times. At least however, they can fight for less terrible ones'.[43]

As noted above, over the course of the trilogy, and indeed the entire series, Haritos changes dramatically, transforming from an approximation of the traditional, tough, terse, independent hardboiled cop and conservative everyman (laden with a predictable repertoire of stereotypical observations about women and gender roles, immigrants and politics), to an increasingly nuanced, sympathetic and empathetic character. His growing likeability derives from his capacity to poke fun at the stereotypes with which, as a policeman, he is invariably surrounded and thereby, relatedly, to address the crimes, not through the 'advanced logic of a Hercule Poirot or a Sherlock Holmes', but by tapping into a 'common psyche,' the 'folk wisdom' of his friend Zisis, as well as the larger community to which he increasingly turns to and collaborates with.[44] Part and parcel of Haritos' transformation in these novels, and what really saves him and his collaborator, Zisis, the leftist who spent time on Makronissos, from frustration and disillusionment – the fate of many of their neo-noir counterparts, who, unable to find their own relevance within the framework of neoliberal ideology are irremediably trapped in a nostalgic yearning for their irretrievable utopian ideals[45] – is Katerina. Indeed, Katerina, who is repeatedly described as extremely similar to Haritos, his child completely, very literally turns Haritos' police narrative of surveillance and disciplining into one of healing and community-building.

Markaris' Crisis Trilogy is as much a domestic, family narrative as it is a detective series, that transforms the bourgeois heteronormative mantra of hygiene, privatization, and consumption into one of ethical responsiveness, socialization and alliance-building. The trilogy begins, significantly, with the wedding of Katerina and her doctor sweetheart, Fanis. The preparations for the wedding are interwoven with Haritos's concerns about buying a new car; not a German brand he decides in discussions with Fanis, but rather a Spanish or Italian one, in a gesture of solidarity with other maligned southern European economies, the so-called PIGS.[46] This embedding of heteronormative, domestic, political and economic narratives to articulate and enable new forms of identity and alliance-building is repeated again and again in a variety of ways – across generations, political proclivities, and social strata – throughout these novels. Most obviously, there is the development of Katerina's marriage plot: her induction into the nuclear family and her temptation to succumb to the siren call of emigration that would enable the economic mandates of this plot. Katerina, however, resists this call; instead, the model of the nuclear family is supplanted by the creation of an *extended* (albeit still solidly heteronormative) family – the addition of Mania and her boyfriend

Uli to the family, for example – and an economics of collective support. This is evident in the 'business' Katerina starts with Mania to aid both Athenian youth driven to addiction and despair and exploited immigrants; as well as the homeless shelter for the destitute and elderly that is organized through her help and oversight and which provides her with bodyguards during the last two volumes of the trilogy when she is targeted by neo-Nazis. This parable-like reworking of domestic models in a way that clearly calls out the economic cooptation of neoliberal institutions – law, medicine, to name just two – is echoed in an even more intimate, domestic setting in the close-knit family dynamic that Markaris models with the Haritos clan: Andriani, Haritos' wife, survives the threat of suicide, by gathering together 'family', biological, adoptive, and extended – Katerina and her husband; Mania and her boyfriend; Zisis, the exiled leftist; even their in-laws, around the dinner table for a home-cooked meal and conversation: 'We haven't been alone as a couple since the crisis started', muses Haritos at one point. While Markaris' novels fully detail the destruction and dehumanization wreaked by the crisis, they also gesture toward the ways that Greek society might not only survive but also be recreated – from Adriani's self-help mantras to Haritos's collaborations and Katerina's advocacy.

After work, as a form of relaxation, Haritos likes to read the dictionary and pore over the shades of meaning of the various words he looks up: violence, debt, bureaucracy. In each case he struggles to fit the words to what he has experienced and witnessed, to both see through and expand the dictionary definition: reading the definition of 'terrorism' in Dimitrakos (one of the definitive Greek dictionaries), Haritos muses, 'Once again Dimitrakos has let me down, but he's not entirely to blame, he lived in different times [. . .] the constant threat of further cuts to our salaries, to our pensions to our benefits, that's a form of terrorism'.[47] Markaris' Crisis Trilogy similarly plumbs the potential of the noir crime genre to both articulate and define the pressing social issues of the moment and also to address them, to demand an ethical responsiveness of the reader that goes beyond a mere consideration and witnessing of the suffering of others. His trilogy, to paraphrase Judith Butler's work on the relationality of the subject, insists on an interdependence that is imagined and articulated as an 'ongoing normative dimension of our social and political [and, I would add, *psychic*] lives'.[48] In so doing it affirms the political power of the imagination, as well as the political function of a new use of noir, that gives shape to a subjecthood that escapes a permanent condition of torment and enslavement to 'crisis' through the creation of alliances that act out and transform the world.

Notes

1. The Crisis Trilogy novels are: *Ληξιπρόθεσμα Δάνεια* [Expiring Loans (Athens, 2010)]; *Περαίωση* [Settling Accounts (Athens, 2011)]; *Ψωμί, Παιδεία, Ελευθερία* [Bread, Education, Freedom (Athens, 2012)]; and *Τίτλοι Τέλους: Ο Επίλογος* [Closing Credits: The Epilogue (Athens, 2014)].
2. See Mark T. Conrad's definition of noir 'Nietzsche and the meaning and definition of noir', *The Philosophy of Film Noir* (Lexington, KY, 2006), p. 12.
3. The mystery fiction columnist Oline Cogdill describes this as the mission of the crime novel, noting that 'crime novels are the social novels of today.' Jason Pinter, 'The State of the Crime Novel' (2010), *The Huffington Post Blog*. Available at http://www.huffingtonpost.com/jason-pinter/the-state-of-the-crime-no_b_342918.html (accessed on 1 May 2016).
4. Lakis Fourouklas, 'Petros Markaris: the Greek master of crime fiction' (2012), *CriminalElement*.com. Available at http://www.criminalelement.com/blogs/2012/06/petros-markaris-the-greek-master-of-crime-fiction-lakis-fourouklas (accessed 2 June 2015); Mark Mazower, 'No Exit? Greece's ongoing crisis' (2013), *The Nation*. Available at https://www.thenation.com/article/no-exit-greeces-ongoing-crisis/ (accessed 20 June 2015).
5. Julian Borger, 'Crime writer Petros Markaris channels Greek rage into fiction,' *Guardian*, 13 May 2012. Available at https://www.theguardian.com/world/2012/may/13/petros-markaris-greek-rage-fiction (accessed 3 June 2015).
6. Petros Markaris, 'Greece: the other side of 1968' in Gassert, Philipp and Klimke, Martin (eds), *1968: Memories and Legacies of a Global Revolt* (Washington, DC, 2009), p. 210.
7. Markaris is a respected Brecht translator, who launched Brecht's reception in Greece with a 'comprehensive rewriting' of the German's work. He is also a playwright who has been greatly influenced by Brecht, including his influential 1971 play *The Story of Ali Retzo*. See Gonda Van Steen, '*The Story of Ali Retzo*: Brecthian theatre in Greece under the military dictatorship' *Journal of Modern Greek Studies*, 31/1 (May 2013), pp. 85–115.
8. For an elegant overview of the tension between these two strands of crisis narrative, see Maria Boletsi's 'From the subject of the crisis to the subject in crisis: Middle voice on Greek walls,' *Journal of Greek Media and Culture* 2/1 (2016), pp. 3–28.
9. Judith Butler, *The Psychic Life of Power* (Stanford, 1997), pp. 18–19.
10. Markaris, *Τίτλοι Τέλους*, p. 20. All translations from the Crisis Trilogy novels are mine.
11. Robin Truth Goodman, *Policing Narratives and the State of Terror* (Albany, NY, 2009) p. 10.

12. William Nichols *Transatlantic Mysteries: Crime, Culture, and Capital In the Noir Novels of Paco Ignacio Taibo Ii and Manuel Vázquez Montalbán* (Lewisburg, PA 2011), p. 15.
13. Christopher Breu, *Hard-boiled Masculinities* (Minneapolis, MN, 2005).
14. Nicholas Christopher, *Somewhere in the Night: Film Noir and the American City* (New York, NY, 1998), p. 37.
15. Kristin Ross, *Fast Cars, Clean Bodies: Decolonization and the Reordering of French Culture* (Cambridge, MA, 1994).
16. Breu, *Hard-boiled*, pp. 175–176.
17. Ibid., p. 5.
18. Quoted in David Anshen, 'Clichés and commodity fetishism: The violence of the real in Jim Thompson's *The Killer Inside Me*', *Journal of Narrative Theory*, 37/3 (Fall 2007), p. 404.
19. As I have argued elsewhere, Markaris' treatment of the femme fatale in the novel that immediately precedes the Crisis Trilogy, *Παλιά, πολύ παλιά* (A Long Long Time Ago [Athens, 2008]), 'systematically undoes the main tropes of nostalgia and consumption of the noir novel by exorcising its main gendered prototypes.' Patricia Felisa Barbeito, 'Telling the ewes from the rams: economics and gender disorder in Petros Markaris' Inspector Haritos Mysteries' in E. Minardi and J. Byron (eds), *Out of Deadlock: Female Emancipation in Sara Paretsky's Novels and her Influence on Contemporary Crime Fiction* (Newcastle Upon Tyne, 2015), p. 83.
20. See, for example, Susan Massey's 'Inheriting the mantle: Wallander and daughter,' in Macah Effron (ed.) *The Millennial Detective: Essays on Trends in Crime Fiction, Film and Television, 1990–2010* (Jefferson, NC, 2011), in which she argues that contemporary detective fiction challenges the 'heroics' of the traditional male detective and often changes the trajectory of the crime series through the introduction of a woman character as co-protagonist.
21. Lakis Dolgeras, 'Από την ηθική του αστυνόμου Χαρίτου στην ηθική των εκδικητών' (From the ethics of Inspector Haritos to the ethics of the avengers), *The books' journal* 68 (July 2016) p. 64.
22. Barbeito, 'Ewes,' pp. 63–64.
23. Dolgeras, 'Ethics', p. 64.
24. Markaris, *Τίτλοι Τέλους*, pp. 284–285.
25. Markaris, *Περαίωση*, p. 11.
26. Ibid., p. 12.
27. Ibid., p. 16.
28. Here I am borrowing from and paraphrasing Nichols' points about some of the main themes in the neo-noir novels systematic critique of globalization in *Transatlantic*, p. 21.
29. In *Settling Accounts* egregious tax evaders are murdered by hemlock; in *Bread, Education, Freedom* the former poster-boy student activists of the Polytechnic generation turned labour racketeers and entrenched government operators are literally hunted down; and in the final volume, *Closing Credits*, the owner of a lucrative *frontistirio* (after-school tutoring business) in a working-class area of

Athens, who used to work as a civil servant in public education and was instrumental in dismantling it so as to necessitate the rise of *frontistiria*, is found shot in the head; as are the following three victims: a nasty type who makes a very luxurious living (while collecting unemployment) by using his contacts to facilitate the passage of various kinds of permits through Greece's notorious bureaucracy; and two big landowners/farmers who live high on the hog off the profits they make from their exploited immigrant farmhands.

30. Markaris, *Τίτλοι Τέλους*, p. 285.
31. Borger, 'Crime writer Petros Markaris channels Greek rage into fiction'.
32. Svetlana Boym, *The Future of Nostalgia* (New York: Basic Books, 2001), p. 44.
33. Ibid., pp. 49–50; p. xvii. Boym describes an 'off-modern' tradition of nostalgia that critiques the 'deterministic narrative of twentieth-century history.' She attributes this more creative use of nostalgia to 'eccentric traditions,' 'those often considered marginal or provincial with respect to the cultural mainstream, from eastern Europe to Latin America', *Nostalgia*, p. xvii.
34. Markaris, *Περαίωση*, p. 396.
35. Markaris, *Τίτλοι Τέλους*, p. 285.
36. Ibid., p. 288.
37. Ibid., p. 290.
38. Nichols, *Transatlantic*, p. 131.
39. Ibid,, p. 120.
40. Haritos's relationship to one of his closest friends in these novels, the leftist Zisis who was tortured under the Junta in the very police station that Haritos was training as a rookie cop, is interesting in this respect. Zisis increasingly becomes a trusted collaborator in the novels, as well as a second father to Katerina and an integral member of the family.
41. In his influential essay 'Notes on Film Noir' (1972), Paul Schrader defines nostalgia, 'a passion for the past and present, but also a fear of the future' as the 'fundamental' noir theme: 'Noir heroes dread to look ahead, but instead try to survive by the day, and if unsuccessful at that, they retreat to the past. Thus film noir's techniques emphasize loss, nostalgia, lack of clear priorities, and insecurity.' In Barry Keith Grant (ed.), *Film Genre Reader III* (Austin, TX, 2003), p. 237.
42. Markaris, *Τίτλοι Τέλους*, p. 290.
43. Markaris, *Περαίωση*, p. 412.
44. Dolgeras, 'Ethics', p. 64.
45. Nichols, *Transatlantic*, p. 15.
46. This conversation occurs during the wedding scene at the very beginning of *Expiring Loans*.
47. Markaris, *Ψωμί, Παιδεία, Ελευθερία*, p. 108.
48. Butler, *Precarious Life: The Power of Mourning and Violence* (London & New York, 2004), p. 27.

CHAPTER 11

THE UNBEARABLE LIGHTNESS OF CRISIS: (ANTI-)UTOPIA AND MIDDLE VOICE IN SOTIRIS DIMITRIOU'S *CLOSE TO THE BELLY*

Maria Boletsi

If political realities in Greece since the government-debt crisis broke out in 2009 allow limited room for imagining the country's future, literature sometimes springs in to take on this task. Sotiris Dimitriou's novella *Κοντά στην κοιλιά* [*Close to the Belly*, henceforth *CttB*] (2014) starts in the present of the crisis-stricken country but stretches out towards the future to imagine a Greek society that oscillates between utopia and anti-utopia.

With the spectre of the crisis in Greece haunting every aspect of everyday life, the tendency to reduce cultural and artistic expression in present-day Greece to a product of the 'crisis' is amplified. This tendency has to be met with scepticism, insofar as it risks turning the 'crisis' into a master-narrative: an overarching framework for understanding every expressive form, which often ends up appropriating cultural products to dominant discourses of the crisis. Dimitriou's novella has not escaped this framing by critics – understandably so, since the narrative explicitly thematizes the crisis in Greece. Thus, one reviewer describes it as a 'surrealist carnival of individuals and groups in the midst of the crisis'.[1] Pari Spinou reads it as 'a parody of our course during the crisis'.[2]

Aristotelis Sainis even suggests 'crisis' as a framework for reading Dimitriou's whole oeuvre: according to him, Dimitriou's fictional universe is always 'in crisis' as it zooms in on 'critical' moments' in the lives of marginalized, idiosyncratic, deviant characters. *CttB*, Sainis notes, generalizes the crisis, showing how suffering and anxiety encompass society as a whole.[3]

This chapter also delves into the novella's staging of crisis, but does not read *CttB* only as a narrative about, or commentary on, 'the' Greek crisis. Omitting the article 'the' in front of 'crisis', I explore the novella's critical engagement with the concept of crisis itself in its multiple meanings – as judgement, decision, binary choice, separation and illness. I am particularly interested in the language through which *CttB* intervenes in the crisis rhetoric today in Greece. The novella's engagement with crisis, I argue, unravels in a discourse in the middle voice, which recasts the Greek present from a future that appears absurdly strange yet uncannily familiar. Through the middle voice, the novella seeks an expressive mode that shuns metaphysical 'truths' and moral predicates, yet also stages the *desire* for new grounds on which the imagination of alternative futures could flourish.

Crisis and (anti-)utopias

In a recent article on Greek 'prose of the crisis', Eleni Papargyriou situates *CttB* in a second wave of Greek literature published since the outbreak of the crisis. Literary prose published in the first four years of the crisis (2009–2013) centred on charting the grim crisis-landscape – debts, suicides, evictions, homelessness – as well as assigning responsibility for the crisis in ways that did not deviate essentially from those followed by mainstream media. Intensely preoccupied with the question of who is to blame, many of these literary narratives generated, as Papargyriou argues, a homogeneous image of the suffering country without any differentiation along class or other lines. After this initial focus on registering the symptoms of the crisis, literary works since 2014 tend to use the crisis as the background of characters' actions: they thematize the crisis 'sideways', through metaphor, synecdoche or allegory. Papargyriou situates Dimitriou's *CttB* in the latter trend, reading it as an allegory that focuses on collectivities rather than individuals.[4]

Dystopian and utopian narratives also pose among fiction of 'the crisis'. Dystopias certainly take the lead over utopias, as Greek fiction – especially from 2009 to 2013 – registers the desolation that overcame the country. Utopian fiction in this context is never straightforwardly optimistic: alternative societies and heterotopias set up in fiction usually lapse into anti-utopias or carry both utopian and dystopian dimensions.[5] Such is the case, for example, in Hristos Oikonomou's collection of interrelated short stories *Το καλό θα 'ρθει από τη θάλασσα* [*The Good will Come from the Sea*] (2014), which narrativizes the attempts at a new beginning and new mode of living on an imaginary island as well as their crushing. An island is the site of another utopian narrative by Sotiris Dimitriou, published three years before *CttB*: *Η σιωπή του ξερόχορτου* [*The Silence of the Dry Weed*] (2011). This novella lays out a future society in the Aegean, in which human relations and social structures are radically re-arranged: traditional Greek patriarchal family structures and the taboos that accompany them are rejected, and so is an anthropocentric view of the universe, in favour of an ethics of care for others, respect for nature, and freedom. Embracing carefreeness and play, the novella's utopian society overcomes hierarchical oppositions and eschews normative judgements. Even though the utopianism in this society is stronger than in *CttB*, which hovers between utopia and anti-utopia, *The Silence of the Dry Weed* is not devoid of anti-utopian elements either: at times the problematic sides of this alternative society shine through, while its final dissolution owing to the vices of human nature gives this society's utopian hopefulness a bitter aftertaste.

The Silence of the Dry Weed can be read as the 'twin narrative' of *CttB*. Unlike *CttB*, this novella does not thematize the Greek crisis, yet this work has also been received as a response to the crisis: reviewers stressed its attempt to offer solace and 'simple recipes for survival and reorganization' in 'a time of gloom, unease and disorientation'.[6] Other reviewers see 'crisis' as the red thread connecting these two novellas. 'It is not the first time Dimitriou writes about the crisis', Hatzivasileiou notes in his review of *CttB*; 'with his novella *The Silence of the Dry Weed* (2011) he sought a transcendent escape from the landscape of sickliness and suffocation'.[7] Although the future societies in both novellas display several commonalities, *CttB* uses a more parodic, self-undermining language that draws the more troubling aspects of the first novella's society to an extreme. Both works, however, are attempts to imagine a future Greece that is both a continuation of, and a break with, the country's past and its present crisis.

Utopian or dystopian narratives of the future usually spring from a critical dialogue or conflict with the present from which they emerge and revise our understandings of the past by revisiting it from unfamiliar perspectives. Utopias and dystopias also bear an intimate relation to crisis, in a twofold way: they tend to flourish in times of social, political or economic crisis that call for the imagination of alternatives; and they usually issue a *krisis* – in the sense of *judgement* or *critique* – of the present, confronting readers with a choice between two (or more) alternatives.[8] But if utopian and dystopian narratives thrive in crisis-times, how do such narratives relate to the contemporary historical moment?

Zooming out of Greece and going back to 1989, the era after the Cold War and the fall of Eastern-bloc communism was supposed to put utopias out of business. To be sure, many critics speak of the 'end' or 'death' of literary utopia already since the second part of the twentieth century, but utopian thinking in Western social theory enjoyed an extended popularity (with some intervals) until the 1990s.[9] The first years after 1989 were met with optimism by many Western liberal thinkers who saw in the global reign of neoliberalism, led by the US, the 'end of history' and the promise for democratic consensus and socio-political stability in a post-political era.[10] There would be no need for alternatives, it seemed, as the best possible model had acquired licence to rule globally. Thus, utopian aspirations would be absorbed into the course towards worldwide liberalization.

If in the first years after 1989 'the West was identified with utopia' in the minds of several Western intellectuals, the fall of the Twin Towers put an end to this optimism.[11] Today, it would be safe to say that history has not come to an end and liberalism as the only alternative does not deliver on its promises. The fear of others, enhanced since '9/11' and the responses it triggered, the global financial crisis of 2007–2008, the Eurozone crisis since 2009, uprisings, riots, terrorist attacks within and outside the West, the currently unfolding European refugee crisis since 2015, have all forged the sense of living in perpetual crisis – a sense that has been instrumentalized by many European countries to implement 'states of emergency', anti-immigration measures, biopolitical control and austerity politics. 'The concept "crisis"', Giorgio Agamben says in an interview, 'has indeed become a motto of modern politics, and for a long time it has been part of normality in any segment of social life'.[12]

The term 'crisis' (κρίσις) for the ancient Greeks functioned in the domains of law, medicine and theology, where it designated a choice: 'crisis' demanded 'choices between stark alternatives – right or wrong, salvation or damnation, life or death'.[13] Following Reinhart Koselleck's history of the concept, in the classical Greek context, crisis signified both an 'objective crisis' (a decisive point 'that would tip the scales', particularly in politics) and 'subjective critique' (a judgement or verdict, in the sense of 'criticism', but also in the juridical sense of 'trial' or 'legal decision'). *Krisis* as judgement assumes a theological dimension in the Greek translation of the Bible: as God becomes the judge of his people, the term is invested with the 'promise of salvation' and 'apocalyptic expectations' in the Final Judgement (*teliki krisis*). In the term's medical meaning, crisis denoted both a medical condition (the illness) as well as the judgement about the course of the illness (the diagnosis).[14]

Many of these connotations resonate in the term's contemporary uses. Yet, our common understanding of crisis today deviates from the word's original meaning in a decisive way. While crisis signified judgement and decision, 'the present understanding of crisis', Agamben says, 'refers to an enduring state. So this uncertainty is extended into the future, indefinitely' and 'is divorced from the idea of resolution'. 'Today crisis', Agamben continues, 'has become an instrument of rule. It serves to legitimize political and economic decisions that in fact dispossess citizens and deprive them of any possibility of decision'.[15] Like coffee without caffeine, this new understanding of crisis is deprived of its defining feature – choice and decision. This withholding of choice is exemplified by the so-called TINA doctrine ('There Is No Alternative'), a slogan often used by Margaret Thatcher to denote that there is no alternative to neoliberalism, and rekindled in Europe during the Eurozone and the Greek crisis. As Athina Athanasiou succinctly puts it:

> Through the doctrine of TINA ('There Is No Alternative'), neoliberalism is established as the only rational and viable mode of governance. Predicated upon this doctrine, discourses of crisis become a way to governmentally produce and manage (rather than

> deter) the crisis. 'Crisis' becomes a perennial state of exception that [. . .] renders critical thinking and acting redundant, irrational, and ultimately unpatriotic.[16]

This becomes palpable in the Greek crisis, where austerity politics is commonly presented in dominant rhetoric as a 'one-way street'.

Against this background, the need for alternative choices and for utopian imagination presents itself with urgency. Yet writers do not privilege the utopian form, while 'utopia's cousin – or alter ego – the dystopia', continues to thrive.[17] Although the reasons for the waning of utopia are too complex to address here in detail, it seems that the confidence needed for imagining comprehensive reconstitutions of society – a confidence that was a key ingredient in many past utopias – is maimed today. The bankruptcy of grand narratives and the sense of living in chronic crisis yields a deadlocked present: a crisis without the decision-making, without the critique. Utopian narratives are faced with the challenge of imagining alternatives against the odds of the TINA-doctrine and in a time that has debunked metaphysical foundations and grand narratives yet desires new narratives for the future.

Staging crisis

'Crisis' rhetoric may be instrumentalized to preclude choice, yet it certainly does not deter judgement. On the contrary, dominant rhetoric on the Greek crisis both in Greece and Europe revolves around the passing of judgement and finger-pointing, taking the form of a 'blame-game'.[18] The first part of *CttB* projects finger-pointing as the citizens' main obsession, setting a vicious circle of blame-transfer in motion:

> When the country went bankrupt our partner countries kept pointing the finger at us; their fingers stiffened.
> So we started, baffled, to point at one another.
> 'This one is to blame', 'and this one, and this one, and that one and the other one there in the corner'.[19]

Then, while the whole world was pointing at the nation until the country got the 'hiccups' from all the bad-mouthing, the blame-game takes another direction, as 'the hands of the fellow Greeks' 'shyly started to point at the Northern partners'.[20] Some Greeks saw the country's denigration by its foreign accusers as proof of the Northerners' envy for the sun-drenched country.[21]

The novella's starting point is a well-known wall-writing that can be found in several cities in Greece, featuring the verb *βασανίζομαι* [*vasanizomai*]. The verb is not easy to translate; 'I am in torment' probably comes the closest to its meaning. The novella's opening lines sketch the wide dissemination of *vasanizomai* in the country since the crisis:

> The word 'vasanizomai' appeared on the walls soon after the country's demise started. Fast as the wind, it filled the whole city. In Ilioupoli, on neoclassical buildings in Exarcheia, on concrete fences in Metaxourgeio, in Piraeus, in Salamina. It came to be used as a location marker.
> 'I pass by Agioi Anargyroi, then by the National Bank, on *vasanizomai* I make a right turn and I arrive at school' a little kid would say to the related question.[22]

While *vasanizomai* in the narrative becomes a measure of the torment of the Greeks as they are subjected to a relentless finger-pointing, soon another wall-writing appears, causing a slight turn:

> The country took heart when, to its good fortune, the word *lathos* appeared on the walls. Like a catalyst, it helped people gain overview of the general picture and find the most beneficial course, like running water does.[23]

The appearance of the wall-writing *λάθος* [*lathos*] – 'mistake' – marks a transit from finger-pointing to 'national self-awareness', taking the form of a generalized self-blaming:

> 'It's my fault, it's my fault' everyone was shouting.
> 'Please, it is more my fault'.
> 'No sir, it's my fault'.
> The 'it's my fault' was about to turn into a self-destructive movement.[24]

In a series of public tirades, 'agitators' expose the 'public sins' of various population groups, extracting confessions, laments, and public displays of penitence. In this satirical staging of a secular Judgement Day during which no-one is spared, the original meaning of the word 'crisis' (*krisis*) as judgement and its theological overtones are rekindled. 'Crisis' here comes down to judging the guilty and separating them from the innocent, although nobody's innocence remains unscathed:

> 'Yes, yes, we have sinned' everyone was shouting by then, bailiffs, dockworkers, drivers, registrars, farmers, minute-takers and lawyers, teachers, professors, pilots and tutors, customs officers, bailiffs and judges – no, not judges, let them be excluded – rectors and hookers.
>
> All the people, one voice of repentance. But the agitator was relentless.
>
> 'Damn you all communistocapitalists'.[25]

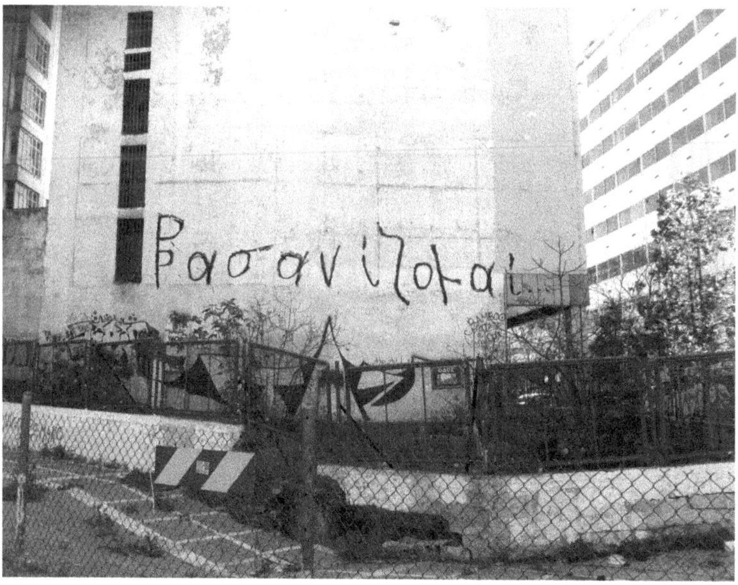

Figure 11.1 Version of the wall-writing *vasanizomai* in Stadiou Street, Athens, 2014. Photograph by Maria Boletsi

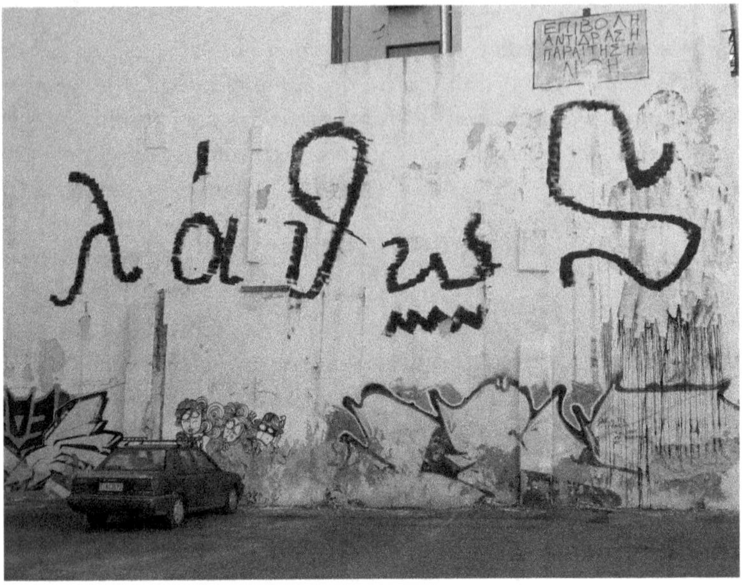

Figure 11.2 Version of the wall-writing *lathos* in Kerameikos/Gkazi, Athens, 2013. Photograph by Julia Tulke

Vasanizomai and *lathos* are widely disseminated wall-writings in Greek cities since the crisis broke out and have become emblematic of the urban landscape shaped by the crisis (Figures 11.1 and 11.2).[26] How do these writings function in Greek public space and in the novella's 'theatre of Justice'? Instead of being symptomatic of the crisis rhetoric, these wall-writings, I contend, deconstruct this rhetoric and challenge its overreliance on *krisis* as judgement and clear-cut assignation of guilt. Their challenge, as I will show, emanates from their grammatical form.

In contrast with the abundant statements of blame in *CttB*, *vasanizomai* does not address an explicit 'you'. The message in *vasanizomai* is introspective and conveys something about the condition of the speaking 'I'. The addresser (the verb's subject) is also the one affected by the action: i.e., the one in torment. This is typical for middle voice constructions, in which the subject remains inside the action and is affected by it. The 'I' is thus involved in the designated process, but the agent causing the torment remains ambiguous: it could be the subject itself – i.e., 'I am tormenting myself' – or an undefined agent external to the subject – i.e., 'I am tormented'. Both readings are concurrently accommodated by the middle voice, resulting in a certain ambiguity regarding positions of victim and perpetrator. This precarious agency and the bracketing of the cause of the action typify *vasanizomai* as a middle voice construction. In the face of the crisis rhetoric, which in *CttB* culminates in the agitators' ludic theatre of Justice, *vasanizomai* generates a crisis in the rhetoric of crisis itself by allowing the entanglement of perpetrator and victim, or the subject issuing the action and the subject affected by it. Middle voice constructions often underscore the event rather than the agent responsible for it.[27] Thus, *vasanizomai* deflects attention away from the cause and emphasizes the torment itself: the individual suffering, that becomes collective by being publicly shared on the city's walls.

The middle voice has disappeared as a grammatical category in modern languages – with very few exceptions – and has been redistributed into the binary distinction between active and passive. But although there is no verb form for the middle voice, some uses of language still constitute middle voice constructions. Moving from grammar to theory, post-structuralist thinkers, particularly Roland Barthes, Jacques Derrida, and Hayden White,[28] have conceptualized a discursive analogue of the middle voice, exploring its potential as a theoretical concept. As such, the middle voice denotes an area of undecidability that resists binary oppositions, such as those between transitive and intransitive or active and passive.[29] In Derrida, the middle voice is inextricable from his notion of *différance*:

> in the usage of our language the ending *-ance* remains undecided *between* the active and the passive. And we will see why that which lets itself be designated *différance* is neither simply active nor simply passive, announcing or rather recalling something like, the middle voice, saying an operation that is not an operation, an operation that cannot be conceived either as passion or as the action of a subject on an object, or on the basis of the categories of agent or patient, neither on the basis of nor moving toward any of these terms. For the middle voice, a certain non-transitivity, may be what philosophy, at its outset, distributed into an active and a passive voice, thereby constituting itself by means of this repression.[30]

The middle voice for Derrida is the operation repressed by the opposition of the active and the passive voice, and, by extension,

Dominick LaCapra writes, 'the "in-between" voice of undecidability and the unavailability or radical ambivalence of clear-cut positions'.[31] The middle voice marks a temporary suspension of pre-determined judgement in binary terms, enabling a multiplication and intertwinement of roles and complex positions of responsibility to emerge. The subject in the middle voice is neither active or passive, agent or victim. This 'and/and' rather than 'either/or' logic allows language to host ambivalent, opposed attitudes and propositions as co-existing (im)possibilities. *Vasanizomai* thus signals an alternative expressive mode that challenges the binary positions and destructive judgement (*krisis*) of the crisis rhetoric.

Lathos intervenes in the crisis rhetoric in a different but comparable manner. This wall-writing denotes a judgement (it signifies 'mistake'). Read as such, it subscribes to the judgement and partition of guilty and innocent in the crisis rhetoric. *Lathos* in *CttB*, some argue, designates the collective or individual mistakes that led to the crisis, and is thus taken as a judgement, comparable to the agitators' chastising or the citizens' self-blame.[32] As *lathos* hints at the nation's wrong course, Dimitriou, critics argue, 'takes it upon himself to correct this mistake' in his narrative by envisioning a new future.[33]

However, in its figurations on Greek walls *lathos* is always misspelled, written with an 'ω' (*omega*) instead of an 'ο' (*omikron*), i.e., λάθως instead of λάθος (comparable with 'misteak'). This misspelling does not 'amplify the magnitude of the mistake' as some contend.[34] Rather, it undercuts the credibility and transparency of the word's judgement by ironically incorporating the mistake the word attributes to an external agent within itself. The word's judgement is thus also directed towards the *medium* of the judgement, language, as inherently fallible, improper, non-transparent, and thus always in crisis. By encompassing the contestation, the mistake, within its structure, the wall-writing casts the crisis rhetoric as unable to convey an uncontestable truth or unwavering *krisis*, already flawed in its judgement, catachrestic. *Lathos*, then, does not aspire to make a wrong right or turn the judgements of the crisis rhetoric into truths. It suspends judgement in dualistic terms, allowing, like *vasanizomai*, more nuanced positions of responsibility, which acknowledge language's role in constructing such 'truths'.

It is noteworthy that in his novella Dimitriou in fact misquotes the word that street artists in Greece misspelled, by spelling it correctly: λάθος instead of λάθως. As the wall-writing's critical force depends on this misspelling, Dimitriou's misquoting is puzzling; it could indicate a desire – whether intentional or not is beside the point – to rectify the mistake and turn a faulty rhetoric into a better truth in his utopian society, by (first) correcting the spelling. However, the misspelled *lathos* on Greek walls, with which Greek readers are likely to be familiar, haunts the writer's correction with the impossibility of erasing language's mis-judgement. It suggests that language's judgements cannot appeal to extra-linguistic certainties. Dimitriou's rectification of the misspelled *lathos* is both a correction *and* a mistake (a misquoting) in the second degree. As such, it is contiguous with the middle voice, which allows the cohabitation of opposed states. Dimitriou's (mis) quoting thereby simultaneously captures the desire for a transparent language – or at least the possibility of justice through a language able to correct 'mistakes' – and the knowledge that every such correction still carries traces of a certain transgression, a hidden but ineradicable violence embedded in language. In this case, then, two wrongs do not make a right: they make right and wrong co-exist in tension.

This suspension of binary judgement and attitude of self-contestation typify not only *vasanizomai* and *lathos*, but several aspects of the narrative in *CttB*. The novella accommodates trust and distrust in language, seriousness and lightness, tragedy and comedy, utopia and anti-utopia, without cancelling the one through the other. In what follows, I trace how the features of the middle voice permeate the novella, both *thematically*, in the way future Greece is laid out, and through the narrator's *language*.

From the weight of the past to the lightness of the future

In *CttB*, *vasanizomai* becomes a historical marker: history is split into the pre- and post-*vasanizomai* era. In the post-*vasanizomai* era, the country escapes the malaise of the crisis and shakes off the guilt from an unbearable *krisis* (judgement) that had thrown the nation into a neurotic state. The newly found state of 'lightness' entails a divorce from grand ideals and political visions. 'Before vasanizomai', the narrator sarcastically notes, 'even the mayors in Ano and Kato Koutrouvaleika had a vision'; post-*vasanizomai*, however, 'politicians [. . .] were not allowed to have a vision'.[35] The goal of politics is not progress or social advancement, but consolation, alleviation of suffering, and pleasant living. In order to prevent the corruption of power, any prospective politician first has to serve ten years as a garbage-collector.[36] Any narrative that claims to hold the truth and promises salvation is mistrusted and old oppositional distinctions, such as left and right, evaporate.[37] *Krisis* as choice, however, is abundant: countless 'parties' and 'sects' offer ideas and worldviews to choose from without imposing laws or compulsory modes of living. Leaving behind an era of pseudo-choice in politics whereby self-appointed saviours imposed recipes for salvation that never worked,[38] the country enters an epoch of happy existential mess.

Here is a sample from the list of parties that competed during this era. There is the 'party of consolation' that strives to put people's suffering in perspective; the 'exonerators" sect, who absolve people from all guilt imposed by judgement and reject the 'illusion' of the autonomous, willing subject by advancing that the human mind simply follows the 'mind of the species'.[39] Then there is the party of those believing in some higher being; the 'agnostics', who eschew any knowledge as certainty; the 'anti-anthropocentrists'; the party of the 'pawns of chance'; the 'optimistic nihilists'; the party 'hallo asshole' which is challenged by the opposed party 'hallo wonderful being'; the 'party of confession'; the 'party of the camel' that advocates a bridging of opposed propositions in a golden middle; and the party 'what would the deceased have said?' that answers every question by speculating on how the deceased would have answered.[40]

None of the alternatives offered by these parties is raised to a grand narrative or truth. The parties criticize each other and expose each other's blind spots in a spirit of lightness and humour. Rekindling *krisis* as critique, this era leaves no 'truth' uncontested. The narrator's humorous and ironic language enhances the contestation of these conflicting worldviews, not allowing them to crystallize into dogmas. For example, the suspension of judgement and absolution of the population's sins, which the exonerators' sect propagates, is presented as an attractive option and simultaneously problematized. During a public speech by someone from the exonerators' sect, an audience member slaps him and says:

> 'Choose' he told him. 'Either the mind of the mind, or the mind of the species, or the sub-mind is responsible. But it is certainly not my fault'.

> 'But this is exactly what I am saying, dear' the propagandist [of the exonerators] said and in his turn gave him two slaps and a kick. What followed was a generalised happy brawl among innocent people.[41]

While political disputes are marked by lightness ('happy brawl') – an attractive antidote to the unbearable 'blame-game' – the ironic designation of the participating people as 'innocent' betrays the narrator's critique of this party's extreme evasion of responsibility.

Some parties even deconstruct themselves: the 'anti-illusionists', for example, have to live with the self-undermining paradox that rejecting all truths as illusions also makes their credo – that everything is an illusion – an illusion. This contradiction is self-consciously embedded in their motto: 'Against illusions, off to the great illusion'.[42]

Nevertheless, one party is singled out as having changed the course of the species: the party of the 'initial serenity' (or 'initial appeasement'), otherwise known as 'close to the belly'.[43] Its title refers to the tranquility, oblivion and bliss of humans when still swimming in the mother's amniotic fluid. The narrator likens this sensation to the feeling of wholeness when one floats in the sea, sun-drenched, surrendering to the water's movement.[44] This party's *locus amoenus* enacts the desire for a full suspension of *krisis*, both as distinction and as judgement: the foetus' oneness with the mother's body activates a desire for the wholeness of the imaginary order that resists the violent distinctions of the symbolic order.[45] This state of sweet oblivion also captures the wish for disengaging from the weight of history and the present as *loci* of guilt, neurosis, repression and pain. The baby's secretion of bodily fluids, shared with the mother's body, constitutes a form of eroticism 'without the slightest guilt or reciprocation'.[46] This desire for a debt-less, guilt-less, weight-less state is stressed by Dimitriou himself in an interview about the book:

> A focal point of remembrance for this novel was my love for the sea. Whenever I was close to her, I felt that in some way I shed my debts. That is, I forgot small miseries, the sea erases them. I drew the connection with the small sea of amniotic fluid in pregnancy and assumed that there is full bliss there.[47]

The Greek verb that Dimitriou uses in this quote, ξεχρέωνα (*xehreona*) – to shed one's debts – is telling, for only when you are free of debt does the judgement of others cease to define you. In the crisis rhetoric, references to debt are usually accompanied by moral judgement: a country's debt, David Graeber writes, becomes 'the rational measure of fiscal morality'. In other words, 'a nation in debt must have done something wrong, just as a nation with surpluses must be doing something right'.[48] This moral judgement sets the tone in the novella's first part. The utopian desire of 'close to the belly' represents a fantasy of escape from the weight of this debt and the judgement it unleashes, towards a lighter state – even literally, since we are lighter in water.

As a *leitmotif* in this future society, lightness takes the form of carefreeness, frugalness, play instead of work, and freedom from guilt and history. Lightness is projected as a remedy to the nation's crisis, understood as illness, as is suggested in the following doctor–patient exchange, which provided the foundations for the 'consolation party':

> As the patient walks out, the doctor tells him
> 'and get rid of stress'
> 'how do I achieve this doctor?'
> 'do not give a fuck about anything'.
> This medical prescription was deemed effective and the doctor in question was proclaimed as a major theoretician of the party.[49]

Echoing the medical meaning of crisis, the remedy here sounds less romanticized but not essentially different from that of 'close to the belly'. Lightness as remedy, however, carries the double edge of *pharmakon*: it provides consolation, yet it is also a poison that numbs the country. The latter dimension crystallizes in the novella's last part, when the nation's longing for lightness culminates in its transformation into a 'coffee republic':

> As we said, they [the Greeks] were not willing to work.
> So they thought they could exploit their comparative advantage.
> The sun and the sea. They decided to turn the country into a café.
> [. . .] They renamed it into a coffee republic and the flag showed a fuming cup.[50]

In this third phase, the stereotype of the lazy Greek drinking frappé coffee all day – so popular in Western European media during the crisis – becomes an official national destiny. Exams for the 'great school of the nation'[51] involve taking multiple coffee orders, coffee-serving skills are decisive for the university entry exams and a 'national coffee card' with stamps is introduced.[52] In this post-political era, conflicts between countries revolve only around commercial disputes. Nationalist discourse is reduced to empty formulas and symbols, as all ties with history have been cut. History becomes a set of simplified fixed stories and images for decorating commercial products. Its purpose is to attract tourists – a phenomenon also witnessed in present-day Greece, which in the novella is drawn to an extreme:

> The cups depicted scenes from the nation's three-thousand-year history. [. . .] Of course the tourists were stealing the cups as souvenirs but boatloads came to us from Taiwan. We had ample currency, thank God.
>
> By painting its history on the cups, the nation was finally relieved from its everlasting burden. It now had the force of a newly born nation.[53]

History becomes part of the cargo thrown overboard to keep the country's ship light enough not to sink. The 'burden of history' is a well-known topos in modern Greek fiction and 'an acute symptom of Greek national ideology'.[54] Setting the novella in an imaginary future allows Dimitriou to test a scenario whereby the longed-for shedding of this burden is fulfilled, while also using humour to hint at the anti-utopianism of the nation's newly found lightness. Reduced to souvenirs and fairytales that story-tellers recite for tourists, history in this capitalist (anti-)utopia is consumed by the present, just like the coffee in those cups. Determined not to let the past 'contaminate' the present with the suffering, guilt, and impotence of the *vasanizomai* era, this future Greece insulates itself from the past, preventing it from becoming an active force in the present. This is the price for starting with a clean slate: the death of history promises the nation's rebirth. This rebirth, however, is not accompanied by growth or change. Babies, we read, 'as soon as they were born, lifted their little hand with grace as if they were holding a tray and shouted "comiiiing"': ironically, the freedom from guilt and from the past comes with a pre-programmed life of servitude.[55] This future society freezes the past *and* the future: it rejects Western modernity's progressive conception of history as moving toward an unknown future – with all its ills and violence. There is only the pursuit of pleasant living in an eternal present.

Soon, the narrator tells us, the words *vasanizomai* and *lathos* cross the Greek borders and spread in other countries.[56] The whole world ends up following Greece's example – its renunciation of judgement and suffering, its surrender to the lightness of a history-less, future-less, depoliticized present. Countries derive their national identity from their key commercial products: Italy's flag boasts a pizza, Turkey's a baclava, Taiwan's, ironically, a replica of the Acropolis. Eventually, national borders fade out and the time of history gives way to the cyclical time of seasons: people become nomads, spending summers in the South and winters in the North or vice versa. They find creative solutions that allow them to live with a little and accept their humble place in the cosmos, indifferent to 'the nonsense-talk of religion but also the far-reaching philosophical questions'.[57]

The nomadic humanity in this future society refuses to live by a general law or metaphysical principle that judges and structures life – the kind of *krisis* that in the novella's first part generates suffering without redemption. They live forcefully without repressing desires. Significantly, they tap into humour and laughter, which, following Gilles Deleuze's take on humour, enable 'the joyous eruption of life'.[58] Their lifestyle carries an attractive utopianism, which is nevertheless thwarted by the uncomfortable contiguity of this carefree living with the quasi-capitalist (anti-)utopia that preceded this phase (the era of Greece as a coffee republic), as well as by the novella's pessimistic ending. The 'course of humanity after the redemptive words vasanizomai and lathos' ends in a brutal war over who gets to stay in the sun the most, leading to humanity's extinction.[59]

Middle voice as crisis: Humour, faith and (anti-)utopia

What kind of alternative or *lysis* – if any – does the novella envision to the present Greek crisis and the rhetoric around it? Its reception by some reviewers as a comically sketched utopia[60] and by others as a dystopian and eschatological narrative, registers a certain confusion.[61] Greece in the narrative passes through different phases: from the theatre of Justice during the crisis to the anarchical co-existence of various parties, then from the Greek 'coffee republic' to the global acceptance of Greece's 'model' and finally from the dissolution of borders and endorsement of nomadism to total war and extinction. Some of these phases are more utopian than others, but none is idealized. The narrator projects their lure as remedies to the crisis – a lure that mainly stems from their *lightness*, their freedom from judgement and history – and simultaneously hints at their anti-utopian dimensions. Like a pendulum moving incessantly between utopia and anti-utopia, *CttB* refuses to rest permanently on either side of a *krisis*. Each alternative model in this fictional universe is constantly at risk of being disproven, criticised or mocked by other worldviews, which expose its internal contradictions or absurdities. The critique that springs from these worldviews rubbing against each other is topped by the narrator's playfully critical language, which carries the lightness of humour and parody.

The middle voice allows opposed, paradoxical states to become intertwined. 'Don't forget that humourists are the most depressed people', Dimitriou said in an interview.[62] As a narrative in the middle voice, the novella suspends moralizing judgement and didacticism without eschewing critique: utopian and anti-utopian, light and serious, full of positive energy and pessimism, it conveys a sense of responsibility towards the future even if its messages are not translatable into moral predicates. As a 'writerly' text (*texte scriptible*) – to use Barthes' term for texts not easily consumed by readers – *CttB* complicates the reader's *krisis*.[63] The novella's *lightness* makes it harder to 'digest': cast in the middle voice, the narrative confuses readers' attempts to classify it or extract its messages in the form of either/or choices or 'do's' and 'don'ts'. In his distinction between the writerly (*scriptible*) and readerly (*lisible*) text, Barthes forges an implicit link between the writerly text and an attitude of lightness, since he views *seriousness* as typical of the reader of the 'readerly text': when the reader approaches the text as a consumer, he 'is plunged into a kind of idleness – he is intransitive; he is, in short, *serious*'. This reader, Barthes continues, 'is left with no more than the poor freedom either to accept or reject the text'.[64] This binary *krisis* – acceptance or rejection – is precisely what *CttB* counters through the middle voice. We cannot decide how to read this text: 'social satire',[65] 'surrealist carnival',[66] political narrative,[67] utopian, dystopian, eschatological, comical are just some of the labels reviewers use to classify it. Thus, the desire to release the weight of *krisis* as judgement does not only pertain to the novella's imagined society, but also to the narrative's own resistance to classification. This desire had already been articulated in Dimitriou's earlier novella about a future society, *The Silence of the Dry Weed*, which decides to abolish the judgement and distinctions of literary criticism:

> Grammatologists in general – especially all those kinds of foreign agents in the body of literature – ceased to exist. Literature was no longer divided in any way into genres, styles, schools, generations. You just listened through the ethereal waves, 'and now we will read you something from the art of speech'. And the whole impact on the listeners was limited to 'I like it,' 'I don't like it,' and even that was rare. They just listened.[68]

I take this disdain for literary criticism as an invitation for forging critical idioms that are not satisfied with clear-cut labels, but listen to the narrative's resistances to easy judgements and classifications. Thus, Dimitriou's lightness and humour in *CttB* also resists being be placed under the banner of a postmodern relativism that refrains from judgement, stresses the groundlessness of all discourse, and detaches itself from a community's 'we'.[69] His choice for humour above moral didacticism has a critical and, indeed, political function. 'Morality,' Claire Colebrook writes:

> is possible when cruelty is given a meaning: the forceful and violent interactions of bodies are subjected to law: *judgement*. By establishing a human, moral or justifying point of view we are able to see cruelty, violence and force as exercises of law or punishment.[70]

This version of *krisis* as moralizing judgement that ascribes meaning to cruelty by seeing it as punishment is precisely at work in the current crisis-rhetoric that casts the politics of austerity as punishment for a 'guilty' nation. 'Humour, by contrast,' Colebrook continues, 'displays the cruelty of violence: the unjustified or meaningless enjoyment of another's suffering'.[71] It is this cruelty that the agitators' tirades in the novella expose, as they inflate the moralizing crisis rhetoric to the absurd.

Humour thus becomes a means for contesting the crisis-rhetoric and unleashing repressed desires, drives and creative forces that disrupt the 'common sense' and 'seriousness' of this rhetoric. By recasting the Greek crisis *preposterously*, as an after-effect of a future that makes and does not make sense,[72] the narrative mobilizes humour to foreground the cruelty in the crisis-rhetoric and the practices it legitimizes. Seeking an alternative to this rhetoric, *CttB* does not propose another measure of morality or proper judgement, as satire often does.[73] There is no consistency and infallible truth to be found in this future society. Yet new ideas, creative forces and inventive practices constantly parade before our eyes, some of which may bear the seeds of a better alternative to the present living-in-crisis. The novella conveys an energising desire for a better future, albeit with the realization that any narrative that responds to this desire should remain open to contestation, including the writer's own.

In the middle voice, 'the subject and object of the action are in some way conflated'.[74] The narrator in the novella, a persona of Dimitriou, does not exclude himself from critique by assuming an external perspective: he remains part of the 'we'. A member of the crowd in the public gatherings during the crisis, he even takes the word from the agitator in order to confess his own public sins, which take up no less than six pages.[75] The narrative itself also performs several gestures of self-contestation, such as in the following passage. Talking about the party of 'close to the belly', the narrator writes:

> Perhaps during sleep – when we approach the amorphous mass before the embryonic state – we seek absolute sweetness and oblivion. Before the advent of the unknown sculptor who will free the fingers, reveal the nails.
>
> Man, the re-creator, may not know his creator, but steals his ways; from the inaccessible whole he paddles on the surface of the partial.
>
> Like for example this text was created when – like rain from the sky of words – the myriad words outside of it fell out and only a little cloud remained.
>
> Neither in this text nor probably in the whole language – in all the possible word combinations – is there any nugget of truth.
>
> 'There is another illusion. That of language' one of the anti-illusionists would say. But perhaps someone from the audience would get annoyed and swear badly at him.

> 'But why are you swearing at me?'
> 'But when, who swore at you? It's an illusion'.
> 'Oh, well ok then'.[76]

In a postmodernist vein, this passage casts the whole narrative as a construct of language and questions its truth-status; but not quite. The humorous dialogue Dimitriou sketches, contests the truth of the narrator's statement that there is no 'nugget of truth' in language, or, in fact, follows this statement to its full consequences. That is, the audience member's answer – 'But when, who swore at you? It's an illusion' – *parodies* a (by now) commonplace tendency ascribed (not always rightly) to postmodern fiction: to appeal to the deceptive nature of language in order to renounce responsibility for one's utterances. Aware that the writer, even if he can make no truth-claims, is still *accountable* for his text, Dimitriou assigns the weight of this accountability here to the lightness of a joke. Moreover, paradoxically, he rejects truth in writing but likens the act of writing to divine creation, investing it with metaphysical undertones. Just like the unknown God-sculptor, the writer also sculpts his text. Yet this betrays no nostalgia for the author as creative genius that creates *ex nihilo*: the writer's material is never original but borrowed from the 'sky of words' in a combinatory process that involves the *krisis* of selection and the violence of exclusion, as rejected words fall out of the writer's 'little cloud'. The resulting image of the writer – not a creator but a 're-creator', operating on the 'surface' of the partial rather than the 'inaccessible whole' – exemplifies the novella's discourse in the middle voice, in which contradictory positions do not reach a harmonious synthesis but co-exist in tension as manifestations of conflicting desires and fantasies that run through every individual and collective body. The writer searches here for traces of the divine, the poetic, in *this* world: on an immanent rather than metaphysical plane (the metaphor of 'surface' is telling) and in the 'partial' rather than in all-encompassing narratives. Thus, even though religion is relentlessly attacked in the novella's future society, humour and parody are not just affirmations of a postmodern nonchalant groundlessness: they convey a desire for another form of faith in literature and in the world, without metaphysical foundations and the arrogance of power. This faith is linked to literature's poetic, world-making power – a power, however, that the narrative also subjects to (self-)contestation.

Literature, Jacques Derrida famously said, is a '*fictive institution* which in principle allows one to say everything' and 'in *every way*', to 'break out of prohibitions' and defy the 'law' of all institutions, including itself.[77] It can create worlds, drive the desires and fears that underlie public rhetoric to their extreme or violent consequences or re-arrange bits and pieces of the past towards new narratives. This freedom, which is particularly palpable in utopian fiction, gives literature agency but can also make it politically impotent: 'The freedom to say everything is a very powerful political weapon but one which might immediately let itself be neutralized as a fiction. This revolutionary power can become very conservative', Derrida writes.[78] Literature's ability to intervene in our political and social realities, which stems from this freedom, can be mitigated and neutralised due to its fictional status ('it's just fiction!') or, put differently, its lightness.

CttB does not suppress this risk by constructing a semblance of seriousness. Rather, it projects the lightness of fiction – its irresponsibility, humour, inconsistency, conflicting desires – as an alternative to the seriousness and clear-cut judgements of the crisis rhetoric. The novella forms a discourse in the middle voice that combines faith in the possibility of a better world without abandoning a postmodern suspicion towards truth and grand narratives. As such, it expresses a *desideratum* of our (post-)postmodern times: the wish to move beyond relativism without reverting to truth-claims and essentialist mindsets. In the middle voice of (anti-)utopia that Dimitriou experiments with, this impossible wish is not a stalemate or an either/or dilemma, but a possible impossibility.

It is perhaps in this light that we can read humanity's self-destruction in the book's end. The narrative's willingness to open itself to *krisis*, contestation, also makes it vulnerable to its potential (self-)destruction. Defiant and provocative to the bitter end, with the unbearable lightness of its *krisis* in a world of unbearable seriousness, literature here does not let tragedy drown its humour, as it exclaims, together the last man before he dies: 'go fuck yourselves, idiots!'.[79] And although the narrator's own last words inform us that nobody survived to write this final message on the walls, we know better than to take him all too seriously, since luckily, in yet another paradox, the narrator must have survived to write this, and so does the reader.

Notes

1. Antonis Frangos, 'Ένα σουρεαλιστικό καρναβάλι προσώπων και ομάδων, εν μέσω κρίσης' [A surrealist carnival of individuals and groups in the midst of the crisis], *To Periodiko*, 7 May 2015. Available at http://www.toperiodiko.gr/κοντά-στην-κοιλιά-σωτήρης-δημητρίου-εκ/#.V5jVwatPjww (accessed 16 June 2016).
2. Pari Spinou, 'Κλαίμε άδαρτοι, δεν περνάμε αυτά που έζησαν οι παλιότεροι' [We cry without having been beaten, we are not going through what previous generations lived through] (interview with Sotiris Dimitriou), *Efimerida ton Syntakton*, 23 January 2015. Available at http://www.efsyn.gr/arthro/klaime-adartoi-den-pername-ayta-poy-ezisan-oi-palioteroi (accessed 16 June 2016). All translations from Greek sources are mine.
3. Aristotelis Sainis, '"Βασανίζομαι" σαν χώρα' [I am in torment as a country], *Efimerida ton Syntakton*, 22 November 2014. Available at https://www.efsyn.gr/arthro/vasanizome-san-hora (accessed 16 June 2016).
4. Eleni Papargyriou, 'Και τώρα τι; Η πεζογραφία της κρίσης (2015–2016)' [And now what? The prose of the crisis (2015–2016)], *Efiermida ton Syntakton*, 2–3 July 2016, pp. 27–28.
5. I treat the terms 'dystopia' and 'anti-utopia' as largely overlapping, yet different in that 'dystopia' denotes a disturbing, non-desirable society, while 'anti-utopia' designates a failed utopia: a utopia that takes a dystopian turn or is shown to not have been that ideal after all. Anti-utopia thus stands in a dialectical relation with utopia and issues a critique thereof.
6. Maria Moira, 'Θερινή ονειροφαντασία' [Summer dream fantasy], *Avgi*, 19 February 2012. Available at http://avgi-anagnoseis.blogspot.nl/2012/02/blog-post_6602.html (accessed 16 June 2016).
7. Vangelis Hatzivasileiou, 'Σωτήρης Δημητρίου: Ανάμεσα στην κωμωδία και στο παράδοξο' [Sotiris Dimitriou: Between comedy and paradox], *To Vima*, 31 January 2015. Available at http://www.tovima.gr/books-ideas/article/?aid=672678 (accessed 16 June 2016).
8. The decision that utopian and dystopian narratives invite readers to make is often a pseudo-decision, especially when readers are presented with a good versus a nightmarish alternative (i.e., no reader would choose to live in the society Orwell sketches in *1984*).
9. For the many ways in which utopia has been proclaimed 'dead', see Krishan Kumar, 'The ends of utopia', *New Literary History*, 41/3 (2010), pp. 549–569. Kumar explores the waning of utopian imagination in literature and social theory in the twentieth and twenty-first centuries.
10. 'End of history' alludes to Francis Fukuyama's book *The End of History and the Last Man* (New York: Free Press, 1992).
11. Kumar, 'The ends of utopia', p. 558. Concerning the period directly following 1989, Kumar differentiates the attitudes of intellectuals in the West and in Eastern Europe: for the latter, the 'discredited Marxist experiment' marked the 'end of utopia'. Ibid., p. 558.

12. Giorgio Agamben, 'The endless crisis as an instrument of power: In conversation with Giorgio Agamben', *Verso Blog*, 4 June 2013. Available at http://www.versobooks.com/blogs/1318-the-endless-crisis-as-an-instrument-of-power-in-conversation-with-giorgio-agamben (accessed 16 June 2016). English translation of the original interview, published in German: 'Die endlose Krise ist ein Machtinstrument', *Frankfurter Allgemeine Zeitung*, 24 May 2013. Available at http://www.faz.net/aktuell/feuilleton/bilder-und-zeiten/giorgio-agamben-im-gespraech-die-endlose-krise-ist-ein-machtinstrument-12193816.html (accessed 27 July 2016).
13. Koselleck refers here to classical Greece, the Hellenistic era, early Christian and Roman contexts. Reinhart Koselleck, 'Crisis', trans. Michaela W. Richter, *Journal of the History of Ideas* 67/2 (2006), p. 358.
14. Koselleck, 'Crisis', pp. 358–360.
15. Agamben, 'The endless crisis as an instrument of power'.
16. Athina Athanasiou in Judith Butler and Athina Athanasiou, *Dispossession: The Political in the Performative* (Cambridge, UK and Malden, MA, 2013), p. 149.
17. Kumar, 'The ends of utopia', p. 555.
18. For a more elaborate analysis of the rhetoric of the Greek crisis, see my article 'From the subject of the crisis to the subject in crisis: Middle voice on Greek walls', *Journal of Greek Media & Culture* 2/1 (2016), pp. 4, 8–11. This article contains an extensive analysis of the wall-writing *vazanizomai* in Greece and in Dimitriou's novella, from which I draw in this essay.
19. All translations of passages from Dimitriou's novella are mine. In Sotiris Dimitriou, *Κοντά στην κοιλιά* [Close to the belly] (Athens, 2014), p. 8.
20. Ibid., pp. 9–10.
21. Ibid., p. 12.
22. Ibid., p. 50.
23. Ibid., p. 9.
24. Ibid., p. 14.
25. Ibid., p. 17.
26. Although I have not been able to determine when the wall-writings vasanizomai and lathos first appeared, 2009 is probably the *terminus post quem* for their emergence. Different versions of both writings circulate, but they are usually written with distinctive calligraphy. *Vasanizomai* is usually followed by three ellipsis marks and sometimes by a full stop. For the various versions of *vasanizomai*, see Boletsi, 'From the subject of crisis to the subject in crisis'.
27. Linda J. Manney, *Middle Voice in Modern Greek: Meaning and Function of an Inflectional Category* (Amsterdam and Philadelphia, 2000), p. 22.
28. Roland Barthes, 'To write: An intransitive verb?', in Richard Macksey and Eugenio Donato (eds), *The Structuralist Controversy: The Languages of Criticism and the Sciences of Man* (Baltimore and London, 1970), pp. 134–145; Jacques Derrida, 'Différance', in *Margins of Philosophy*, trans. Alan Bass (Chicago, 1982), pp. 1–27; Hayden White, 'Writing in the middle voice', in *The Fiction of*

Narrative: Essays on History, Literature, and Theory 1957–2007 (Baltimore, 2010 [1992]), pp. 255–262.

29. Dominick LaCapra, *Writing History, Writing Trauma* (Baltimore and London, 2001), p. 20.
30. Jacques Derrida, 'Différance', p. 9.
31. LaCapra, *Writing History, Writing Trauma*, p. 20.
32. See Spinou, 'Κλαίμε άδαρτοι'.
33. Lina Pantaleon, 'Ένας ηλιόλουστος κόσμος' [A sun-bathed world], *Kathimerini*, 1 February 2015. Available at http://www.kathimerini.gr/801399/article/politismos/vivlio/enas-hlioloystos-kosmos (accessed 20 July 2016).
34. Lina Pantaleon, 'Ένας ηλιόλουστος κόσμος'.
35. Dimitriou, *Κοντά στην κοιλιά*, pp. 44–45.
36. Ibid., p. 45.
37. Ibid., p. 51.
38. The narrator's re-enactment of the following pre-*vasanizomai* scene parodies the lack of choice in these saviours' narratives:
"'Good morning, I'm here to save you".
'Oh, I see. Go sweep your yard sir. I have my own work to finish".
"Oh but you don't have the right to choose. On the one hand, you don't know the truth, and on the other, your heart does not have room for the whole humanity"'. Ibid., pp. 51–52 (my translation).
39. Ibid., p. 47.
40. The parties and sects are elaborately laid out in pp. 47–77.
41. Ibid., pp. 49–50.
42. Ibid., p. 52.
43. Ibid., p. 63.
44. Ibid., p. 65.
45. My use of the terms 'imaginary' and 'symbolic order' follows Jacques Lacan's well-known distinction.
46. Ibid., p. 63.
47. Dimitriou in Spinou, 'Κλαίμε άδαρτοι'.
48. David Graeber, 'The Greek debt crisis in almost unimaginably long-term historical perspective', in Antonis Vradis and Dimitris Dalakoglou (eds), *Revolt and Crisis in Greece: Between a Present Yet to Pass and a Future Still to Come* (Oakland and Edinburgh, 2011), p. 229.
49. Dimitriou, *Κοντά στην κοιλιά*, p. 73.
50. Ibid., p. 78.
51. Ibid., p. 79.
52. Ibid., pp. 80, 82.
53. Ibid., p. 85.
54. Gerasimus Katsan, *History and National Ideology in Greek Postmodernist Fiction* (Madison, Teaneck, 2013), p. 1.
55. Sotiris Dimitriou, *Κοντά στην κοιλιά*, p. 87.
56. Ibid., p. 88.

57. Ibid., p. 92.
58. Deleuze presented in Claire Colebrook, *Irony* (London and New York, 2004), p. 146.
59. Dimitriou, *Κοντά στην κοιλιά*, p. 94.
60. See Michel Fais, 'Πεζογραφία σε πρώτο πρόσωπο' [Prose in the first person], *Efimerida ton Syntakton*, 20 September 2014. Available at http://archive.efsyn.gr/?p=236079 (accessed 16 June 2016); and Spinou, 'Κλαίμε άδαρτοι'.
61. Sainis, '"Βασανίζομαι" σαν χώρα'.
62. Dimitriou in Yannis Baskozos, 'Σωτήρης Δημητρίου: Ας κάνουν μια κωλοτούμπα' [Sotiris Dimitriou: let them turn a somersault] (interview with Sotiris Dimitriou), *O Anagnostis*, 17 February 2015. Available at http://www.oanagnostis.gr/sotiris-dimitriou-as-kanoun-mia-kolotoumpa/ (accessed 16 June 2016).
63. Roland Barthes, *S/Z*, trans. Richard Miller (Oxford, 1990), pp. 4–5.
64. Barthes, *S/Z*, p. 4.
65. Fais, 'Πεζογραφία σε πρώτο πρόσωπο'.
66. Frangos, 'Ένα σουρεαλιστικό καρναβάλι προσώπων και ομάδων, εν μέσω κρίσης'.
67. Spinou, 'Κλαίμε άδαρτοι'.
68. Dimitriou, *Η σιωπή του ξερόχορτου*, p. 50.
69. Colebrook, *Irony*, p. 120.
70. Ibid., p. 148 (emphasis added).
71. Ibid., p. 149.
72. I use 'preposterously' in the way Mieke Bal uses the term for an act of reversal that 'puts the chronologically first (pre-) as an aftereffect behind (post-) its later recycling'. Mieke Bal, *Quoting Caravaggio: Contemporary Art, Preposterous History* (Chicago, 1999), pp. 6–7.
73. Hatzivasileiou also notes that *CttB* refrains from the moralizing tone of satire. Hatzivasileiou, 'Σωτήρης Δημητρίου: Ανάμεσα στην κωμωδία και στο παράδοξο'.
74. White, 'Writing in the middle voice', p. 260. White discusses here Barthes, who traces this subject/object conflation in modernist writing, in which the writing subject is constituted in and by the text as 'contemporary with the writing'. Ibid., p. 262.
75. Dimitriou, *Κοντά στην κοιλιά*, pp. 21–26.
76. Ibid., pp. 63–64.
77. Derrida encapsulates this freedom in the phrase 'tout dire'. Jacques Derrida, 'This strange institution called literature: An Interview with Jacques Derrida', in Jacques Derrida, *Acts of Literature*, ed. Derek Attridge (London, 1992), p. 36.
78. Ibid., p. 38.
79. Dimitriou, *Κοντά στην κοιλιά*, p. 95.

CHAPTER 12

DISCOURSES AND COUNTER-DISCOURSES OF THE GREEK CRISIS: A CRITICAL LINGUISTIC PERSPECTIVE

Dionysis Goutsos and Ourania Hatzidaki

Introduction

Irrespective of whether one subscribes to an essentialist or a constructivist view of what a crisis is,[1] it is difficult to disagree with Hay that a crisis crucially involves a process of bringing itself into existence 'through narrative and discourse'.[2] It is not necessary to fully agree with Falkheimer and Heide that 'a crisis is a crisis due to the fact that different groups, interested parties, and institutions perceive and experience it as a crisis'[3] in order to recognize this discursive dimension of a crisis. Material aspects of particular socio-economic and political events, such as rising unemployment, income reduction and property devaluation or loss, which raise substantial issues of survival, welfare, self-realization or social participation, usually concur with, or give impetus to, important symbolic aspects concerning the representation of these events through language and discourse.

Three emblematic episodes in the course of the last seven years can be considered illustrative of the discursive dimension of the Greek crisis. First, George Papandreou's reassurance during the October 2009 election campaign that *λεφτά υπάρχουν* (there's money aplenty), uttered immediately before the Greek crisis erupted. This is a discursive event that decisively influenced the course of actual political developments, by representing a grand but unsubstantiated electoral promise, exploiting the emerging crisis towards short-term party-political ends. Its swift and spectacular falsification by subsequent events contributed to one of the sharpest tectonic shifts in Greece's recent (party-)political history, namely the practical collapse of a major party (PASOK), along with the concurrent ideology of the so-called political 'middle' (*μεσαίος χώρος*) and the firmly established 30-year bi-partisan system. The phrase was to be interepreted as betraying, variously, blissful ignorance, denial or public obfuscation of the real depth of the crisis on the part of highly experienced and involved politician agents.

The onset of the Greek crisis itself coincides with the notorious aphorism by 2010 deputy prime minister Theodoros Pangalos *μαζί τα φάγαμε* (we all got a piece of the pie), which spurred a flurry of reactions and re-textualizations, still unfolding several years after its utterance. The phrase neatly encapsulates the predominant discourse of the attribution of blame for the Greek crisis and constitutes the argumentative core behind the austerity measures imposed by successive governments that signed Memoranda with the Greek creditors, by emphasizing the moral dimension of the financial debt. As such, it has served as a means of formulating and, at the same time, concealing the premises underlying the advocacy of austerity measures, namely 'we are all guilty', 'the guilty should be punished' and 'there is no alternative'.[4] Its function is that of an enthymeme or syllogism that misses an unstated premise and is thus taken for granted. Needless to say, Pangalos' sweeping generalization obscures the critical and much debated issue of the nature and proportionality of the 'guilt' per social actor and also of the 'punishment' eventually inflicted (the austerity policies) and its, for many, unjust apportionment.

The third example concerns the decision of the 2015 Minister of Finance Yanis Varoufakis to rename the *μνημόνιο* (Memorandum of Understanding or MoU) into *συμφωνία* (agreement) and the so-called 'Troika', that is the supervisory body formed by the European Commission, the European Central Bank and the International Monetary Fund, into 'institutions'. This discursive intervention illustrates the performative dimension of politics and its limits, since the strategy of response to the austerity policies was deemed as passing through a reformulation of basic entities and agents, although in the long run this proved ineffectual and beside the point.[5]

It is obvious that all three episodes require a more extensive analysis, which lies beyond the scope of this chapter; however, they have been brought here because they mark crucial moments in the way the Greek crisis has been understood and debated by the parties involved and thus highlight the importance of analysing the discursive dimensions of what a crisis entails. This chapter attempts to outline the principal ways in which the Greek crisis has been perceived and experienced through opposing discourses. Our emphasis is on the relationships between language use, and especially lexicogrammatical choices, and the social conditions underlying its production, including the different ideologies represented in and through language. This is the perspective of critical linguistics, which we take to be a practice rather than a branch of linguistics, incorporating, but not limited to, many of the concerns of Critical Discourse Analysis, as well as its synergy with methods such as Corpus Linguistics.[6] Our aim is to provide a synthesis of what has been found on the representation of opposing positions in discourse with regard to the Greek crisis.

As this is an issue that potentially requires a book-length treatment, our discussion will necessarily be concise in order to place emphasis on prominent discourses and counter-discourses. For this reason, we have decided to focus on the analysis of four major agents in the discourse production concerning the Greek crisis, namely that of politicians who have had an active role in the exercise of power, the mass media which mediate between positions of power and the general public, agents resisting dominant discourses, and neo-fascist organizations. In the following we analyse the discourse of each of these agents and try to draw some general conclusions about their stance throughout the period of the crisis.

The discourse of power

A central issue in the case of agents with an active role in the exercise of power is that of legitimation, that is the public argumentative process through which an action is justified.[7] Although many prominent politicians and public figures were eventually involved in the process of justifying the austerity measures brought on by the successive MoUs, there is a paucity of studies on the actual legitimation practices followed by them. As an exception, a study of the speeches delivered by Kostas Karamanlis and George Papandreou in three national election campaigns (2004, 2007 and 2009) finds that both politicians use increasingly fewer positively loaded words like *όραμα* (vision), *όνειρο* (dream) or *εμπιστοσύνη* (trust), whereas they gradually employ more negative words like *κρίση* (crisis), *χρέος* (debt) or *μέτρα* (measures) as the Greek crisis deepens.[8] Words like *αλήθεια* (truth) are preferred by each of these politicians when in the opposition rather than in government, a practice suggesting a tendency to manipulate audiences' opinions. In general, discourse formulations of PMs and leaders of the opposition seem to suggest that these high-profile political actors have been aware of problems that could lead (or can be interpreted as leading) to a crisis, but have systematically avoided their foregrounding, opting instead for vague and schematic representations of the country's situation.

This change in the positions of the agents in order to fit the changing circumstances and their evolved role in them is typical of political discourse in the Greek crisis and should be expected to be found across the political spectrum. For instance, it has been shown that Alexis Tsipras as the leader of SYRIZA increasingly used the word *λαός* (the people) in his central 2009 and 2012 election campaigns in order to fit the changing perceptions of the party with regard to its potential audiences.[9] In particular, these claims of general representation have coincided with the extraordinary transformation of a minor party that represented 4.6 per cent of the Greek votes into a ruling party, ready to become a 'government of the left'. There is evidently much scope for further research, especially as concerns the discourse of SYRIZA in the height of the crisis and after the assumption of power by this party.

A further strategy expected to be present in politicians' discourse concerns blame allocation, a notion used by Angouri and Wodak whilst investigating the *Guardian*'s representation of the rise of Golden Dawn in Greece.[10] In their analysis, a range of imagined groups such as political institutions and particularly Greek and non-Greek governments, as well as the EU and the IMF, are held accountable by language users for the situation in Greece and the party's growth. As is suggested by the parallel case of Portugal,[11] this is a central issue in the discourse representation of the crisis on the part of agents like PMs or other government agents. In our view and in relation to our discussion of

Pangalos' quote above, this widespread allocation of blame is a typical strategy aiming at diluting responsibility for the crisis.

At the same time, such strategies are inscribed within the more general frame of the so-called ideological square, in van Dijk's term,[12] which involves positive self-presentation and negative other-presentation, namely the positive evaluation of 'us' and our actions and the negative evaluation of 'them' and their actions, and the concomitant highlighting of our positive and de-emphasizing of our negative aspects, and the converse for 'them'. This is a long-standing feature of the Greek political discourse, not exclusively related to the crisis context,[13] and as such, is also found in different discourses on the Greek crisis (see sections below). Among else, it has been suggested that the two main parties in the political scene in Greece at the time of the emergence of the crisis, conservative New Democracy and social-democratic PASOK, attempted to revive the historical dichotomies of the past in order to discursively reintroduce the distinction between 'us' as 'Greek patriots' and 'them' as 'traitors' or 'national enemies', and thus legitimate their own political actions and reactions.[14]

Furthermore, naturalization, i.e. presenting one's point of view as the only one possible, the 'natural' option, has also been found to play a prominent role in the discourse of government officials at the outbreak of the crisis. As indicated by an investigation of official statements to the press, parliamentary and other speeches by Prime Minister George Papandreou and his Minister of Finance George Papakonstantinou in 2010, what is objective or not is itself a construction; in other words, subjective and objective representations of a situation are manipulated for rhetorical purposes, employed as a means of enhancing the policymakers' authority and credibility. Specifically, these two politicians employ discursively constructed aspects of government knowledge on the Greek debt crisis across different communicative settings, as well as specific complement structures of the cognitive factive verbs *ξέρω* and *γνωρίζω* (to know) in order to present their stance as natural and self-evident.[15] Analyses like this underline the fact that knowledge is a central issue, since agents who assume a position of the 'subject supposed to know' (to use Lacan's terms) can also control what is taken for granted or considered to be a shared assumption.

Finally, research has suggested that politicians in positions of power can set the discursive agenda, by introducing, for example, an issue towards which all agents are forced to take a stance. This is the case of the 'theory of the two extremes', which dominated the public discourse of major political actors in Greece between 2012 and 2014. As has been pointed out, the collective actors who participated in the debate could be clearly divided into stigmatizers and stigmatized, with both parties striving 'to discursively establish their own central/distinctive and diachronically enduring self- and other-identification features'.[16] In particular, New Democracy and PASOK branded the left and SYRIZA as the most significant exponents of the extremes, who, together with, but to a markedly lesser extent, the far right and Golden Dawn, were depicted as the collective, irregular agent of violence and instability. What is important is that the reproached, rather than returning the accusation of extremism, strove to debunk such arguments by downplaying the charge, probably being conscious of the fact that association with the concept of extremism comes with a high political cost.

A similar case concerns the use of the label 'populist' to describe a vast array of policies, politicians, parties or rhetorical styles, which supposedly are opposed to the 'enlightened' view of European democracy. Relevant studies have found a basic opposition between 'populist' and 'anti-populist' newspapers.[17] Specifically, while both relate the lemma *λαός* (the people) to lemmas like *ελληνικός* (Greek), *Ελλάδα* (Greece), *έθνος* (nation), *χώρα* (country), in the former the lemma co-occurs with *κυρίαρχος* (sovereign) or other words related to power/authority (εντολή 'mandate', *αποφασίσει* 'decides') or movements (*τάξη* 'class', *εργατική* 'working', *κίνημα* 'movement'), whereas in the latter it is commonly found together with *λαϊκισμός* (populism). Evaluative adjectives are, correspondingly, positive and negative, in the latter case being related to metaphors presenting populism as disease, madness or natural disaster. This is another case of dominant discourses, deciding what is positive and negative, and thus highlighting the manipulative dimension of political discourse.

Media discourses

The discourses generated and circulated by the media are perhaps those that have been most extensively studied, with – more or less – uniform results. Both representations of the Greek crisis abroad and in the local press have been investigated, although with a prevalence of the former and an emphasis to mainstream media, especially newspapers, in both cases. Content analysis, which is mainly used for this investigation, usually does not allow for insight into the exact linguistic means by which these are realized. Despite this, certain trends can be gleaned as, for instance, in an extensive study of the international press, including British, French, German, Italian and US newspapers from 2005 to 2011, which observes an explosion of articles in the coverage of events in Greece in 2010 and 2011 and a marked preference for this over events in other European countries facing similar problems. More importantly, 'a remarkable degree of consensus in criticizing the Hellenic Republic for its crisis' has been found in this study, along with a strong interest of international newspapers 'in the future of their own states'.[18]

As expected by the well-known emphasis of newspapers on negative events, the Greek crisis has also been covered in the press through stories focusing on negative rather than positive developments. In addition, the analysis of individual newspapers in various countries shows a remarkable degree of polarized and contradictory discourses, negative stereotyping, or even patterns of racism in the media perception of Greece abroad.[19] At the same time, it is obvious that the construction of the crisis is directly related to the political affiliation of each newspaper, and this is corroborated by the analysis of the domestic press. In particular, media of a conservative political orientation in both Greece and abroad have been found to reproduce the dominant view of conservatives in Europe, exclusively blaming Greece and arguing that the crisis is local and can be handled by austerity policies and measures, whereas centre-left media are more ambivalent and view the crisis also 'as political rather than merely economic and call for a European, systemic treatment'.[20]

A dominant trend in the newspaper treatment of the Greek crisis is what has been called the moralist/culturalist understanding, which is ascribed to the neoliberal ideology.[21] This approach attributes the roots of the crisis to the Greek culture and, as has been suggested, it has been 'disseminated systematically by international and national economic and political elites and mainstream media since the beginning of the crisis'.[22] This view has been based on an extensive analysis of local and international media. For example, the analysis of mainstream newspapers such as the conservative *Kathimerini* suggests that the neoliberal explanation of the economic crisis as something concerning the pathologies of the Greek society is adopted wholesale.[23] This dominant discourse has served the business interests of mainstream media magnates, who dictated editorial decisions 'to limit coverage to pro-EC, ECB and IMF agendas and to censor alternative opinions'[24] and this accords well with the overwhelming opinion of the Greek audience, something which accounts for the extensive discrediting of the media in public opinion, further exacerbated by the scandalously one-sided coverage of the July 2015 referendum in favour of the pro-EU, pro-MoU agenda.[25]

Whether one agrees with the view of the total control of the media by the powerful elites or not, what cannot be doubted is the lack of critical voices or means of reflection in mainstream media discourses. This has been borne out, for instance, in the press coverage of the so-called 'indignant' or 'squares' movement by Greek newspapers during and after the massive protests of May to September 2011. Contrary to the view that mainstream media were 'uncharacteristically sympathetic' to the movement,[26] a close analysis has found that contemporary newspaper data 'project an obvious embarrassment as to how to classify the protesters, as well as a hastiness to map them onto far-left or far-right groups', in a way reminiscent of how earlier protests were treated in the Greek press.[27] That is, media representations of the movement were embedded in received interpretative patterns and were later used as a means of propaganda amidst party power conflicts. Moreover, the media texts mentioning the events in the following three years further perpetuated and expanded on this strategy by systematically ignoring the novel political aspects of the movement, by assimilating it into related foreign movements and by embedding it in the local context of political antagonism, including its interpretation as a version of the 'theory of the two extremes'.[28]

Equally interesting with what mainstream media did or did not do is the question of how they managed to put forward a dominant representation of the Greek crisis. It is in this that metaphors have played a central role, as suggested by several studies of media, parliamentary, technocratic, political or everyday discourse:[29] thus, the crisis is construed as a disease or as a natural disaster, the Eurozone countries as victims or rescuers and the solution to the crisis as mechanical repair or a teaching process, inscribing the crisis discourse among didactic or disciplinary discourses. Most of these metaphors serve the discourses of power as discussed above, namely the legitimation of austerity measures (conceptualized as medicine for the sick or punishment for unruly children) and the naturalization of the crisis and the solution to it (by presenting it as a natural phenomenon or a mechanical process and not as the conscious choice of specific individuals or institutions).

With the proviso that mainstream newspapers have received the lion's share in the analysis, whereas TV and radio, as well as alternative media have not been thoroughly analysed, we can conclude that, as regards the Greek crisis, the media have aligned with prevailing ideologies and mostly engaged with current affairs, strictly conceived of in terms of party politics. Perceptions of Self and Other also seem to have been opportunistically managed by newspapers in order to fit political exigencies and interpret novel developments in the light of received knowledge and stereotypes. This has foreclosed any question about their constructive employment as a means of challenging readers to make informed decisions and has turned them into instruments of retaining the status quo.

Discourses of resistance

The discourse of politicians or other citizens identifying themselves with opposition to power has not been as thoroughly analysed as the discourse of those in power or of the mainstream mass media. This is not only due to the inherent analytical bias of models, including critical linguistics, towards the criticism of dominant discourses. It can also be accounted for by the much lower visibility of alternative discourses, mainly because of the role of the mainstream mass media, as discussed above. Furthermore, as has also been observed, 'the "anti-memorandum" bloc hosts an increasing number of discourses on the crisis, which are often contradictory'.[30] In this sense, we need to distinguish between discourses of opposition, which are self-proclaimed as opposing power, and discourses of resistance, which attempt to systematically act against the grain. For instance, neo-fascist discourse is self-proclaimed as anti-establishment but, as will be argued below, like the discourses of the elites, is crucially concerned with self-legitimation, whereas protest movements have initiated alternative text and discourse practices, which are inscribed within alternative social practices.

Thus, we lack a fully-fledged analysis of oppositional or anti-establishment discourses concerning the Greek crisis, including SYRIZA discourse before as compared to after its coming to power. At the same time, as has been pointed out,[31] resistance discourses also resort to strategies of identification which involve positive self-appraisal and the denigration of the Other, fitting broadly into van Dijk's model of the ideological square which emphasizes the opposition between the positive perception of the in-group and the negative evaluation of the out-group. The attraction of the in-group vs. out-group schema does not only lie in its polarizing simplicity but also in its potential to be skilfully handled so as to accommodate an assortment of different entities in the 'us' and 'them' poles. Thus, along with findings about the far Left using sophisticated and inventive strategies to discursively defend itself against its detractors, it has been observed that the discourse strategies of the far Right demonstrate significant complexity and thus offer themselves up for further analysis.

One example of resistant discourses that has been analysed to a certain extent concerns the 'squares movement', made widely known by the media as the movement of the indignants.[32] The protesters' own Public Assembly minutes and statements suggest that their self-identity was based on the construction of a bipolar 'us' and 'them' representation, in which the 'us' includes other anti-government and anti-memorandum groups, as well as international movements, whereas the 'them' involves agents such as the Greek government, the banks, the Troika and occasionally all parliamentary parties, even if some supported the movement's goals. It is interesting that in newspaper data covering the protests, the protesters are emphatically found in the 'them' pole and are collectively given the name *αγανακτισμένοι* (indignants), a name which, as mentioned above, the protesters specifically disown. In their own words, *είμαστε αποφασισμένοι, όχι αγανακτισμένοι* (we are determined, not indignant). What seems to be particularly significant in the protesters' data is an emphasis on a self-reflecting identity that is related to space. For example, especially frequent and significant are not only words like *συνέλευση* (assembly) and *πλατεία* (square), but also personal pronouns in the first person plural (*μας* 'us'/'our'), the related verb *είμαστε* (we are) and the adverb *εδώ* (here). Particularly prominent phrases are *είμαστε εδώ* (we are here) and *είμαστε στην πλατεία/στις πλατείες* (we are in the square/squares), a further indication that the protesters' constructed identity was fundamentally realized in terms of space. Location in space is itself constituted by the events taking place in the square and the people participating. This makes for a circular definition of identity, which prescribes the limits of the movement.

Another example of a resistance discourse that has been studied concerns the lyrics of songs written on the topic of the crisis.[33] It is unclear whether this discourse falls in the resistance end of the pole, as songwriters use both similar and dissimilar discourse strategies with the people who participated in the squares movement. Thus, although both protesters and songwriters adopt a general anti-memorandum stance and regard politicians as the main culprits for the Greek crisis, the former construct a self that takes its force from the process of the assembly itself, whereas the latter resort to a nationalist image of the 'glory that was Greece' and claim a return to this as a way out of the crisis. In this sense, songwriting seems to, perhaps unwittingly, inscribe itself within the culturalist argument of the neoliberal ideology that attributes the crisis to cultural reasons, as mentioned above, although it expressly and adamantly opposes austerity measures. It may be suggested that this basic contradiction generally characterizes the anti-MoU version of oppositional discourses, although much more research is needed before reaching such a conclusion.

Finally, the pro-memorandum vs. anti-memorandum dichotomy is actively debated by individual agents who do not assume a public voice claiming to represent larger collectivities but try to make sense of the crisis through informal debate and communication. For instance, informal Facebook conversations are a privileged site for understanding how citizens perceive and talk about the crisis and, contrary to expectations, their contributions display reflexivity and a heightened awareness of the contexts involved, as well as a variety of argumentation and stance-expressing techniques which seem to balance affiliative and disaffiliative positions.[34] Similarly, an analysis of massive amounts of Twitter data has concluded that this medium is 'used primarily by citizens for the purpose of discussing and communicating the movement's aims and agendas, and less so by organizations', as is commonly believed.[35] As a result, its significance lies in expanding the discourse through the use of newspaper pieces, videos and links to other social media and online content rather than in crowd mobilization and coordination.

The discourse of neo-fascism

It is a common assumption in the literature that the economic crisis has significantly contributed to the rise of right-wing extremism, including neo-Nazi and neo-fascist discourses. Ignazi notes that 'in every period of growing economic crisis the degree of confidence in the system diminishes and the extremist tendencies develop'.[36] With reference to Greece, Georgiadou points out that '[h]idden under the cloak of anti-capitalist, anti-globalization rhetoric, euro-scepticism, and opposition to multiculturalism, far-right attitudes proved to have appeal across a large swath of the political spectrum'.[37] As a result, neo-fascist discourses must be seen as an integral part of the political landscape in crisis-ridden Greece.

The fairly recent broadening of Golden Dawn's electoral base in Greece probably accounts for the relative scarcity of studies, which have concentrated on the rhetorical construction of the party's collective identity and in-group boundaries, its discursive practices in relation to emotions or the retextualization of fascist discourses.[38] Content analysis, which has focused on the polarizing effects of the speeches by Golden Dawn's leader, Nikolaos Michaloliakos, has found aggressive, extreme and straightforward strategies used in the party's discourse.[39] By contrast, other studies, including that of the discourse of the Cypriot far-right party ELAM, draw a more nuanced picture, involving a combination of subtle and dense discourse tactics with simplistic, clear-cut dichotomies. For instance, a study of Golden Dawn's webpage texts suggests that they mainly aim at presenting the party as the victim and transferring the blame to others.[40] It is also significant that, contrary to expectation, Golden Dawn avoids presenting Pavlos Fyssas, who was stabbed to death by one of its members, negatively or evaluating his murderer positively and adopts a distancing approach towards the Fyssas incident as a whole. Thus, Fyssas is not placed in the them pole, which is reserved for Golden Dawn's alleged opponents and critics; the latter are characterized as criminal by extending the definition of 'criminal' to include political corruption, and economic, ecological, sexual and other crimes. The party thus prepares the ground for representing itself as a victim and the subsequent murder of its two members suitably reinforces this claim. Similarly, the party's official discourse has been found to be lexically dense and highly informative, affording its texts a guise of authority, credibility and seriousness.[41] At the same time, there is an emphasis on the 'enemies of the people' (which include Zionism, Marxism, liberalism, capitalism, the corrupt political system and immigration), against which Golden Dawn allegedly stands. Emotion seems to play an important role in cementing in-group cohesion and promoting out-group aversion in such a way as to reinforce the self-truth of dichotomies.[42]

In all, the discourse of the far right seems to present a much subtler picture than is commonly or stereotypically assumed. Entities represented as commonly accepted to be good or bad (e.g. the nation/people or the elites) are easily placed in opposite poles, whereas those towards which it is less easy to adopt an unequivocal stance are kept at a distance, as the example of Pavlos Fyssas indicates. This allows for the (discursively sophisticated) attribution of blame to others, which immediately implies self-legitimization, and, at the same time, is in line with the dual strategy that Wodak and Richardson have found with regard to extreme-right parties, namely their dissociation from, *and* rehabilitation of, fascism.[43]

Conclusion and scope for further research

As must have become clear from the discussion above, the representation of the Greek crisis is intimately related to basic parameters of discourse production, for instance binary entities such as official vs. non-official, collective vs. individual, positional vs. oppositional, normative vs. resistant, as well as the attribution/assumption of responsibility and the related issues of (self- and other-)identity. Our distinction between discourses and counter-discourses is necessarily schematic and does not do justice to the full spectrum of contradictory representations of the Greek crisis. Having said that, it is surprising that most research on the issue converges on some basic findings. First, the discourse of the elites or the powerful, including politicians in power, shows a homogeneous tendency to legitimate their position and present austerity measures as natural and thus inevitable. The central, unstated premise of related arguments lies in the equal sharing of the guilt and blame by all social agents, thus subverting any oppositional or alternative voice. At the same time, it is the discourse of the powerful that sets the agenda, mainly through its stronghold over the media, which intervene between political power and the public, and thus impose the 'us' vs. 'them' opposition of their choice in public debate. In this manner, even oppositional forces are made to participate in dilemmas and dichotomies that others have created for them.

Furthermore, the role of the media in their alignment with powerful discourses has been repeatedly argued in the Greek case, suggesting a potential collusion with the elites and their bias against any voice of resistance. This is a major factor in delegitimating or distorting any counter-discourses that are mounted against the prevailing opinion. Fragmentation and lack of a more widely conceived set of imperatives seem to be contributing factors in the stifling of resistant discourses. By contrast, neo-fascist discourses, which apparently have found an easy outlet in the mainstream and social media, are, despite appearances and stereotypes, quite sophisticated in their strategy of subterfuge.

It is obvious that further research is needed on several issues relating to the discourses of the Greek crisis including and beyond those mentioned in this chapter. For instance, texts of central importance such as the MoUs have not yet been extensively investigated either as sources of argumentation or of vernacularization of technical politico-economic discourses. Discourses of resistance need to be further explored, including a variety of sites like traditional media, and especially radio and TV channels, to the extent that they host anti-memorandum/anti-austerity perspectives, as well as alternative, local or digital media, including the social media, blogs and other sites, which do not share the limitations of the former. Finally, everyday conversation in its various manifestations can be a rich locus of discourse strategies and techniques, involving a wide spectrum of linguistic phenomena with respect to crisis and its representations.

Notes

1. Of course, there is a continuum between these two opposing views with several points in the middle; on the constructive pole a crisis consists of material events in the 'real' world, whereas on the other pole crisis constitutes a fundamentally discursive event, which depends on one's representation of events, including what a crisis is.
2. Colin Hay, 'Narrating crisis: The discursive construction of the "Winter of Discontent"', *Sociology* 30/2 (1996), pp. 254–255.

3. Jesper Falkheimer and Mats Heide, 'Crisis communicators in change: From plans to improvisations', in W. T. Coombs and S. J. Holladay (eds), *The Handbook of Crisis Communication* (Oxford, 2010), p. 514.
4. On the moral dimension of the debt with regard to the Greek crisis, see Wolfgang Streeck, 'The construction of a moral duty for the Greek people to repay their national debt', in M. Fourcade, P. Steiner, W. Streeck and C. Woll (eds), *Moral Categories in the Financial Crisis* (Paris, 2013).
5. A similar point could be made with regard to the term 'Grexit', coined to describe a prospective/possible exit of Greece from the euro and/or the EU. This highly significant discursive event would require an extensive treatment, possibly also in association with the discursive and material event of the Brexit, which, however, lies beyond the scope of this paper.
6. Critical linguistics has its origins in the East Anglia group of researchers in the 1970s, see e.g. Roger Fowler, Bob Hodge, Gunther Kress and Tony Trew (eds), *Language and Control* (London,1979). A good discussion of its scope and relation to Critical Discourse Analysis can be found in Ruth Wodak, 'Critical Linguistics and Critical Discourse Analysis', in J. Verschueren, J.-O. Östman and J. Blommaert (eds), *Handbook of Pragmatics: Manual* (1995), pp. 204–210.
7. See Norman Fairclough & Isabelle Fairclough, *Political Discourse Analysis: A Method for Advanced Students* (London, 2012), p. 242.
8. Georgia Kostopoulou, 'The dream that turned into a nightmare: Addressing the Greek voters long and right before the crisis', in O. Hatzidaki & D. Goutsos (eds), *Greece in Crisis: Combining Critical Discourse and Corpus Linguistics Perspectives* (Amsterdam, forthcoming).
9. Yorgos Katsambekis, *ΣΥΡΙΖΑ 2004–2012: Από τη «νεολαία» στον «λαό». Μια λογο-θεωρητική προσέγγιση του λαϊκισμού της ριζοσπαστικής αριστεράς.* [SYRIZA 2004–2012: From "youth" to "the people". A discourse-theoretical approach to the populism of the radical left] (Athens, 2014).
10. Jo Angouri and Ruth Wodak 'They became big in the shadow of the crisis: The Greek success story and the rise of the far Right', *Discourse & Society* 25/4 (2014), pp. 540–566.
11. See Pedro Fonseca and Maria João Ferreira, 'Through 'seas never before sailed': Portuguese government discursive legitimation strategies in a context of financial crisis', *Discourse & Society* 26/6 (2015), pp. 682–711.
12. One of the best presentations of the model can be found in Teun A. van Dijk, 'Opinions and ideologies in the Press', in A. Bell and P. Garrett (eds), *Approaches to Media Discourse* (Oxford, 1998), pp. 21–63.
13. This is suggested by a thorough analysis of Greek newspapers in Georgia Fragaki, 'Evaluative adjectives in a corpus of Greek opinion articles', in M. L. Carrió Pastor and M. Á. Candel Mora (eds), *Las tecnologías de la información y las comunicaciones: Presente y futuro en el análisis de córpora. Actas del III Congreso Internacional de Lingüística de Corpus* (Valencia, 2011), pp. 169–176.

14. Salomi Boukala, 'Waiting for democracy: Political crisis and the discursive (re) invention of the "national enemy" in times of "Grecovery"', *Discourse & Society* 25/4 (2014), pp. 483–499.
15. George Polymeneas, '"[T]oday I know, we know, that these sacrifices are heavy, but necessary": Constructing governmental knowledge on Greece's sovereign debt crisis', in O. Hatzidaki and D. Goutsos (eds), *Greece in Crisis*, op.cit.
16. Ourania Hatzidaki, 'The "theory of the two extremes": A rhetorical topography for self- and other-identification across the Greek political spectrum', in O. Hatzidaki and D. Goutsos (eds), *Greece in Crisis*, op.cit.
17. Research in the *Populismus* project have closely looked into this opposition; see, among else, Yannis Stavrakakis, Nikos Nikisianis, Alexandros Kioupkolis, Giorgos Katsambekis and Thomas Siomos, 'Λαϊκιστικός λόγος και δημοκρατία'. [Populist discourse and democracy]. *Ελληνική Επιθεώρηση Πολιτικής Επιστήμης* 43 (2015), pp. 49–80 and Nikos Nikisianis, Thomas Siomos, Yannis Stavrakakis & Titika Dimitroulia, 'Λαϊκισμός εναντίον αντιλαϊκισμού στον ελληνικό Τύπο' [Populism vs. anti-populism in the Greek press], *Σύγχρονα Θέματα* 132–133 (2016), pp. 52–70.
18. George Tzogopoulos, *The Greek Crisis in the Media: Stereotyping in the International Press* (Farnham, 2013).
19. See e.g. Yiannis Mylonas, 'Media and the economic crisis of the EU: The "culturalization" of a systemic crisis and Bild-Zeitung's framing of Greece.' *TripleC – Cognition, Communication, Co-operation: Open Access Journal for a Global Sustainable Information Society* 10/2 (2012), pp. 646–671, Amelie Kutter, 'A catalytic moment: The Greek crisis in the German financial press'. *Discourse & Society* 25/4 (2014), pp. 446–466, Sofia Lampropoulou, '"Greece will decide the future of Europe": The recontextualisation of the Greek national elections in a British broadsheet newspaper.' *Discourse & Society* 25/4 (2014), pp. 467–482, Bessie Mitsikopoulou and Christina Lykou, 'The discursive construction of the recent European economic crisis in two political magazines', *On the Horizon* 23/3 (2015), pp. 190–201, Eero Vaara, 'Struggles over legitimacy in the Eurozone crisis: Discursive legitimation strategies and their ideological underpinnings', *Discourse & Society* 25/4 (2014), pp. 500–518.
20. Bessie Mitsikopoulou and Christina Lykou, 'The chronicle of an ongoing crisis: Diachronic media representations of Greece and Europe in the Greek press', in O. Hatzidaki and D. Goutsos (eds), *Greece in Crisis*, op.cit.
21. Mylonas, ibid.
22. Hara Kouki, 'European crisis discourses: The case of Greece', in T. Murray-Leach et al. *Crisis Discourses in Europe. Media EU-phemisms and Alternative Narratives* (London, 2014), p. 17.
23. George Pleios, 'Τα ΜΜΕ απέναντι στην κρίση: Έντονη υιοθέτηση της λογικής των ελίτ' [The media against the crisis: Extensive adoption of the elite logic], in G. Pleios (ed.), *Η κρίση και τα ΜΜΕ* [Crisis and the Mass Media] (Athens, 2013), Yiannis Mylonas, 'Crisis, austerity and opposition in

mainstream media discourses of Greece', *Critical Discourse Studies* 11/3 (2014), pp. 305–321.

24. Kouki, ibid, p. 17, cf. Pleios, ibid.
25. The need to take disciplinary measures by the journalists' trade union (ΕΣΗΕΑ) against specific high-profile journalists and anchor people because of the public outcry justifies this characterization: see, for instance, the discussion and the public complaints in: https://www.esiea.gr/apofasi-yp-arithm-62016-toy-protovathmioy.
26. As stated in Maria Kaika and Lazaros Karaliotas, 'The spatialization of democratic politics: Insights from Indignant Squares', *European Urban and Regional Studies* 23/4 (2016), p. 561.
27. Dionysis Goutsos and George Polymeneas, 'Self-constructed and ascribed identity of the Greek protesters at Syntagma Square: From "where we are" to "who they are"', in O. Hatzidaki and D. Goutsos (eds), *Greece in Crisis*, op.cit.
28. See Hatzidaki, ibid.
29. See, among else, Villy Tsakona, 'The Greek patient and the plaster cast: From the Greek military junta of 21 April 1967 to the IMF and EU's rescue mechanism', *Metaphor and the Social World* 2/1 (2012), pp. 61–85, Hans Bickes, Tina Otten and Laura Chelsea Weymann, 'The financial crisis in the German and English Press. Metaphorical structures in the media coverage on Greece, Spain and Italy', *Discourse & Society* 25/4 (2014), pp. 424–445, Mylonas, ibid.
30. Kouki, ibid.
31. Hatzidaki, ibid.
32. See Dionysis Goutsos and George Polymeneas, 'Identity as space: Localism in the Greek protests of Syntagma square', *Journal of Language and Politics* 13/4 (2014), pp. 675–701, ibid., Kaika & Karaliotas, ibid. On the slogans used see Nicoletta Tsitsanoudi-Mallidi, '«Αγανακτισμένων Συνθήματα»: Γλωσσικές πραγματώσεις και ιδεολογικό πλαίσιο.' [Slogans of the Indignant: Linguistic realizations and ideological framework]. *Νέα Παιδεία* 143 (2012), pp. 47–64.
33. Stamatia Koutsoulelou, '"Crisis written all over me": Greek songs in times of crisis', in O. Hatzidaki and D. Goutsos (eds), *Greece in Crisis*, op.cit. For instance, see the song '*Melina*' by Kyriakos Doumos, sung by Melina Aslanidou, available at: https://www.youtube.com/watch?v = uhS_9_eSlBM.
34. Mariza Georgalou, 'Taking stances on the Greek crisis: Expertise, opinions and contradiction on Facebook', in O. Hatzidaki and D. Goutsos (eds), *Greece in Crisis*, op.cit.
35. Yannis Theocharis, Will Lowe, Jan W. van Deth and Gema García-Albacete, 'Using Twitter to mobilize protest action: Online mobilization patterns and action repertoires in the Occupy Wall Street, Indignados, and Aganaktismenoi movements', *Information, Communication & Society* 18/2 (2015), pp. 202–220.
36. Piero Ignazi, *Extreme Right Parties in Western Europe* (Oxford, 2003), p. 63.
37. Vassiliki Georgiadou, 'Right-wing populism and extremism: The rapid rise of olden Dawn in crisis–ridden Greece', in R. Melzer and S. Serafin (eds),

Right-wing Extremism in Europe. Country Analyses, Counter-strategies and Labor-market Oriented Exit Strategies (Berlin, 2013), p. 75.

38. Lia Figgou, Ioanna Mylopoulou & Alexandra Birbili–Karaleka, 'Κατασκευές της ιδεολογικής ακρότητας και "μειονοτικοποίηση" στην προεκλογική ρητορική του ακροδεξιού κόμματος "Χρυσή Αυγή"' [Construction of ideological extremism and 'minoritization' in the pre–electoral rhetoric of the far right party 'Golden Dawn'], *10th Scientific Yearbook of the Psychology Department* (Thessaloniki, 2014), pp. 499–527, Fabienne H. Baider and Maria Constantinou, '"How to make people feel good when wishing hell": Golden Dawn and National Front discourse, emotions and argumentation', in J. Romero-Trillo (ed.), *Yearbook of Corpus Linguistics and Pragmatics 2014: New Empirical and Theoretical Paradigms* (Dordrecht, 2014), Angouri & Wodak, ibid.
39. Despoina Paraskeva-Veloudoyanni, *Ο εχθρός, το αίμα, ο τιμωρός. Αναλύοντας δεκατρείς λόγους του «αρχηγού» της Χρυσής Αυγής* [The enemy, the blood, the punisher. Analysing thirteen speeches of the leader of Golden Dawn] (Athens, 2014).
40. Georgia Fragaki, '"Tragic event" vs. "cowardly murder": A longitudinal study of Golden Dawn's lexicogrammatical choices and discourse strategies', in O. Hatzidaki and D. Goutsos (eds), *Greece in Crisis*, op.cit.
41. Ioannis Saridakis, 'Golden Dawn and the traits of extreme right-wing discourse amidst the Greek crisis', in O. Hatzidaki and D. Goutsos (eds), *Greece in Crisis*, op.cit.
42. Fabienne Baider and Maria Constantinou, '"We'll come at night and find you, traitors." Cybercommunication in the Greek-Cypriot ultra-nationalist space', in O. Hatzidaki and D. Goutsos (eds) *Greece in Crisis*, op.cit.
43. Ruth Wodak and John E. Richardson, 'European fascism in text and talk. Introduction.', in R. Wodak and J. E. Richardson (eds), *Analysing Fascist Discourse: European Fascism in Talk and Text.* (London/New York, 2013). Cf. Georgiadou's, ibid, p. 77 observation of a dual strategy that aims to blur the distinction between rejecting the system and delegitimizing it.

BIBLIOGRAPHY

Adam-Veleni, Polyxeni 2013, 'Εκπαιδεύοντας τη Ρίτα: η επικοινωνιακή και εκθεσιακή πολιτική του Αρχαιολογικού Μουσείου Θεσσαλονίκης 2007–2009' ['Educating Rita: the communication and exhibition policy of the Archaeological Museum of Thessaloniki, 2007–2009'] in *Το Αρχαιολογικό Έργο στη Μακεδονία και τη Θράκη* 23, Thessaloniki, 2013, pp. 303–318.

Agamben, Giorgio, *Homo Sacer. Sovereign Power and Bare Life* (Stanford, 1998).

——— *State of Exception*, trans. Kevin Attell (Chicago and London, 2003).

Agnew, John, 'No borders, no nations: making Greece in Macedonia', *Annals of the Association of American Geographers* 97/2 (2007), pp. 398–422.

Amnesty International, *The Human Cost of Fortress Europe. Human Rights Violations Against Immigrants and Refugees at Europe's Borders* (London, 2014).

Anagnostou Yiorgos, 'The Diaspora as a usable past for a nation-in-crisis: Media readings of Palikari: Louis Tikas and the Ludlow Massacre', *Filmicon*: Journal of Greek Film Studies, Occasional Papers, November 5 (2014). Available at http://filmiconjournal.com/blog/post/32/the_diaspora_as_a_usable_past_for_a_nation_in_crisis] (accessed 5 November 2014).

——— 'Re/collecting Greek America: Reflections on ethnic struggle, success and survival', *Journal of Modern Hellenism* 31/ Fall (2015), pp. 148–175.

Anderson, Benedict, *The Spectre of Comparisons: Nationalism, Southeast Asia, and the World* (London & New York, 1998).

Angouri, Jo and Ruth Wodak, '"They became big in the shadow of the crisis": The Greek success story and the rise of the far right', *Discourse & Society* 25/4 (2004), pp. 540–566.

Anshen, David, 'Clichés and Commodity Fetishism: The Violence of the Real in Jim Thompson's the Killer Inside Me', *Journal of Narrative Theory* 37/3 (Autumn 2007), pp. 400–426.

Avdikos, Vassilis, *Οι πολιτιστικές και δημιουργικές βιομηχανίες στην Ελλάδα* [*Cultural and Creative Industries in Greece*] (Athens, 2014).

Badiou, Alain, *Being and Event*, translated by Oliver Feltham (London, 2005).

Baider, Fabienne H. and Maria Constantinou, '"How to make people feel good when wishing hell": Golden Dawn and National Front discourse, emotions and argumentation', in J. Romero-Trillo (ed.), *Yearbook of Corpus Linguistics and*

Pragmatics 2014: New Empirical and Theoretical Paradigms (Dordrecht, 2014), 179–210.

——— '"At night we'll come and find you, traitors": Cybercommunication in the Greek-Cypriot ultra-nationalist space', in O. Hatzidaki and D. Goutsos (eds), *Greece in Crisis: Combining Critical Discourse and Corpus Linguistics Perspectives* (Amsterdam, forthcoming).

Bal, Mieke, *Quoting Caravaggio: Contemporary Art, Preposterous History* (Chicago, 1999).

Barbeito, Patricia Felisa, 'Telling the ewes from the rams: economics and gender disorder in Petros Markaris's Inspector Haritos mysteries', in E. Minardi and J. Byron (eds), *Out of Deadlock: Female Emancipation in Sara Paretsky's Novels and her Influence on Contemporary Crime Fiction* (Newcastle Upon Tyne, 2015), pp. 67–86.

Barro, Robert J. and Xavier Sala-i-Martin, *Economic Growth* (New York, 1995).

Barthes, Roland, 'To write: An intransitive verb?', in Richard Macksey and Eugenio Donato (eds), *The Structuralist Controversy: The Languages of Criticism and the Sciences of Man* (Baltimore and London, 1970), pp. 134–145.

———, *S/Z*, trans. Richard Miller (Oxford, 1990).

Bartsiokas, Antonios and Elizabeth Carney, 'The Royal skeletal remains from Tomb I at Vergina', *Deltos. Journal of the History of Hellenic Medicine* 36 (2008), pp. 15–19.

——— and Juan-Luis Arsuaga, 'The lameness of King Philip II and Royal Tomb I at Vergina, Macedonia', *Proceedings of the National Academy of Sciences of the United States of America* 112/32 (2015), pp. 9844–9848.

Baudrillard, Jean, 'Kool Killer or the Insurrection of Signs', in Jean Baudrillard, *Symbolic Exchange and Death* (London, 1993), pp. 76–84.

Bauman, Zygmunt and Carlo Bordoni, *State of Crisis* (Cambridge, 2014).

Benjamin, Walter, 'Theses on the philosophy of history' in *Illuminations*, trans. Harry Zohn (London, 1979), pp. 255–266.

Bickes, Hans, Tina Otten and Laura Chelsea Weymann, 'The financial crisis in the German and English Press: Metaphorical structures in the media coverage on Greece, Spain and Italy', *Discourse & Society* 25/4 (2014), pp. 424–445.

Boletsi, Maria, 'From the subject of the crisis to the subject in crisis: Middle voice on Greek walls', *Journal of Greek Media and Culture* 2/1 (2016), pp. 3–28.

Borza, Eugene N. and Olga Palagia, 'The chronology of the Macedonian royal tombs at Vergina', *Jahrbuch des Deutschen Archaeologischen Instituts* 122 (2007), pp. 81–125.

Boukala, Salomi, 'Waiting for democracy: Political crisis and the discursive (re) invention of the "national enemy" in times of "Grecovery"', *Discourse & Society* 25/4 (2014), pp. 483–499.

Bounia, Aleka, 'Cultural Policy in Greece, the Case of the National Museums (1990–2010): an Overview' in L. Eilersten and A. Bugge Amundsen (eds), *Museum Policies in Europe 1990–2010: Negotiating Professional and Political Utopia* (Linköping, 2012), pp. 127–156.

Boura, Eleni and Mikela Hartoulari, *Το αποτύπωμα της κρίσης* [*The trace of crisis*] (Athens, 2012).

Boym, Svetlana, *The Future of Nostalgia* (New York, 2001).

Bramall, Rebecca, *The Cultural Politics of Austerity: Past and present in austere times* (Basingstoke, 2013).

——— Introduction: The Future of Austerity', *New Formations* 87 (2016), pp. 1–10

Brinkerhoff, Jennifer M., 'Creating an Enabling Environment for Diasporas' Participation in Homeland Development', *International Migration* 50/1 (2012), pp. 75–95.

Breu, Christopher, *Hard-boiled Masculinities* (Minneapolis, MN, 2005).

Brennan, Vicki L., 'Chamber Music in the Barn: Tourism, Nostalgia, and the Reproduction of Social Class', *The World of Music* 41/3 (1999), pp. 11–29.

Brown, Wendy, *Undoing the Demos. Neoliberalism's Stealth Revolution* (Cambridge MA and London, 2015).

Butler, Judith, *The Psychic Life of Power* (Stanford, CA, 1997).

——— *Precarious Life: The Power of Mourning and Violence* (New York, 2006).

Butler, Judith and Athina Athanasiou, *Dispossession: The Political in the Performative* (Cambridge, UK and Malden, MA, 2013).

Caruth, Cathy, *Unclaimed Experience: Trauma, Narrative, and History* (Baltimore, 1996).

Chaffee, Lyman G., *Political Protest and Street Art: Popular Tools for Democratization in Hispanic Countries* (Westport, 1993).

Chalkou, Maria, 'A New Cinema of "Emancipation": Tendencies of Independence in Greek Cinema of the 2000s', *Interactions* 3/2 (2012), pp. 243–261.

Chiotis, Theodoros (ed.), *Futures: Poetry of the Greek Crisis* (London, 2015).

Christodoulakis, Nicos, *Germany's War Debt to Greece: A Burden Unsettled* (Basingstoke, 2014).

Christopher, Nicholas. *Somewhere in the Night: Film Noir and the American City* (New York, 1998).

Colebrook, Claire, *Irony* (London and New York, 2004).

Conrad, Mark T., 'Nietzsche and the Meaning and Definition of Noir', *The Philosophy of Film Noir* (Lexington, KY, 2006), pp. 7–22.

Cottrell, Stephen, *Professional Music-Making in London: Ethnography and Experience* (London, 2004).

Damaskos, Dimitris and Dimitris Plantzos (eds), *A Singular Antiquity. Archaeology and Hellenic Identity in Twentieth-Century Greece* (Athens, 2008).

De Haas, Hein, 'Engaging Diasporas. how Governments and Development Agencies can Support Diaspora Involvement in the Development of their Origin Countries', *International Migration Institute (IMI), University of Oxford, for OXFAM NOVIB* (2006). Available at http://www.heindehaas.com/Publications/de%20Haas%202006%20-%20Engaging%20Diasporas.pdf.

——— 'Migration and Development: A Theoretical perspective1', *International Migration Review* 44/1 (2010), pp. 227–264.

——— 'The Migration and Development Pendulum: A Critical View on Research and Policy', *International Migration* 50/3 (2012), pp. 8–25.

Delanty, Gerard 'Conclusion: On the Cultural Significance of Arts Festivals', in Liana Giorgi, Monica Sassatelli and Gerard Delanty (eds), *Festivals and the Cultural Public Sphere* (London and New York, 2011), pp. 190–198.

Derrida, Jacques, *Margins of Philosophy*, trans. Alan Bass (Chicago, 1982).

———, 'This Strange Institution Called Literature: An Interview with Jacques Derrida', in Jacques Derrida, *Acts of Literature*, ed. Derek Attridge (London, 1992), pp. 33–75.

Deutsche, Rosalyn, 'Art and Public Space: Questions of Democracy', *Social Text* 33 (1992), pp. 34–53.

Dickens, Luke, '"Finders Keepers": Performing the Street, the Gallery and the Spaces In-Between', *Liminalities: A Journal of Performance Studies* 4/1 (2008), pp. 2–30.

Dimitriou, Alinda, *Πουλιά στο Βάλτο* [*Birds in the Mire*] (Athens, 2008).

——— *Η ζωή στους Βράχους* [*Life Among the Rocks*] (Athens, 2009).

——— *Τα Κορίτσια της Βροχής* [*Girls of the Rain*] (Athens, 2012).

Dimitriou, Sotiris, *Η σιωπή του ξερόχορτου* [*The silence of the dry weed*] (Athens, 2011).

_______ *Κοντά στην κοιλιά* [Close to the belly] (Athens, 2014).

Dolgeras, Lakis, 'Από την ηθική του αστυνόμου Χαρίτου στην ηθική των εκδικητών' ['From the ethics of Inspector Haritos to the ethics of avengers'], *The books' journal* 68 (July 2016).

Douzinas, Costas, *Philosophy and Resistance in the Crisis* (Cambridge, 2013).

Doxanaki, Anastasia, 'Τα αρχαιολογικά μουσεία και η επικοινωνία τους με το κοινό: Ανασταλτικοί παράγοντες επιρροής στο μοτίβο της επισκεψιμότητας των αρχαιολογικών μουσείων της Αθήνας' ['Archaeological museums and their communication to the public: prohibiting factors of influence to the pattern of archaeological museum visiting in Athens'], *Mouseio* 8 & 9, pp. 60–71.

Doyle, Gillian, *Understanding Media Economics* (London, 2013) (2nd edition).

Ducat, Jean, *Spartan Education: Youth and Society in the Classical Period* (Swansea, 2006).

Dufoix Stéphane, 'From nationals abroad to "diaspora": The rise and progress of extra-territorial and over-state nations', *Diaspora Studies* 4/1 (2011), pp. 1–20.

Dumont, Jean-Christophe, Gilles Spielvogel, and Sarah Widmaier, *International Migrants in Developed, Emerging and Developing Countries: An Extended Profile*: OECD Social, Employment and Migration Working Papers, 2010.

Easton Ellis, Brett, *American Psycho* (New York, 1991).

Elsaesser, Thomas, *European Cinema: Face to Face with Hollywood* (Amsterdam, 2005).

Eyerman, Ron, *Cultural Trauma: Slavery and the Formation of African American Identity* (Cambridge, 2001).

Fairclough, Norman and Isabelle Fairclough, *Political Discourse Analysis: A Method for Advanced Students* (London, 2012).

Faist, Thomas, 'Migrants as transnational development agents: An inquiry into the newest round of the migration–development nexus', *Population, Space and Place* 14/1 (2008), pp. 21–42.

Falassi, Alessandro, 'Festival: Definition and Morphology', in Alessandro Falassi (ed.), *Time out of Time: Essays on the Festival* (Albuquerque, 1987), pp. 1–2.

Falkheimer, Jesper and Mats Heide, 'Crisis communicators in change: From plans to improvisations', in W.T. Coombs & S.J. Holladay (eds), *The Handbook of Crisis Communication* (Oxford, 2010), pp. 511–526.

Featherstone, Kevin, 'The Greek Crisis', *Journal of Modern Greek Studies* 28/2 (2010), pp. 298–301.

——— 'The Greek sovereign debt crisis and EMU: a failing state in a skewed regime', *Journal of Common Market Studies*, 49/2 (2011), pp. 193–217.

Figgou, Lia, Ioanna Mylopoulou and Alexandra Birbili–Karaleka, 'Κατασκευές της ιδεολογικής ακρότητας και "μειονοτικοποίηση" στην προεκλογική ρητορική του ακροδεξιού κόμματος "Χρυσή Αυγή"' ['Construction of ideological extremism and "minoritization" in the pre–electoral rhetoric of the far right party "Golden Dawn"'] *10th Scientific Yearbook of the Psychology Department* (Thessaloniki, 2014), pp. 499–527.

Filippou, Filippos, 'Crime fiction during the crisis' and Marlena Politopoulou, 'When the Crisis Wears Noir' in Natasha Lemos & Eleni Yannakakis (eds), *Critical Times, Critical Thoughts: Contemporary Greek Writers Discuss Facts and Fiction* (Newcastle upon Tyne, 2015), pp. 144–173.

Fleischer, Hagen and Despina Konstantinakou, 'Ad calendas graecas? Griechenland und die deutsche Wiedergutmachung', in Hans Günter Hockerts, Claudia Moisel, and Tobias Winstel (eds), *Grenzen der Wiedergutmachung* (Göttingen, 2006), pp. 375–457.

Fleischer, Hagen, Karl Heinz Roth & Christoph Schminck-Gustavus, 'Die Opfer und nicht die Täter sollen in der Bringschuld sein?', *Zeitschrift für Geschichtswissenschaft* 64/4 (2016), pp. 379–388.

Fonseca, Pedro and Maria João Ferreira, 'Through "seas never before sailed": Portuguese government discursive legitimation strategies in a context of financial crisis', *Discourse & Society* 26/6 (2015), pp. 682–711.

Forkert, Kirtsen, 'Austere Creativity and Volunteer-run Public Services: the Case of Lewisham's Libraries', *New Formations* 87 (2016), pp. 11–28.

Forster, E.M., 'The Complete Poems of C.P. Cavafy', in *Two Cheers for Democracy* (London, 1951), pp. 243–248.

Fotiadi, Eva, 'State Interventions in Public Space in Athens and the Mediatization of the Crisis: Sustaining the Unsustainable Using Precarity as a Tool', *European Journal of Cultural Studies* (2015), pp. 1–16.

Foucault, Michel, *History of Sexuality*, Vol. 1: An Introduction (London, 1979).

——— *Power / Knowledge. Selected Interviews and Other Writings 1972–1977* (New York, 1980).

——— *Security, Territory, Population. Lectures at the Collège de France 1977–1978* (New York, 2007).

——— *The Birth of Biopolitics. Lectures at the Collège de France 1978–1979* (New York, 2008).

——— *Power. The Essential Works of Foucault, 1954–1984*, vol. 3 (London, 2010).

——— 'The Subject in Power', in H. Dreyfus and P. Rabinow (eds), *Michel Foucault: Beyond Structuralism and Hermeneutics* (Chicago, 1982), pp. 208–226.

——— 'Technologies of the self', in L.H. Martin, H. Gutman and P.H. Hutton (eds), *Technologies of the Self* (London, 1988), pp. 16–49.

Fragaki, Georgia, 'Evaluative adjectives in a corpus of Greek opinion articles', in M.L. Carrió Pastor and M.Á. Candel Mora (eds), *Las tecnologías de la información y las comunicaciones: Presente y futuro en el análisis de córpora. Actas del III Congreso Internacional de Lingüística de Corpus*, (Valencia, 2011). Available at: www.editorial.upv.es/publicacion/6032.

——— '"Tragic event" vs. "cowardly murder": A study of Golden Dawn's lexicogrammatical choices and discourse strategies', in O. Hatzidaki and D. Goutsos (eds), *Greece in Crisis: Combining Critical Discourse and Corpus Linguistics Perspectives* (Amsterdam, forthcoming).

Fukuyama, Francis, *The End of History and the Last Man* (New York, 1992).

Galanaki, Rhea, *Η Άκρα Ταπείνωση* [*Utmost Humiliation*] (Athens, 2015).

Galt, John, *Letters From the Levant: containing views of the state of society, manner, opinions and commerce in Greece and several of the principal islands of the archipelago* (London, 1813).

Georgalou, Mariza, 'Taking stances on the Greek crisis: Expertise, opinions and contradiction on Facebook', in O. Hatzidaki and D. Goutsos (eds), *Greece in Crisis: Combining Critical Discourse and Corpus Linguistics Perspectives* (Amsterdam, forthcoming).

Georganas, Ioannes, 'The effects of the economic crisis on Greek heritage: A view from the private cultural sector', *Journal of Eastern Mediterranean Archaeology and Heritage Studies* 1/3 (2013), pp. 242–245.

Georgiadou, Vassiliki 'Right-wing populism and extremism: The rapid rise of "Golden Dawn" in crisis–ridden Greece', in R. Melzer and S. Serafin (eds), *Right-wing Extremism in Europe. Country Analyses, Counter-strategies and Labor-market Oriented Exit Strategies* (Berlin, 2013).

Gerodimos, Roman and Georgios Karyotis, 'Austerity Politics and Crisis Governance: Lessons from Greece' in Georgios Karyotis & Roman Gerodimos (eds), *The Politics of Extreme Austerity: Greece in the Eurozone Crisis* (Basingstoke, 2015), pp. 259–271.

Getz, Donald, 'The Nature and Scope of Festival Studies', *International Journal of Event Management Research* 5/1 (2010), 1–47.

Giannitsis, Tassos and Stavros Zografakis, 'Greece: solidarity and adjustment in times of crisis', Hans-Böckler-Stiftung, IMK Studies, Nr. 38, Düsseldorf March 2015.

Giorgi, Liana and Monica Sassatelli, 'Introduction', in Liana Giorgi, Monica Sassatelli and Gerard Delanty (eds), *Festivals and the Cultural Public Sphere* (London and New York, 2011), pp. 1–10.

Glăvan, Bogdan, 'Brain Drain: A Management Or a Property Problem?' *American Journal of Economics and Sociology* 67/4 (2008), pp. 719–737.

Goodman, Robin T., *Policing Narratives and the State of Terror* (Albany, NY, 2009).

Goutsos, Dionysis and George Polymeneas, 'Identity as space: Localism in the Greek protests of Syntagma square', *Journal of Language and Politics* 13/4 (2014), pp. 675–701.

——— 'Constructed and ascribed identity of the Greek protesters at Syntagma Square: From "where we are" to "who they are"', in O. Hatzidaki and D. Goutsos (eds), *Greece in Crisis: Combining Critical Discourse and Corpus Linguistics Perspectives* (Amsterdam, forthcoming).

Graeber, David, 'The Greek Debt Crisis in Almost Unimaginably Long-term Historical Perspective', in Antonis Vradis and Dimitris Dalakoglou (eds), *Revolt and Crisis in Greece: Between a Present Yet to Pass and a Future Still to Come* (Oakland, Edinburgh, London and Athens, 2011), pp. 229–243.

Gruber, Christiane, 'The Visual Emergence of the Occupy Gezi Movement', *JADmag* 1/4 (2013), pp. 29–36.

Haiven, Max, *Crises of Imagination, Crises of Power: Capitalism, Culture and Resistance in a Post-Crash World* (London, 2014).

Hamdy, Basma and Don Karl Stone (eds), *Walls of Freedom: Street Art of the Egyptian Revolution* (Berlin, 2014).

Hamilakis, Yannis, *The Nation and its Ruins. Antiquity, Archaeology, and National Imagination in Greece* (Oxford, 2007).

——— 'Some debts can never be repaid: the archaeo-politics of the crisis', *Journal of Modern Greek Studies* 34/2 (2016), pp. 227–264.

Hapsoulas, Anastasios, 'Εντεχνη δυτική μουσική και ελληνική μουσική εκπαίδευση: Κρίση και προοπτικές' ['Western Art Music and Greek Music Education: Crisis and Prospects'], *Polyphonia* 26 (Spring 2015), 82–95.

Hatzidaki, Ourania, 'The "theory of the two extremes": A rhetorical topography for self- and other-identification across the Greek political spectrum', in O. Hatzidaki and D. Goutsos (eds), *Greece in Crisis: Combining Critical Discourse and Corpus Linguistics Perspectives* (Amsterdam, forthcoming).

Hay, Colin, 'Narrating crisis: The discursive construction of the "Winter of Discontent"', *Sociology* 30/2 (1996), pp. 253–277.

Herzfeld, Michael, 'Crisis Attack: Impromptu Ethnography in the Greek Maelstrom', *Anthropology Today* 27/5 (2011), pp. 22–26.

——— 'The European Crisis and Cultural Intimacy', *Studies in Ethnicity and Nationalism* 13/3 (2013), pp. 491–497.

Hirsch, Marianne, *Family frames: photography, narrative, and postmemory* (Cambridge, Mass. & London, 1997).

——— 'The Generation of Postmemory', *Poetics Today* 29/1 (Spring 2008), pp. 103–128.

Howery, Cherkea, 'The effects of the economic crisis on archaeology in Greece', *Journal of Eastern Mediterranean Archaeology and Heritage Studies* 1/3 (2013), pp. 228–233.

Ignazi, Piero, *Extreme Right Parties in Western Europe* (Oxford, 2003).

Johnson, Julian, *Who Needs Classical Music?* (Oxford and New York, 2002).

Kaika, Maria and Lazaros Karaliotas, 'The spatialization of democratic politics: Insights from Indignant Squares', *European Urban and Regional Studies* 23/4 (2016), pp. 556–570.

Kalantzis, Konstantinos '"Fak Germani": materialities of nationhood and transgression in the Greek crisis', *Comparative Studies in Society and History* 57/4 (2015), pp. 1037–1069.

Kalyvas, Stathis N, *Modern Greece: What Everyone Needs to Know* (Oxford, 2015).

Kapur, Devesh and John McHale, *Give Us Your Best and Brightest: The Global Hunt for Talent and its Impact on the Developing World* (Washington DC, 2005).

Karamessini, Maria, 'Life Stage Transitions and the Still-Critical Role of the Family in Greece', *The Welfare State and Life Transitions. A European Perspective* (Cheltenham, 2010), pp. 257–283.

Karyotis, Georgios and Wolfgang Rüdig, 'Protest Participation, Electoral Choices and Public Attitudes towards Austerity in Greece' in Georgios Karyotis & Roman Gerodimos (eds), *The Politics of Extreme Austerity: Greece in the Eurozone Crisis* (Basingstoke, 2015), pp. 123–141.

Katsambekis, Yorgos, *ΣΥΡΙΖΑ 2004–2012: Από τη «νεολαία» στον «λαό». Μια λογο-θεωρητική προσέγγιση του λαϊκισμού της ριζοσπαστικής αριστεράς {SYRIZA 2004–2012 From 'youth' to 'the people': A discourse-theoretical approach to the populism of the radical left*} (Athens, 2014).

Katsan, Gerasimus, *History and National Ideology in Greek Postmodernist Fiction* (Madison, Teaneck, 2013).

Kavouras, Pavlos, 'Η έντεχνη δυτική μουσική στην περίοδο της κρίσης: Μία διεπιστημονική μελέτη του σύγχρονου ελληνικού πολιτισμού και της ευρωπαϊκής ολοκλήρωσης' {'Western Art Music at the Time of Crisis: An Interdisciplinary Study of Contemporary Greek Culture and European Integration'}, *Polyphonia* 26 (Spring 2015), pp. 7–64.

Kentikelenis, Alexander and Irene Papanikolas, 'Economic crisis, austerity and the Greek public health', *European Journal of Public Health* 22/1 (2011), pp. 4–5.

Kentikelenis, Alexander, Marina Karanikolos, Aaron Reeves, Martin McKee, David Stuckler, 'Greece's health crisis: from austerity to denialism', *Lancet* 383 (22 February 2014), pp. 748–753.

Knight, Daniel M., 'Turn of the screw: narratives of history and economy in the Greek crisis', *Journal of Mediterranean Studies*, 21/1 (2012), pp. 53–76.

——— 'Cultural proximity: crisis, time and social memory in central Greece', *History and Anthropology* 23/3 (2012), pp. 349–374.

——— *History, Time, and Economic Crisis in Central Greece* (London & New York, 2015).

——— 'Wit and Greece's economic crisis: ironic slogans, food, and antiausterity sentiments', *American Ethnologist* 42/2 (2015), 230–246.

Knight, Daniel M. and Charles Stewart, 'Ethnographies of Austerity: Temporality, Crisis and Affect in Southern Europe', *History and Anthropology* 27/1 (2016), pp. 1–18.

Kirtsoglou Elisavet and D. Theodossopoulos, 'The poetics of anti-Americanism in Greece: rhetoric, agency, and local meaning', *Social Analysis* 54/1 (2010), pp. 106–124.

Kitromilides, Paschalis, M., *Enlightenment and Revolution: The Making of Modern Greece* (Cambridge, Mass, 2013).

Kokonis, Michalis, 'Is there such a thing as a Greek Blockbuster? The revival of contemporary Greek cinema' in Lydia Papadimitriou and Yannis Tzioumakis (eds), *Greek Cinema: Texts, Histories, Identities* (Bristol, 2011), pp. 37–54.

Konstantinakou, Despina-Georgia, *Πολεμικές οφειλές και εγκληματίες πολέμου στην Ελλάδα* [*War reparations and war criminals in Greece*] (Athens, 2015),

Konstantios, Dimitris, 'Μια άλλη πολιτική είναι εφικτή' ['Another policy is feasible'], *ILISSIA* 1 (2007), pp. 4–13.

Kornetis, Kostis, 'No more heroes? Rejection and reverberation of the past in the 2008 events in Greece', *Journal of Modern Greek Studies* 28/2 (2010), pp. 173–197.

——— *Children of the Dictatorship: Student Resistance, Cultural Politics, and the 'Long 1960s' in Greece* (New York, 2013).

Koselleck, Reinhart, 'Crisis', trans. Michaela W. Richter, *Journal of the History of Ideas* 67/2 (2006), pp. 357–400.

Kostopoulou, Georgia, 'The dream that turned into a nightmare: Addressing the Greek voters long and right before the crisis', in O. Hatzidaki and D. Goutsos (eds), *Greece in Crisis: Combining Critical Discourse and Corpus Linguistics Perspectives* (Amsterdam, forthcoming).

Kotsakis, Kostas, 'The past is ours: images of Greek Macedonia', in L. Meskell (ed.), *Archaeology under fire. Nationalism, Politics and Heritage in the Eastern Mediterranean and Middle East* (London and New York, 1998), pp. 44–67.

Kouki, Hara, 'European crisis discourses: The case of Greece', in T. Murray-Leach et al., *Crisis Discourses in Europe: Media EU-phemisms and Alternative Narratives* (London, 2014).

Koundoura, Maria, *The Greek Idea: The Formation of National and Transnational Identities* (London, 2007).

Kourelou, Olga, Mariana Liz, and Belén Vidal, 'Crisis and Creativity: The New Cinemas of Portugal, Greece and Spain', *New Cinemas: Journal of Contemporary Film* 12/1 & 2 (2014), pp. 133–151.

Kousis Maria, 'The transnational dimension of the Greek protest campaign against troika memoranda and austerity policies, 2010–2012', in Donatella della Porta and Alice Mattoni (eds), *Spreading Protest: Social Movements in Times of Crisis* (Colchester, UK, 2014), pp. 137–169.

Koutsoulelou, Stamatia, '"Crisis written all over me": Greek songs in times of crisis', in O. Hatzidaki and D. Goutsos (eds), *Greece in Crisis: Combining Critical Discourse and Corpus Linguistics Perspectives* (Amsterdam, forthcoming).

Kumar, Krishan, 'The ends of utopia', *New Literary History* 41/3 (2010), pp. 549–569.

Kutter, Amelie, 'A catalytic moment: The Greek crisis in the German financial press', *Discourse & Society* 25/4 (2014), pp. 446–466.

Kuvik, Aimee, 'The Race for Global Talent, EU Enlargement and the Implications for Migration Policies and Processes in European Labour Markets', in Brigit Glorius, Izabela Grabowska-Lusinka and Aimee Kuvik (eds), *Mobility in Transition: Migration Patterns After EU Enlargement* (Amsterdam, 2014), pp. 113–132.

Labrianidis, Lois, *Επενδύοντας στη φυγή: Η διαρροή επιστημόνων από την Ελλάδα την εποχή της παγκοσμιοποίηση* [*Investing in Leaving: The Greek Case of International Migration of Professionals in the Globalization Era*] (Athens, 2011).

——— 'Investing in Leaving: The Greek Case of International Migration of Professionals' *Mobilities* 9/2 (2014), pp. 314–335.

Labrianidis, Lois and Nikos Vogiatzis, 'The Mutually Reinforcing Relation between International Migration of Highly Educated Labour Force and Economic Crisis: The Case of Greece' *Southeast European and Black Sea Studies* 13/4 (2013), pp. 525–551.

Labrianidis, Lois and Manolis Pratsinakis, 'Greece's New Emigration at Times of Crisis' *GreeSE: Hellenic Observatory Papers on Greece and Southeast Europe* paper 99, (2016).

LaCapra, Dominick, *Writing History, Writing Trauma* (Baltimore and London, 2001).

Ladino, Jennifer K., *Reclaiming Nostalgia: Longing for Nature in American Literature* (Charlottesville and London, 2012).

Lampropoulou, Sofia, '"Greece will decide the future of Europe": The recontextualisation of the Greek national elections in a British broadsheet newspaper', *Discourse & Society* 25/4 (2014), pp. 467–482.

Lane Fox, Robin J. (ed.), *Brill's Companion to Ancient Macedon. Studies in the Archaeology and History of Macedon, 650 BC – 300 AD* (Leiden and Boston, 2011).

Lapavitsas, Costas, 'The Greek crisis – politics, economics, ethics: a debate held at the Birkbeck Institute for the Humanities, Birkbeck College, University of London, 5 May 2010', *Journal of Modern Greek Studies* 28/2 (2010), pp. 293–310.

Lazzarato, Maurizio, *The Making of the Indebted Man: An Essay on the Neoliberal Condition* (Los Angeles, 2012).

Lemos, Natasha and Eleni Yannakakis (eds), *Critical Times, Critical Thoughts: Contemporary Greek Writers Discuss Facts and Fiction* (Newcastle upon Tyne, 2015).

Leontis, Artemis, *Topographies of Hellenism. Mapping the Homeland* (Ithaca and London, 1995).

Leventis, Panos, 'Walls of Crisis: Street Art and Urban Fabric in Central Athens, 2000–2012', *Architectural Histories* 1/1 (2012), pp. 1–10.

Levidou, Katerina, 'Επιβιώνοντας στην κρίση: Θερινά φεστιβάλ έντεχνης δυτικής μουσικής στη σύγχρονη Ελλάδα' ['Surviving the Crisis: Summer Festivals of Western Art Music in Contemporary Greece'], *Polyphonia* 26 (Spring 2015), pp. 124–155.

Levidou, Katerina and Georgia Vavva, 'Παράρτημα: Φεστιβάλ με έντεχνη δυτική μουσική στην Ελλάδα, από το 2008 έως σήμερα (ενδεικτικός κατάλογος)' ['Appendix: Festivals with Western art music in Greece, from 2008 up to the present (indicative catalogue)'], *Polyphonia* 26 (Spring 2015), pp. 224–245.

Lewisohn, Cedar, *Street Art: The Graffiti Revolution* (London, 2008).

Liakos, Antonis, 'Greek narratives of crisis', *Humaniora. Czasopismo Internetowe*, 3/3 (2013), pp. 79–86.

Lindqvist, Katja, 'Museum finances: challenges beyond economic crises', *Museum Management and Curatorship* 27/1 (2012), 1–15.

Litsas, Spyridon, N. 'The Greek failing state and its "smart power" prospects: a theoretical approach', *Mediterranean Quarterly* 26/3 (2014), pp. 52–73.

Lykidis, Alex, 'Crisis of sovereignty in recent Greek cinema', *Journal of Greek Media & Culture* 1/1 (2015), 9–27.

Makridakis, Yannis, *Ανάμισης ντενεκές* [*One and a Half Tin*] (Athens, 2008).

——— *Το ζουμί του πετεινού* [*Cockerel's Soup*] (Athens, 2012).

——— *Του Θεού το μάτι* [*God's Eye*] (Athens, 2013).

——— *Αντί Στεφάνου* [*Instead of a Wreath*] (Athens, 2015).

Malakos, Tolis, 'Greece facing herself: the past and present as fate', *Journal of Balkan and Near Eastern Studies* 15/1 (2013), pp. 1–15.

Malkki Liisa H., 'National Geographic: The rooting of peoples and the territorialization of national identity among scholars and refugees', in Akhil Gupta and James Ferguson (eds), *Culture, Power, Place: Explorations in Critical Anthropology* (Durham, NC, 1997), pp. 52–74.

Manney, Linda J., *Middle Voice in Modern Greek: Meaning and Function of an Inflectional Category* (Amsterdam and Philadelphia, 2000).

Margomenou, Despina and Faidra Papavasiliou, 'Times of Crisis and Seeds of New Intimacies on a North Aegean Island: Activism, Alternative Exchange Networks, and Re-Imagined Communities', *Studies in Ethnicity and Nationalism* 13/3 (2013), pp. 523–529.

Markaris, Petros, *Παλιά, Πολύ Παλιά* [*A Long Long Time Ago*] (Athens, 2008).

——— 'Greece: the other side of 1968' in Gassert, Philipp and Klimke, Martin (eds), *1968: Memories and Legacies of a Global Revolt* (Washington, DC, 2009).

——— *Ληξιπρόθεσμα Δάνεια* [*Expiring Loans*] (Athens, 2010).

——— *Περαίωση* [*Settling Accounts*] (Athens, 2011).

——— *Ψωμί, Παιδεία, Ελευθερία* [*Bread, Education, Freedom*] (Athens, 2012).

——— *Τίτλοι Τέλους: Ο Επίλογος* [*Closing Credits: the Epilogue*] (Athens, 2014).

Massey, Douglas S., Joaquin Arango, Graeme Hugo, Ali Kouaouci, Adela Pellegrino, and J. Edward Taylor, 'Theories of International Migration: A Review and Appraisal', *Population and Development Review* 19/3 (1993), pp. 451–454.

Massey, Susan, 'Inheriting the Mantle: Wallander and Daughter' in Macah Effron (ed.), *The Millennial Detective: Essays on Trends in Crime Fiction, Film and Television, 1990–2010*. (Jefferson, NC, 2011), pp. 50–65.

Mathur, Vijay K., 'Human Capital-Based Strategy for Regional Economic Development', *Economic Development Quarterly* 13/3 (1999), pp. 203–216.

Mavroudi Elizabeth, 'Helping the homeland? Diasporic Greeks in Australia and the potential for homeland-oriented development as a time of economic crisis', in Anastasia Christou and Elizabeth Mavroudi (eds), *Dismantling Diasporas: Rethinking the Geographies of Diasporic Identity, Connection and Development* (New York, 2015), pp. 175–187.

Mbembe, Achille, 'Necropolitics', *Public Culture* 15/1 (2003), pp. 11–40.

Metaxas, Theodore and Alexis Deffner, 'Marketing, management and promotion policies of city image: defining the role and the contribution of public museums in Greece', in A. Bounia, N. Nikonanou and M. Economou (eds), *Technology in the Service of Cultural Heritage: Management, Education, Communication* (Athens, 2008), pp. 117–129.

Meyer, Jean Baptiste, 'Network Approach Versus Brain Drain: Lessons from the Diaspora', *International Migration* 39/5 (2001), pp. 91–110.

Mitsikopoulou, Bessie and Christina Lykou, 'The discursive construction of the recent European economic crisis in two political magazines', *On the Horizon* 23/3 (2015), pp. 190–201.

——— 'The chronicle of an ongoing crisis: Diachronic media representations of Greece and Europe in the Greek press', in O. Hatzidaki and D. Goutsos (eds), *Greece in Crisis: Combining Critical Discourse and Corpus Linguistics Perspectives* (Amsterdam, forthcoming).

Morton, Dudley J., 'Metatarsus atavicus: the identification of a distinct type of foot disorder', *The Journal of Bone and Joint Surgery* 9 (1927), pp. 531–544.

Moskos Peter C., and Charles C. Moskos, *Greek Americans: Struggle and Success* (New Brunswick, NJ, 2014) (3rd edition).

Mouliou, Maria, 'Το μουσείο ως ποιότητα, εμπειρία, αστικό σύμβολο και ήπια δύναμη. Παραδείγματα από τη διεθνή και εγχώρια μουσειακή πρακτική' ['The museum as quality, experience, civic symbol and soft power. Examples from international and local museum practice'] in I. Poulios et al. (eds), *Πολιτισμική διαχείριση, τοπική κοινωνία και βιώσιμη ανάπτυξη* (Athens, 2015), pp. 74–79.

Mouliou, Maria and Despoina Kalessopoulou, 'Emblematic museum objects of national significance: In search of their multiple meanings and values', in S. Dudley, J. Binnie and J. Petrov (eds), *The Thing about Museums* (London, 2011), pp. 47–68.

Mylonas, Yiannis, 'Media and the economic crisis of the EU: The "culturalization" of a systemic crisis and Bild-Zeitung's framing of Greece', *TripleC – Cognition, Communication, Co-operation: Open Access Journal for a Global Sustainable Information Society* 10/2 (2012), pp. 646–671.

——— 'Crisis, austerity and opposition in mainstream media discourses of Greece', *Critical Discourse Studies* 11/3, pp. 305–321.

Nichols, William J., *Transatlantic Mysteries: Crime, Culture, and Capital In the Noir Novels of Paco Ignacio Taibo Ii and Manuel Vázquez Montalbán* (Lewisburg, PA, 2011).

Nicoarea, Georgiana, 'Interrogating the Dynamic of Egyptian Graffiti: From Neglected Marginality to Image Politics', *Revista Română de Studii Eurasiatice* X/1–2 (2014), pp. 171–186.

Nielsen, Peter and Bengt-Åke Lundvall, *Innovation, Learning Organizations and Industrial Relations*, DRUID Working Paper, 2003.

Nikisianis, Nikos, Thomas Siomos, Yannis, Stavrakakis and Titika Dimitroulia, 'Λαϊκισμός εναντίον αντιλαϊκισμού στον ελληνικό Τύπο' ['Populism vs. anti-populism in the Greek press'], *Σύγχρονα Θέματα* 132–133 (2016), pp. 52–70.

Nooshin, Laudan, 'Introduction to the Special Issue: The Ethnomusicology of Western Art Music', *Ethnomusicology Forum* XX/3 (2011), 285–300.

OECD, *Better Skills, Better Jobs, Better Lives: A Strategic Approach to Skills Policies* OECD, 2012.

Oikonomou, Hristos, *Το καλό θα 'ρθει από τη θάλασσα* [*The good will come from the sea*] (Athens 2014).

Ong Aihwa, *Buddha Is Hiding: Refugees, Citizenship, the New America* (Berkeley, 2003).

——— *Flexible Citizenship: The Cultural Logics of Transnationality* (Durham, NC, 1999).

Pangalos, Orestis, 'Testimonies and Appraisals on Athens Graffiti, Before and After the Crisis', in M. Tsilimpounidi and A. Walsh (eds), *Remapping 'Crisis': A Guide to Athens* (London, 2014), pp. 154–176.

Papadimitriou, Lydia, 'The National and the Transnational in Contemporary Greek Cinema', *New Review of Film and Television Studies* 9/4 (2011), pp. 493–512.

——— 'Locating Contemporary Greek Film Cultures: Past, Present, Future and the Crisis', *Filmicon:* Journal of Greek Film Studies 2 (September 2014), pp. 1–19.

——— 'In the Shadow of the Studios, the State and the Multiplexes: Independent Filmmaking in Greece', in M. Erickson and D. Baltruschat (eds), *The Meaning of Independence: Independent Filmmaking around the Globe* (Toronto, 2014), pp. 113–130.

——— 'Film Distribution in Greece: Formal and Informal Networks of Exchange since the crisis', *Screen* 59/4 (2018) (forthcoming).

——— 'Transitions in the periphery: Funding film production in Greece since the financial crisis', *International Journal of Media Management* 19/2 (2017) (forthcoming).

Papanikolaou, Panagiota, 'The economic crisis in Greece and its effects on culture (2010–2015). The case of museums and art galleries', *International Journal of Research in Humanities and Social Sciences* 2/10 (2015), pp. 55–60.

Papathanassopoulos, Stelios, 'The Politics and the Effects of the Deregulation of Greek Television, *European Journal of Communication* 12/3 (1997), pp. 351–368.

Pappas, Takis S., 'Why Greece failed', *Journal of Democracy*, 24/2 (2013), pp. 31–45.

Paraskeva-Veloudoyanni, Despoina, *Ο εχθρός, το αίμα, ο τιμωρός: Αναλύοντας δεκατρείς λόγους του «αρχηγού» της Χρυσής Αυγής* [*The enemy, the blood, the punisher. Analysing thirteen speeches of the "leader" of Golden Dawn*] (Athens, 2014).

Pellerin, Hélène and Beverley Mullings, 'The "Diaspora Option", Migration and the Changing Political Economy of Development' *Review of International Political Economy* 20/1 (2013), pp. 89–120.

Plantzos, Dimitris, 'Archaeology and Hellenic identity, 1896–2004: the frustrated vision', in D. Damaskos and D. Plantzos (eds), *A Singular Antiquity: Archaeology and Hellenic Identity in Twentieth-Century Greece* (Athens, 2008), pp. 10–30.

——— 'Τα ορφανά του Αλέξανδρου' ['Alexander's orphans'], *The Athens Review of Books* 30, 2012 (Jun.), pp. 51–54.

——— 'The glory that was not: embodying the classical in contemporary Greece', *Interactions* 3/2 (2012), pp. 147–171.

——— 'The *kouros* of Keratea: constructing subaltern pasts in contemporary Greece', *Journal of Social Archaeology* 12 (2012), pp. 220–244.

——— 'Amphipolitics', *The Athens Review of Books* 55, 2014 (Oct.), p. 10.

——— 'Των Ελλήνων τα ιερά' ['On the Sacred Bones of the Greeks'], *Unfollow* 33, 2014 (Sept.) pp. 114–119.

——— Το Πρόσφατο Μέλλον [*The Recent Future*] (Athens 2016).

Pleios, George, 'Τα ΜΜΕ απέναντι στην κρίση: Έντονη υιοθέτηση της λογικής των ελίτ' ['The media against the crisis: Extensive adoption of the elite logic"'], in G. Pleios (ed.), *Η κρίση και τα ΜΜΕ* [*Crisis and the Mass Media*] (Athens, 2013).

Polymeneas, George '"[T]oday I know, we know, that these sacrifices are heavy, but necessary": Constructing governmental knowledge on Greece's sovereign debt crisis', in O. Hatzidaki and D. Goutsos (eds), *Greece in Crisis: Combining Critical Discourse and Corpus Linguistics Perspectives* (Amsterdam, forthcoming).

Poulakis, Nikos, 'Θεσμοί σε κρίση Μουσικά σύνολα και πολιτιστικοί οργανισμοί στην Ελλάδα του 21ου αιώνα' ['Institutions in Crisis; Music Ensembles and Cultural Organisations in Greece of the 21st century'], *Polyphonia* 26 (Spring 2015), 96–123.

Pratsinakis, Manolis, Hatziprokopiou, Panos, Grammatikas, Dimitris, Labrianidis, Lois. 'Crisis and the resurgence of emigration from Greece: trends, representations, and the multiplicity of migrant trajectories' in Brigit Glorius, B. and Josefina Domínguez-Mujica (eds), *European Mobility in Times of Crisis: The new context of European South-North Migration* (Bielefeld 2017), pp. 75–102.

Quinn, Bernadette, 'Symbols, Practices and Myth-Making: Cultural Perspectives on the Wexford Festival Opera', *Tourism Geographies* 5/3 (2003), 329–349.

Ragkos, Athanasios, Stavariani Koutsou and Theodoros Manousidis, 'In Search of Strategies to Face the Economic Crisis: Evidence from Greek Farms', *South European Society and Politics* 21/3 (2016), pp. 319–337.

Rancière, Jacques, *The Emancipated Spectator*, trans. Gregory Elliott (London, 2011).

Raymond, Richard, 'The Interregional Brain Drain and Public Education', *Growth and Change* 4/3 (1973), pp. 28–34.

Romanou, Keti, *Έντεχνη ελληνική μουσική στους νεότερους χρόνους* ['Greek Art Music in Modern Times'] (Athens, 2006).

Romp, Ward and Jakob De Haan, 'Public Capital and Economic Growth: A Critical Survey' *Perspektiven Der Wirtschaftspolitik* 8/1 (2007), pp. 6–52.

Rose Nikolas, 'Governing the Enterprising Self', in Paul Heelas, Paul Morris, and Paul M. Morris (eds), *Values of the Enterprise Culture: The Moral Debate* (New York, 1992), pp. 141–164.

Ross, Kristin, *Fast Cars, Clean Bodies: Decolonization and the Reordering of French Culture* (Cambridge, MA, 1994).

Roth, Karl Heinz, *Griechenland am Abgrund. Die deutsche Reparationsschuld* (Hamburg, 2015).

Rust, Stephen, Salma Monani and Sean Cubitt, *Ecocinema Theory and Practice* (London, 2013).

Samson, Jim, 'Music in Crisis: Key Terms and Concepts', in Pavlos Kavouras (ed.), *Η έντεχνη δυτική μουσική στην περίοδο της κρίσης: Μία διεπιστημονική μελέτη του σύγχρονου ελληνικού πολιτισμού και της ευρωπαϊκής ολοκλήρωσης* [*Western Art Music at the Time of Crisis: An Interdisciplinary Study of Contemporary Greek Culture and European Integration*] (Athens, 2015), pp. 42–49. Available at http://westartmusinenglish.weebly.com/uploads/4/2/1/4/42143431/westartmusvolume.pdf (accessed 17 August 2016).

Saridakis, Ioannis, 'Golden Dawn and the traits of extreme right-wing discourse amidst the Greek crisis', in O. Hatzidaki and D. Goutsos (eds), *Greece in Crisis: Combining Critical Discourse and Corpus Linguistics Perspectives* (Amsterdam, forthcoming).

Saxenian, AnnaLee, *Silicon Valley's New Immigrant Entrepreneurs*, Vol. 32 (San Francisco, 1999).

Schacter, Rafael, *Ornament and Order: Graffiti, Street Art and the Parergon* (Surrey, 2014).

Schrader, Paul, 'Notes on Film Noir' in Grant, Barry Keith (ed.), *Film Genre Reader III* (Austin, TX, 2003), pp. 221–242.

Seremetakis, C. Nadia, 'Implications', in C.N. Seremetakis (ed.), *The Senses Still. Perception and Memory as Material Culture in Modernity* (Chicago and London, 1994), pp. 123–145.

Serres, Michel, *Conversations on Science, Culture, and Time* (Ann Arbor, 1995).

Shachar, Ayelet, 'The Race for Talent: Highly-Skilled Migrants and Competitive Immigration Regimes' *New York University Law Review* 81, (2006), pp. 148–206.

Sinatti, Giulia and Cindy Horst, 'Migrants as Agents of Development: Diaspora Engagement Discourse and Practice in Europe', *Ethnicities* 15/1 (2015), pp. 134–152.

Singer, Milton, *When a Great Tradition Modernizes: An Anthropological Approach to Modern Civilization* (New York, 1972).

Skeldon, Ronald, 'International Migration as a Tool in Development Policy: A Passing Phase?', *Population and Development Review* 34/1 (2008), pp. 1–18.

Stampoulidis, Georgios, 'Rethinking Athens as Text: The Linguistic Context of Athenian Graffiti During the Crisis', *Journal of Language Works* 1/1 (2016), pp. 10–23.

Stavrakakis, Yannis, Nikos Nikisianis, Aleksandros Kioupkolis, Giorgos Katsambekis and Thomas Siomos, 'Λαϊκιστικός λόγος και δημοκρατία' ['Populist discourse and democracy'], *Ελληνική Επιθεώρηση Πολιτικής Επιστήμης* 43 (2015), pp. 49–80.

Stefanidis, Ioannis D., *Stirring the Greek Nation: Political Culture, Irredentism and Anti-Americanism in Post-war Greece, 1945–1967* (Aldershot, 2007).

Straubhaar, Thomas, 'International Mobility of the Highly Skilled: Brain Gain, Brain Drain Or Brain Exchange' *Hamburgisches Welt-Wirtschafts-Archiv (HWWA)* Discussion Paper 88 (2000), pp. 1–23.

Streeck, Wolfgang, 'The construction of a moral duty for the Greek people to repay their national debt', in M. Fourcade, P. Steiner, W. Streeck and C. Woll (eds), *Moral Categories in the Financial Crisis* (Paris, 2013). Available at: http://www.maxpo.eu/pub/maxpo_dp/maxpodp13-1.pdf.

Sutton, David, *Remembrance of Repasts: An Anthropology of Food and Memory* (Oxford, 2001).

Taibo, Paco Ignacio and Subcomandante Marcos, *The Uncomfortable Dead* (New York, NY 2006).

Talalay, Lauren E., 'Drawing conclusions: Greek antiquity, the €conomic crisis, and political cartoons', *Journal of Modern Greek Studies* 31/2 (2013), pp. 249–276.

Theocharis, Yannis, Will Lowe, Jan W. van Deth and Gema García-Albacete, 'Using Twitter to mobilize protest action: Online mobilization patterns and action repertoires in the Occupy Wall Street, Indignados, and Aganaktismenoi movements', *Information, Communication & Society* 18/2 (2015), pp. 202–220.

Theodossopoulos, Dimitrios 'Infuriated with the Infuriated? Blaming Tactics and Discontent about the Greek Financial Crisis', *Current Anthropology* 54/2 (2013), pp. 200–221,

——— 'The Ambivalence of Anti-Austerity Indignation in Greece: Resistance, Hegemony and Complicity', *History and Anthropology* 25/4 (2014), pp. 488–506.

Thompson, Jim, *The Killer Inside Me* (Robbinsdale, MN, 1952).

Tonkiss, Fran, 'Austerity Urbanism and the Makeshift City' *City* 17/3 (2013), pp. 312–324.

Triadafilopoulos, Triadafilos (ed.), *Wanted and Welcome?: Policies for Highly Skilled Immigrants in Comparative Perspective* (New York, 2013).

Triandafyllidou, Anna, Ruby Gropas, and Hara Kouki (eds), *The Greek Crisis and European Modernity* (Basingstoke, 2013).

Tsakona, Villy, 'The Greek patient and the plaster cast: From the Greek military junta of 21 April 1967 to the IMF and EU's rescue mechanism', *Metaphor and the Social World* 2/1 (2012), pp. 61–85.

Tsangari, Athina, 'On Solidarity, Collaboration and Independence: Athina Rachel Tsangari discusses her films and Greek cinema with Vangelis Calotychos, Lydia Papadimitriou and Yannis Tzioumakis' *Journal of Greek Media and Culture* 2/2 (2016), pp. 237–253.

Tsiara, Syrago, 'Contemporary Greek Art in Times of Crisis: Cuts and Changes', *Journal of Visual Culture* 14/2 (2015), pp. 176–181.

Tsilimpounidi, Myrto, '"If These Walls Could Talk": Street Art and Urban Belonging', *Laboratorium* 7/2 (2015), pp. 71–91.

Tsitsanoudi-Mallidi, Nicoletta, '«Αγανακτισμένων Συνθήματα»: Γλωσσικές πραγματώσεις και ιδεολογικό πλαίσιο.' ['Slogans of the Indignant: Linguistic realizations and ideological framework'], *Νέα Παιδεία* 143 (2012), pp. 47–64.

Tsoukalis, Loukas, 'International bubbles, European currency union, and national failures: the case of Greece and the euro crisis', in Anna Triandafyllidou, Ruby Gropas and Hara Kouki (eds), *The Greek Crisis and European Modernity* (Basingstoke, 2013), pp. 25–43.

Tziovas, Dimitris, 'Beyond the Acropolis: rethinking neohellenism', *Journal of Modern Greek Studies* 19/2 (2001), pp. 189 –220.

——— 'Decolonizing antiquity, heritage politics, and performing the past', in D. Tziovas (ed.), *Re-imagining the Past. Antiquity and Modern Greek Culture* (Oxford, 2014), pp. 1–26.

Tzogopoulos George, *The Greek Crisis in the Media: Stereotyping in the International Press* (Farnham, UK & Burlington, VT, 2013).

Vaara, Eero, 'Struggles over legitimacy in the Eurozone crisis: Discursive legitimation strategies and their ideological underpinnings', *Discourse & Society* 25/4 (2014), pp. 500–518.

Vamiedakis, Stefanos, 'Επιστροφή στο χωριό: Το νέο success story' ['Return to the village: The new success story'], *Λεύγα* 7 (2012), pp. 4–8. Available at https://issuu.com/levga/docs/levga7?viewMode=doublePage&e=3506162/2973984 (accessed 1 September 2016).

Van Dijk, Teun A., 'Opinions and ideologies in the Press', in A. Bell and P. Garrett (eds), *Approaches to Media Discourse* (Oxford, 1998).

Van Dyck, Karen (ed.), *Austerity Measures* (London, 2016).

Van Steen, Gonda, '*The Story of Ali Retzo*: Brecthian theatre in Greece under the military dictatorship', *Journal of Modern Greek Studies* 31/1 (May 2013), pp. 85–115.

Varoufakis, Yanis, 'We are all Greeks Now! The crisis in Greece in its European and global context', in Anna Triandafyllidou, Ruby Gropas and Hara Kouki (eds), *The Greek Crisis and European Modernity* (New York, 2013), pp. 44–58.

______ 'Being Greek and an economist while Greece is burning! An intimate account of a peculiar tragedy', *Journal of Modern Greek Studies* 32/1 (2014), pp. 1–23.

Vasilopoulou, Sofia, Daphne Halikiopoulou & Theofanis Exadaktylos, 'Greece in Crisis: Austerity, Populism and the Politics of Blame', *Journal of Common Market Studies* 52/2 (2014), pp. 388–402.

Vasilopoulou, Sofia and Daphne Halikiopoulou, *The Golden Dawn's 'Nationalist Solution': Explaining the Rise of the Far Right in Greece* (New York, 2015).

Vavva, Georgia, 'Η έντεχνη δυτική μουσική στην «κοινότητα»: Η περίπτωση του Μουσικού Χωριού' ['Western Art Music in the "Community": The Case of the Music Village'], *Polyphonia* 26 (Spring 2015), 209–223.

Venturas, Lina, '"Deterritorializing" the Nation: The Greek State and "Ecumenical Hellenism"', in Dimitris Tziovas (ed.), *Greek Diaspora and Migration since 1700: Society, Politics and Culture* (Farnham, UK; Burlington, VT, 2009), pp. 125–140.

Verney, Susannah, 'Waking the "sleeping giant" or expressing domestic dissent? Mainstreaming Euroscepticism in crisis-stricken Greece', *International Political Science Review* 36/3 (2015), pp. 279–295.

Visconti, Luca M., John F. Sherry, Stefania Borghini, and Laurel Anderson, 'Street Art, Sweet Art? Reclaiming the "Public" in Public Place', *Journal of Consumer Research* 37/3 (2010), pp. 511–529.

Vlastos, Giorgos, *Η πρόσληψη της ελληνικής αρχαιότητας στη γαλλική μουσική του 20ου αιώνα: 1900–1918* [*The Reception of Greek Antiquity in French Music of the Early Twentieth Century: 1900–1918*], PhD dissertation (Athens, 2005).

Vogli Elpida, 'The making of Greece abroad: Continuity and change in the modern diaspora politics of a "historical" irredentist homeland', *Nationalism and Ethnic Politics* 17 (2011), pp. 14–33.

Voudouri, Daphne, *Κράτος και μουσεία: Το θεσμικό πλαίσιο των αρχαιολογικών μουσείων* [*State and Museums: The institutional framework of archaeological museums*] (Athens, 2003).

Vournelis Leonidas V., *Living the Crisis: Identities and Materialities in a Transnational Greek Setting*, Diss. (Southern Illinois University Carbondale, 2013).

———, 'Alexander's great treasure: wonder and mistrust in neoliberal Greece', *History and Anthropology* 27/1 (2016), pp. 121–133.

Vradis, Antonis and Dimitris Dalakoglou, *Revolt and Crisis in Greece: Between a present yet to pass and a future still to come* (Oakland & Edinburgh, 2011).

Waclawek, Anna, *Graffiti and Street Art* (London, 2011).

White, Hayden, 'Writing in the middle voice', in *The Fiction of Narrative: Essays on History, Literature, and Theory 1957–2007* (Baltimore 2010 [1992]), pp. 255–262.

——— *The Practical Past* (Evanston 2014).

Williams, Allan and Vladimír Baláž, *International Migration and Knowledge* (London, 2014).

Wills, David, 'Reinventing Paradise: the Greek crisis and contemporary British travel narratives', *Byzantine and Modern Greek Studies* 39/2 (2015), pp. 286–301.

Wodak, Ruth, 'Critical Linguistics and Critical Discourse Analysis', in J. Verschueren, J.-O. Östman and J. Blommaert (eds), *Handbook of Pragmatics: Manual* (Amsterdam, 1995).

Wodak, Ruth and John E. Richardson, 'European fascism in text and talk. Introduction.', in R. Wodak and J.E. Richardson (eds), *Analysing Fascist Discourse: European Fascism in Talk and Text* (London/New York, 2013).

Xenakis, Sappho & L.K. Cheliotis, 'Crime and Economic Downturn: The Complexity of Crime and Crime Politics in Greece since 2009', *British Journal of Criminology* 53/5 (2013), pp. 719–745.

Yalouri, Eleana, *The Acropolis: Global Fame, Local Claim* (Oxford, 2001).

Zois, Antonis, *Η Αρχαιολογία στην Ελλάδα* [*Archaeology in Greece*] (Athens, 1990).

Zorba, Myrsini, 'Conceptualizing Greek cultural policy: the non democratization of public culture', *International Journal of Cultural Policy* 15/3 (2009), pp. 245–259.

INDEX

Illustrations are denoted by the use of *italics*. Endnotes not included.

www.ingramcontent.com/pod-product-compliance
Lightning Source LLC
LaVergne TN
LVHW052246200926
848481LV00002B/289
9780755601097